THE CHANGING PROFILE OF THE NATURAL LAW

THE CHANGING PROFILE OF THE NATURAL LAW

by

MICHAEL BERTRAM CROWE

MARTINUS NIJHOFF/THE HAGUE/1977

PATRIS MATRISQUE
ALMAE MEMORIAE

ISBN 90 247 1992 5

TYPESET IN GREAT BRITAIN

ACKNOWLEDGMENTS

It is my pleasant duty to record my indebtedness to the many whose help has made the writing of this book possible. Many of my more obvious debts are recorded in the footnotes and the bibliography. But I would not have go unacknowledged the help of the very great number of scholars in the field of the natural law, who are not named simply because I have not cited them explicitly in the text or in the notes. Their assistance has been nonetheless real and appreciated for being silent.

Of the many more personal debts to teachers and colleagues I single out two. The late Professor Denis O'Keeffe, Professor of Ethics and Politics at University College, Dublin, first directed my attention to the study of the natural law. And the late Professor Jacques Leclercq was the kindly and inspiring promotor of my doctoral studies on the same topic at the *Institut supérieur de philosophie* in the University of Louvain.

As to the text, part of Chapter VIII was read as a paper to the *III Congresso internazionale di filosofia medievale* in 1964; and part of Chapter IX was a paper given to the *XII Congresso internazionale di Filosofia* in 1958. I also wish to thank the Editors of the following periodicals for permission to make use of material that has appeared in their pages: *Irish Ecclesiastical Record, Irish Theological Quarterly, Tijdschrift voor Filosofie.* In addition I acknowledge the kind permission of Argus Communications to use material originally published by them in *The Future of Ethics and Moral Theology* (Chicago, 1968).

I thank the Dean and professors of the Harvard Divinity School who welcomed me as a Visiting Scholar in 1973–1974 and, with their colleagues in the Boston Theological Institute (particularly the Faculty at St. John's Seminary), encouraged the beginnings of this book. Its completion was made possible by the generosity of my *Alma Mater Lovaniensis.* I was Visiting

Professor at the Higher Institute of Philosophy in 1975–1976; I thank its former President, Professor A. Wylleman, his successor Professor U. Dhondt and their colleagues who made my stay in Louvain pleasant and, I trust, fruitful. I also enjoyed a Research Fellowship of the University of Louvain and here acknowledge, in particular, the good offices of the former Dean of the Faculty of Philosophy and Letters, Professor Gérard Verbeke. The National University of Ireland has made a grant towards the costs of publication, for which I wish to express my appreciation.

I thank successive Presidents and Governing Bodies of University College, Dublin for leave of absence generously granted and extended; and my colleagues in the Department of Ethics and Politics for their ready cooperation.

Lastly, there are the relatives and friends whose support and encouragement have meant – and continue to mean – so much to me. The greatest and the least repayable of all my debts is indicated in the dedication of this work.

M.B.C.
University College, Dublin
December, 1976

TABLE OF CONTENTS

INTRODUCTION

It has more than once been observed that funeral orations for the natural law have always been premature.[1] The implication that the concept has a continuing vitality, giving the lie to the prophets of its doom, is justification for yet another book on a subject, now as much as ever in the two and a half millenia of its history a matter of controversy.

The history of the natural law has often been written – or at least the history of the concept in the Western European Greco-Roman tradition.[2] This study does not claim to be a history, although its method is primarily historical and its subject is an idea that, more perhaps than most, has been shaped by its history. The omissions, Hobbes, Vico, Kant, Hegel for example, amply demonstrate that this is not a systematic history. On the other hand it accepts that

> In an orderly preparation for the study of natural law the most important step would be to list the main modifications undergone by the notion of natural law as a result of doctrinal and historical circumstances.[3]

[1] Bergbohm, *Jurisprudenz und Rechtsphilosophie*, cited in G.M. Manser, *Das Naturrecht in Thomistischer Beleuchtung*, p. 1; cf. A.P. d'Entrèves, *Natural Law*, p. 13: "It was declared dead, never to rise again from its ashes. Yet natural law has survived and still calls for discussion."

[2] A. Truyol y Serra, *Historia de la filosofia del derecho y del estado de los origenes a la baja Edad Media*, pp. 1–85, after an introductory chapter, studies Egyptian, Babylonian, Assyrian, Persian and Jewish notions of political wisdom and follows with chapters on Chinese and Indian culture. The *Proceedings of the Natural Law Institute*, vol. V, Notre-Dame, 1953, study the natural law in the Jewish, Moslem, Hindu, Buddhist and Chinese traditions.

[3] Yves, R. Simon, *The Tradition of Natural Law: A Philosopher's Reflections*, pp. 10–11. Simon gives some examples of the meaning of natural law in different systems of reference, the diverse but not unrelated meanings of the word in the Stoics, Aquinas, Tom Paine and Adam Smith; also the way in which historical situations may work for and against the natural law, as in the eighteenth century, in the American and French Revolutions, the appeal was to nature as against constituted authority, whereas in the nineteenth century the problem of nationalities, in some circumstances, worked against natural law in favour of what came to be called 'historical law.'

and also that

Any study of the natural law must take account of its paradoxical rôle in human history. It has served both as a stimulus to reform and a bulwark against change. The medieval church used natural law arguments to bulwark its supremacy over the civil state. Dante used related arguments to establish the primacy of the civil state. The church used St. Thomas's arguments against the rising tide of Protestantism; later Protestant jurist-theologians were to use the same premises and method to vindicate the Reformation.... To critics of natural law thinking this is proof of the scientific falsity of the entire doctrine ....[4]

Against the last statement in the paragraph just quoted, this book argues that the "persistence of the notion of natural law," in the words of the same author, "supports a possible inference of its validity, however questionable may be some of the methods employed and some of the contents developed."[5]

The danger in such an approach is that of falling into the perennial temptation of historians of thought – hindsight or wisdom after the event. It is the danger, for example, of reading too much significance into the elements of the pre-history of the natural law precisely because they are the *disjecta membra*, the building-stones of subsequent systems. The ambiguity of the term natural law itself and its lack of a continuous history help to guard against that danger.

Nevertheless it will be argued that the scholastic influence upon the history of the natural law has been decisive. The great thirteenth century thinkers and their sixteenth and seventeenth century successors made a weighty and inescapable, but not overpowering, contribution to the history of the notion. What resulted was a profile; and a profile is not a full portrait. If the essential features by which the natural law can be recognised are sketched, that is already a great advance. The details may and must change with the passage of time and differences in culture; nor can there ever be a final portrait complete in every detail.

The statements in the foregoing paragraph will, it is hoped, find their justification in what follows. But there are some preliminary points to be made. It will be clear, for instance, that the natural law is treated as an ethical concept rather than a legal one – although the philosophical and the juridical are, especially in

[4] A.L. Harding, "A Reviving Natural Law" in *Natural Law and Natural Rights*, p. 71.

[5] A.L. Harding, Introduction to *Origins of the Natural Law Tradition*, p. vi.

modern times, almost inextricably intertwined in its history.[6] This enables us to give short shrift to sterile discussions about whether natural law is law in the lawyers' sense of the word and whether or not human law, not in agreement with natural law, is law, bad law or not law at all. The persistence of this problem is probably due to an assertion, attributed to Plato (in the *Minos*), to the effect that law is not law unless it is good and re-echoed in St. Thomas's proposition that the ruler's will, unless regulated by reason, is wickedness rather than law.[7] This does not allow the jurist to escape from the "ever-recurring dilemma," as W. Luijpen has called it. One may take the view that the concept of a natural law is harmful and leads only to confused thinking; that it is based, for instance, upon a notion of 'nature' taken out of its original context in Greek philosophy and foisted upon men as normative and the touchstone of moral good and evil. Even to reject the natural law in these or similar terms means to address oneself to that "ever-recurring dilemma." Luijpen makes the point that the questions raised by living philosophy are somehow always the same; they remain the eternal questions of mankind, despite the variety of answers that have been offered to them. The natural law is one kind of answer to the fundamental questions about good and evil, rights and duties, justice and law. Such questions cannot be avoided; for human existence is co-existence:

> As soon as man manages to reach the level of authentic existence, it becomes obvious to him that even the most elementary level of authenticity is impossible unless existence is co-existence. To be man is to be a fellow-man. But even the most simple and most elementary level of coexistence calls for rules and regulations to make this coexistence possible and to preserve it when it has been achieved.[8]

The question arises, then, about the foundation of those rules and regulations; and not merely as a theoretical necessity but as a matter of fact, man has questioned the means by which order is introduced into society. One answer, with a venerable tradition behind it, is the natural law with its connected notions of justice and the objectivity of moral values; and it retains a relevance as

[6] F.H. Eterovich, *Approaches to Natural Law from Plato to Kant*, pp. 15–16.

[7] H. Cairns, *Legal Philosophy from Plato to Hegel*, pp. 33–34, 38; cf. H.L.A. Hart, *The Concept of Law*, pp. 182–183; St. Thomas, *Summa theologiae*, 1–2ae, q. 90, a. 1 ad 3.

[8] W. Luijpen, *Phenomenology of Natural Law*, pp. 17–18.

long as the relevance of the questions, to which it claims to provide the answer, remains.

Luijpen goes on to discuss the "untenability of legal positivism" on the ground that questions properly arise which are unanswerable within the bounds of juristic science. This upsets the presupposition of positivism, namely that all problems must be solved within the law and not by appeal to ideologies outside it. The dichotomy that emerges between a natural law and a legal positivism is basically – and this is one of the themes of the book – the same as that between the intellectualist and nominalist positions in the thirteenth and fourteenth centuries, between the *via antiqua* and the *via moderna*, between (in many cases) Catholic and Protestant after the Reformation; and it bears more than a passing resemblance to the differences between moral essentialists and situationists on the contemporary scene.

There is at the very least a *prima facie* case that what the scholastic has to say retains an importance. The underlying thesis of this book, then, is relatively simple and, it is hoped, will not be obscured by the detail judged necessary to sustain it. It is that the profile of the natural law, after several false starts and wrong turnings, was established in the second half of the thirteenth century, notably in the work of St. Thomas Aquinas. It was painfully constructed on a basis of tradition – but some traditional obstructions, like the authoritative definitions of Ulpian and Gratian, had to be removed. The profile was not definitive – none can be. It was attacked in the fourteenth century. It was damaged in another way by the rigidity and inflexibility resulting from the Age of Reason. The hope of the present day lies in getting behind the disfigurements of history to discover the lineaments which can be measured to the moral perplexities and dilemmas of our time. The crucial stages in this long story are indicated in the chapter headings; and the last chapter endeavours to draw the conclusion. It is for the reader to judge.[9]

[9] If one were to look for a motto for the enterprise one might take this striking phrase from Kant (cited in H. Welzel, *Naturrecht und materiale Gerechtigkeit*, p. 236): "Alles geht wie in einem Fluss vor uns vorüber, und der wandelbare Geschmack und die verschiedenen Gestalten des Menschen machen das ganze Spiel ungewiss und trüglich. Wo finde ich feste Punkte der Natur, die der Mensch niemals verrücken kann, und wo ich Merkzeichen geben kann, an welches Ufer er sich zu halten hat?"

CHAPTER I

BEGINNINGS

A. THE PRE-SOCRATICS

The influence upon Greco-Roman civilization of certain legal terms like those covering the notions of 'justice,' 'injustice' and 'law' has been enormous. Yet the systematic study of those terms is a comparatively late phenomenon. We find it in the later dialogues of Plato and in Aristotle and his school. Aristotle's pupil and successor at the Lyceum, Theophrastus, was the author of a formal treatise *De Legibus.* In classical times generally there was a whole series of tracts *peri nomou,* mostly, however, lost to us.[1] But if the systematic study of legal concepts had to wait until the fourth century B.C., the concepts had been there and were known and discussed by the Greeks long before.

Among these terms those translated by 'justice' have played an important rôle from earliest times; they are found in the mythologies and cosmogonies of the pre-philosophic age, linked with the idea of order or organisation in the universe. The goddesses Themis and Dikè of the mythologies are personifications of the different aspects of this notion of 'justice',[2] aspects corresponding more or less with the later developments in the direction of positive law, on the one hand, and of morality, even natural law, on the other.[3] The germs of those developments are discernible in the history of 'justice' even before its emergence as a

[1] Titles etc. in A. Boeckh, *In Platonis qui vulgo fertur Minoen,* pp. 73 ff., cited by W. Jaeger, "Die Anfänge der Rechtsphilosophie und die Griechen" in *Zeitschrift für philosophische Forschung,* 3 (1948), pp. 321–328, 512–520.

[2] R. Hirzel, *Themis, Dikè und Verwandtes,* passim; E. Wolf, *Griechisches Rechtsdenken,* I, pp. 70–151; W. Jaeger, *op. cit.,* pp. 323–326.

[3] Cf. P. Guerin, *L'idée de justice dans la conception de l'universe chez les Grecs, de Thales à Heracleite,* p. 21.

philosophical term in the nature-philosophy of the Milesian school.[4]

The beginnings of philosophy in the Ionian school, Thales of Miletus, Anaximander and Anaximenes, in the 6th century B.C., the so-called 'Greek miracle,' can scarcely be expected to provide a fully-fledged articulation of a natural law theory. The transition from superstition and pre-scientific modes of thought to science and philosophy was indeed a mighty step forward in the history of thought, which fact has tended to inflate our expectations concerning the actual achievements of the Ionians. Their achievement was to have asked the philosophic question: What is the nature of reality? That remains a colossal achievement even if their answers now appear naive – Thales said that the world was made of water, Anaximander that it was made of a 'boundless material' the *apeiron*, Anaximenes that it was made of air.[5] But in philosophy asking questions is more important than getting answers; some questions are philosophical and to pose them is to philosophize even if the answers are unsatisfactory. That is precisely why we contrast the Ionians with their predecessors, whose superstitious cosmogonies were not, whatever their literary, aesthetic or religious appeal, based upon rational speculation; they were a far remove from cosmology. Another major step, however, is required before the philosophy which has now appeared on the scene turns to problems other than the purely cosmological.

With the beginning of philosophy, a new stage has been reached in the approach to 'justice.' Anaximander, (611–548 B.C.) the second of the Milesians, sees a justice and an injustice in the separating-out of the elements from the primal Boundless (*apeiron*).[6] This is 'cosmic justice.' To Anaximenes, a generation after Anaximander, is attributed a far-reaching distinction between written or state law and unwritten or universal natural

[4] P. Guerin, *op. cit.*, p. 30: "C'est alors que la justice sera ni un personnage mythique, ni un fait social, ni un fait de conscience, ni un Ideal moral, mais une conception philosophique." Cf. E. Wolf, *op. cit.*, I, pp. 22 ff.

[5] Our knowledge of the pre-Socratic philosophers is hampered by the fact that the sources are fragmentary and have suffered various vicissitudes of transmission. The standard collection is H. Diels, *Die Fragmente der Vorsokratiker*, 6th ed., vols. I–III, Berlin, 1951–1952.

[6] H. Diels, *op. cit.*, I, p. 89, n. 1: "And into that from which things take their rise they pass away once more, as is meet, for they make reparation and satisfaction to one another for their *injustice* according to the ordering of time...." Cf. J. Burnet, *Early Greek Philosophy*, pp. 50–71; P. Guerin, *op. cit.*, pp. 33–43; E. Wolf, *op. cit.*, I, p. 219.

law.[7] For disciples of Pythagoras of Samos (c. 580–500 B.C.) justice becomes a harmony to be understood in the light of their number-theory of reality, an equilibrium symbolised by the lyric diapason.[8] One of the later Pythagorean extravagances was the bizarre identification of justice with the number four because, being the product of equal factors and returning two for two, it is an example of the perfect reciprocity required by justice.[9]

Parmenides (c. 530–444 B.C.) writing in the first quarter of the fifth century B.C., speaks in his allegorical way of Avenging Justice who holds the keys to the mighty doors at the end of the Way of Truth that she and Themis have led him to follow. Probably the exact sense of the passage will never be discovered.[10] Elsewhere Parmenides speaks of a justice that guarantees the absoluteness of being – his characteristic contribution to philosophy – but nowhere, in the extant fragments of his poem, does he define this justice more explicitly.[11]

Heracleitus of Ephesus (c. 540–475 B.C.) has come to be considered of the first importance in the history of the natural law, as presenting the idea if not the term itself. He was probably the first to envisage the philosophical problem as a human as well as a cosmological one; his work, we are told, was divided into three parts or three discourses, one dealing with the universe, one political and one theological.[12] All through his thought there runs the emphasis upon the value of his 'word'; although men do not understand it, yet it will explain all things.[13] What precisely this *logos* was is not clear; but it would seem that it must be connected with Heracleitus's leading idea that all things are in flux, a position taken up in diametric opposition to Parmenides and summarized in the celebrated paradox about not being able to step twice into the same river "for fresh waters are ever flowing in upon you.[14]" Perhaps the secret and saving word was Heracleitus's discovery that the strife and flux of nature is really a

[7] Cf. Aristotle, *Rhet. ad Alex.*, II, 1421 b 35; R. Hirzel, *Agraphos Nomos*, pp. 24–25.

[8] H. Diels, *op. cit.*, I, pp. 408–410 (Fragment n. 6 from Philolaus); P. Guerin, *op. cit.*, pp. 46–48.

[9] Cf. J. Burnet, *Greek Philosophy: Thales to Plato*, p. 90; P. Guerin, *op. cit.*, pp. 55–58.

[10] H. Diels, *op. cit.*, I, pp. 228–230, n. 1. See the various interpretations, including that of M. Heidegger, in E. Wolf, *op. cit.*, I, pp. 238–239.

[11] H. Diels, *op. cit.*, I, pp. 227–246; J. Burnet, *Early Greek Philosophy*, p. 175.

[12] Diogenes Laertius, *Lives of the Philosophers*, IX, 5.

[13] H. Diels, *op. cit.*, I, pp. 150–151, nn. 1–2.

[14] H. Diels, *op. cit.*, I, p. 154, n. 12.

tension of locked forces, that there is, after all, a fundamental unity behind the ever-changing façade of appearance, that the strife is at the same time a harmony.[15] In the human and social sphere the place of this unity is taken by justice – "men would not have known the name of justice if these things were not."[16]

The relevance of "universal and divine reason" (*koinos kai theios logos*) governing the universe to the history of the natural law is clear. It is also clear that this conception should not be pressed too far in a Christian-latin sense of natural law, which would certainly be foreign to a Greek in the age of Heracleitus. It is probably something much more in the nature of a world-order.[17] Nevertheless some of the fragments of Heracleitus that have survived are very striking. For example there is the pronouncement that "all human laws are fed by the one divine law."[18] This distinction between the laws of the city and something superior, universal, enduring and unchanging is a distinction that will perfectly fit the later conceptions of the natural law; it is, according to Heracleitus, an ideal of law for which a people must be prepared to fight as for their city-walls. It is his conceptions of this kind that make many see in Heracleitus the true founder of natural law.[19]

From what has been said it should be clear that, already at the opening of the classical age, Greek thought was enriched with a variety of speculation about natural justice and a law of nature. A complete study of this speculation would require an exhaustive examination of the extant texts and a discussion of the great

[15] H. Diels, *op. cit.*, I, pp. 150–152, nn. 1,8; p. 162, n 51; cf. J. Sauter, *Die philosophischen Grundlagen des Naturrechts, p.* 7. Plato, *Cratylus,* 402A and Aristotle, *Metaph.*, III, 5, 1010 a 66 ff, are responsible for the attribution of pure relativism, even in ethics, to Heracleitus. The *panta rei* does not occur in extant fragments; but it does epitomize one side of Heracleitus's thought. Cf. Aristotle, *Top.*, I, 11, 104b 22; *De coelo,* III, 1, 298 b 30; *Phys.*, VII, 3, 253 b 2. Also J. Burnet, *Early Greek Philosophy*, pp. 143, 146, 163; K. Freeman, *The Pre-Socratic Philosophers,* p. 113.

[16] H. Diels, *op. cit.*, I, p. 169, n. 80; J. Burnet, *Early Greek Philosophy*, p. 137, note 5 says that by 'those things' Heracleitus probably meant all kinds of injustice; E. Wolf, *op. cit.*, I, pp. 239–240 says that it is not the term 'justice' that is in question but its *divinity*.

[17] E. Wolf, *op. cit.*, I, p. 274: "nicht Gesetz sondern Daseinsordnung, Verfassung." J. Burnet, *Early Greek Philosophy*, p. 168, sees here a preparation for the Stoic world-state. Cf. H. Welzel, *Naturrecht und materiale Gerechtigkeit,* pp. 9–10.

[18] H. Diels, *op. cit.*, I, p. 176, n. 114.

[19] Cf. E. Calán y Gutierrez, *Jus Naturae,* pp. 21–32; H. Rommen, *Natural Law*, p. 6.

questions arising out of them. Such, for example, would be the relation between the ontological law of nature, of the kind first suggested by Anaximander, and the ethical-moral concepts in the mythologies and cosmogonies that preceded; the influence of the hieratic codes of laws in the 7th and 6th centuries, constructed following the ideal of *isonomia* or equality of the citizens before the law[20]; and, more generally, the play of the Greek capacity for generalisation which first took a term, 'justice,' from the world of human social values to apply it to nature at large[21] and would later argue from the rule of law in nature to a law in man as part of the system, from the macrocosm to the microcosm. One could deal also with such interesting subsidiary questions as that of the cross-fertilization between medical and politico-legal thinking, involving the ideas of harmony and balance[22] or the examination of the terms *anagkè* and *nomos.*[23]

These great questions lie well beyond the limits of this book.[24] One such question must, however, be considered, however briefly – the *physis-nomos* controversy in the time of the Sophists and Plato. But before going on to this it will be well to conclude the present section by listing some of the classical references to the natural law.

The great classical dramatists reflect, as one would expect, the leading ideas of their age, including that of a natural law; and, in

[20] Cf. W. Jaeger, "Die Anfänge der Rechtsphilosophie und die Griechen," p. 327: "Die Schlagworte der sozialen Revolution, die die feudale Ordnung der frühgriechischen Welt während des 7. und 6. Jahrhunderts verwandelte, waren *dikè* und *nomos* der (um die Gleichheit der Rechte der einzelnen Bürger zu betonen) *isonomia.*"

[21] Cf. W. Jaeger, *op. cit.*, p. 330; R. Hirzel, *Themis, Dikè* und *Verwandtes*, pp. 386–387.

[22] W. Jaeger, *op. cit.*, pp. 329, 332–333. One may connect this with the later doctrine of the mixed constitution, i.e. one in which the elements are balanced, as in a healthy body; or with Empedocles's doctrine of the elements; or with the theory of the humours in the Sicilian school of medicine, attributed to Alcmaeon, in virtue of which health was an *isonomia* and disease the 'monarchy' of one of the elements. Compare also Aristotle's diagnosis of unhealthy constitutions in the *Politics* and his description of the manner in which to treat them. Cf. E. Barker, *The Politics of Aristotle*, p. 242, note uu; H. Welzel, *op. cit.*, p. 10.

[23] Cf. R. Hirzel, *op. cit.*, p.390.

[24] There is no lack of literature on the subject. See E. Wolf, *op. cit.*; S.V. Ehrenberg, *Die Rechtsidee im frühen Griechentum*; R. Hirzel, *Agraphos Nomos*; B. Horvath, "Die Gerechtigkeitslehre der Vorsokratiker" in *Studi dedicati a G. Del Vecchio*, I, 336–372; W. Jaeger, *Paideia;* A. Sánchez de la Torre, *Los Griegos y el derecho natural;* A. Verdross, *Abendländische Rechtsphilosophie*, 1. Abschnitt, etc.

addition, a natural law easily provides situations that are inherently dramatic. Aeschylus (525–458 B.C.) for example, builds his play *Seven against Thebes* upon a conflict between brothers each of whom thinks that the other is acting unjustly. At the end of the play the dramatist makes what looks like a distinction between positive laws (*ta dikaia*) which vary in different states and at different times, and a natural law (*to dikaion*) which does not.[25] Perhaps it is no more than a suggestion. Sophocles (490–405 B.C.) puts the same problem, the clash of laws, more acutely in his *Antigone*.[26] The climax of the tragedy is Antigone's defiance of the edict forbidding burial honours to her brother. She justifies herself, invoking "the unwritten and unfailing statutes of heaven... (whose) life is not of today or yesterday but from all time; and no man knows when they were first put forth."[27] This is a *locus classicus* and has been cited by almost every writer on the natural law since Aristotle.[28] In the *Oedipus Tyrannus* Sophocles refers to "laws of range sublime whose parent was no race of mortal men."[29] This 'divine law' of Sophocles has the qualities that are precisely those assigned by his contemporaries the Sophists to the *physei dikaion* as distinct from, *nomo dikaion*.[30] Euripides reflects the opposition between *physis* and *nomos* in allegorical terms when he remarks that "in nature is commandment; she does not ask for laws."[31]

B THE SOPHISTS AND SOCRATES

The idea of a natural law – or rather of an unwritten law which is superior to and is the measure of man-made law – did not gain

[25] Aeschylus, *Seven against Thebes*, 1071–1073; cf. E. Wolf, *op. cit.*, I, 366: "Es ist ein Wissen, zwar noch nicht um das *physei dikaion*, wohl aber um das *theio dikaion*."

[26] W. Jaeger, "Die Anfänge der Rechtsphilosophie und die Griechen," pp. 337–338; M. Tierney, "The Antigone of Sophocles – A Problem Reviewed" in *Studies*, 37 (1943), p. 330: "... The limitation of state-authority by the law of nature."

[27] Sophocles, *Antigone*, 454 ff.

[28] *Rhet.*, I, 13, 1373 b 1 ff.; I, 15, 1375 a 25 ff.; cf. R. Hirzel, *Agraphos nomos*, pp. 6, 10.

[29] Sophocles, *Oedipus Tyrannus*, 863–871; cf. Th. Meyer, *Institutiones Iuris Naturalis*, I, n. 251.

[30] E. Wolf, *op. cit.*, II, p. 263: "das von den Sophisten gesuchte Richtmass und der legitimierende, unverteilbare Grund aller menschlich-politischen *nomoi* also längst schon vorhanden und gefunden sei, nämlich in Gestalt des *nomos theios*."

[31] Euripides, *Frag.* 912 cited in M. Hamburger, *Morals and Law: the Growth of Aristotle's Legal Theory*, p. 60. Cf. H. Cairns, *Legal Philosophy from Plato to Hegel*, pp. 45–46.

the day without a struggle. The conceptions of law and of natural justice, in the cosmological as well as in the moral sense, had to keep pace with the social evolution of the Greek world. The city-states began to enjoy highly-developed systems of law; and wars and commerce, by multiplying the relations between the cities, made possible a comparison between those various codes. What we have loosely called 'natural law' or 'natural justice' was the ideal, by and large, of these codes. Solon, for example, the great Athenian lawgiver of the early sixth century B.C. was a firm believer in the ideal of justice. The early mythologists like Hesiod had seen in calamities like floods, fires, storms and war the punishment of the gods upon the unjust city. Solon's view was less naive; he saw in the social evils of political unrest, party-faction, sedition, conspiracy and so on the consequences of injustice. Justice was for him the good health, the well-being of society. Pericles in the great Funeral Oration refers to "that code which, although unwritten, yet cannot be broken without acknowledged disgrace"[32]; Demosthenes (c. 384–322 B.C.) speaks of the "whole life of man . . . governed by nature and by law"[33] and of a "law valid for all men given by nature."[34] And the quotations could be multiplied.

This latter development came under strong attack from the Sophists, in whose *Weltanschauung* state-law became the very antithesis of natural law. The word 'sophist' is usually taken in the pejorative sense it has had since Plato. But it is worth recalling that its origin, in *sophos* a wise man, was thoroughly respectable. Plato himself says that the sophist is on the border between the philosopher and the statesman; and elsewhere he says that God himself is the "complete and accomplished sophist."[35] But by the end of the fifth century B.C. 'sophist' had come to mean a professional teacher providing the kind of training (mostly in eloquence) required by those entering upon public life. They travelled about, taking fees for their instruction, and they acquired the reputation of being more interested in persuasion than

[32] Thucydides, II, 35–46.

[33] Demosthenes, *Contra Aristog.*, I,: "Haec lex est cui omnes homines convenit obtemperare, cum propter alia pleraque tum maxime, quod omnis lex inventum est et donum Dei, placitum vero sapientum hominum coercitioque peccatorum tam voluntariorum quam non voluntariorum, civitatis autem pactum commune, secundum autem quod convenit vivere quicunque in ea sunt." This passage, quoted by the jurist Marcianus, found its way into the *Institutes* of Justinian, I, iii, 2.

[34] Demosthenes, *Contra Aristog.*, 61.

[35] Plato, *Euthydemus*, 305C; *Cratylus*, 403C.

in truth, in 'making the worse appear the better reason.' Plato also gave expression to this low opinion of the sophists, and thus became responsible for the derogatory meaning of the term. "They (the sophists) are a manifest pest and a corrupting influence on all that have to do with them"; "They deal wholesale and retail in the food of the soul (i.e. knowledge) hawking it about and praising it up without knowing whether the various items are beneficial or hurtful to the customers." He makes Hippocrates blush at the idea of becoming a sophist. And, in the dialogue *Sophistes*, he defines the sophist as a word-spinner, a conscious deceiver who presents the appearance of truth by juggling with words, a paid hunter of the young and rich, a trafficker in learning. Aristotle shared this prejudice – a sophist deals, he said, in 'pseudo-science.'[36]

The most important of the Sophists were Protagoras and Gorgias. Protagoras of Abdera, who flourished in the latter half of the fifth century B.C., spent his life in an extended lecture-tour. He visited Athens twice (or possibly thrice); his second visit, in 432 B.C. is described in Plato's dialogue named after him. Little is known about the number and titles of his works. His outstanding doctrine that 'man is the measure' (*anthropos metron; homo mensura*) is, however, well attested. "Man is the measure of all things, of things that are that they are, and of things that are not that they are not."[37] The meaning commonly given to this is that things are for each man as they appear to him; this is the meaning taken by Plato in the *Theaetetus*[38] Others have suggested that by 'man' Protagoras may have meant 'mankind.'[39] The assertion, however, that all percepts are equally true pointed to the denial of the law of contradiction, and offered the ground for the severe criticism of Protagoras in Plato and Aristotle.[40] The only qualification seemingly admitted by Protagoras was that one opinion might be better, not truer, than another; to the jaundiced all things are yellow, but it is better not to be jaundiced. This relativism, extended into ethics, is clearly a radical rejection of the distinction between good and evil or, one might say, a denial

[36] Plato, *Meno*, 91; *Protagoras*, 313; *Sophistes* passim; Aristotle, *Soph. Elench.*, I, 3 a 7.

[37] H. Diels, *Die Fragmente der Vorsokratiker*, II, p. 263.

[38] 152 ff.

[39] E.g. J. Burnet, *Greek Philosophy: Thales to Plato*, pp. 114 ff.

[40] Plato, *Theaetetus*, 151E; Aristotle, *Metaphys.*, IV, 2–7 1005 a 5–1011 b 25: K. Freeman, *The Pre-Socratic Philosophers*, pp. 349–352.

of a natural moral law. And this was an implication seen by Socrates and Plato.

Protagoras's contemporary, Gorgias of Leontini (483–375 B.C.), said to have been the pupil of Empedocles, was famous for a florid, euphuistic style, tricked out with various figures of speech. In contrast with Protagoras's teaching that everything is true, Gorgias maintained that there was no truth at all. Using arguments taken mainly from Zeno the Eleatic and Melissus, he purports to show (i) that nothing exists; (ii) that if anything existed it could not be known; and (iii) that if anything were known, knowledge could not be communicated. He may or may not have been serious about the arguments; his position may have been simply a dialectical tour-de-force. It is notable that Plato does not regard him as a nihilist (as he does Protagoras) but treats him as a rhetorician. In ethics such nihilistic views would amount to a denial of the distinction between right and wrong; but Gorgias himself appears not to have advanced to that position. That was left to Callicles and Thrasymachus who appear in Plato's discussion of justice in the *Republic.*[41] Hippias of Elis (460–399 B.C.), a third member of the older generation of sophists, made a more positive contribution to what was to become the great debate. He stressed the equality of men, which he saw as a creation of nature. Human law, on the contrary, created inequality: "I count you all," he said to the other participants in Plato's dialogue *Protagoras*, "my kinsmen, family and fellow-citizens – by nature, not by convention. By nature like is kin to like; but custom, the tyrant of mankind, does much violence to nature."[42] This leads to the paradox of the sophists' attack upon existing institutions, made in the name of natural justice, of *physei dikaion.* So it came about that the Sophists, in spite of their relativistic conceptions of moral matters and their support of 'natural laws' ranging from an identification of might with right (Thrasymachus, Callicles, Critias) to a defence of the weak against exploitation (Lycophron, Alcidemas), yet find themselves named among the founders of the doctrine of the natural law.[43] Natural law for the sophists, far from being a standard to apply for the improvement and justification of positive law, became instead the instrument of a reckless criticism of the existing order. A parallel may be seen in the

[41] Gorgias' arguments are discussed in K. Freeman, *op. cit.*, pp. 359–361. Callicles and Thrasymachus appear in *Republic*, Book I.

[42] Plato, *Protagoras*, 337C

[43] Cf. E. Wolf, *Griechisches Rechtsdenken*, II, pp. 18–171 for a full study.

explosive effect of the Rousseauistic theory of natural rights in 18th century Europe.[44]

The shift in the meaning of the terms *physis* and *nomos* provoked by the Sophist attack on natural law merits careful study. At times both Plato and Aristotle speak of *nomos* in such a way as to imply its identification, more or less, with arbitrariness[45] and of *physis* as something quite apart from law. One of the great advances that Aristotle will make will be to replace the concept of natural justice within the framework of law – as will be seen in its place.

The influence of the Sophists was not, however, entirely negative and destructive. We must make allowance for the fact that we know their opinions largely from caricatures like those of Aristophanes (who in the *Clouds* takes Socrates as the typical Sophist) and from the adverse criticisms of Plato.[46] The Sophists must be credited with accentuating the distinction between what is merely legal and what is naturally and morally just, with furthering the ideas of freedom and equality of all men by nature and, in consequence, adumbrating a theory of the rights of man. They too prepared the way for the Stoic notion of a world-state (with its corollary the artificiality of the city-state). Less happily they fathered the conception of a 'state of nature' (portrayed optimistically or pessimistically) before the advent of the organised polity, a state in which the only writ that ran was that of the law of nature. This is an idea that will be taken up by the Fathers (who Christianised it) and by the followers of Rousseau (who repaganised it).[47]

The Sophists set the stage for Socrates. There can be no question of his importance or of his achievement in changing the course of Greek philosophy. The change, already begun with Heracleitus, focussed interest upon man rather than upon the universe; with Socrates the change becomes irreversible. From now on philosophy will be concerned with the great issues of the

[44] Cf. Plato, *Protagoras*, 337C–D; H. Rommen, *Natural law*, pp. 8–11; D.G. Ritchie, *Natural Rights*, pp. 21–27; A.P. d'Entrèves, *Natural Law*, p. 16.

[45] Cf. W. Siegfried, *Der Rechtsgedanke bei Aristoteles*, pp. 62–63 and note 157. See also A. Mansion, *Introduction à la physique aristotélicienne*, p. 109, note 14.

[46] See the useful corrective in M.S. Shellens, "der Gerechtigkeitsbegriff des Thrasymachus" in *Zeitschrift für philosophische Forschung*, 8(1953), pp. 481–492.

[47] H. Rommen, *op. cit.*, pp. 9–10; H. Welzel, *Naturrecht und materiale Gerechtigkeit*, p. 16.

good and of conduct and of conscience. The Sophists had already endeavoured to meet the new conditions of thought. It was precisely because he conceived their answer to be the wrong one that Socrates devoted his life to opposing their relativism.

Our sources for the life and career of Socrates are mainly three – Xenophon, Aristophanes and Plato. Xenophon, in the *Memorabilia* has left examples of 'Socratic discourses'; and Aristophanes, in the *Clouds*, presents a caricature of Socrates. But far the most important source is Plato, who makes his master, Socrates, figure in so many of his dialogues. This is not the place to embark upon a discussion of the 'Socratic problem,' to ask whether the Socrates of Plato's dialogues is the historical Socrates or merely a sounding-board for Plato's own personal teachings. Those are, it is safe to say, the extremes between which the truth of the matter lies. It is nowadays fairly well accepted by scholars that the Socrates of the early (historical) dialogues is the real Socrates, while in the middle and later dialogues Plato puts his own views, notably the Theory of Forms, into the mouth of Socrates.[48]

Socrates' life of 'intellectual midwifery' changed the course of philosophy and focussed attention inescapably upon the problems of man and morals. He was himself aware of this and at his trial shows that he is proud of his 'offence': "I believe that to this day no greater good has ever happened in the state than my service to the god." He refers to himself as the "gadfly of the state."[49] In technical philosophy Socrates was responsible for two things, inductive arguments and universal definition.[50]

In the field of ethics these innovations were of great importance. It is characteristic of the Socrates of Plato's dialogues to engage in the search for the definition of goodness, justice, courage and so on. It was not simply a theoretical exercise, but a practical, and, one must add, ethical investigation-and usually without result, apart from the vital conclusion that what is ethically right must be the object of objectively valid knowledge.[51]

This meant that Socrates took a stand against the nihilism of the Sophists, whose views he regarded as intellectually mistaken and morally harmful. His own views are expressed in the famous

[48] W.D. Ross, *Plato's Theory of Ideas*, p. 157; Id., "The Greek Philosophers" in M. Platnauer (ed.), *Fifty Years of Classical Scholarship*, p. 132.

[49] Plato, *Apologia*, 24–30.

[50] Aristotle, *Metaphys.* XIII, 4, 1078 b 27.

[51] H. Welzel, *Naturrecht und materiale Gerechtigkeit*, p. 20.

dictum that virtue is knowledge. This was a direct challenge to the Sophists, for whom communicable knowledge was a chimera. '*arete*' (virtue) means primarily efficiency at a task – hence Socrates' constant references to cobblers, bridle-makers etc. – and efficiency depends upon knowledge, having a definite job and understanding what is to be done. What is the *arete* of man as such? It is the knowledge of what man is and of man's function. To discover this was the object of Socrates' questionings. "But we must remember that, first of all, Socrates did not mean by 'knowledge' simply abstract knowledge of a proposition. He meant full and immediate realization, sight or intuition, an opening or turning of the 'eye of the soul' to a direct and therefore compelling vision of the good."[52]

The Socratic identification of virtue and knowledge prepared the way for Plato's emphasis upon reason and for Aristotle's doctrine of practical wisdom and, ultimately, for the idea of natural law in the Stoics and their successors.

It would, however, be excessively optimistic to identify the daimon that inspired Socrates with a sort of *a priori*, intuitive knowledge of objective moral values, of what, in effect, is the natural law.[53] Nevertheless one should recall Socrates' appeal, recorded by Xenophon, to 'unwritten laws.'[54] And it is undoubtedly true that Socrates spent his life arguing for a kind of society that would give weight to the natural law – even if he were, as has been pointed out, apt to identify the laws of the polis with natural justice and to demand for them the obedience we would give to our parents.[55] This view, shared also by Plato, explains how the attacks of the Sophists upon the *nomoi* of the Athenian democracy, attacks made in the name of natural law, were regarded as attacks upon every principle of good government. Even Aristotle, who was such a political realist, lived to see the Greek *poleis* pass under the Macedonian hegemony and failed to see the consequence of this for the too-close association of the notions of state-law and natural-law.

[52] Xenophon, *Memorabilia*, III, 9, 4; cf. A.H. Armstrong, *Introduction to Ancient Philosophy*, p. 30; W.K.C. Guthrie, *The Greek Philosophers*, pp. 71–80.

[53] J. Sauter, *Die Philosophischen Grundlagen des Naturrechts*, p. 13: "Das Daimonion, auf das er sich viel berief, kann man also wertkognitives Aprioriwissen verstehen."

[54] Xenophon, *Memorabilia*, IV, 4, 19–25. But this 'unwritten law' is said not to forbid – for example – sexual intercourse between parents and children 'because many do it.'

[55] Plato, *Crito*, 50C–54E

C. PLATO

With Plato (428–348 B.C.) and the Platonic Academy a new stage is reached in the history of thought; the era of the great systematic philosophies is ushered in, with all its consequences for the development of the conception of a natural moral law. Plato was born just after the death of Pericles and some three or four years after the beginning of the Peloponnesian War which put an end to the golden age of Athens. He was of a distinguished family and, as a matter of course, aspired to play a part in public life. Socrates had known the family of Plato since about 431 B.C. and his trial and death, in 399 B.C., effectively put an end to Plato's political career in Athens. Plato had already written some of the early dialogues. He now travelled, to Italy and to Sicily. On returning to Athens, about 388 B.C., he founded the Academy which, although he could hardly have foreseen this, was to last down to the year 529 A.D. when it was suppressed by the Emperor Justinian. It was to be for almost all of its long life a vitally important centre of philosophy. For about twenty years Plato presided over the Academy and wrote the great dialogues, the *Phaedo, Symposium, Phaedrus, Republic.* In 368–7 B.C. he paid a visit to Sicily and made an unsuccessful intervention in the politics of the place. He returned to Athens once again and wrote the later dialogues, *Theaetetus, Parmenides, Sophist, Politicus, Philebus.* In 361 B.C. he was persuaded, against his better judgment, to go yet again to Syracuse and to advise on Sicilian affairs; but this intervention was no more successful than the first. In his last years at Athens he composed the final dialogues, *Timaeus, Critias, Laws* and *Epinomis.* Plato's influence upon the course of philosophy has been enormous. A.N. Whitehead once wrote: "The safest general characterisation of the European philosophical tradition is that it consists of a series of footnotes to Plato." Which provoked the inevitable comment that most of the footnotes were written by Aristotle![56]

Nothing quite like the Academy had previously existed. The school of Plato's contemporary, Isocrates, himself a pupil of Gorgias, was probably slightly prior to the Academy; but it differed from the Academy in important respects.[57] In the Academy there appear to have been three grades of

[56] A.N. Whitehead, *Process and Reality,* p. 63; the comment is attributed to M. Adler, cf. A.C. Pegis, *St. Thomas and the Greeks.*

[57] Cf. T.R. Glover, *The Ancient World,* pp. 152–153.

membership – probationers, those who spent some years in the Academy before entering upon public life, and those who spent their lives in the Academy. The latter were members in the fullest sense.[58] The kind of study is described by Plato in *Epistle 7*:

(Philosophical truth) can only be grasped by devoting every effort and a great deal of time.... All these different things must be, as it were, rubbed together, words and statements, visual images and sense-perceptions; they must be tried and tested in friendly disputation by the ungrudging use of questions and answers. Only then, if even then, when the mind has been strained as far as is humanly possible, does the understanding of each thing stand out.[59]

Mathematics was an essential discipline in the Academy; also studied were philosophy in all its branches, empirical sciences, and politics.

These details have their importance for Plato's system of thought and for his place in the history of the philosophy of the natural law. The theory of ideas or forms is Plato's specific and fundamental contribution to philosophy, in metaphysics, epistemology, morals and politics. It has been suggested that the theory of ideas was Plato's answer to the dilemma posed by the contradiction between the thought of Heracleitus, for whom all was in flux, the universe in ceaseless change, and Parmenides, who stressed the permanence of being and the illusory nature of change. The Platonic ideas are changeless; our experience of change is in the world about us, which reflects the world of the Ideas.

If a graph were drawn of the appearance of the theory it would stay at zero for several of the earliest works, rise doubtfully in some of the so-called Socratic dialogues, leap to a maximum with the *Phaedo* and *Symposium*, stay at that level in the central books of the *Republic*, *Phaedrus*, *Parmenides* and then settle down to a level where the existence of some transcendental realities is definitely taken for granted but no full explanation of the extent of that belief is given in spite of several outstanding questions clamouring for solution.[60]

Plato's moral philosophy cannot be divorced from the theory of ideas. And, very much to our purpose, the ideas provide the ground for objective morality. Good and evil are not the result of

[58] Cf. G.C. Field, *Plato and his Contemporaries*, p. 35.

[59] *Epistle 7*.

[60] G.M.A. Grube, *Plato's Thought*, p. 7; W.D. Ross, *Plato's Theory of Ideas*, passim.

any arbitrary distinction or individual experience; they correspond to eternal and unchangeable truths. In the early dialogue, *Euthyphro*, indeed, Plato anticipates the kind of question that later was taken to provide the acid test of a natural law approach to ethics: Is a religious act religious because the gods approve it, or do they approve it because it is religious?[61] Is an act good, one might insist, because it is commanded? Or is it commanded because it is good? Or, still more insistently, are all evil actions evil because they are forbidden? Or are there some actions which are forbidden because they are evil? The denial of the *quaedam prohibita quia mala* will become the touchstone of the nominalism (and denial of the natural law) of the fourteenth century – as will be seen. But much development lies between Plato and, say, William of Ockham.

The problem of the status of pleasure is a useful focus for Plato's application of the theory of ideas to moral matters. Where there is a conflict (as we would express it) between pleasure and duty, why should we come down on the side of duty? The problem reflects in its own way the sophists' distinction between *physis* and *nomos*. The argument that a man should choose pleasure, if he is strong enough to ride above the legal obstacles and the punishments the weaker set in his way, is presented by Callicles in the *Gorgias* and by Thrasymachus in the *Republic*. It is rejected by Plato (and Socrates). But there remains a real problem, which is discussed and progressively refined in a number of the Platonic dialogues – the *Protagoras*, the *Phaedo*, the *Symposium*, the *Republic*, the *Philebus* (in which is found the longest and most detailed discussion) and, finally, the *Laws*. In the long run the problem proves to be that of the Good, eventually said to consist of the mingling of the truest pleasure with the truest wisdom.[62]

In the discussion of pleasure Plato's terms of reference in the ideas emerge and, even more significantly, his emphasis upon the

[61] *Euthyphro*, 8B–11A: cf. A.E. Taylor, *Plato: the Man and his Work*, p. 151; H. Welzel, *op. cit.*, pp. 22–23: "Platons Ideenlehre als Lehre von den apriorischen Wesensgehalten der Welt bildet das theoretische Rückgrat jeder ideellen Naturrechtslehre. Denn sie enthält drei Momente: Die Ideen sind erstens Erkenntnisgegenstände von strengster Allgemeingültigkeit, da sie unabhängig von der Einzelerfahrung für jede Einzelerfahrung gültig sind. Diese Inhalte ermöglichen zweitens eine Sacherkenntnis von absoluter Gewissheit und Sicherheit. Sie sind drittens ewige Vernunftwahrheiten, nicht wandelbare Willensentscheidungen."

[62] Cf. *Philebus*, 59E–66D; J. Burnet, *Greek Philosophy: Thales to Plato*, p. 324; A.H. Armstrong, *Introduction to Ancient Philosophy*, pp. 67 ff.

importance of wisdom. The same emphasis appears when the larger questions of law and of political organisation are faced. For Plato, as for Socrates, the great problem here was twofold: What is the good? and: How is it to be realised in private and in public life? He had written: "Two considerations go to the foundations of the philosophy of law: What pleasures ought not to be sought? and: What pains ought to be avoided?";[63] and in the practice of legislation the legislator must "often ask himself these questions: What am I aiming at? and secondly, Am I hitting the mark or missing it? In this way and in this only, he may possibly so discharge his task as to leave nothing for others to do after him."[64] The measure of realisation is the standard of 'justice'; and that realisation depends upon the predominance of the element of reason. The problem of the *Republic* is to discover the essence of justice (*dikaiosyne*), the investigation on the state-scale being undertaken because it promises to be easier to find justice "writ large."[65] And the conclusion is that justice, in the individual as in the state, will consist in the harmony of the parts, under the predominance of the element of reason.[66]

Just as there is a harmony in the soul, called individual justice, when its parts, the appetitive, the spirited and the rational, are in harmony, so there is justice in the state, political justice, when the three classes, the artisans the military and the rulers or perfect guardians, work in harmony.[67] All this is clearly germane to a theory of natural law, particularly when it is understood, as it must be, in terms of Plato's theory of ideas. Justice – human justice – must be referred to a supramundane justice, an ideal justice of which it is the pale reflection. The human lawgiver must try to see this justice in order to imitate it in his legislation;[68] he must leave out of consideration all human and variable legislation, all empirical knowledge of laws (which is knowledge appertaining to the world of sense) in order to arrive at the true, intellectual knowledge of 'justice in itself' (*to auto dikaion, to haplos dikaion*).[69]

[63] *Laws,* 636D–E.

[64] *Laws,* 744A, 719, 769D, 885B, 916E, cited in H. Cairns, *Legal Philosophy from Plato to Hegel,* p. 49.

[65] *Republic,* II, 368E–369B.

[66] *Republic,* IV, 431E–443A.

[67] *Republic,* IV, 441D–E.

[68] *Republic* VI, 514A (the myth of the cave), 501B; *Statesman,* 300C–E. Cf. J. Sauter, *Die philosophischen Grundlagen des Naturrechts,* p. 15, and note 4.

[69] *Phaedo,* 65D; cf. *Republic* V, 476A.

This may appear to be a very unrealistic programme. But Plato elsewhere shows that he was a realistic political philosopher and was not prepared to push his theory of ideas to the lengths of political absurdity. In the detail of his legislation he had an eye to human nature when giving an empirical content to the abstract ideal of justice; and, in particular, when he came to write the *Laws* in his old age, his views had mellowed somewhat from the apparent authoritarianism of the *Republic*, written in his maturity.[70] "At the root of Plato's theory of legislation is the idea, developed later by the proponents of natural law, that the legislator through reason alone is able to formulate a set of rules which will be adequate for the needs of the community."[71] More than once he even suggests that a law which is not a good law, in the sense of producing justice, is not a law at all: "Keep watch on my present law-making" says the Athenian, "in case I should enact any law either not tending to goodness at all, or tending only to part of it."[72]

Here are almost all the elements of a fully-formed theory of the natural law as it was to appear in the Stoics and those who came after them. It is small wonder that it has been argued that the natural law really begins with Plato (and Aristotle), rather than with the Stoics, who are usually given the credit of having been first to formulate the doctrine.[73] Bearing in mind that the way was shown by Socrates, Plato's claim to be the first philosopher to set up an objective standard of right and wrong independently of the individual conscience, is a serious one. This is clearly the province of the natural law; and in giving a new meaning to the *physei dikaion* of the Sophists, Plato provides the context for what A.E. Taylor has called with some hyperbole, "the first occurrence . . . in extant literature of the ominous phrase 'Law of Nature'."[74]

Great, however, as was Plato's importance for the growth of a

[70] *Laws*, 804; H. Welzel, *Naturrecht und materiale Gerechtigkeit*, p. 27: "Keine apriorische Ideenschau, sondern die empirische Beobachtung der menschlichen Natur stützt die Einzelthesen der platonischen Staatslehre. Platon hat auch hier der weiteren Naturrechtslehre den methodischen Weg gewiesen."

[71] H. Cairns, *op. cit.*, p. 44.

[72] *Laws*, 705E. The idea that a bad law is no law at all is more clearly adumbrated in the *Minos*, 314E; but this work is of doubtful authenticity. Cf. *Hippias Maj.* 284B–E; *Laws*, 715B; Xenophon, *Memorabilia*, I, 2, 40–66, cited by H. Cairns, *op. cit.*, p. 38 and note 22.

[73] See for example J. Wild, *Plato's Modern Enemies and the Theory of Natural Law*, pp. 134–171.

[74] A.E. Taylor, *Plato: The Man and His Work*, p. 117; Cf. *Gorgias*, 483E; *Republic*, 517C; *Phaedrus*, 247D; *Parmenides*, 130B; J. Sauter, *op. cit.*, p. 16.

teaching on the natural law, the influence of his pupil Aristotle, although he had less directly to say on the subject, was greater. This was partly due to the historical accident that, as far as Western Europe was concerned and, above all for the thirteenth century, the works of Aristotle were known and those of Plato were not. This will serve as a generalisation, to be qualified later to take account of the indirect influence of Platonism on the Christian centuries down to the Middle Ages and of the fact that the greater part of Aristotle's works were only re-discovered to the West in the late twelfth and early thirteenth century. But, historical contingencies apart, it should be fruitful to enquire whether the little Aristotle directly had to say about the natural law does not constitute one of those vital 'footnotes to Plato' which have so affected the history of thought.

D. ARISTOTLE

Aristotle was born in 383 B.C. at Stageira of a family with connections at the court of Macedon (he was at one stage in his career to be tutor to the future Alexander the Great). The details of his life are well known and only the outline need be recalled here. He began his active philosophical life in the Platonic Academy, arriving in 367 B.C. at the age of seventeen and remaining until the death of Plato twenty years later. This long apprenticeship and the close association with Plato left their mark on Aristotle, despite the fact that, in some important ways, he was fundamentally out of sympathy with the approach to philosophy in the Academy. When Plato was succeeded by Speusippus as head of the Academy, Aristotle left Athens and crossed the Aegean. He spent the next twelve years of his life at Assos, at Mitylene and, finally, at Pella (where he tutored Alexander). Lastly, in 335 B.C. shortly after the death of Philip of Macedon and the accession of Alexander, he returned to Athens and founded the Lyceum. The remaining twelve years of his life were spent in the Lyceum and to this period belong most of his extant works. On the fall of Athens to the Macedonians in 323 B.C. Aristotle left for Chalcis, where he died in the following year.[75]

[75] W.D. Ross, *Aristotle*, 5th edition, ch. 1, pp. 1–19; E. Barker, *The Politics of Aristotle* Introduction, pp. xi–xxvi: R.A. Gauthier-J.Y. Jolif, *L'Ethique à Nicomaque*, t. I, pp. 5–62.

The influence of Aristotle – the 'master of those that know' as Dante described him –, has been so pervasive and so decisive in practically all the areas of philosophy that it is not surprising to find him being credited with being "the father of natural law." Some justify this honorific title by the fact that "his metaphysics have provided ethics and consequently the doctrine of natural law with so excellent a fundation"[76] rather than by any striking innovation on Aristotle's part. This seems less than just; the celebrated distinction between natural and legal justice in the *Nicomachean Ethics,* to be considered presently, cannot be so easily dismissed. Before citing the vital passage, however, it will be well to sketch the outlines of Aristotle's system, the metaphysical and moral background to his teaching on the natural law. This is all the more necessary as his ethical works have little directly to do with metaphysics – in contrast with, for example, the *Republic* of Plato.

One capital point is that Aristotle's metaphysics is teleological. The idea of 'nature' is linked to that of 'end' – the nature of anything is determined by the end to which it is directed, as the nature of the acorn is understood by reference to the oak-tree into which it can develop. The complexities and difficulties of the Aristotelian 'nature,' and its damaging as well as its beneficial consequences in the history of philosophy, need not detain us here. It will be obvious, however, that the results for a 'law of nature' will be important.[77] It might also be pointed out that Aristotle himself consciously used the concept of 'nature' in laying down the fundamental themes of his moral philosophy, his politics and his ethics, including that of an 'intrinsic' morality.

From this metaphysical position Aristotle arrived at his teleological method of handling social phenomena. In the *Ethics* he sets the stage for that approach in the first sentence: 'Every art and every enquiry, and similarly every action and pursuit, is thought to aim at some good; and for this reason the good has rightly been declared to be that at which all things aim.' All that follows is a development and a deduction from that

[76] H. Rommen, *Natural Law,* p. 16; E. Galan y Gutierrez, *Jus Naturae,* p. 42; M. Salamon, "Le droit naturel chez Aristote" in *Archives de philosophie de droit et de sociologie juridique* 7 (1937), p. 121: "Aristote . . . n'a formulé cette idée (du droit naturel) ni le premier ni avec la conviction la plus forte"; contrast R. Voggensperger, *Der Begriff des 'jus naturale' im römischen Recht,* p. 71: "Aristoteles, der erste Dogmatiker des Naturrechts . . . ."

[77] H. Welzel, *Naturrecht und materiale Gerechtigkeit,* p. 31: "In engstem Zusammenhange mit dieser teleologischen Metaphysik sind die rechtsphilosophischen Grundthesen des Aristoteles zu verstehen . . . ."

principle. Similarly the opening sentence of the *Politics* is again teleological; 'Every state is a community of some kind, and every community is established with a view to some good; for mankind always act in order to obtain that which they think good.' And the rest of the discussion is an effort to determine the end of the state, and the nature of the matter or means which is necessary to a realization of that end. This view led him to see the function of education and law as instruments for the achievement of the good life. . . .[78]

Like Plato, Aristotle rejects any merely conventional source for the distinction between good ad evil. Like Plato, he speaks of an absolute good and even sets the transcendent good at the summit of being; but he understands these propositions in a way proper to himself.[79] In the *Nicomachean Ethics* he refers to the analogy of goodness; concrete, individual goods, in this context friendship, are values only incidentally and insofar as they resemble the supreme value.[80]

More closely concerned with the development of natural law theory are some of the general positions adopted by Aristotle in epistemology. There is his conception of the *intellectus agens* as a natural light which enables us to have right knowledge of first principles. With this may be compared the doctrine concerning the intuitive reason brought into play in the acquisition of the first principles of moral reasoning.[81] There is here some affinity with the scholastic teaching on *synderesis* and the habit of first practical principles but, as will be seen, it cannot be pushed too far.

Specifically with relation to law there is Aristotle's constant insistence upon reason. Law is a "rule proceeding from a sort of practical wisdom and reason"[82] which makes one think of later

[78] H. Cairns, *Legal Philosophy from Plato to Hegel*, pp. 89–90; cf. Ph. Delhaye, *Permanence du droit naturel*, pp. 25–28.

[79] *Metaph.*, XIV, 4, 1091 a 30 – 1092 a 4; *Eud. Eth.*, VII, 2, 1235 b 30–1237 a 9.

[80] *Nic. Eth.*, VIII, 4, 1157 a 30 – 1157 b 4.

[81] *De anima*, III, 18, 430 a 15–16: *Nic. Eth.*, VI, 12, 1143 a 35–1143 b 14; VII, 9, 1151 a 17–19. Cf. J. Sauter, *Die Philosophischen Grundlagen des Naturrechts*, p. 42 and note 2.

[82] *Nic. Eth.*, X, 9, 1180 a 23; cf. W. Siegfried, *Der Rechtsgedanke bei Aristoteles*, p. 50: "Das Gesetz ist ein Stück ordnender Vernunft ohne triebhaftes Begehren; *Id.*, p. 63, note 157: "Dass das Naturrecht ein Vernunftrecht sei, ist zwar bei Aristoteles, so viel ich sehe, nirgendswo ausdrücklich bemerkt (vgl. für das Verhältnis von logos und physis immerhin *Eud. Eth.*, 1221 a 22 und b 7) aber offenbar nur deshalb, weil diese Gleichsetzung für Aristoteles sich von selbst versteht; die Natur ist die oberste Norm für das richtige, die Vernunft die oberste Instanz, uns zu sagen, worin es besteht."

controversies about whether law is essentially an act of intellect or of will. For Aristotle the social ideal is the rule of law even more than the rule of men in conformity with the law; "we do not allow a *man* to rule, but a *rational principle*"[83]; or again, in a celebrated passage from the *Politics*:

He who commands that law should rule may thus be regarded as commanding that God and Reason alone should rule; he who commands that a *man* should rule adds the character of the beast. Appetite has that character and high spirit too, perverts the holders of office, even when they are the best of men. Law may thus be defined as 'reason free from all passion.'[84]

Such conceptions are highly relevant to Aristotle's thought on the natural law. The central notion, however, is that of justice (*dikaiosyne*) which, for him, is inseparable from law. It is discussed at length in the fifth book of the *Nicomachean Ethics.* In a wide sense, justice is synonymous with virtue in general, or at least with the sum of those virtues required for social intercourse.[85] It is, however, justice in the narrower sense, the specific virtue of justice, that concerns us here. Aristotle deals with it in detail all through Book V, where he gives its kinds (in the main, distributive and remedial justice, political justice and its divisions), examines the kind of equality required by justice (geometrical or arithmetical) and so on. It is in the part dealing with political justice, or the justice that obtains between citizens, that Aristotle introduces the term *dikaion physikon* which, if not its synonym, at least directly involves the natural law.

Of political justice part is natural, part legal, – natural, that which everywhere has the same force and does not exist by people's thinking this or that; legal, that which is originally indifferent, but when it has been laid down is not indifferent, e.g. that a prisoner's ransom shall be a mina, or that a goat and not two sheep shall be sacrificed, and again all the laws that are passed for particular cases, e.g. that sacrifice shall be made in honour of Brasidas, and the provisions of decrees. Now some think that all justice is of this sort, because that which is by nature is unchangeable and has everywhere the same force (as fire burns both

[83] *Nic. Eth.*, V, 6, 1134 a 35. For a discussion of the rule of law in Aristotle see W. Siegfried, *op. cit.*, pp. 44–45 and especially note 103.

[84] *Pol.*, III, 5, 1273 a 28–32.

[85] *Nic. Eth.*, V, 2, 1130 b 5 ff. Cf. W. Siegfried, *op. cit.*, p. 9, note 18. Compare the Biblical usage of 'justice' for the sum of the virtues; see also Cicero, *De off.*, I. 7, 20 – "justitia in qua virtutis splendor est maximus, ex qua boni viri nominantur." Cf. P. Trude, *Der Begriff der Gerechtigkeit in der aristotelischen Rechts- und Staatsphilosophie*, passim.

here and in Persia). While they see change in the things recognized as just. This, however, is not true in this unqualified way, but is true in a sense; or rather, with the gods it is perhaps not true at all, while with us there is something that is just even by nature, yet all of it is changeable; but still some is by nature, some not by nature. It is evident which sort of thing, among things capable of being otherwise, is by nature; and which is not but is legal and conventional, assuming that both are equally changeable. And in all other things the same distinction will apply; by nature the right hand is stronger, yet it is possible that all men should come to be ambidextrous. The things which are just by virtue of convention and expediency are like measures; for wine and corn measures are not everywhere equal, but larger in wholesale and smaller in retail markets. Similarly, the things which are just not by nature but by human enactment are not everywhere the same, since constitutions also are not the same, though there is but one which is everywhere by nature the best.[86]

The very importance of this passage, because it has always attracted commentators, makes it difficult to determine exactly what Aristotle meant. There seem to be two extremes to avoid in the interpretation. On the one hand it is reading too much into the passage to make it a kind of charter of natural rights. Natural and legal justice, it must be remembered, are for Aristotle, parts of political justice. And political justice is the justice of the citizenry, found "among men who share their life with a view to self-sufficiency, men who are free and either proportionately or arithmetically equal, so that between those who do not fulfil this condition there is no political justice but justice in a special sense and by analogy."[87] Women, children and slaves will not, therefore, come within the ambit of political justice here defined – for where these classes are concerned equality is not in question but subordination. And a natural justice that is part of political justice is a far cry from a theory of natural law or natural rights in the modern sense. On the other hand one minimises unduly the importance of the passage by regarding it as if the only criterion Aristotle had in mind, when he distinguished between natural and legal justice, were that of legal validity – natural law having its principle in nature ("unchangeable and has everywhere the same force") whereas the validity of positive law depends upon the act

[86] *Nic. Eth.*, V. 7, 1134 b 18–1135 a 5.

[87] *Nic. Eth.*, V. 6, 1134 a 26–30. Aristotle does not, however, deny all justice between citizens and slaves. Cf. *Nic. Eth.*, VIII, 11 – "... the slave is a living tool, and the tool a lifeless slave. *Qua* slave, then, one cannot be friends with him. But *qua* man can; for there seems to be some justice between any man and any other who can share a system of law...."

of a human will choosing between alternatives that, before the choice, are indifferent ("that a prisoner's ransom shall be a mina, or that a goat and not two sheep shall be sacrificed").[88] It is true that Aristotle is dealing with legal terms and that he is perfectly aware of contemporary legal ideas and practice.[89] Still, the distinction he makes between legal and natural justice does not fit into a purely legal context.

In fact this passage in which Aristotle distinguishes between natural and legal justice contains two major innovations. The first is the recognition that natural justice is not immutable – a point that is made more succinctly in the parallel passage in the *Magna Moralia.*[90] The second and more far-reaching innovation is the inclusion of natural justice as a variety of political.

The first of these points is clearly made; Aristotle extends the concept of 'nature,' the domain of scientific investigation and proof, to the matter of justice. In the process he expressly refutes the Sophists' view that all law is conventional; for the Sophists' argument depended upon a sharp antithesis between the supposed immutability of nature and the widely differing conceptions of justice that obtained in different communities. Since laws vary and nature does not, the Sophists' opposition between the two seemed complete. Aristotle's answer was that it is only true with qualification to say that nature is unchangeable. The gods may have an immutable natural justice, but not so man. For us nature does not exclude all possibility of change. The example, common to the *Nicomachean Ethics* and to the *Magna Moralia*, is not, perhaps, very convincing. "By nature" the right hand is stronger than the left, but that does not exclude the possibility that some, or even all, men should become ambidextrous.[91] Still, in spite of this variability, the things that are just by nature are clearly distinguishable from the things that are so as the result of free,

[88] M. Salomon, "Le droit naturel chez Aristote" in *Archives de philosophie du droit et de sociologie juridique*, 7 (1937), pp. 122–125.

[89] Cf. H.D.P. Lees, "The Legal Background to two Passages in the Nicomachean Ethics" in *Classical Quarterly*, 41 (1937), pp. 129–140; E. Barker, *The Politics of Aristotle*, p. 149, note FF.

[90] *Magn. Mor.*, I, 33, 1194 b 30–1195 a 7: "Things are just either by nature or by law. But we must not regard the natural as being something which cannot by any possibility change; for even the things which are by nature partake of change.... Nor because things change does it follow that they are not by nature...."

[91] It is suggested that the example may be a tilt at Plato who had said (*Laws;* 794D 5–795D 5) that both hands are equal, implying that it is unnatural for the right to be stronger.

although not arbitrary, choice like the decision establishing legal measures for wine and corn on the basis of convenience. Such choice could perfectly well be otherwise; one cannot prove that one particular set of measures should be used. By contrast if it is a question of a constitution we are within the domain of proof, for, in Aristotle's view, "there is but one which is everywhere by nature the best."[92]

The second innovation of Aristotle, in the passage we are considering, is really a consequence of the first. Once it was conceded that natural justice could vary there was no further good reason for excluding it from the sphere of political justice; a natural justice changeable as are all things human, yet found everywhere, can be a part of political justice – for only its supposed immutability prevented people linking it with the obviously variable political justice. And this is the conception that will pass into Roman law; there we shall find that *jus naturale* and *jus gentium* are not entities outside, but integral parts of the system.[93]

Aristotle's distinction between natural and legal justice is, therefore, a pregnant one; we shall see in the sequel some of its fruits. To complete the account of Aristotle we must refer to another distinction, which at first sight appears equally promising – that between written and unwritten law (*nomos gegrammenos; nomos agraphos*) with which is associated the distinction between general and particular law (*nomos koinos; nomos idios*).[94] Aristotle returns more than once to these distinctions in the *Rhetoric* but his treatment of them is not consistent. On the whole he appears to equiparate particular with written and general with unwritten law. This would agree with the distinction between natural and legal justice in the *Nicomachean Ethics*,[95]

[92] Cf. M. Salamon, *op. cit.*, pp. 124–126.

[93] Cf. M. Hamburger, *Morals and Law–The growth of Aristotle's Legal Theory*, pp. 60–63. Contrast Aristotle's statement in *Soph. Elench.*, 12, 173 a 7–16 that nature and law are generally in conflict.

[94] *Rhet.*, I, 10, 1368 b 7–10: "Now the law is particular or general. By particular I mean the written law in accordance with which a state is administered; by general, the unwritten regulations which appear to be universally recognised; I, 13, 1374 a 27–1375 b 8: "For it is evident that if the written law is counter to our case we must have recourse to the general law and equity as more in accordance with justice . . . that equity is ever constant and never changes, even as the general law which is based on nature, whereas written laws often vary . . . it is the part of a better man to make use of and abide by the unwritten rather than the written law. . . ."

[95] *Nic. Eth.*, V, 7, 1134 b 18; VIII, 13, 1162 b 21.

although it is difficult to reconcile it with the fact that the *Nicomachean Ethics* makes natural and legal justice divisions of political justice. Elsewhere in the *Rhetoric* Aristotle seems to imply that both written and unwritten law may be the work of a human legislator – a view which, incidentally, is even more clearly expressed in the *Nicomachean Ethics.*[96] It is not to our present purpose to pursue these distinctions further or to attempt their final reconciliation.[97] It should, however, be remarked that the *Rhetoric* is not a scientific treatise on moral philosophy; the distinctions mentioned are given by way of illustration so that a certain fluidity of terminology is to be expected.[98]

Aristotle's discussion of *dikaion physikon* leaves more than one tantalising question unanswered. In one way, perhaps, this fact has contributed to the history of the concept of the natural law; for where there is ambiguity commentators sometimes find what they wish to find. And what they find may prove to be as important as anything indubitably in the text itself. We shall find that this passage from the fifth book of the *Nicomachean Ethics* will recur in the history of the natural law.

There is, however, another doctrine of Aristotle in the *Ethics*, that of the 'practical syllogism,' which has likewise greatly influenced the development of the natural law; and in this instance it is clear that subsequent thinkers have, wittingly or unwittingly, attributed to Aristotle views that he certainly did not hold. The doctrine appears in the seventh book of the *Nicomachean Ethics*, when Aristotle is discussing the problem of incontinence (*akrasia*); but it is found elsewhere too.[99] The question is whether Aristotle attributed the importance to the practical syllogism that

[96] *Rhet.*, I, 15, 1376 b 24–27: "In addition to this, we must examine whether the contract is contrary to any written law of our own or foreign countries, to any general law, or to other previous or subsequent contracts"; cf. *Nic. Eth.*, X, 9, 1180 a 35.

[97] For various attempts to reconcile the distinctions cf. R. Hirzel, *Agraphos nomos*, pp. 1–14; W. Siegfried, *Der Rechtsgedanke bei Aristoteles*, p. 63, note 158; J. Sauter, *Die Philosophischen Grundlagen des Naturrechts*, p. 42, note 1; S. Gagner, *Studien zur Ideengeschichte der Gesetzgebung*, pp. 252–256.

[98] Contrast the view of M. Hambuger, *op. cit.*, p. 65, for whom the *Rhetoric* contains "the consummation of Aristotle's legal philosophy and theory" and where "perfect harmony is established between the various legal spheres."

[99] *Nic. Eth.*, VII, 1147 a 4 ff.; cf. VI, 1143 a 35 – b 5, 1144 a 31–36; *De motu anim.*, 6–7, 700 b 4–701 b 1: *De anima*, III, 434 a 16–21: cf. D.J. Allan, "The Practical Syllogism" in *Autour d'Aristote: Recueil d'études de philosophie ancienne et médiévale offert à A. Mansion*, 1955, pp. 325–340.

some of his commentators have given it. It has been pointed out[100] that he does not speak explicitly of the 'practical syllogism' and his statements are easily interpreted as offering patterns of reasoning in moral matters which are syllogistic, without making the assumption that all moral reasoning must be syllogistic, or that all moral situations can be cast into the form of a syllogism or a sorites. Furthermore, his main use of the syllogism is in the specific question of 'incontinence' or 'unrestraint': How is it that a man yields to passion although he knows what is right? The problem arises when one departs, as Aristotle did, from the Socratic identification of virtue and knowledge. Aristotle's discussion, it is fair to say, bristles with difficulties. These, fortunately, need not detain us; nor need Aristotle's answer to the problem.

The practical syllogism, to which he makes appeal, was taken over after Aristotle and pressed into the service of the natural law in a way that is foreign to his thinking. The medievals' doctrine of *synderesis*, itself to make a powerful contribution to the development of the natural law, as will be seen in its place, is not to be found in Aristotle. Whatever may be thought of Aristotle's solution of the problem of the unrestrained man who acts, not in accordance with what he knows to be right, but in accordance with his passions, whatever one thinks of the suggestion that the conclusion of the syllogism is action (and not simply a proposition about action), and, indeed, whatever one thinks of the entire analogy between speculative and practical reasoning, Aristotle does not say there is a special *habitus* of first practical principles (the scholastic *synderesis*) which provides the major premiss of the practical syllogism. It is easy to see how attractive to a natural law thinker is such an idea. It explains in a tidy and acceptable fashion the mechanism of applying the principles of the law to particular cases and it underlines the fundamental character of those first principles; the practical principles are compared with the first principles of reasoning in general (the so-called first principles of logic) in their function and in the special and unmistakable way in which they are known. It was, however, Albert the Great, in the thirteenth century, who posited this habit of first principles in the practical intellect, thereby marking an important innovation for the theory of the natural law. It would be a mistake to attribute this view to Aristotle.[101]

[100] Cf. W.F.R. Hardie, *Aristotle's Ethical Theory*, p. 228; cf. H. Cairns, *Legal Philosophy from Plato to Hegel*, pp. 81–82.

[101] Cf. R.A. Gauthier-J.Y. Jolif, *L'Ethique à Nicomaque*, T. II, pp. 563–568, especially p. 564, citing O. Lottin, *Psychologie et morale aux XIIe et XIIIe siècles*, t. II, pp. 212–224.

For a complete account of Aristotle's thought on the natural law it would be necessary to follow up his conception of the relations between natural and positive law, his use of the distinction between natural and unnatural action in the opening chapters of the *Politics* already mentioned, his insistence upon the fact that laws bind the magistrates as well as the people and a host of other connected questions.[102] Such a study, however, would lead one too far afield from the influence of Aristotle in the matter of *defining* the natural law. The same may be said of Aristotle's views concerning the structure of the moral act, the rôle of right reason as the rule of morality and the organisation of moral problems under the virtues. We shall find many of these conceptions will play a part later, mediated by other thinkers. The rôle of right reason, for example, will be capital:

> ... that which is proper to each thing is by nature best and most pleasant for each thing; for man, therefore, the life according to reason is best and pleasantest, since reason more than anything else *is* man. This life therefore is also the happiest.[103]

This conception, supplemented by the Stoic precept of living according to nature, and connected with a conception of law as a "rule proceeding from a sort of practical wisdom and reason"[104] will later serve as a resumé of almost all that the doctrine of a natural law implies.

The picture that has begun to emerge is that of a natural law, a standard of moral rectitude connected with human reason. The primitive intuitions concerning justice, mythologised or personified, were the first gropings towards this standard. The Sophists' undermining of the notion of a moral standard provoked reactions: Socrates and, following him Plato, rallied to the defence of morality against relativism. Here reason comes to the fore, whether in the Socratic identification of virtue with reason, or in Plato's stress upon the rule of reason, in the individual and in the state. And for Aristotle, despite his critique of the Socratic notion of virtue and his much greater realism in recognising the non-rational factors in human moral behaviour, the 'naturally just' was also bound up with reason. In these elements there is not yet a developed theory of natural law; they are the *disjecta membra*, 'nature' and 'reason,' 'good' and 'evil,' features that diverse thinkers will, in their various fashions, form into a profile of the natural law.

[102] *Pol.*, I, 5, 1254 a 20–1255 a 2; IV, 1, 1289 a. For a full panoply of texts see W. Siegfried, *Der Rechtsgedanke bei Aristoteles*, pp. 66–81.

[103] *Nic. Eth.*, X, 7, 1178 a 5–8.

[104] *Nic. Eth.*, X, 9, 1180 a 23.

CHAPTER II

THE PROFILE EMERGES

A. THE STOICS

In any history of the natural law the Stoics occupy an important place. There is general agreement that they were the first to systematize the concept, although not all would agree with the comment of Samuel Pufendorf (1632–1694), himself a key-figure in the modern shaping of the natural law, that the Stoic concept had been narrowed by the substitution of Aristotle's philosophy of law and politics for the Stoic ideas.[1] But which Stoics? And what was their conception of the natural law? These are questions not easily answered when one recalls that the school stretches over half a millenium and includes thinkers that differ even on matters one would have thought essential. Zeno of Citium (c. 336–264 B.C.) appeared at Athens, teaching at the painted porch (*stoa poikile*, whence the name 'stoic') about the year 300 B.C. He and his first successors, Cleanthes (c. 331–233 B.C.) and Chrysippus (281–208 B.C.) constitute the Early Stoa. The Middle Stoa is represented mainly by Panaetius of Rhodes (c. 185–110 B.C.) and Poseidonius of Apamea (135–51 B.C.); and the Late or New Stoa covers the first to the third centuries A.D., the age of Seneca (3–65 A.D.), the former slave Epictetus (c. 60–100 A.D.) and the Emperor Marcus Aurelius Antoninus who reigned from 161 to 180 A.D. This long time-span and the diversity of thinkers it includes already make it difficult to interpret the Stoic philosophy. But one must add the fact that the philosophy was transplanted from the Greek to the Roman world and the further fact that, since the writings of the Early and Middle Stoa have disappeared or survive only in fragmentary form, we depend for

[1] Cf. S. Pufendorf, *Specimen controversiarum*, I, 4; V, 22 cited in J. Sauter, *Die philosophischen Grundlagen des Naturrechts*, pp. 54–55 and notes 1, 2.

our knowledge of Stoicism upon the later Roman Stoics and upon the testimony of writers like Cicero (106–44 B.C.), Plutarch (50–120 A.D.), Sextus Empiricus (second half of the second century A.D.) and Diogenes Laertius (third century A.D.).[2]

In general the Stoics (like the Epicureans) divided philosophy into three parts: logic, natural science and ethics. After Aristotle's death there was no thinker of his calibre to carry on the great metaphysical tradition represented by his and Plato's speculative thought; and the practical bent of post-Aristotelian philosophy was shown in the concentration of the Stoics (and of the Epicureans) on moral philosophy or ethics. Ethics is the crowning part of philosophy and the other two branches prepare the way. Of the Stoic logic it is sufficient to note that it consists of two parts, the dialectic and the theory of knowledge, the latter being mainly the search for the criterion of truth. The Stoic natural science, including a metaphysics borrowed in part from Heracleitus, is constructed around three themes – materialism, dynamism and pantheism. The materialism in thorough-going; everything, even qualities, thought, and the soul itself, is ultimately three-dimensional matter of varying degrees of subtlety. The dynamism indicates that matter is of itself inert and requires force to reduce it to shape. And the pantheism identifies the world, thought of as an organic unity, with God, otherwise called the primary matter, the substrate of the universe, the reason of the world, even the primal fire.

The Stoic ethic is based upon an understanding of the nature of man in conformity with the general principles of their philosophy of nature. The soul of man is material, the mind a fiery breath. The seat of the soul is the breast, where the blood is warmed and whence comes the voice, the expression of thought. There are seven derivative powers of the soul – the five senses and the powers of reproduction and of speech. The dominant power of the soul is reason; and emotions, "when reason is hurried into what is contrary to nature by excess of impulse," have no part in the life of reason, which is the good life. So much seems common ground of all the Stoics.[3] When it comes to the detail of their ethical system there are many more difficulties and uncertainties in our knowledge. Two points of relevance for our theme may be

[2] Cf. M. Pohlenz, *Die Stoa*, passim; the texts of the Stoics are found in Johannes ab Arnim, *Stoicorum veterum fragmenta*, 4 vols.

[3] Cf. J. Sauter, *op. cit.*, pp. 44–54; A. Verdross, *Abendländische Rechtsphilosophie*, pp. 44–46; E. Zeller, *Stoics, Epicureans and Sceptics*, pp. 126-180.

noted. Firstly, freedom is denied to man: there can be no exception to the general law of determinism and man, like every other being, is bound into the chain of natural causes. And secondly, the notions of virtue, the highest good and the ideal of the wise man dominate the moral teaching of the Stoics. Virtue has two aspects; positively it is subjection to the law of nature and negatively it is independence of irrational impulse (as represented by the emotions). The highest good lies in conformity with nature. And the wise man, the Stoic sage, is he who has achieved virtue, is wholly conformed to nature and reason. On these matters the early Stoics were uncompromising. Virtue, for example, was one and indivisible – either you possessed it or you did not, as a statement is either true or false (there is no third possibility), a shot hits or misses the mark (whether it misses by an inch or a mile is irrelevant), a man drowns or he does not (whether he is a handsbreadth below the surface or a hundred fathoms deep does not matter).

These uncompromising principles were somewhat modified by the later Stoics, notably when they realised that no one, not even Socrates, had measured up to the ideal of the wise man and that complete *apatheia* or indifference to feeling was an impossible state. The latter Stoics were the first to develop a science of casuistry, tempering the severity of the general principles. Nevertheless the eulogy of the wise man remains the characteristic feature of the expositions of Stoic moral philosophy. The ideal of heroic insensibility, of severity, rigidity, duty had its own appeal. The wise man's independence of externals finds dramatic expression in suicide, in his being able to leave life at will: "The door is open" said Epictetus, "there is one entry to life but many exits."[4]

In a word, Stoicism is an eclectic system marked by a stern practical and moral bent. The real business of philosophy is the moral conduct of man – according to Chrysippus the life of pure speculation, lauded by Plato and Aristotle, is equivalent to living only for pleasure.[5] Virtue is the primary object of philosophy; ethics, therefore, is the most important branch.

Now virtue, as Socrates had taught, is identical with knowledge; and for the Stoics the other branches of philosophy, namely logic and natural science, will be subordinate to ethics and

[4] Epictetus, *Discourses*, I, 9.

[5] Seneca, *Ep.*, 89, 8 – "Philosophia studium virtutis est, sed per ipsam virtutem"; cf. E. Zeller, *Stoics, Epicureans and Sceptics*, p. 57.

will have as their *raison d'être* the production of that knowledge which is virtue. Specifically this knowledge is knowledge of the world-order or of the universal law to which the individual must submit himself – and here is the point of insertion of the natural law in the system. We must know nature in order to follow nature's law; the universal law is the *law of nature* and the Stoic morality is epitomised in the maxim: "Live according to nature" (*homologoumenos tè physei zen*).

This precept is a radical identification of *nomos* and *physis* and will become a cornerstone of the edifice of natural law. It requires to be examined more closely. It has been suggested that in the phrase "Live in harmony with nature" the words "with nature" were a later addition; the original maxim would, therefore, have meant "Live in a way that is self-consistent,"[6] Be that as it may, it is the phrase that passed into currency that is important here. Clearly its meaning will follow the sense given to nature. The Stoics were materialists and pantheists; their entire science of nature is materialist and pantheist and their doctrine concerning the nature of man is in character. The human soul is material and is diffused throughout the body; it is the bond of union of the body just as the world-soul is the bond of union of the world at large; it is of the most subtle kind of matter, like the particles of fire (an idea the Stoics borrowed from Heracleitus).[7] The dominant power of the soul is reason and following human nature was identical with following reason. Chrysippus, the 'second founder' of Stoicism, had already posed the question whether it was universal nature or human nature that was to be followed, and answered that they came to much the same thing.[8]

The notion of obligation presents a difficulty for the Stoic; or rather, since Stoicism leaves no room for freewill, obligation and duty must be given a meaning different from the usual.[9] In the final analysis doing one's duty seems to mean willing to do what one will, in any event, be forced to do by the nature of things; he

[6] M. Pohlenz, *op. cit.*, I, pp. 116–119; J. Sauter, *op. cit.*, p. 48; D.G. Ritchie, *Natural Rights*, p. 34, citing Stobaeus, *Ecl.*, II, c. 6, n. 6.

[7] H. Welzel, *Naturrecht und materiale Gerechtigkeit*, p. 38.

[8] J. ab Arnim, *op. cit.*, I, n. 555; cf. Diogenes Laertius, *Lives of the Philosophers*, VII, 89: "Naturam autem Chrysippi quidem eam cui convenienter oporteat vivere et communem intelligit et proprie humanam. At vero Cleanthes communen tantummodo naturam suscipit, quam sequi oporteat, non etiam particularem."

[9] The difficulty is, of course, common to all determinist moral philosophies – in modern times those of Spinoza, say, or J.S. Mill.

does his duty who cooperates with the inexorable causes. The sage, the favourite subject of Stoic eulogies, is the man who willingly submits to the rule of nature; in which he distinguishes himself from the fool who is dragged in the train of events. Seneca put it in a phrase: Fate leads the willing and drags the unwilling: *fata volentem ducunt nolentem trahunt.* More prosaically, if vividly, the situation is compared with that of the dog tied behind a cart; he may run with the cart's progress or sit upon his hind legs and be dragged ignominiously.[10]

Even Cicero's lifelong acquaintance with the problems of human freewill and spontaneity, in the courtroom and in the practice of the law, does not seem to have suggested to him that the Stoic notion of inexorable fate needed revising. "Things which are to be do not suddenly spring into existence, but the evolution of time is like the unwinding of a cable: it creates nothing new and only unfolds each event in its order." Gerard Watson, who quotes this passage, goes on to comment: "What then about our ordinary ways of thought and language which presume personal responsibility for one's actions?"[11]

There is no immortality of the soul-materialism excludes that – nor is there any need for it. Virtue, which is within the power of man, is identical with happiness. What are commonly thought to be the misfortunes of life are simply irrelevant. The sage, who has acquired complete independence of all that is irrational, notably all emotion, is godlike and, indeed, indistinguishable from God.[12]

The foregoing has no pretensions to be an account of Stoicism; it is no more than a sketch of some leading ideas of the school in order to suggest the need for caution in assessing the significance of Stoicism in the history of the natural law. What appears to be a conventional description of the law of nature is seen differently when set against its proper Stoic background; and, on the other hand, the importance of some such passages may be measured by their capacity of surviving when the specific Stoic meanings of terms like 'God,' 'nature,' 'right reason,' 'law' have been lost sight of. Take, for example, the following description from Diogenes Laertius' life of Zeno:

And nature, they (the Stoics) say, made no difference originally between plants and animals for it regulates the life of plants too – in their case

[10] Seneca, *Ep.*, 107, 11; J. ab Arnim, *op. cit.*, II, n. 975; cf. Ph. Delhaye, *Permanence du droit naturel*, p. 29 for commentary on similar passages in Epictetus and Marcus Aurelius.

[11] G. Watson, "The Natural Law and Stoicism," in A.A. Long (ed.) *Problems in Stoicism*, p. 231.

[12] J. ab Arnim, *op. cit.*, III, n. 526.

without impulse or sensation – just as certain processes of a vegetative kind go on in us. But when, in the case of animals, impulse enabling then to go in quest of their proper food has been added, for them, according to the Stoics the rule of nature is to follow the direction of impulse, and when reason, by way of a more perfect leadership, has been bestowed upon the beings we call rational, for them life according to reason rightly becomes the natural life .... This is why Zeno was the first to designate as the goal "life in agreement with nature" which is the same as a virtuous life, because virtue is the end to which nature guides us...."

Living virtuously is equivalent to living in accordance with experience of the actual course of nature, as Chrysippus says in the first book of his *About Ends;* for our undivided natures are parts of the nature of the whole universe. And this is why the end may be defined as life in accordance with nature or, in other words, in accordance with our own human nature as well as that of the universe, a life in which we refrain from every action forbidden by the law common to all things, that is to say, the right reason which pervades all things and is identical with Zeus, lord and ruler of all that is.[13]

Here there is not merely the dramatic identification of *nomos* and *physis,* but the practical identification of the human nature with the nature of the universe. It may, indeed, be that the principle of following nature does not, in practice, offer much guidance concerning human behaviour because it becomes, within the system, something of a tautology. It may, further, be true that some at least of the Stoic philosophers condoned incest, community of wives, homosexuality, prostitution, masturbation or cannibalism; and the Stoic justification of suicide is notorious.[14] Nevertheless

[13] *Lives of the Philosophers* VII, 86–88; cf. Cicero, *Acad.* I, 10, 38; J. Stelzenberger, *Die Beziehungen der frühchristlichen Sittenlehre zur Ethik der Stoa,* p. 100; J.T.C. Arntz, "Natural Law and its History" in *Concilium,* 5 (1965), pp. 23–32.

[14] Cf. G. Watson, "The Early History of Natural Law" in *Irish Theological Quarterly,* 33 (1966) pp. 72–73 for detailed references and the observation that allowance must be made for the polemics of the witnesses. The theme of suicide in Stoicism has attracted much attention, cf. supra, note 4.: Thus Seneca says "Malum est in necessitate vivere. Sed in necessitate vivere nulla necessitas est. Quidni nulla sit? Patent undique ad libertatem viae multae, breves, faciles. Agamus Deo gratias quod nemo in vita teneri potest..."; Epictetus says I, 9 "The door is open"; cf. I, 2; and Marcus Aurelius, *Meditations,* V, 29, says that "the philosopher chooses the mode of his death just as he chooses a ship for a journey or a house to live in. He leaves life as he would leave a banquet – when it is time. He lays aside his body when it no longer suits him, as he would lay aside worn-out clothes and withdraws from life as he would withdraw from a house no longer weather-proof". Of the leading Stoics Zeno, Cleanthes, Antipater and Seneca are said to have committed suicide; and the classical example of Stoic suicide was that of Cato the Younger.

there was a very great deal in Stoicism that could be, and was, adopted into Christian thought. The Stoic eulogies of law, for instance, when purged of pantheism and corrected by reflection on the transcendence of God, will be found acceptable as we shall see, by the Church Fathers. So, for instance, the well-known gloss by Chrysippus on Pindar's hymn to law as king (*nomos basileus*)

The natural law is king over everything, divine and human alike. It must be the authority that determines what is good and what is evil, the leader of men destined to live in communities; it lays down standards for right and wrong, and it does so by commanding what is to be done and forbidding what is not to be done.[15]

It has been pointed out that even this does not give concrete guidance; and that Chrysippus, "a philosopher learned in history, delighted in collecting examples of historical relativism; but like all the Stoics he was undisturbed by the diversity of the phenomena, for behind all the variety there is agreement at least about the basic issues, the agreement of reasonable men of all times and countries. As Epictetus put it in one of his pithy sayings: the formulation of what is lawful is not the province of fools. Plato in the *Republic* and in the *Philebus* had ventured the same opinion."[16] In a word, Chrysippus's saying can not merely be detached from its Stoic background, unacceptable to Christians, but that background itself, with its reference to the *logos* of Heracleitus and the 'law' of Pindar, may be seen to yield the pattern for future development in the schema 'eternal law – natural law – human law.'[17]

In this connection one might also cite Cleanthes's praise of law "rational, eternal, all-governing ... than which nothing higher exists for man or God."[18] Leaving aside the Stoic fatalism, there is here a concept of a universal law, the measure of particular laws. In this connection it is interesting to notice that Chrysippus regarded all human laws as mistaken, even those of the great lawgivers, Cleisthenes, Lycurgus, Solon.[19] This outlook resembles

[15] J. ab Arnim, *Stoicorum veterum fragmenta*, III, n. 354.

[16] L. Edelstein, *The Meaning of Stoicism*, p. 84, citing Epictetus, *Discourses*, IV, 7, 33–34.

[17] Cf. H. Welzel, *op. cit.*, p. 39.

[18] J. ab Arnim, *op. cit.*, I, p. 537.

[19] J. ab Arnim, *op. cit.*, III, n. 324; cf. Plutarch, *De stoicorum repugnantia*, 1033 F; Seneca, *Controv.*, II, 13, 7: "sui juris rerum natura est nec ad leges humanas componitur"; cf. J. Sauter, *Die philosophischen Grundlagen des Naturrechts*, p. 53.

that of the Sophists already seen. In the critique of existing institutions, however, the advantage lay with the Stoics because of their much more developed concepts of universality of law, of the brotherhood of all men, Greek, slave and barbarian, and of the cosmopolitan ideal of the world-state.

Perhaps the single most important contribution of the Stoics to the development of the doctrine of the natural law was their insistence upon the universal brotherhood of men; by this "the Stoics exploded the framework of the *polis*."[20] The *Politeia* of Zeno, is, according, to Plutarch, "directed to this one main point, that our life should not be based on cities or peoples each with its view of right and wrong, but we should regard all men as our fellow-countrymen and fellow-citizens . . ."[21] How far changed political conditions – the passing of the city-states of Greece and the hellenization of the world in the wake of the conquests of Alexander the Great – brought about the acceptance of such views is not important. What is important is that the original Stoic notion of *oikeiosis*, the process by which the individual assimilates to himself what is beneficial and rejects what is harmful, a process which lies at the back of all development of thought and of morals, has been broadened to take account of society and of mankind at large.

> One of the most striking features of the Stoics' teaching in ethics is their universalism, their sense of human unity, their belief that human affairs are governed by rules that hold universally. The Stoics are citizens of the world, citizens of the human republic, and they are strongly inclined to believe in propositions that are equally true and good in all parts of the world. After Plato and Aristotle they are the main founders of moral universalism.[22]

This is not, however, the whole picture; besides this universalizing tendency in the interpretation of human nature one should set the complementary tendency to see law in a more individual fashion. As a broad generalisation it may be said that the early Stoa stressed nature, the Middle Stoa human reason, while "the younger Stoics heard the voice of the natural law, not only in reason but in the human conscience also. 'I do nothing,'

[20] C.J. Friederich, *The Philosophy of Law in Historical Perspective*, pp. 27–28.

[21] Plutarch, *De Alex. Magni fortuna aut virtute*, 329 a–b, cited by G. Watson, "The Natural Law and Stoicism," p. 220; cf. Marcus Aurelius, *Meditations*, VI, 44: "my nature is rational and civic; my city and country, as Antoninus, is Rome; as a man, the world."

[22] Y.R.M. Simon, *The Tradition of Natural Law*, p. 30.

Seneca says, 'on account of opinions commonly held; I do everything for conscience's sake.''[23]

The Stoic philosophy, then, has come to articulate the natural law in a new and systematic way, a way that will survive, not merely in its phraseology but in a great part of its structure, into the Christian and later formulations of the doctrine.[24] And not alone the explicit teaching on the natural law, but other Stoic moral doctrines, such as that of evident principles, common to all men and prior to experience, principles that include a certain knowledge of good and evil, the elements of the virtues, the recognition of the goodness and eternity of God, will be taken up, corrected and developed by Christians. And so the claim of the Stoics to be the founders of the doctrine of the natural law will be substantiated. This formative influence of Stoicism was transmitted to the Fathers and later to the scholastics by Cicero and by the Roman law. As each is considered in turn, the outlines of the doctrine will be seen to come into sharper focus.

B. CICERO

Marcus Tullius Cicero (106–43 B.C.) was not a great original thinker; but he was very great popularizer of the natural law philosophy of the Greek Stoics. He has some inkling of this when, although not an unduly self-deprecatory character, he said of some of his writings: "They are merely copies and cost me comparatively little labour. I supply only the words, of which I have a copious flow." It was, however, through Cicero more than anyone else that the natural law of the Stoics passed to the Latin west. He knew the writings of the School. He says expressly that he followed Panaetius in the first two books of his *De officiis;* and, as a young man in 97 B.C., he had made the journey to Rhodes to consult Poseidonius, the greatest Stoic of his time. Nor was Cicero an uncritical popularizer; again we have his own testimony: "For our part we do not play the rôle of mere translator, but, while preserving the doctrines of our chosen au-

[23] Seneca, *Dial.* VIII, 20, 4; L. Edelstein, *op. cit.*, p. 84; J. Stelzenberger, *Die Beziehungen der frühchristlichen Sittenlehre zur Ethik der Stoa*, p. 104.

[24] V.J. Bourke, *St. Thomas and the Greek Moralists*, pp. 27–28: "Though the Greek Stoics are materialistic, naturalistic and pantheistic in their concept of divinity, at least they conceived of a deity which could be an immutable guide for moral action. It is a case of low-grade metaphysics accompanied by high-grade moral ideals."

thorities, add thereto our own criticism and our own arrangement."[25] It is not surprising that many expositions of the Stoic teaching on natural law should rely so heavily on Cicero. It has even been argued, with a good deal of force, that the Stoic natural law is really a creation of Cicero's – at least in the sense that the older Stoics, according to our admittedly defective knowledge, were no more natural law theorists than, say, Plato or Aristotle:

> To write about natural law, then, in Stoicism would be to write about Stoic morality. But Plato and Aristotle also had systems of morality and yet their names are not linked in the way that the Stoics' are with the natural law. For later ages the Stoics were particularly associated with natural law mainly because of one man, Cicero.[26]

What is certain is that it was largely due to the writings of Cicero that the Stoic theory of laws made its impact upon Roman law and, later, upon Christian legal thought. One of the most celebrated passages, expressing a theory of natural law, is preserved by Lactantius from the lost third book of Cicero's *Republic*. It is a eulogy of the eternal and unchanging law, the expression of right reason, that will find a ready echo in the philosophers, the moralists, the theologians and the lawyers in the centuries between Cicero and the coming of modern times. Lactantius quotes, as he says, the "almost divine words" of Cicero; and Cicero is paraphrasing and developing Chrysippus's definition.[27]

> There is a true law, right reason, agreeable to nature, known to all men, constant and eternal, which calls to duty by its precepts, deters from evil by its prohibitions.... This law cannot be departed from without guilt; it is not allowable to abolish any part of it, nor is it possible entirely to abrogate it. Neither can the Senate or the people loose us from this law.... Nor is there one law at Rome and another at Athens, one thing now and another afterwards; but the same law, unchanging and eternal, binds all races of men and all times; and there is one common, as it were, master and ruler – God, the author, promulgator and mover of

[25] *De offic.* I, 2, 6; II, 17, 60: "... hic ipse Panaetius, quem multum in his libris secutus sum"; III, 7, 33; H. Cairns, *Legal Philosophy from Plato to Hegel*, p. 130. E. Levy, "Natural Law in Roman Thought" in *Studia et documenta Historiae et Juris*, 15 (1949), pp. 2–6.

[26] G. Watson, "The Natural Law and Stoicism," pp. 217–218.

[27] The definition is preserved by the jurist Marcian, Dig., I, 3, 2: "Sed et philosophus summae stoicae sapientiae Chrysippus sic incipit libro quem fecit de lege: Lex est omnium regina rerum divinarum humanarumque, oportet autem praeesse eam tam bonis quam malis et ducem et magistram esse animalium quae natura civilia esse voluit, indeque normam esse justi et injusti, quae jubeat fieri facienda, vetet fieri non facienda."

this law. Whoever does not obey it departs from (his true) self, contemns the nature of man and inflicts upon himself the greatest penalties even though he escapes other things which are considered punishments.[28]

This passage has been many times commented upon. Unfortunately the development of ideas it contains, and replies to obvious objections, which one would have expected to read in the remaining parts of the *Republic*, have been lost. But Cicero, in his other great contribution to the philosophy of law, the *De legibus*, provides his own commentary. The universal, eternal law of Chrysippus becomes the all-governing right reason which, in the final analysis, is the divine reason. This law is founded neither upon arbitrary choice, nor upon private opinion, but upon a natural and divine order and sanction.[29] It is, as he puts it in more eloquent, if less technical terms in the *Pro Milone, non scripta sed nata lex* – not the law written for us but rather the law born in us.[30] The quotations from the first book of the *De legibus* could be multiplied and it is easily seen that it is an extended and eloquent plea for the naturalness of this natural law, for its independence of convention, for the need of such a concept of law if we are to explain the difference between good and evil, right and wrong, justice and injustice.[31] The tracing of Cicero's

[28] *De rep.* III, 22 cf. Lactantius, *Inst. Div.*, VI, 8, (Migne, P. L., 6; 660–661): "Est quidem vera lex recta ratio naturae congruens, diffusa in omnes, constans, sempiterna, quae vocet ad officium jubendo, vetando a fraude deterreat; quae tamen neque probos frustra jubet aut vetat, nec improbos jubendo aut vetando movet. Huic legi nec abrogari fas est nec derogari ex hac aliquid licet, neque tota abrogari potest, nec vero aut per senatum aut per populum solvi hac lege possumus, neque est quaerendus explanator aut interpres ejus alius, nec erit alia lex Romae, alia Athenis, alia nunc, alia posthac, sed et omnes gentes et omni tempore una lex et sempiterna et immutabilis continebit, unusque erit quasi magister et imperator omnium deus, ille legis hujus inventor, disceptator, lator; cui qui non parebit, ipse se fugiet ac natura hominis aspernatus hoc ipso luet maximas poenas, etiamsi cetera supplicia, quae putantur effugerit." For a discussion of the authenticity of this passage cf. J. Galbiati, *De fontibus M.T. Ciceronis librorum qui manserunt de republica et de legibus quaestiones*, pp. 379 ff. R. Voggensperger, *Der Begriff des 'ius naturale' im römischen Recht.* p. 74, note 29, remarks that, even if aprocryphal, the passage probably goes back to Panaetius; and it is in perfect agreement with the first book of Cicero's *De legibus.*

[29] *De leg.* I, 7, 23: "Est igitur quoniam nihil est ratione melius eaque est et in homine et in deo, prima homini cum deo rationis societas; inter quos autem ratio, inter eosdem etiam recta ratio communis est; quae cum sit lex, lege quoque consociati homines cum diis putandi sumus"; I, 10, 28: "Nihil est profecto praestabilius quam plane intelligi nos ad justitiam esse natos, neque opinione sed natura constitutum esse jus."

[30] IV, 10.

[31] *De leg.*, I, 6, 19; 1, 15, 17; I, 17, 46, etc.

authorities for this or that view, whether he is following Panaetius or Antiochus of Ascalon for instance, is of secondary importance. He may not have been following any single author for his argument; what is important is his conclusion – that the law of which he speaks must be based upon human nature.[32]

The supposition in all this is that the nature in question is human nature, in which alone right reason is exercised. There is, however, an ambiguity that will have its importance later on with the Roman jurists of the second and third centuries A.D. The ambiguity of the word 'nature' was nothing new, even in Cicero's time; nor, perhaps, will it ever be absent from discussions of the natural law. The universe, for example, is a nature with its laws, while man is a nature in another sense and has his law. The Stoic way of dealing with this ambiguity was to identify the law of human nature with that of the universe – this is what was meant by life in accordance with nature. Here, however, the reference is to another of the ambiguities of 'nature.' Cicero follows Chrysippus, Panaetius and Posidonius in assigning nature as the cause of parental affection and the urge towards the education of offspring both in the human and in the animal world.[33] But he had no use for a law common to man and animals, such as he attributed to Pythagoras and to Empedocles.[34] We shall see that when the Roman jurisconsult Ulpian, at the end of the second century A.D., defined the natural law as 'what nature has taught all animals' he was perpetuating a serious confusion. There is nothing of the kind in Cicero, who had no doubts about the supremacy of man, lifted above the brutes precisely by his possession of reason; man alone in nature is capable of *jus* – and here Cicero cites Chrysippus in support.[35]

"To those to whom reason is given, there is given also right

[32] *De leg.*, I, 5, 17: "natura enim juris explicanda nobis est eaque a hominis repetenda natura"; cf. I, 12, 34.

[33] *De fin.*, III, 19, 62: "Pertinere autem ad rem arbitrantur intelligi natura fieri ut liberi a parentibus amentur ... neque vero inter se congruere possunt, ut natura et procreari vellet et diligi procreatos non curaret. Atque etiam in bestiis vis naturae perspici potest; quarum in fetu et in educatione laborem cum cernimus, naturae ipsius vocem videmur audire ... "; cf. *De off.*, I, 4, 11; *Auctor ad Herenn.* II, 13, 19 apud R. Voggensperger, *op. cit.*, p. 75.

[34] *De rep.*, III, 11, 19; cf. E. Levy, "Natural Law in Roman Thought" in *Studia et Documenta Historiae et Juris*, 15 (1949), p. 18.

[35] De fin. III, 20, 67: "Praeclare etiam Chrysippus cetera nata esse hominum causa et deorum, eos autem communitatis et societatis suae; ut bestiis homines uti ad utilitatem suam possint sine injuria." Cf. *De invent.*, I, 24–34; *De leg.*, I, 7, 22; also the passages in J. ab Arnim, *Stoicorum Veterum Fragmenta*, III, pp. 367–376: "Iuris communionem non pertinere ad bruta-animalia."

reason and, in consequence, law which is right reason commanding and forbidding."[36] This phrase, from the *De legibus*, will serve as well as any to convey Cicero's characteristic view of the natural law, as right reason wherein are the principles by which human behaviour is to be guided. Cicero many times returns to the subject and his lapidary phrases describing the natural law will keep on recurring in the subsequent history of the concept. "Law," he says, "is the supreme reason, implanted in nature, which commands what ought to be done and forbids the opposite"[37] and this is one of his many phrases that will re-echo down the ages. He has a phrase linking the natural law with the divine reason which simply cries out for adoption into the Christian scheme of things: "the true and primal law, applied to command and prohibition, is the right reason of supreme Jupiter."[38] Finally, there is Cicero's description, this time from the *De inventione*, of natural law as "something which is implanted in us, not by opinion, but by a kind of innate instinct."[39] This, like the others just quoted, is a description of the natural law that will find favour with author after author down the centuries.

The natural law, thus described, must be known to all men. Cicero at times suggests that universal consent is to be considered the voice or law of nature and he explains aberrations and apparent ignorance of the law as the corruption of good manners by evil customs; in the young, he says, who are as yet uncorrupted, we see nature as in a mirror.[40]

Stress has been laid upon the phraseology of Cicero for the good reason that, as will be seen in the sequel, his influence can frequently be traced in the verbal dependence of his successors. He wrote in Latin, which was the language of the Roman law and was the vehicle for speculation about the natural law down at least to the end of the seventeenth century; his writings were accessible in a way in which those of his Greek models, had they survived, could never have been. And the fact that Cicero was a

[36] *De leg.*, I, 12, 33: "Quibus enim ratio a natura data est iisdem etiam recta ratio data est, ergo etiam lex, quae est recta ratio in jubendo et vetando"; cf. I, 25, 42.

[37] *De leg.*, I, 6, 18.

[38] *De leg.*, II, 4, 10: "lex vera atque princeps apta ad jubendum et ad vetandum ratio est recta summi Iovis."

[39] *De invent.*, II, 22, 65: "... naturae quidem jus esse quod nobis non opinio sed quaedam innata vis adferat."

[40] *Tusc. disp.* III, 1, 2; *De fin.*, V, 22, 61: "pueri in quibus ut in speculis natura cernitur."

consummate stylist ensured that his re-phrasing and re-thinking of the Stoic natural law philosophy made the maximum impact.

C. THE ROMAN JURISCONSULTS

The importance of the classical Roman jurisprudence for subsequent juridical thought and the philosophy of law can hardly be exaggerated. The writings of the second and third century jurisconsults, especially Gaius, Paulus and Ulpian, were enshrined in the *Corpus Juris Civilis*, compiled under the Emperor Justinian in the sixth century, and so had their authority confirmed and enhanced for centuries of legislators, jurists and philosophers. In particular, their definitions of natural law, *jus gentium* and civil law were to exert enormous influence.

It has been seen that, despite the limpidity of his style, Cicero was not altogether clear and consistent in his concept of natural law; while it is usually an ideal and supra-human law, in passages where he appeals to the universal consent of mankind he tends to identify it with the *jus gentium*. And there is some reason for supposing that he occasionally felt uneasy with the twofold division of law into civil law, on the one hand, and natural law (or *jus gentium*), on the other; in the *De finibus* he makes use of the remarkable phrase *quasi civile jus cum genere humano*, a circumlocution for a law that fits into neither category and points to the inadequacy of the bipartite division.[41] The lawyers of the first century, however, who rely heavily upon the Stoics and Cicero, seem as far as one can judge from the relatively few juristic texts that have survived, to have been happy enough with the identification of natural law and *jus gentium*.[42] At least it is not until the end of the second century A.D. that the problem of distinguishing between the two notions presented itself with any acuteness. A sharp distinction, embodying a definition of the natural law as "what nature has taught all animals" was made by the jurist

[41] *Tusc. disp.* I, 13, 30: "Omni autem in re consensio omnium gentium lex naturae est"; I, 15–35 "omnium consensus naturae vox est"; *De fin.*, III, 20, 67.

[42] F. Senn, *De la justice et du droit.* Appendix, "De la distinction du jus naturale et du jus gentium," p. 77; M. Villey, *Leçons d'histoire de la philosophie du droit*, pp. 121–123; J.K.B.M. Nicholas, *An Introduction to Roman Law*, pp. 54–59.

Ulpian and was to have a dramatic impact upon the history of the natural law. To understand the situation to which Ulpian brought this radical solution it will be useful to consider the more pragmatic and less philosophical features of the development of the *jus gentium*.

Up to about the middle of the third century B.C. Roman treaties frequently included commercial clauses extending, for example, the privilege of Roman law to Carthaginian merchants at Rome; the condition, of course, was reciprocity in respect of Roman merchants at Carthage. In other words, Roman law was extended in part (the *jus commercii*) to some who were not Roman citizens. But when Rome became supreme, she no longer needed to be so considerate and the privilege of Roman law was jealously restricted to her citizens. This situation presented a problem; there was no law to govern litigation where one of the parties was not a Roman citizen. To meet such cases there gradually grew up, side by side with the development of Roman law, a body of informal legal rules, based on the concept of *bona fides*, which came to be called the *jus gentium*. From 242 B.C. a special Peregrine Praetor had been designated to look after matters affecting peregrines and he it was who administered the *jus gentium*.

As to its content this *jus gentium* seems to have been a body of empirical case-law; the edicts of the praetor had the force of precedent and were based upon considerations of general good sense and upon custom.[43] The custom in question may in the beginning have been that found literally common to various races, but development inevitably occurred and gradually not alone the sphere but also the meaning of *jus gentium* widened until it became, in the spirit, if not in the letter, a kind of natural law.[44] Its development cannot fail to have been influenced by Greek thought; from the first it would have been in contact with the Greek law of southern Italy (*Magna Graecia*) and Sicily, and afterwards, as the Romans conquered the east, it must have been still further influenced by the Hellenistic law established there.

[43] W. Friedmann, *Legal Theory*, pp. 50–51.

[44] H.F. Jolowicz, *Historical Introduction to the Study of Roman Law*, pp. 100–105; J.K.B.M. Nicholas, *Introduction to Roman Law*, pp. 54–58; A.F. Utz, *Recht und Gerechtigkeit-Kommentar in 2-2ae*, p. 446; E. Barker, Translator's Introduction to O. Gierke, *Natural Law and the Theory of Society 1500–1800*, pp. xxxvi–xxxvii.

And in its ultimate apotheosis *jus gentium* is not far removed from the ideal natural law.[45]

It is not surprising, therefore, that the jurist Gaius writing about 180 A.D., should distinguish only two kinds of law, *jus civile* and *jus gentium*, the latter being the work of natural reason and getting its name from the fact that all peoples observed it.[46] Paulus, writing slightly later, similarly recognises no opposition between *jus naturale* and *jus gentium*.[47] At the end of the century there is a change; for in the writings of the jurisconsults Tryphoninus, Florentinus and Ulpian, a sharp distinction appears.[48]

Of these far the most important is Domitius Ulpianus who has been described as the last of the classical jurists. He was born about 170 A.D., the exact date being unknown. He had some connection with Tyre in Phoenicia – it is more likely that his family came from there than that he was a native of the place. Like his great contemporary Julius Paulus, he was a disciple of Emilius Papinianus (c. 146–212 A.D.). His major works are the *Ad Edictum libri LXXXIII* and the *Libri LI ad Sabinum*, written for the most part under Caracalla. Ulpian was banished under Elagabalus, who became Emperor in 217 A.D., but he returned as adviser-in-chief under Septimius Severus in 222 A.D., became

[45] Cf. R. Sohm, *Institutionen, Geschichte und System des römischen Privatrechts*, p. 84, apud A.F. Utz, *op. cit.*, p. 447: "Das jus gentium war der Teil des römischen Privatrechts, welcher mit dem Recht anderer Völker (insbesondere mit dem griechischen Recht, das an den Gestaden des Mittelmeers eine natürliche Vorherrschaft ausübte) in seinem Grundgedanken übereinstimmte. Mit anderen Worten, das jus gentium war derjenige Teil des römischen Rechts, welcher schon den Römern als eine Art von ratio scripta, als gemeingültiges und gemeinmenschliches Recht erschien"; M. Villey, *Leçons d'histoire de la philosophie du droit*, p. 131, note 28.

[46] Gaius, *Dig.* I, 1, 9: "...quod quisque populus ipse sibi jus constituit id ipsius proprium civitatis est; vocaturque jus civile quasi jus proprium ipsius civitatis. Quod vero naturalis ratio inter omnes homines constituit, id apud omnes peraeque custoditur; vocaturque jus gentium, quasi quo jure omnes gentes utuntur."

[47] *Dig.*, I, 7, 11: "Jus pluribus modis dicitur, uno modo cum in quod semper aequum ac bonum est jus dicitur, ut est jus naturale...."

[48] Tryphoninus and Florentinus make the distinction when they refer to slavery. *Dig.*, 6, 64 (Tryphoninus): "Ut enim libertas naturali jure continetur et dominatio ex jure gentium introducta est"; *Dig.* I, 5, 4 (Florentinus): "Servitus est constitutio juris gentium, qua quis dominio alieno contra naturam subjicitur." Cf. R.W. and A.J. Carlyle, *History of Medieval Political Theory in the West*, Vol. I, p. 39; R. Voggensperger, *Der Begriff des 'jus naturale' im römischen Recht*, pp. 17–24, 112–113.

Praefectus annonae and *Praefectus praetorio* before being assassinated by soldiers, who forced their way into the palace by night and killed him in the presence of the Emperor and of his mother, Mammaea, in 228 A.D.

To Ulpian are attributed a number of well-known definitions and aphorisms in the Roman law; so, for instance, the description of jurisprudence as the *ars equi et boni* (a description Ulpian takes from Celsus) or the definition of justice as the *constans et perpetua voluntas ius suum cuique tribuendi* (also borrowed from Celsus).[49] But Ulpian's influence extended far beyond these attributions. One might say that the great part of the codification of Roman law undertaken by Justinian in the sixth century was indebted to him. Much of his writing was still extant in the time of Justinian; and by quantity Ulpian contributed more than any other jurist to the *Digest*, about a third of the whole. The reason is possibly that he was less difficult than the other jurists excerpted in the *Digest*. But even before Justinian set his hand to the "arduous but indispensable task" of the reformation of the Roman jurisprudence, an indulgent edict of Theodosius the younger helped the judge whose conscience was perplexed by the "number and weight of discordant testimonies, by the infinite variety of laws and legal opinions that in the space of ten centuries had filled many thousand volumes which no fortune could purchase and no capacity could digest" by nominating five civilians, Gaius, Papinian, Paulus, Ulpianus and Modestinus as the "oracles of jurisprudence."[50]

Ulpian's definition of the natural law is embodied in the tripartite division of laws into natural law, *jus gentium* and civil law. The reconciliation of this tripartite division with the bipartite division, into *jus gentium* and civil law, with which Ulpian's

[49] Other phrases attributed to Ulpian are the list of the law's precepts as *honeste vivere, alterum non laedare, suum cuique tribuere;* the maxims *quod principi placuit legis habet vigorem*, and *princeps legibus solutus*; and possibly the definition of fear as *instantis vel futuri periculi mentis tribulatio.* Ulpian, too, it was who described jurists as "priests of the art of knowing what is good and equitable." *Dig.*, I, 1, 1; I, 1, 10; I, 3, 31; I, 4, 1 etc.

[50] E. Gibbon, *The Decline and Fall of the Roman Empire* (ed. J.B. Bury), Vol. IV, p. 461. When the opinions of the 'oracles of jurisprudence' were divided, the casting vote was ascribed to the superior wisdom of Papinian. Like Ulpian after him, Papinian had held the office of *Praefectus praetorio*, and, as was also to be the fate of Ulpian, died miserably at the hands of the soldiers, Cf. W. Ennslin in *Cambridge Ancient History*, XII, pp. 62–64; W.W. Buckland, *Text Book of Roman Law from Augustus to Justinian*, pp. 31–32.

predecessors were content, was to present many problems.[51] For the moment, however, we need only to consider Ulpian's natural law in its setting.

Here is how it appears in the *Digest*:

Natural law is what nature has taught all animals. For this law is not proper to man but is common to all animals whether born on land or in the sea, and birds also. Whence comes the conjunction of male and female, which we call marriage; whence the procreation of children and their education; we see that other animals also, even wild animals, come under this law. *Jus gentium* is that which is observed by human peoples and is easily seen to fall short of the natural law because natural law is common to all animals while this is proper to man alone....[52]

The tripartite division of laws, in which these definitions figure, exerted enormous influence because of its conspicuous adoption at the beginning both of the *Digest* and of the *Institutes* of Justinian. What is curious is that for the text of the *Institutes*, in A.D. 533, Ulpian's definition of natural law was retained but his definition of the *jus gentium* was discarded for that of Gaius. The procedure sinned flagrantly against the rules laid down by Justinian for his compilers, one of the principal of which was that the *Corpus Juris* was to be pruned of discrepancies and contradictions.[53] The result could not but be confusing. Whatever value Ulpian's distinction between *jus naturale*, *jus gentium* and *jus civile* may have had, it had at least the merit of being clean-cut.

[51] For discussion and bibliography, see F. Senn, *De la justice et du droit*, Appendix *De la distinction du jus naturale et du jus gentium*, p. 66, note 7; R. Voggensperger, *Der Begriff des 'jus naturale' im römischen Recht*, p. 64. The *Digest* in fact presented three divisions of law—a bipartite division of Gaius (*jus gentium; jus civile* in *Dig.* I, i, 9); and two tripartite divisions, Ulpian's and Hermogenian's, the former distinguishing *jus naturale; jus gentium; jus civile* on the philosophical-theoretical plane (*Dig.* I, 1, 1, 6; 1, 3) and the latter on the historical plane (*Dig.* I, 1, 5). Cf. J.M. Aubert, *Le droit romain dans l'oeuvre de Saint Thomas* pp. 92–93; V. Cathrein, *Recht, Naturrecht und positives Recht*, pp. 192–193 apud O. Lottin, *Le droit naturel chez St. Thomas d'Aquin et ses prédécesseurs*, p. 8, note 1.

[52] *Dig.*, I, 1, 1, 3: "Jus naturale est quod natura omnia animalia docuit. Nam istud jus non humani generis proprium, sed omnium animalium quae in terra, quae in mari nascuntur, avium quoque commune est. Hinc descendit maris atque feminae conjunctio, quam nos matrimonium appellamus; hinc liberorum procreatio, hinc educatio; videmus enim coetera quoque animalia, feras etiam, istius juris peritia censeri. Jus gentium est quo gentes humanae utuntur; quod a naturali recedere facile intelligere licet, quia illud omnibus animalibus, hoc solis hominibus inter se commune sit."

[53] Cf. H.J. Roby, *Roman Law*, in *Cambridge Medieval History* vol. II, p. 59; J.K.B.M. Nicholas, *An Introduction to Roman Law*, pp. 38–45.

In the *Institutes* the *jus gentium* moves closer to positive law – the sketch given of its field of operation, the consequences of war, contracts, etc., (taken from Hermogenianus) makes it even resemble modern positive international law.[54] The question was not merely a speculative one; it had its importance in the sphere of practical administration. From the time of Caracalla, who reigned from 212 to 217 A.D., Roman citizenship had become almost universal in the Empire, a fact which promoted in a practical way the *rapprochement* between *jus gentium* and *jus civile.*[55] The *jus gentium* has come a long way from its virtual identification with natural law in Cicero and the older jurists.

The confusion created by the eclecticism of the *Institutes* is further increased by the adoption of a text of Marcianus which after the older fashion, speaks of *jus naturale* and *jus gentium* in more or less the same terms.[56] The net result of all this is to isolate Ulpian's definition of the natural law, as what nature has taught all animals, by depriving it of the support of the complementary definition of *jus gentium* as the natural law proper to mankind.

D. THE SPECIAL CASE OF ULPIAN

Whatever its origin and merits, the place in the history of the natural law of Ulpian's definition was assured by its conspicuous adoption in the *Corpus Juris* of Justinian. By the Middle Ages it had acquired an almost irrefragable authority. And it was to continue to exercise the ingenuity of commentators down to comparatively modern times. It cannot be dismissed as easily as

[54] *Inst.*, I, 2, 2: "Jus gentium omni humano generi commune est. Nam usu exigente et humanis necessitatibus, gentes humanae quaedam sibi constituerunt; bella etenim orta sunt et captivitates secutae et servitutes quae sunt naturali juri contrariae. Jure enim naturali omnes homines ab initio liberi nascebantur. Et ex hoc jure gentium omnes pene contractus introducti sunt ut emptio, venditio, locatio, conductio, societas, depositum et alii innumerabiles." The text of Hermogenianus is in *Dig.* 1, 1, 1, 5.

[55] W. Friedmann, *Legal Theory*, p. 51.

[56] *Instit.* 21, 1: '*Naturali jure* communia sunt omnium haec, aer, aqua profluens et mare et per hoc littera maris. Nemo igitur ad litus maris accedere prohibetur, dum tamen a villis et monumentis abstineat; quia non sunt *juris gentium*, sicut est mare." Cf. also the texts of Gaius identifying *jus naturale* and *jus gentium* reproduced in the *Institutes* and cited by O. Lottin, *Le droit naturel chez s. Thomas d'Aquin et ses prédécesseurs*, p. 9.

Austin thought, writing, more than a century ago, that Ulpian's definition

> accords with an admired conceit of Hooker and Montesquieu (and) seems to have been taken by the good Ulpian from certain inept speculations of certain stoic philosophers. Since it is peculiar to Ulpian, and since no attempt to apply it occurs in the *Pandects* or *Institutes*, it can scarcely be considered the *natural law of the Romans*, nor can it be fairly imputed to the body of the Classical Jurists. Did it not stand at the *beginning* of the *Institutes* and *Pandects*, and were it not the source of certain conceits which have gotten good success, I should have dismissed it without examination. But since it occupies the foremost place in Justinian's *Institutes* and *Pandects* and since it is manifestly the groundwork of more imposing nonsense it possesses an extrinsic or accidental importance which demands a passing and brief notice.[57]

Perhaps Ulpian's was, indeed, "merely a piece of over-ambitious generalization" one of those useless ornaments that it pleased Justinian to have at the beginning of the *Corpus Iuris*, "an artificial preamble, a porch added without regard to the rest of the edifice."[58]

One may include under the conceits referred to by Austin certain opinions of ancient and Patristic writers, which later authors used in support of Ulpian's definition. They include appeals to the Bible, theological considerations on the prelapsarian harmony of man and animals, philosophical elaborations of the analogy between animal and human nature and so on. Some of these considerations will prove relevant to the later history of the natural law. For the moment, however, we must turn our attention to speculations about the origin of Ulpian's definition, which have been many and various.[59]

The obvious explanation is that the definition is spurious; it is

now usually considered a post-classical insertion; and so is the trichotomy *ius civile, ius gentium ius naturale* as opposed to the dichotomy *ius civile, ius gentium* (= *ius naturale*). All the blame would then rest on the Byzantine compilers. They had been ordered by Justinian to omit, and even to alter 'everything in the ancient books that

[57] J. Austin, *Lectures on Jurisprudence*, II, p. 567, Lecture XXXI in fine.

[58] F. Pollock, "History of the Law of Nature," in *Jurisprudence and Legal Essays*, p. 128; M. Villey, *Leçons d'histoire de la philosophie du droit*, p. 121.

[59] "Explications aussi savantes et diverses qu'invraisemblables" in the phrase of M. Villey, *op. cit.*, p. 144.

ye shall find badly stayed or superfluous or imperfect" (Const. Deo Auctore). They made the issues only more obscure in their endeavour *solliciter doucement les textes....*[60]

This view that the definition was interpolated by or before Justinian's imperial chancellor Tribonian, who was responsible for the *Corpus Juris*, has been held by distinguished scholars like Perozzi, Beseler, Alberatio, Monier, Senn, Lombardi, and others.[61] Van Hove and others have held what amounts to the same view, namely that the definition, admitted by Byzantine jurists and wrongly attributed to Ulpian, was possibly a gloss that found its way into the text.[62] Others still have held that the text is genuine and not interpolated.[63] This matter need not be further pursued; the subsequent influence of the definition going under the name of Ulpian does not depend in any noticeable degree upon the question of its authenticity; it was enough that it figured prominently in the *Corpus Iuris* and, as Onclin points out, was taken as genuine by the medieval commentators.[64] The question of possible sources of Ulpian's "what nature has taught all animals" is, however, worth examining briefly.

One may neglect the more far-fetched suggestions about the origin of the definition.[65] Reference has already been made to a vague doctrine, of Pythagorean origin, allowing a community of law between man and beasts, a doctrine probably connected with the Pythagorean transmigration of souls. Aristotle alleged that this was the view of Empedocles; Cicero attributes a similar idea to Pythagoras and Empedocles; and there is a passage in the same

[60] A.P. d'Entreves, *Natural Law*, p. 31.

[61] E.Levy–E. Rabel, *Index Interpolationum quae in Iustiniani digestis inesse dicuntur*, I, ad D. I, 1, 1, 1, 3; R. Voggensperger, *Der Begriff des 'ius naturale' im römischen Recht*, p. 64; F. Senn, *De la justice et du droit*, p. 66 note 1; J.M. Aubert, *Le droit romain dans l'oeuvre de saint Thomas*, p. 93 note 1.

[62] A. Van Hove, *Commentarium Lovaniense in Codicem Iuris Canonici*, Vol. I, tome 1. *Prolegomena*, p. 54; Clementinus a Vlissingen, *De evolutione definitionis iuris gentium*, pp. 36–37.

[63] Cf. F. Senn, *De la justice et du droit* (Paris 1927) p. 66, note 1; G. Ambrosetti, *Diritto naturale cristiano*, pp. 54–57.

[64] W. Onclin, "Le droit naturel selon les romanistes des XIIe et XIIIe siècles," in *Miscellanea Moralia A. Janssen*, II, p. 329.

[65] Homer's "law of horses" (*nomos hippon*), *Iliad*, VI, 511, for example; or similar phrases in Hesiod, *Works and Days*, 276; Virgil, *Georgics*, IV, 219–221; Ovid, *Metamorphoses*, XV, 60–76. A little more weight might be attached to Xenophon, *Memorabilia*, II, 3, 4 or to Demosthenes, *Contra Aristog.*, XXV, 65–66. But clearly these are far-fetched suggestions.

sense in Chrysippus which, through the medium of the jurist Marcian, found its way into the *Digest* of Justinian.[66]

These passing references may be indicative of a more general – even a philosophical – view of a law of animals and of men. Pythagoras's doctrine of metempsychosis, for instance, could be taken to provide the basis for an assertion that animals, no less than men, are capable of rights and duties; if the animal body is simply the temporary housing of a soul that has in the past, or may in the future, inhabit a human body, then there is some reason for treating animals as subjects of law. Empedocles's universal palingenesis, indeed, leads him to count animals as kinsmen to the extent that laying hands upon an animal for sacrificial purposes is parricide.[67]

The doctrine of transmigration, according to Burnet, "is most easily to be explained as a development of the primitive belief in the kinship of men and beasts."[68] Cicero, then, was well-informed when he said that "those not ordinary but rather great and distinguished men, Pythagoras and Empedocles, held that all living creatures enjoyed the same juridical status" so that violation of an animal brought inexpiable punishment.[69] The same teaching, pushed to the point of imposing vegetarianism, may be found in the neo-Platonist Porphyry (c. 233–304 A.D.) who was, of course, born some years after Ulpian's death. In this context Porphyry seems to echo Ulpian's phrase that "nature has taught (*physis edidaze*) all animals."[70]

[66] Aristote, *Rhet.*, I, 13, 1373 b 15–17: "Empedocles has the same idea when he speaks of our not killing anything that has life; he regards this not as a matter which some have a right to do and others are wrong in doing.

No, but a rule for all, unbroken spread

Through heaven's wide realm and all the range of earth" Cicero, *De rep.* III, 11, 10; Marcianus *Dig.* I, 3, 2; Diogenes Laertius, *Lives of the Philosophers,* VIII, 1, 3; F. Senn, *De la justice et du droit,* Appendix *De la distinction du jus naturale et du jus gentium,* pp. 67–70; R. Voggensperger, *Der Begriff des 'jus naturale' im römischen Recht,* pp. 80–81 (who points out that the idea died out at the end of the third century, probably under Christian influence; Ulpian's definition, however, remained influential for many centuries more); R. Hirzel, *Themis, Dikè und Verwandtes,* p. 390.

[67] J. Burnet, *Early Greek Philosophy,* pp. 225–6, 250.

[68] J. Burnet, *op. cit.*, p. 93. One of Pythagoras's ancient biographers, Dikaiarchos of Messene, says that Pythagoras held this doctrine.

[69] *De rep.*, III, 11, 78–79: "Non enim mediocres viri, sed maximi et docti, Pythagoras et Empedocles, unam omnium animantium conditionem iuris esse denuntiant, clamantque inexpiabiles paenas impendere iis a quibus violatum sit animal. Scelus est igitur nocere bestiae."

[70] *De abstinentia,* I, 4; III, 9, 10.

Stoic philosophy, for a number of reasons, would appear a much more likely source for Ulpian. There is the general and pervading influence of Stoicism upon the Roman law; and, more particularly, there is the Stoic insistence on the universal law of nature, to which Ulpian's natural law is easily matched. The well-known description of this universal law, in Diogenes Laertius' *Life of Zeno,* has already been cited.[71] Cicero, in his popularizing of the Stoic legal philosophy, does indeed refer to the Stoic doctrine concerning the nature that makes parents love their children "just as in the beasts the force of nature may be perceived."[72] And he speaks of the common appetite of all living things to join the sexes and to look after the offspring.[73] Whether these and other references substantiate the notion of a law common to man and animals, is, however, another question. As Villey justly remarks[74] the Stoic theme of a single law that regulates the instinct of animals and the reason of man need not imply that man and beast form a juridical community. And here is perhaps the most important point in all this discussion. For it seems clear that the consensus of Stoic opinion was against any idea of a law genuinely common to men and animals. Diogenes Laertius, a late witness and often unreliable but yet one of our few sources of information about the early Stoics, expressly denies that Chrysippus or Poseidonius allowed a law common to man and beast.[75] And in this view the jurists, and possibly Ulpian himself in one passage, concurred. Ulpian says, in fact, that an

[71] *Lives of the Philosophers,* VII, 86–88; cf. supra note 13.

[72] *De fin.,* III, 19, 62: "Perrinere autem ad rem arbitrantur intelligi natura fieri ut liberi a parentibus amentur . . . neque vero haec inter se congruere possent, ut natura et procreari vellet et diligi procreatos non curaret, atque etiam in bestiis vis naturae perspici potest, quarum in fetu et in educatione laborem cum cernimus, naturae ipsius vocem videmur audire." Cf. *De natura deorum,* II, 51–52; supra notes 33, 34, p 39.

[73] *De off.,* I, 4, 11: "Commune item animantium omnium est coniunctionis appetitus procreandi causa et cura quaedam eorum quae procreata sint."

[74] *Leçons d'histoire de la philosophie du droit,* p. 144 and note 70.

[75] *Lives of the Philosophers,* VII, 129: "Placet item illis nulla non lege naturae teneri adversus reliqua animalia, ob naturae dissimilitudinem ut Chrysippus in primo de justitia et Poseidonius in primo de officiis tradunt." Cf. Seneca, *Ep. ad Lucil,* 121, 124; *De ira,* ii, 26, 4. The Stoic view is described by Max Pohlenz, *Die Stoa,* p. 137: "Von der Gemeinschaft der Vernunftwesen sind selbstverständlich die Tiere ausgeschlossen und gegenüber den Pythagoreern und ihren Gesinnungsgenossen, die aus religiösen Grunden den Fleischgenuss verboten, haben die Stoiker nachdrücklich den Satz verfochten, dass es keinerlei rechtliche oder sittliche Bindung gegenüber dem Tiere gebe". c. *ibid.,* p. 227.

animal cannot suffer an injury *quod sensu caret.*[76] But despite all this, there remains the feeling that there must be something to be said for Ulpian's definition. Is there no sense in which law can be said to be common to man and animals? This idea of a community of men and animals was current in Greek speculation and has, as Aubert describes it, *une saveur plus philosophique que juridique.*[77] Graneris, speaking of Ulpian's definition of *jus*, and his suggestion that to teach law is to teach true philosophy, senses "the nostalgic sigh of the fugitive of some Greek school" (in contrast with Celsus, whose description of law "transports us to the feet of the Roman praetor").[78]

There remains the question of what it was that Ulpian was trying to express. Perhaps he did have a hankering after Greek philosophy and glimpsed an important truth which he expressed rather ineptly in his formula. Man does share something of his nature with animals – man is, after all, a rational animal. And there ought to be some way of indicating that human patterns of conduct in matters like self-preservation, marriage, procreation and education of children, resemble patterns imposed upon animals by instinct. But here one must tread very warily indeed between the metaphors and the similes that have misled many besides Ulpian. It may be fruitful to suggest that there is here a confusion not unlike that which, according to John Stuart Mill, vitiated Montesquieu's *De l'esprit des lois*, the confusion between descriptive and prescriptive laws, between laws of nature like Newton's Law of Gravitation on the one hand, and, on the other hand, natural laws of morality, such as are expressed in, say, some precepts of the Decalogue. Ulpian would not be the first nor the last to have been deceived by the resemblance; *on fut dupe d'une homonymie.*[79]

[76] *Liber ad Edictum* partially reproduced in *Institutes*, IV, 9. The argument would have been stronger had the phrase been *quod ratione* (or *intellectu*) *caret.*

[77] J.M. Aubert, *Le droit romain dans l'oeuvre de saint Thomas*, p. 120.

[78] G. Graneris, *La filosofia del diritto*, p. 38: "Ci sembra di sentire il gemito nostalgico di un profugo di qualche scuola greca. . . ." Ulpian has been described as "etwas schulmeisterlicher Rechtslehrer" by E. E. Hölscher, *Vom römischen zum christlichen Naturrecht*, ch. 1.

[79] M. Villey, *Leçons d'histoire de la philosophie du droit*, p. 140.

CHAPTER III

THE CHRISTIAN FACE OF THE NATURAL LAW

Cicero's exposition of the doctrine of a natural law on the Stoic model and the various definitions of the natural law that found their way into the Roman law constitute important strands in the developing tradition. They are joined by another strand which, although not invariably distinct from them, is nonetheless of the first importance. It will be useful to consider the Christian contribution to the growing insistence upon the natural law first of all in the New Testament, particularly in St. Paul, and then in the Fathers and the ecclesiastical writers of the early Christian centuries.

A. ST. PAUL AND THE NEW TESTAMENT

In the *Epistle to the Romans* (2; 14–15) St. Paul has a well-known reference to the natural law. It comes after his excoriation of the Romans, in chapter I, for their depravities and sexual excesses and in answer to the implied objection that the pagans, not having the benefit of Revelation (the Mosaic law), are not to be castigated for not having observed the law. There is another law which they were bound to know and to observe:

> ... when the Gentiles, who have not the law, do by nature those things that are of the law, these having not the law, are a law to themselves; who shew the work of the law written in their hearts, their conscience bearing witness to them.

The passage is justly celebrated, for it emphasises two fundamental aspects of the natural law, its foundation upon nature and its immediacy to human conscience. There can be little doubt of the law in St. Paul's mind when he speaks of the pagans;[1] the

[1] For the senses of the word law (*nomos* with and without the article) in St. Paul, cf. P. Bläser, *Das Gesetz bei Paulus*, passim.

whole context of the passage makes it clear that the heathens, who have not the (Mosaic) law, have nevertheless another law which teaches them the difference between right and wrong; a law which is the very *foundation* of the distinction of good and evil and not merely an indicator; a law which, although not reinforced by any special revelation to the Gentiles, yet obliges them and makes them blameworthy in rejecting it. The two verses quoted above are no more than a pithy summary of one of the fundamentals of St. Paul's preaching.[2] They are not an isolated or chance expression although their exploitation in the ages of texts and authorities, with the Fathers and the medievals, might give that impression. St. Paul makes considerable use of the idea of 'nature' and 'natural' in his preaching; and he is perfectly aware of the distinction to be made between what in the Old Law is merely ritual or positive and what is of permanent binding force. It can hardly be a distortion to label this a comprehension of the natural law.

It is true that Bible commentators are divided on the issue, some allowing and others denying that Paul, particularly in the second chapter of *Romans*, refers to the natural law. And not merely the Scripture scholars. One of the most influential of contemporary theologians, Karl Barth, rejects the interpretation that would see a reference to the natural law in St. Paul; and he is followed in this by a number of Protestant theologians.[3] One may fairly ask, however, whether this may not be as much the inference drawn from a theological position regarding the radical corruption of human nature by sin and the consequent need for grace, as an interpretation of St. Paul. Felix Flückiger denies that the natural law in question is the 'metaphysical natural law' and suggests Paul's perspective is purely that of 'salvation history.' But, as has frequently been pointed out, the metaphysical and the salvation-history natural law are complementary rather than contradictory.[4]

More fundamentally, Hans Welzel, without referring to *Romans* 2; 14–15, argues that Paul's general views are as much opposed to a justice claimed by the Greek rationalist wisdom as

[2] See the full discussion in J. Fuchs, *Natural Law—a Theological Investigation*, pp. 14–37. Cf. also J. Quirmbach, *Die Lehre des hl. Paulus von der natürlichen Gotteserkenntnis und dem natürlichen Sittengesetz*, passim.

[3] D. Composta, "Il diritto naturale neo-testamentario" in *Monitor Ecclesiasticus*, 96 (1972), pp. 99–100, lists Jacques Ellul, Helmut Thielicke, Karl Barth and Felix Flückiger.

[4] J. Fuchs, *op. cit.*, pp. 29–32.

to the justice claimed by the Jews on the basis of the Old Law; neither can replace the will of God which is the ultimate determinant, for St. Paul, of right and wrong. The concept of will, Welzel points out, had not been developed by the Greeks. When it was developed in later Christian writers–when, for instance, the free creative will of God was contrasted with the Platonic demiurge, or the Word of God was taken as God's will (by Marius Victorinus, a convert to Christianity from neo-Platonism) rather than God's reason–there was also the consequence that the divine will was opposed to the Greek rationalism. The contrast was to receive its full expression in the fourteenth century moral nominalism associated with the names of John Duns Scotus and William of Ockham; but it is already in germ in St. Paul.[5] More will be seen of this question when we come to the medieval nominalism. And as a matter of interpreting St. Paul the question need not here be further pursued. For the fact is that many, if not most, of the early Christian interpreters of St. Paul's *Epistle to the Romans* took him to refer to the natural law. The question of Paul's sources is of more moment for the history of the idea of the natural law.

There is an intriguing reminiscence of Aristotle in the phrase about the Gentiles "being a law to themselves" (*heautois eisin nomos*). A propos of this Greenwood writes:

> It is impossible to state apodictically that he (Paul) had or had not been somehow influenced by the teachings of Aristotle, but his choice of phraseology is undeniably close to that of the Stagyrite in the *Nicomachean Ethics* 1128 a: 'The cultivated and free-minded man will behave as being a law to himself.'[6]

However, a much more obvious source is the Stoic philosophy, the popular Stoicism current in the Roman Empire, perhaps, rather than the technical philosophical teaching of the Stoic philosophers. One should not forget, nevertheless, that Tarsus was an important centre of Stoicism; it was associated with Chrysippus (281–208 B.C.) often called the second founder of the school, and it was the birthplace of his successor as head of the school, Zeno of Tarsus (fl. c. 204 B.C.) and of Antipater of Tarsus (died c. 130 B.C.). One of Paul's contemporaries, whom he may well have known, was the Stoic Athenodorus Calvus (1st cent. B.C.). It would be clearly excessive to think of St. Paul as a late

[5] H. Welzel, *Naturrecht und materiale Gerechtigkeit*, pp. 48–52.

[6] D. Greenwood, "Saint Paul and the Natural Law" in *Biblical Theology Bulletin*, 1 (1971), p. 264.

Stoic, although something of the sort has been argued.[7] On the other hand it would be absurd to deny Stoic influence and, indeed, other philosophical and religious influences in the formation of his thought.[8] This influence has been discerned in his use of images, which were also Stoic models–the city, the body etc.[9]–and likewise in his independent development of ideas of equality, the absolute freedom of man, the natural knowledge of God and so on. It must be remembered that St. Paul was an educated man as well as an intelligent one. If on occasion he borrows the terms current in more or less cultured circles, it is to turn them to his own purpose and, perhaps, give them a new meaning. That is the background of the word 'conscience' (*syneidesis*) in the verses quoted above from *Romans:* it is a word that, in all probability, he took from the cynico-stoic syncretism of his time.[10] Incidentally, it is a word destined to play a great part, masquerading as *synderesis*, in the scholastic discussions of the natural law. Again, St. Paul, even if not familiar with the more recondite technicalities of the Roman law, yet uses legal metaphors and references deliberately and not vaguely–examples are 'adoption', 'inheritance,' 'testament,' 'witness.'[11] One may therefore suspect that St. Paul may have garnered something from Roman law sources, in addition to what he would have known from his experience of the Greek world, concerning the natural law.[12] And the same is surely true of the teachings of Stoic philosophy regarding the natural law.

Outside of the limits of revelation, there is a knowledge of God which is not derived from his covenant with Israel; as also a moral law which

[7] E.g. by Ernst Troeltsch and others cited in D. Composta, *op. cit.*, p. 101.

[8] E. Hamel, *Loi naturelle et loi du Christ*, p. 18: "... l'étude comparative des religions a relevé des parallèles frappants entre la loi de Moise et la loi d'Hammurabi qui était en vigueur, depuis longtemps déjà, dans les régions où la loi de Moise s'est établie. Et ces ressemblances ne portent pas seulement sur la forme, mais aussi sur le contenu des préceptes. Si la morale évangélique ne rend pas le même son que la morale stoïcienne, il n'en reste pas moins vrai que bien des préceptes formulés dans l'Ecriture se retrouvent tels quels dans la morale stoicienne."

[9] M. Spanneut, in *New Catholic Encyclopaedia*, s.v. 'Stoicism.'

[10] J. Dupont, "*Syneidesis*: Aux origines de la notion chrétienne de la conscience morale" in *Studia Hellenistica*, 5(1948), p. 146.

[11] W. S. Muntz, "Rome, St. Paul and the early Church – the Influence of Roman Law on St. Paul's Teaching and Phraseology," p. 58; W.E. Ball, *St. Paul and the Roman Law*, ch. 1–2.

[12] C. Schneider, *Geistesgeschichte des antiken Christentums*, I, p. 117, suggests certain schemata of Plato as one of Paul's sources for his doctrine of law.

binds all men. This is no more than what St. Paul asserts in the two classical passages on the natural law in the *Epistle to the Romans* (*Rom.* 1; 19–21, 2; 15). The Pauline moral teaching is not easily understood unless one takes account of the priority of the major natural moral precepts. In the lists of vices found there (*Rom.*, 1; 24, *1 Cor.*, 6; 9, *Gal.*, 5; 19–20, *Eph.*, 5; 5, *Col.*, 3; 5–6) one must not see a new revelation of the culpability of actions which, apart from revelation, were not considered such. Paul is content to recall the precepts of the natural law, as they were known and diffused among the people by the Stoic teaching. That such actions, already forbidden in virtue of natural morality, remain forbidden under the law of grace, shows the permanence of the natural law in the supernatural order and its ever-present binding-force for Christians.[13]

And what is said of St. Paul may, *mutatis mutandis*, be said of the other parts of the *New Testament*, and even of the teaching of Christ himself. One must beware of foisting an essentially Hellenic and philosophical outlook on passages of quite a different character; but, making allowance for Hebrew thought-patterns, there seems no reason for supposing that the moral teaching of the *New Testament*, in general, departs in any essential from that of the Stoics. That there are great differences no one can deny. But the fact that St. Paul not merely rejected the pantheism of the Stoics but had also supernatural sources of information for the transcendence of God, does not mean that he was uninfluenced by the Stoic approach to morality or that, in his appeal to nature or in his delineation of the capital vices he contradicted Stoic teaching.[14] This, too, can be said of Christ's teaching. The Sermon on the Mount, which has often been contrasted with the idea of the natural law to the disadvantage of the latter, comments upon inner dispositions, not the external moral order. These, too, are complementary, not contradictory. While one may say that what is characteristic of Christian moral teaching is to be found in the Sermon on the Mount, it is also true that no moral teaching can do without legislation. Christ himself said that he came not to destroy the law but to fulfil; and his statements in the Sermon on the Mount presuppose a knowledge of good and evil and man's ability to judge for himself.[15]

The contemporary quarrel between situation-ethics and the so-called legalism of the traditional systems is a variation on this

[13] E. Hamel, *op. cit.*, p. 18.

[14] J. Fuchs, *op. cit.*, pp. 15–22 and the literature there cited; cf. also M. Villey, "Le droit naturel chez Gratien" in *Studia Gratiana*, 3(1954), pp. 83–90.

[15] J. Fuchs, *op. cit.*, pp. 33–38; E. Hamel, *op. cit.*, pp. 19–23.

theme and shows that the questions raised here are among the perennial problems of moral philososphy. For that reason they are likely to remain unresolved. What is important, however, for our present purposes is not whether St. Paul adopted or rejected the Stoic natural law but what the early Christian writers and the Fathers thought he did.

B. THE CHURCH FATHERS

The outlook of the earliest Christian writers is, as one would expect, pre-eminently supernatural. These men would view with some suspicion a purely natural moral law as they would suspect any other importation from pagan philosophy. One therefore should not expect to find much evidence of the natural law at first, despite the example of St. Paul. The apostolic Fathers Ignatius of Antioch, Clement of Rome, Polycarp of Smyrna, Barnabas, the author of the *Didache*, the *Pastor* of Hermas – agree in finding the norm of morality in the will of God or the will and example of Christ or in God's commandments as found in the *New Testament.*[16] Flückiger who, as already seen, denies the natural law reference of *Romans*, 2; 14–15, argues that the Christian writers who speak of a natural law cannot claim the *New Testament* in support and are more in the tradition of Philo of Alexandria (born c. 20 B.C.) who had tried to make a synthesis of Old Testament theology and hellenistic philosophy. Flückiger, nevertheless concedes that some of the Christian writers and Fathers did find a *New Testament* basis for the natural law. He says that the first to do so were the gnostic writers Valentinus and Basileides, both mentioned in the *Stromata* of Clement of Alexandria (c. 150–215).[17]

Whatever be the justice of imputing a natural law theory to St. Paul, later writers had little difficulty in seeing the natural law in the phrase about the Gentiles' 'law written in their hearts' in *Romans*, 2; 14–15. Here it must suffice to remark upon some of the Fathers and ecclesiastical writers whose influence on following ages was greatest in order to see something of their rôle as transmitters of a conception of the natural law. Some of these

[16] K. Hörmann, '*Leben in Christus:*' *Zusammenhänge zwischen Dogma und Sitte bei den apostolischen Vätern*, passim; J. Liebaert, *Les enseignements moraux des pères apostoliques*, passim.

[17] F. Flückiger, *Geschichte des Naturrechtes*, I, pp. 295–299, 297 note 46.

references–particularly those in St. Augustine who will be considered separately in the next section–became classical. It is to these our attention will be directed. This, needless to say, cannot constitute a systematic study of the natural law in the Fathers. Such a study, which would be a considerable undertaking, would have to take into account a number of factors that may be passed over here. There is, for example, the distinction made by many of the Fathers between a primary and a secondary natural law, a distinction connected with their views about the original state of justice and man's condition after the fall. A similar distinction was known to Roman lawyers in later times; and it is not unlike the distinction between 'thesis' and 'hypothesis' that governed discussions of the relations between Church and state until very recent times. The distinction is found, to take one example, in St. John Chrysostom (c. 406) in his *6th Homily on Romans.*[18] Likewise there is the Golden Rule: Do unto others as you would wish others to do to you and: Do *not* to others what you would not have others do to you.[19] This not alone appears in the teaching of Jesus as a summary of the Christian life, but it has a long history in popular ethics too. Many of the Fathers take it as epitomizing the moral life, conveying, one might say, the essence of the natural law.[20]

As for the history of the natural law–and the Christian lineaments of the concept emerge only gradually–it must suffice to refer briefly to some of the major figures of the patristic age, in east and west.

Broadly speaking the Fathers seem to have been content with a conception of the natural law similar to that of Cicero. This conception was, of course, now put into a Christian setting; the impersonal deity or nature of the Stoics gives way to the Christian God, sovereign lord and lawgiver; and the knowledge of the

[18] J. Fuchs, *op. cit.*, pp. 85–122; S. Verosta, *Johannes Chrysostomus, Staatsphilosoph und Geschichtstheologe*, pp. 35–45. The *6th Homily* is in Migne, P.G. 60; 428 f.

[19] Lc., 6; 31, Mc., 7; 12, Tob., 4: 16. cf. A. Dihle, *Die goldene Regel: Eine Einführung in die Geschichte der antiken und frühchristlichen Vulgärethik;* L.J. Philippidis, *Die 'goldene Regel' religionsgeschichtlich untersucht;* H. Reiner, "Die 'goldene Regel': die Bedeutung einer sittlichen Grundformel der Menschheit" in *Zeitschrift fü philosophische Forschung*, 3(1948), 74–105.

[20] A. Dihle, *op. cit.*, p. 107 lists 27 references in patristic literature, including the *Didache*, Justin, Tertullian, Irenaeus, Clement of Alexandria, Lactantius, John Chrysostom, Jerome, Augustine and others.

natural law and its precepts becomes more intimately a matter of conscience.[21]

Tertullian (c. 160–245) who was a jurist by training and played an important part in fashioning the theological terminology of the west, speaks of a natural law that makes all men brothers–good and evil brothers because, by natural law sons of the same mother nature.[22] Elsewhere he says that the natural law enables all men to know God, however distantly; and he speaks of the natural law which is the law of God.[23] Irenaeus of Lyons (c. 203) treats of the natural law at length in his *Adversus Haereses.* His perspective is theological; for him human nature is created nature and the law of human nature is the law of God the lawgiver and is given to man to help out the Mosaic Law, itself completed in the Gospel.[24] But despite the theological preoccupations Irenaeus, who after all was writing a polemic against the heretics, insists upon the naturalness of the moral law. Phrases like *naturalia praecepta* and *naturalia legis* flow easily from his pen.[25] On one occasion he says, apropos of the unity of the old and the new law as coming from the same legislator, God, that the first and greatest precept, namely love the lord with your whole heart and the second like to

[21] F. Flückiger, *op. cit.*, I, pp. 360–361; M. Spanneut, "(Stoic) Influence on Christian Thought" in *New Catholic Encyclopedia*, s.v. 'Stoicism.'

[22] *Liber apologet.*, c. 39 (Migne, P. L., 1; 471): "Fratres autem etiam vestri sumus, jure naturae matris unius, etsi parum homines, quia mali fratres."

[23] *De spectaculis*, c. 2 (P.L., 7; 631–632): "...sed quia non penitus Deum norunt, nisi naturali jure, non etiam de familiari, de longinquo non de proximo...."; *De corona*, c. 6 (P.L., 2; 83): "Quaeris igitur Dei legem? Habes communem istem in publico mundi, in naturalibus tabulis, ad quas et Apostolus solet provocare, ut cum in velamine feminae, 'Nec natura vos,' inquit, docet (I Cor., 11; 14) et cum ad Romanos (2; 14) natura facere dicens nationes ea quae sunt legis et legem naturalem suggerit et naturalem legalem...."; cf. also *Adv. Judaeos*, c. 2 (P.L., 2; 599–601). Other references in J. Stelzenberger, *Conscientia bei Tertullianus*, pp. 28–43.

[24] D. Composta, "Il diritto naturale in S. Ireneo" in *Apollinaris*, 45 (1072), pp. 5–9.

[25] *Adv. Haereses*, IV, 13, 1 (Migne, P.G., 7; 1006–7): "Et quia Dominus naturalia legis per quae homo justificatur, quae etiam ante legislationem custodiebant... non dissolvit sed extendit et implevit...."; *Id.*, IV. 13, 4 (P.G., 7: 1009): "Quia igitur naturalia omnia praecepta communia sunt nobis et illis, in illis quidem initium et ortum habuerunt, in nobis autem augmentum et adimpletionem perceperunt"; *Id.*, IV, 15, 1 (P.G., 7: 1012): "Itaque lex et disciplina erat illis et prophetia futurorum. Nam Deus primo quidem per naturalia praecepta quae ab initio infixa dedit hominibus, admonens eos id est per Decalogum (quae si quis non fecerit non habet salutem), nihil plus ab eis exquisivit...."

it, love your neighbour as yourself, is found *in lege et Evangelio*. The phrase, in the context, is innocuous. But it is intriguing to think that the same phrase was to be the keynote of one of the most influential–and misleading–definitions of the natural law in the Middle Ages, Gratian's assertion that natural law is what is contained in the law and the gospel.

Clement of Alexandria (c. 158–215) has a chapter in the *Stromata* taking up a theme reminiscent of Philo: "How Plato in his lawgiving imitated Moses." In the course of this chapter he mentions the opinion that law is right reason, commanding what ought to be done and forbidding what ought to be avoided.[26] Despite the chapter heading, it seems unnecessary to appeal to Philo[27] for the phrase has a familiar and Ciceronian ring. Clement's pupil, Origen (c. 185–254) also has a phrase with historical associations; he speaks of a law that is "by nature king over all things" in a phrase that would be understood very well by the Stoics, by Cleanthes, for example, whose paean to law it echoes.[28]

Lactantius (d. 320), as we have seen, explicitly acknowledges Cicero as his source (and in fact preserves for us the description of "that sacred and heavenly law which M. Tullius describes in his Republic III").[29] Lactantius can be critical too. He deals in rather a captious way with Zeno's principle: Live according to nature. He criticises it as too vague. There are many kinds of nature; does the principle mean that man is to live like an animal? He does, however, allow that the principle can have an acceptable meaning; man, born to virtue, should follow his own nature.[30] Hilary of Poitiers (d. 366) lays down the basic precepts of the law, which he sees as that described by St. Paul in the *Epistle to the Romans*, the law of the gentiles who do by nature what is of the

[26] *Stromata* I, 25 (P.G., 8; 913): "Cui consequenter, bonae scilicet opinioni, quidem dixerunt legem esse rectam rationem (*orthos logos*) quae jubet quidem ea quae sunt facienda, prohibet autem quae non sunt facienda."

[27] Migne (P.G., 8: 913) refers to Philo, *De vita Moysi*, II, paulo a princ.: "Regis officium est jubere quae oportet fieri, et vetere a quibus abstinere decet. Caeterorum jussio faciendorum et interdictio cavendorum proprie ad legem spectat. Atque ita sequitur ut rex animata lex sit, lex vero sit rex justissimus"; *Id.*, *De migratione Abrahami*, 408: "Lex porro nihil aliud est quam divinum eloquium facienda praecipiens vitanda prohibens". The phraseology is a commonplace and will become increasingly so.

[28] *Contra Celsum*, V, 40 (P.G., 11; 1243): cf. W.A. Banner, *Origen and the Tradition of Natural Law Concepts*, passim; H. Emond, *La notion de loi naturelle chez Origène*, passim.

[29] *Div. Inst.* VI, 8 (P.L. 6; 660)

[30] *Div. Inst.*, III, 8 (P.L., 6; 365–371)

law.[31] The author known as Ambrosiaster finds occasion to mention the natural law in a schematism dealing with the laws of the Old Testament; there is a meaning for 'law' which is consonant with "the natural law forbidding sin".[32]

An important thinker by any standard, and particularly important because of his influence upon natural law thinking, was Ambrose of Milan (c. 340–397). Like Tertullian he was a lawyer with a lawyer's sense of terminology. He was much influenced by Stoic thought; his *Offices* was modelled upon Cicero's work of the same name which, in its turn, depends upon Panaetius. He also came under the influence of Philo's combination of Stoic and Biblical thinking.[33] Ambrose frequently refers to the natural law – to its universality, its innateness, its tendency to bring men closer together.[34] And like many others of the Fathers, Ambrose considered that the Mosaic law became necessary because man had not observed the natural law already given to him.[35] Similar

[31] *Tr. in Ps. 118,* litt xv, 119 (P.L., 9: 604): "Lex enim veluti naturalis est iniuriam nemini inferre, nil alienum praecipere, fraude ac perjurio abstinere, alieno conjugio non insidiari. Novit et hanc Apostolus legem, dicens: cum enim nationes, quae legem non habent, naturaliter secundum legem faciunt. . . ."

[32] *Comm. in Ep. ad Rom.*, III, 20, cited in R.W. and A.J. Carlyle, *A History of Medieval Political Theory in the West,* I, p. 104: "Triplex quidem lex est, ita ut prima pars de sacramentis divinitatis sit Dei; secunda autem quae congruit legi naturali, quae interdicit peccatum; tertia vero factorum, id est sabbati, noemeniae, circumcisionis et cetera. Haec est ergo lex naturalis, quae per Moysen partim reformata, partim auctoritate ejus firmata in vitiis cohibendis, cognitum fecit peccatum."

[33] R. Thamin, *Saint Ambroise et la morale chrétienne du IVe siècle*: *Etude comparée 'des devoirs' de Cicéron et de s. Ambroise,* pp. 189–217; M. Pohlenz, *Die Stoa,* II, p. 218; Th. Deman, "Le *De officiis* de saint Ambroise dans l'histoire de la théologie morale" in *Revue des sciences philosophiques et théologiques*" 37 (1953), pp. 409–424; B. Maes, *La loi naturelle selon Ambroise de Milan,* passim.

[34] *De off.*, III, 4, 25 (P.L., 16; 152): ". . . una lex naturae omnibus, una utique utilitas universorum, ad consulendum utique omnibus naturae leges constringimur"; *Epist.*, 73, 2 (P.L., 16; 1251): "Esse autem legem naturalem in cordibus nostris etiam Apostolus docet, qui scripsit quia plerumque 'et gentes naturaliter ea quae legis sunt faciunt et cum legem non legerint, opus tamen legis scriptum habent in cordibus suis.' Ea igitur lex non scribitur sed innascitur; nec aliqua percipitur lectione, sed profluo quodam fonte in singulis exprimitur, et humanis ingeniis hausitur"; *De off.*, III, 3, 19 (P.L., 16; 150): "Haec utique lex naturae est quae nos ad omnem adstringit humanitatem, ut alter alteri tamquam unius partes corporis invicem deferamus. Nec detrahendum quidquam putamus, cum contra naturae legem sit non juvare."

[35] *Epist.*, 73, 10 (P.L., 16; 1253): "Accipe aliud. Non fuit necessaria lex per Moysen. Denique subintravit, quod utique non ordinarium sed velut furtivus significare videtur introitum; eo quod in locum naturalis legis intraverit. Itaque si illa suum servasset locum, haec lex scripta nequaquam esset ingressa."

conceptions are easily found in St. John Chrysostom (d. 406) or in St. Jerome (d. 420); but there is no need to labour the point.[36] St. Augustine, however, is a special case and may be treated apart.

C. ST. AUGUSTINE

Although St. Augustine (354–431) wrote no distinct treatise on law he provided almost all the elements of a formal scholastic *Tractatus de legibus.* His concept of the natural law is best approached through the notions of divine providence and of the order in creation which results from it.[37]

(i) *Divine Providence and Order in the Universe*

It has been seen that Christianity contributed to the problem of law the idea of the rule of a personal and transcendent God. This necessary modification of Stoic conceptions is clearly found in Augustine, in his formal identification of the "law of the universe" with the divine wisdom.[38] He is conscious, too, of borrowing from neo-Platonism in the matter of providence:

> With sure touch Plotinus, the disciple of Plato, treated of providence and showed it to be the intelligible and ineffable beauty of God, from whom it stretched to the very least things of this earth.[39]

The indebtedness is well-known and has been much studied. A. Schubert, for instance, in his study of the eternal law in Augustine, organises the investigation about the three ideas of order, law and eternal law and identifies as direct sources Cicero, Plotinus, and the New Testament (St. Paul and St. John), and as indirect sources the Stoics and Heracleitus's doctrine of the *logos.*[40] Schubert wrote over thirty years ago; but the most recent

[36] On Chrysostom see S. Verosta, *op. cit.*; E. Osborn, *Ethical Patterns in Early Christian Thought,* pp. 118–119. On Jerome see G. Violardo, *Il pensiero giuridico di san Girolamo,* pp. 39–40.

[37] A. Schubert, *Augustins Lex-aeterna-Lehre nach Inhalt und Quellen,* pp. 3–20; A. Truyol y Serra, *El derecho y el estado en San Agustín,* pp. 80–88.

[38] *De div. quaest. LXXXIII,* 1 (P.L., 40; 90): "Est enim lex universitatis divina sapientiae." See the discussion of this and other similar texts in K. Demmer, *Ius Caritatis: Zur christologischen Grundlegung der augustinischen Naturrechtslehre,* pp. 124–125.

[39] *De civ. Dei,* X, 14 (P.L., 41; 292). On the influence of Plotinus see A. Truyol y Serra, *op. cit.,* pp. 77–79.

[40] A. Schubert, *op. cit.,* II Teil passim.

scholarship has only a different emphasis to add to this picture:

Augustine links the natural law of the Stoics, which since Philo had been identified with the law of Moses, with a Platonic theory of values and gives it a future reference.[41]

In the *De ordine* the conception of order is proved, indirectly, in connection with the problem of evil. Evil is a reality. Therefore it seems either that providence does not extend to everything or that there is evil in the will of God–*utrumque impium sed magis posterius.* St Augustine comes down decisively on the side of an all-embracing providence, and explains evil as due to a partial viewpoint–like that of the man whose view is limited to one square of a mosaic so that he cannot see how its apparent disorder fits into the design and symmetry of the whole.[42] In a similar way there is a providence in everything, even the most unlikely, although it may not be readily apparent. The rains fall plentifully upon the sea, which apparently does not need them, while vast tracts are infertile through lack of moisture. But even in this the workings of providence may be discerned. The drought brings home to the inhabitants of the parched tracts the bitterness of this life, and encourages them to stretch forward to the life to come. Further–a more practical point–what their region does produce is longer preserved and less easily corrupted than the produce of a region which enjoys yearly rains.[43]

In particular, divine providence has care for the actions of men. Those who deny this, desert God and bear their own ruin about with them.[44]

(ii) *The Eternal Law*

The superb order seen by Augustine in creation points to a law, an ineffable law that may be known, but not criticised, by minds suitably purified.[45] This is the law that orders all things–*ea qua*

[41] E. Osborn, *op. cit.*, p. 147.

[42] *De ord.*, I, 1 (P.L., 32; 977–979).

[43] *Enarr. in Ps. 148* (P.L., 37; 1943–1945). See the other references in A. Schubert, *op. cit.*, pp. 8–9.

[44] *Enarr. in Ps. 145* (P.L., 37; 1892): "deserunt Deum . . . quia non credunt Deum curare quid agant"; cf. *Enarr. in Ps. 109* (P.L., 37; 1446): ". . . hanc habent perniciem cogitationis suae in seipsis ut dicant Deum res humanas non curare."

[45] *De vera relig.*, c. 31 (P.L., 34; 147–148): "Deus summa ista lex est secundum quam ratio judicat, sed quam judicare non licet . . . aeternam igitur legem mundis animis fas est cognoscere, judicare non fas est." Cf. K. Demmer, *op. cit.*, p. 132.

justum est ut omnia sint ordinatissima.[46] It is referred to variously as the will of God or the Divine Wisdom;[47] but most often it is described as the *summa ratio.* In a well-known passage, St. Augustine discusses the *lex aeterna moderatrix humanarum.*

A law is right and just which, for the administration of the commonweal, gives the power of creating magistracies, to a people which possesses a sense of moderation and responsibility. Equally just is a law depriving the people of this power, should it become corrupt, venal in voting and apt to commit the government to the most abandoned criminals. Yet these laws are opposed. Is either, therefore, unjust? How is it that in different circumstances contradictory laws may be equally just? The answer is found in the concept of the eternal law:

> Can that law which is called the supreme reason, always to be obeyed, by which the bad merit misery, the good happiness, in reference to which temporal law is rightly enacted, rightly altered – can that law appear to an intelligent being as otherwise than immutable and eternal? Can it sometimes be unjust that the evil should be unhappy, the good happy, or that a moderate and responsible people should create its own magistracies, or that an evil and dissolute people should lack this power? ... At the same time I would have you see that in temporal law there is nothing just and right that men do not derive for themselves from this eternal law.[48]

This eternal law is, of course, immutable and universal.[49] St. Augustine thinks of it in terms of his teaching on the ideas in the mind of God, the archetypal Platonic forms that he saw, not in a world apart but in the Divine Intellect, as "the enduring and unchanging forms of everything that comes to be or could come to be." All in creation that has existence or life, that is preserved or ordered, is contained in and is ruled by these "laws of the most high God."[50]

[46] *De lib. arb.*, I, 6, 15 (P.L., 32; 1228).

[47] *Enarr. in Ps. 36* (P.L., 40; 90); "Voluntas Dei ipsa lex est ... Est enim lex universitatis divina sapientia." Cf. supra note 38, p. 62.

[48] *De lib. arb.*, I, 6 (P.L., 32; 1228–1229). For commentary see K. Demmer, *op. cit.*, pp. 129–134. In his articles on eternal law in the *Summa theologiae* St. Thomas Aquinas refers five times to this passage.

[49] A. Schubert, *op. cit.*, pp. 6–9; A. Truyol y Serra, *op. cit.*, pp. 84–87; J. Mausbach, *Die Ethik des hl. Augustinus*, I. Teil, pp. 101, 125, 128, 327, etc.

[50] *De div. quaest., LXXXIII*, q. 46 (P.L., 40; 29–31): "... Summi Dei legibus contineri et gubernari."

(iii) *The Natural Law*

Augustine uses the term 'natural law' comparatively seldom but he frequently deals with the reality which is the natural law in equivalent terms. He distinguishes, for example, between the eternal law and the *lex temporalis.*[51] He says that the eternal law is "impressed upon us," going on immediately to discuss how man can be ordered in the highest degree in himself. Human nature excels the brute in being endowed with reason; intellectual activity is preferable to mere life. Consequently man is *ordinatissimus* when all his faculties are subjected to the sway of reason.[52] This comes very close to saying that the natural law is the "participation of the eternal law in a rational creature."[53]

In a characteristic passage St. Augustine discusses the immutable rules in virtue of which even the wicked can judge how a man ought to live and the unjust can appreciate what is just. These rules are the source of every just law and are impressed upon the heart of man, just as the image of a signet ring is transferred to the wax and yet remains in the ring.[54] And, in another connexion, he refers to the natural law (this time using the actual term) in a very similar way as "transcribed, as it were, in the rational soul."[55] He even connects this law with an intrinsic standard of good and evil – adultery, he says, is not evil because forbidden by law; rather does the law forbid it because it is evil. This recalls a passage in Plato's *Euthyphron* already referred to; but, more importantly, it anticipates the celebrated scholastic adage, to be so much a bone of contention in the fourteenth century nominalistic controversies, about some things being evil because forbidden and others forbidden because evil (*quaedam mala quia prohibita, quaedam prohibita quia mala*).[56]

[51] *De lib. arb.*, I, 6 (P.L., 32; 1229): "Lex alia aeterna, alia est temporalis"; *Enarr. in Ps. 118,* n. 25 (P.L., 37; 1574): ". . . lex in paradiso data naturaliter insita, in litteris promulgata."

[52] *De lib. arb.*, I, 7–8 (P.L., 32; 1229–1233); cf. *Contra Faust.*, XXII, 27 (P.L., 42; 418).

[53] St. Thomas Aquinas, *Summa theologiae,* 1–2, 91, 2. *Cf. G. Fassò, La legge della ragione*, P. 39; A.H. Chroust, "The Philosophy of Law from St. Augustine to St. Thomas Aquinas," in *The New Scholasticism,* 20 (1946), pp. 26–27.

[54] *De Trin.*, XIV, 15, 21 (P.L., 42; 1052); cf. K. Demmer, *op. cit.*, pp. 115–116.

[55] *De div. quaest. LXXXIII*, q. 43, 2 (P.L., 40; 36): "Ex hac igitur ineffabili atque sublimi rerum administratione, quae fit per divinam providentiam, quasi transcripta est naturalis lex in animam rationalem. . . ."

[56] *De lib. arb.*, I, 3 (P.L., 32; 1224): "Non sane ideo malum est (adulterium) quia vetatur lege, sed ideo vetatur lege quia malum est"; cf. *Quaest. in Hept.* III, 68 (P.L., 34; 707–8) where the same observation is made of lying.

This is not the only passage which makes difficulties for those who, like Hans Welzel, argue that Augustine's approach to natural law opens the way to voluntarism. Here we have the direct opposite of voluntarism; good and evil do not depend upon will, not even upon the will of God.[57] It is true, however, that Augustine was not invariably so precise in his language – and, indeed, as will be noted presently, he defines the eternal law in terms of the divine reason *or will*. This is not the place to go into the matter of the identity of intellect and will with God's essence; it is sufficient to observe that the vagueness of his terminology on the point allows some purchase to those who, in the fourteenth century and after, would make a voluntarist of St. Augustine.

The Golden Rule of doing to others what we would have others do to us is also found in Augustine as an expression of the natural law; it is a theme he several times returns to.[58] As has been noticed, this theme of popular ethical teaching found in the New Testament, was popular with the Fathers. It may serve as a reminder that Augustine, far the most influential of the Latin Fathers on the course of theology in the West, shared many of his views with his Christian predecessors and contemporaries. One of those views was that there is a natural moral law. Augustine's doctrine of the natural law was well-developed, if not systematised in the later scholastic way. One may conclude by referring to two passages (among the many that might be chosen) which reappear in that later scholastic elaboration and provide an index of his influence. The first contains two definitions that became celebrated in the Middle Ages, that of sin as "any saying, deed or desire against the eternal law" (*dictum, factum vel concupitum contra legem aeternam*); and that of the eternal law itself as "the divine reason or the will of God commanding that the natural order be preserved and forbidding its disturbance" (*ratio divina vel voluntas Dei ordinem naturalem conservari jubens, perturbari vetans*). In elaborating what he understands by the "natural

[57] H. Welzel, *Naturrecht und materiale Gerechtigkeit*, pp. 51–56. See the criticism in K. Demmer, *op. cit.*, p. 125; G. Fassò, *op. cit.*, p. 40: "Il linguaggio giusnaturalistico di sant' Agostino – qui tanto preciso da condurre ad escludere dunque anche una concezione del diritto naturale voluntaristica, che faccia dipendere la validità di esso dalla sua posizione da parte del commando divino. Tuttavia, probabilmente, . . . l'atteggiamento agostiniano non fu sempre tanto risoluto. . . ."

[58] For example, *Enarr. in Ps.* 118, 25, 4 (P.L., 37; 1574): "Nullus enim est qui facit alteri injuriam nisi qui fieri nolit sibi; et in hoc transgreditur naturae legem quam non sinitur ignorari dum id quod facit non vult pati"; cf. also the texts cited in K. Demmer, *op. cit.*, pp. 116–117, 141–142, 147–148.

order" Augustine has an interesting reference to the natural law – interesting in view of the Roman law definition of Ulpian which extended the natural law to animals and was to have such a success with the medievals. Augustine, no less than Cicero, rejects any such idea:

There is no doubt that in the natural order the soul is to be preferred to the body. In the soul of man there is reason which is not present in animals. Whence, just as the soul is to be preferred to the body, so reason is to be preferred, *in natural law*, to the other parts of the soul which are common to animals. . . .[59]

Finally, in one of his letters Augustine repeats in one short paragraph three views of the natural law that were common to the Fathers – it is written in the heart of man, it consists fundamentally in the precept of doing as one would be done by, and it had to be supplemented by the Mosaic law.[60] Here Augustine speaks for the tradition of the natural law, now well on the way to being established.

D. ST. ISIDORE OF SEVILLE

St. Augustine, who in so many ways represented the culture of the Roman Empire in the West, died in his episcopal city of Hippo in 431 while the Vandals were actually hammering at the gates, an event whose symbolism can hardly be ignored. The period usually described as the Dark Ages was to follow, in which the transmission of the cultural riches of antiquity and the elaboration of Christian thought itself, were to depend to some considerable degree upon the accidents of historical survival. The contingent fact that Boethius's (c. 480–524) project of translating (and reconciling) the works of Plato and Aristotle was only carried out to the extent of providing the West with a Latin version and commentaries on Aristotle's logic (the *Organon*) has had an incalculable effect upon the course of the history of thought. What might not have been the history of medieval thought had Aristotle's other works been known in good translation and not tardily and at first in piecemeal and unreliable

[59] *Contra Faust.*, XXII, 27, (P.L., 42; 418).

[60] *Ep.*, 158, 3, 16 (P.L., 33; 681): "Proinde quoniam lex est in ratione hominis, qui iam utitur arbitrio libertatis, naturaliter in corde conscripta est, qua suggeritur, ne aliquid faciat quisque alteri quod ipse pati non vult, secundum hanc legem praevaricatores sunt omnes, etiam qui legem per Moysen non acceperunt."

versions? And what might not the medievals have made of the great Platonic dialogues? Boethius's contemporary, Cassiodorus (c. 477–570) tried to make provision for the coming cataclysm by founding the monastery of the Vivarium, at Squillace in southern Italy, giving it his own magnificent library and making provision for the preservation and copying of manuscripts there. To this fact our present day knowledge of the literature of classical antiquity is greatly indebted. It is in this context of the preservation of the past that we must place Isidore of Seville (c. 570–636). He was less important than either Boethius or Cassiodorus in general; but on the particular topic of law he was more important. For he provided the link between the second century Roman lawyers and the medieval civilians and canonists and was the main transmitter of the legal ideas of the jurisconsults to the Middle Ages.[61]

His *Book of Etymologies*, at which he worked for at least nine years before his death, is what would nowadays be called an encyclopaedia; it is a vast and uncritical compilation, whose great merit is that it preserved so much that would otherwise have been lost.

> One may ask whether it was not in the books of the Roman jurists especially the Stoic jurists, that our encyclopedist discovered the idea of his work; for nowhere else can one find such frequent and artificial etymologies.[62]

The *Etymologies* is made up so largely of citations that it is difficult to discover any personal style of Isidore's – difficult even to remark that he has exercised a choice between the authorities he quotes. Nevertheless he did make a choice in the question of the natural law, which interests us; and his choice, because of the disproportionate influence of his book as one of the great

[61] Cf. J. Tardif, "Un abrégé juridique des Etymologies d'Isidore de Seville" in *Mélanges Julien Havet*, pp. 659–680, cited by P. Sejourné, *St. Isidore de Séville*, p. 7.

[62] P. Sejourné, *op. cit.*, p. 62; cf. L.D. Reynolds-N.G. Wilson, *Scribes and Scholars: A Guide to the Transmission of Greek and Latin Literature*, pp. 74–75: "Owing to the phenomenally rapid spread of his works throughout Europe . . . Isidore was quickly established as one of the most influential agents in the transmission and elucidation of ancient learning. His *Etymologies* was at the same time the last product of the Roman encyclopaedic tradition and the starting-point for most medieval compilations. . . . This systematically arranged encyclopaedia, packed with information and misinformation on every topic from angels to the parts of the saddle, descends so often into false etymologizing and the uncritical parade of absurd bric-à-brac, that it cannot be read without a smile. . . ."

educators of the Middle Ages,[63] was an exceedingly important one.

In Book V legal terms find their place. Isidore knew the definitions of the great jurists of the second century either directly or through an otherwise unknown juridical document, current in Spain and dependent upon the Theodosian Code of 438 A.D., upon which he drew heavily.[64] He accepts the tripartite division of Ulpian – *jus naturale: jus gentium: jus civile.* He probably found it either in the *Digest* or in the *Institutes* of Justinian; his use of it, in fact, is one of the indications that he knew Justinian's *Corpus Juris.*[65] But in adopting the division, Isidore effectively changed the terms; on this point he was more than a mere compiler and not with the happiest results.[66]

He abandons entirely the natural law of Ulpian, common to all animals. Isidore, it must be remembered, was a bishop and a distinguished canonist, writing for a Christian milieu in the seventh century; he could be expected to have little sympathy for a conception that had some appeal in the second century when Stoicism was a force. In fact he returns to something not unlike the natural law of Cicero – and his mixture of Ulpian and Gaius has a good deal in common with the *Institutes*' definition of the *jus gentium.* One even finds an echo of the natural law of Aristotle, independent of human conventions;[67] natural law is "what is common to all nations and is set up by a natural instinct and not by any positive institution."[68]

One of the few things clear in this confused picture is that Isidore rejected Ulpian's definition of the natural law. In the Middle Ages, as we shall see, that definition was commonly described as "the jurists' definition" or "the definition of the

[63] One recalls that Dante placed Isidore in the fourth heaven, that of the sun or light, in the excellent company of St. Thomas, St. Albert the Great, Peter Lombard, Gratian, Boethius, Dionysius the Areopagite and others. Cf. *Paradiso,* X, 131.

[64] P. Sejourné, *op. cit.*, p. 62.

[65] P. Sejourné, *op. cit.*, p. 65.

[66] G. Fassò's judgment, however, seems excessive – *Storia della filosofia del diritto,* I, p. 211: "La definizione isidoriana del diritto naturale ha, comunque, scarsa importanza."

[67] G. Fassò, *op. cit.*, I, p. 210; A.F. Utz, *Recht und Gerechtigkeit-Kommentar in 2-2ae,* Bd. 18, p. 448.

[68] *Etym.* V, 4 (P.L., 82; 199): "Jus naturale est commune omne nationum, et quod ubique instinctu naturae, non constitutione aliqua habeatur ut viri et feminae conjunctio, librorum susceptio et educatio, communis omnium possessio et omnium una libertas, acquisitio eorum quae coelo, terra, marique capiuntur. Item depositae rei vel commodatae restitutio. . . ."

law"; and there is a certain irony in the fact that it is occasionally attributed to Isidore, who had little use for it. His retention of the "instinct of nature" – his gesture towards Ulpian? – has its own difficulties. For some of the institutions he puts under the natural law, such as the common ownership of goods, the acquisition of things taken "in the sky, on earth or in the sea," the restitution of goods held in trust, are difficult to reduce to an "instinct of nature."

Isidore changes Ulpian's *jus gentium* in an even more thorough-going way than did the *Institutes* of Justinian. The term takes on much more of the character of positive law and is said to be common to almost all nations.[69] Isidore's examples of matters coming under the *jus gentium* embrace mainly war and its consequences – which may not be unconnected with the fact that in the *Institutes* of Ulpian the *jus gentium* and the *jus militare* are found side by side.[70] This definition is very close to some modern conceptions of international law.

In addition to the threefold division of laws attributed to Ulpian, Isidore had another division, which likewise found favour with the Middle Ages. It is the division of all laws into human and divine, which is later to become the frontispiece of the *Corpus Juris Canonici.* The relation between the two divisions in Isidore is not clear. The distinction between divine and human laws would appear to be the overriding one; but the question is complicated by the narrow view Isidore took of law as a species of *jus* (*lex est jus scriptum*).[71]

The identification of the natural law with the divine law, for which precedent can be discovered in the Fathers, influenced perhaps by Philo's eclecticism, was to find dramatic expression in Gratian's *Decretum* and therefore in much of the canon law of the twelfth and following centuries. It was, as will be seen, a dead end in the history of the natural law. Gratian's definition of natural law, as what is contained in the law and the Gospel, consecrated this misunderstanding; and it was almost as influential as the equally unfortunate definition of Ulpian. Both may be

[69] *Etym.*, V, 6 (P.L., 82; 199–200): "Jus gentium est sedium occupatio, aedificatio, munitio, bella, captivitatem, servitutes . . . et inde jus gentium quod eo jure omnes *fere* gentes utuntur."

[70] The actual examples are found in Ulpian, Hermogenianus, Florentinus, and Marcian. Livy makes a similar use of the *jus gentium* he found in Cicero, i.e. he applies it to matters of war, embassies etc. Cf. S. Ramirez, *El derecho de gentes*, p. 31.

[71] *Etym.*, V, 3 (P.L., 82; 199).

said to have influenced the history of the natural law negatively – by offering definitions that could not, in the last resort, be sustained. Another interpretation of Isidore's division of laws into human and divine would make natural law the positive law of God, opening the way to voluntarism; this, too, as will be seen in its place, was a dead end. The third possibility is a pantheistic interpretation that would identify nature and God; and we shall find some of the medievals, attracted by this interpretation of Isidore, speaking of "nature, that is God" (*natura idest Deus*).[72]

One should not, perhaps, be over-critical of Isidore. He may have been inconsistent or even confused, but he did preserve much that helped the education of the Middle Ages and his contribution to the Christian contour of the natural law is an irreplaceable one.

[72] G. Fassò, *La legge della ragione*, pp. 49–51.

CHAPTER IV

MEDIEVAL CANONISTS AND CIVILIANS

It should by now be evident that tradition, the handing on of the achievements of the past, plays an all-important part in the formulation of a theory of natural law. For this reason Isidore of Seville has an importance out of all proportion to his personal achievement in that he preserved so much of antiquity. An excellent example of use made of materials so preserved is found in the twelfth century canonist Gratian. The influence of Isidore upon Gratian is palpable in the matter of the natural law; and Gratian and his commentators were to influence the theologians of the High Middle Age.[1]

A. GRATIAN

Gratian (d. 1160) was, seemingly, a Camaldolese monk. Not much is known of his life.[2] Even the date of his *Concordia discordantium canonum*, commonly known as the *Decretum* is disputed. It is usually accepted that it was first published about 1140 or at any rate between 1139 and 1142. It was already well

[1] St. Thomas in *Contra pestiferam doctrinam retrahentium a religionis ingressu*, c. 13, says "inconsonum et derisibile quod sacrae doctrinae professores juristarum glossulas in auctoritatem inducant vel de eis disceptant." But, as has been pointed out, it is a statement made in the heat of controversy; cf. B.C. Kuhlmann, *Der Gesetzesbegriff beim hl. Thomas von Aquin im Licht des Rechtsstudiums seiner Zeit*, p. 103; V.J. Bourke, *St. Thomas and the Greek Moralists*, p. 46 note 8.

[2] He seems to have come from the village of Carraria, near Orvieto. Cf. A. Lazzarini, "Gratianus de Urbeveteri" in *Studia Gratiana*, 4 (1956), pp. 1–15. Lazzarini suggests that the passage of Henry V in 1110 in his campaign against Pope Paschal II may have been the occasion of Gratian's vocation; his family may have taken refuge in the Camaldolese monastery of St. Nicholas (or the Holy Cross).

known in 1152 but by then it had been revised and augmented. A much earlier date was argued by the Polish scholar, A. Vetulani, who said that the *Decretum* was written about the beginning of the twelfth century and published about 1120. This view necessitated regarding certain texts, certainly later than the beginning of the century, the decisions of Innocent II at the Lateran Council of 1139 for instance, as interpolations. The fact of the matter is that Gratian spent the great part of his life in the compilation of the *Decretum* so that it is not surprising that the work should show 'layers'; but the additions and revisions made in the course of composition should be distinguished from those made after its publication.[3] The majority of canonists seem to accept the traditional date.

From the time of its publication, and despite the fact that it was never officially recognised by the Church or enjoyed any juridical status greater than that of a private collection of canons,[4] the *Decretum Gratiani* dominated the canon law of the Middle Ages and after. We need not go into the reasons for this beyond the obvious one; that the thicket of canonical legislation of over eleven centuries' of Church history – papal decrees, laws of synods, councils provincial or oecumenical – urgently needed, some kind of codification, rather as the Roman law, by the sixth century under Justinian, had needed to be set in order. An important difference was that Justinian was an Emperor and could give legal effect to his codification; Gratian was acting in no such public capacity. But his achievement, humbler though it was, deserves comparison with that of Justinian's compilers. And Gratian's *Decretum* had an immediate influence upon theology: Peter Lombard, that theological authority par excellence of the Middle Ages, was impressed by the Decretum.[5]

At the time of the writing of the *Decretum* canon law and moral theology had not yet gone their separate ways. In fact

[3] G. Fransen, "La date du Décret de Gratien" in *Revue d'histoire ecclésiastique* 51 (1956), pp. 521–531; G. Le Bras, "Le triomphe de Gratien" in *Studia Gratiana*, 1 (1953), 1–14, at p. 1 and note 1.

[4] A. Van Hove, *Commentarium Lovaniense in Codicem Iuris Canonici: Prolegomena*, pp. 345–346; G. Fassò, *Storia della filosofia del diritto*, II, p. 232.

[5] B.C. Kuhlmann, *Der Gesetzbegriff beim hl. Thomas van Aquin im Lichte des Rechtsstudiums seiner Zeit*, pp. 14–18, 96; E.E. Hölscher, *Vom römischen zum christlichen Naturrecht*, pp. 51–52, 63; O. Lottin, *Psychologie et morale aux XIIe et XIIIe siècles*, II, p. 73; *Id.*, *Le droit naturel chez saint Thomas d'Aquin et ses prédécesseurs*, p. 28; A.H. Chroust, "The Philosophy of Law from St. Augustine to St. Thomas Aquinas," in *The New Scholasticism*, 20 (1946), p. 38.

Gratian himself seems to have been the last great figure to write on canon law from the point of view of a moral theologian, his main preoccupations being sacramental, looking to marriage and ordination as the two sacraments having to do with status and function in the Church.[6] Certainly there is no opposition between theology and canon law in Gratian; only later in his commentators, will the distinction be made. The fact that Gratian wrote from the standpoint of theology no less than that of canon law should be kept in mind when we come to discuss his identification of natural law with what is in Revelation. The fact of the matter, as Arnold points out, seems to be that he simply did not have terminology adequate to express the relationship between the revealed law of God and the law of God available to human unaided reason; and, because the terminology was inadequate, confusion arose, and very speedily, in Gratian's successors. One is tempted to compare the situation with that arising, for a similar reason, from Abelard's handling of moral problems, such as that of the influence of ignorance upon culpability, in the twelfth century. The matter was more important in Gratian because of his direct influence upon the thirteenth century which, in matters of natural law, was clearly much greater than that of Abelard. This influence of Gratian was not merely direct – through his personal definition of natural law – but indirect in his transmitting the Roman law conceptions he found in Isidore of Seville.[7]

In the *Decretum* Gratian twice defines the natural law; but, far from clarifying a situation already confused, he may be said to have made confusion worse confounded. For one of the definitions is taken from Isidore and can, therefore, be placed within a recognised tradition, to whose continuity it contributes; but the other definition, Gratian's personal contribution to the subject, is

[6] Cf. F. Arnold, "Die Rechtslehre des Magister Gratianus" in *Studia Gratiana*, 1 (1953), pp. 457–460. There is uncertainty about the actual organisation of the *Decretum* by Gratian, who nowhere indicates the general divisions of his work. Even the *Distinctiones* by which it is quoted may have been introduced by Gratian's commentator Paucapalea. Cf. A. Van Hove, *op. cit.*, pp. 340–341.

[7] M. Grabmann, "Das Naturrecht der Scholastik von Gratian bis Thomas von Aquin" in *Mittelalterliches Geistesleben*, I, p. 69: "Die Definition des jus naturale in den *Etymologien* des Isidor ist von Gratian übernommen und dadurch auch Gemeingut der Scholastik geworden. Thomas zitiert sowohl Isidor wie auch das Corpus Iuris Civilis und römische Rechtsgelehrte." It should be stressed, however, that St. Thomas, although he used and deferred to Gratian, knew the classical Roman texts independently of Gratian and of Isidore. Cf. J.M. Aubert, *Le droit romain dans l'oeuvre de saint Thomas d'Aquin*, pp. 19–23; E.E. Hölscher, *op. cit.*, pp. 57–58; B.C. Kuhlmann, *op. cit.*, p. 104 note 2.

at first sight at odds with the Isidorian one. It will be well to set out the two definitions.

The *Decretum* begins:

The human race is governed in two ways, by natural law and by custom. Natural law is what is contained in the law and the gospel, in virtue of which each is commanded to do to others as he would wish to be done to himself and is forbidden to do to another what he would not have done to himself.[8]

This, on the face of it, is a challenge and certainly risks being what Dom Lottin called "a regrettable confusion between natural law and divine law."[9] The second definition given by Gratian is the Roman law one, which he found in Isidore:

Natural law is common to all nations by reason of its universal origin in a natural instinct and not in any (positive) constitution.[10]

The relationship between these two definitions has given rise to considerable disagreement amongst scholars.

First, it ought to be noted that Gratian did not proceed systematically. As Composta expresses it, his approach was less methodological than phenomenological, his search for definitions inductive rather than apriori or deductive and he was more impressed by the Biblical account of the nature of man than by the *zoon politikon* of Aristotle.[11] This does go some way towards explaining why, for Gratian, the natural law becomes God's law. And it does seem true that Gratian was free of the systematizing tendencies of many of his followers. Nevertheless the discrepancy between the two definitions remains to be explained. Here there are really two questions: Are the definitions irreconcilable? and: Which, if either, is to be deemed Gratian's own definition? The second question is the more easily answered, at least in the sense that the definition quoted in the tradition as Gratian's is always identified as that which says that the natural law is what is

[8] *Decretum*, D.I, 1: "Humanum genus duobus regitur, naturali videlicet jure et moribus. Jus naturale est quod in lege et evangelio continetur quo quisque jubetur alii facere quod sibi vult fieri et prohibetur alii inferre quod sibi nolit fieri."

[9] O. Lottin, *Le droit naturel chez saint Thomas d'Aquin et ses prédécesseurs*, p. 11 "... Gratien ... soulignait une fâcheuse confusion entre le droit naturel et le droit divin."

[10] *Decretum*, D.I, 7: "Ius naturale est commune omnium nationum eo quod ubique instinctu nature non constitutione aliqua habetur."

[11] D. Composta "Il diritto naturale in Graziano" in *Studio Gratiana*, 2 (1954), 156.

contained in the law and the gospel. This is Gratian's in a way in which the other, taken from the Roman lawyers, through Isidore, is not. The *Decretum*, after all, begins with the phrase about the two laws that govern the human race, of which one, the natural law, is contained in the law and the gospel. Nor is this the only occurrence of the definition – if it were it might be dismissed as a rhetorical flourish or a gesture of piety. Other places in the *Decretum* in which the definition recurs are well known – Rudolf Weigand lists and cites three express reiterations of the definition and one in which it is implicit.[12] The definition is, then, not simply a passing phrase of Gratian's. Furthermore, Gratian was perfectly aware of the paradox of seeming to identify the natural law with what is revealed in the Scriptures; he points out that not all in the Scriptures is of natural law and, in fact, confines the natural law to the moral precepts of the Old Testament and to the summary, positive and negative, of neighbourly love in the New Testament.[13]

Gratian's other definition of the natural law insists more upon its universal presence in mankind. It is what is ingrained by natural instinct and not the result of human making. He takes the phrase from Isidore of Seville – from whom also comes the bipartite division of all laws which inspires the opening phrase of the Decretum: "The human race is governed in two ways. . . .". But the reference to the 'natural instinct,' as we have seen, takes one back behind Isidore to the Roman lawyers and further back to the Stoics; the phrase sits easily with Cicero's *quaedam innata vis* which, and not opinion of men, generates the natural law. To this definition Gratian accords a secondary place – "there is," he says,

[12] R. Wiegand, *Die Naturrechtslehre der Legisten und Dekretisten von Irnerius bis Accursius und von Gratian bis Johannes Teutonicus*, pp. 134–5. The references are: DG p. D.9, c. 11: "Cum ergo naturali iure nichil aliud precipiatur quam quod Deus vult fieri, nichilque vetetur, quam quod Deus prohibet fieri; denique cum in canonica scriptura nichil aliud, quam in divinis legibus inveniatur, divine vero leges natura consistant; patet quod quecumque divinae voluntati seu canonicae scripturae contraria probantur, eadem et naturali iuri inveniuntur adversa. Unde quecumque divinae voluntati seu canonice scripture, seu divinis legibus postponenda censentur, eisdem naturale ius preferri oportet"; D.5 r.n. 2: "Sed cum naturale ius lege et evangelio supra dicatur esse comprehensum. . . ."; DG p. D.6, c. 3: "In lege et evangelio naturale ius continetur. . . ."; D.7 pr.: "Ius autem constitutionis cepit a iustificationibus quas dominus tradidit Moisi dicens 'Si emeris servum ebreum. . . ."

[13] R. Weigand, *op. cit.*; the continuation of DG p. D. 6, c. 3 (preceding note) is: "Sunt enim in lege quedam moralia, ut: non occides etcetera, quedam mistica, utpote sacrificiorum precepta, et alia his similia. Moralia mandata ad naturale ius spectant atque ideo nullam mutabilitatem recepisse monstrantur."

"another division of law" and he introduces Isidore's definition.[14] This 'other division' need not here concern us, beyond insisting that it is not necessarily, and certainly not in the eyes of Gratian, inconsistent with the definition that places the natural law in 'the Law and the gospel'. Gratian, in making use of Isidore (or rather in taking from the *Panormia* of Ivo of Chartres some texts of Isidore) is simply continuing a chain of tradition, stretching back to the Romans. There are in this 'Roman' definition two elements – the idea of the universality of the natural law, traceable to Gaius and the *Institutes* of Justinian and the idea of a 'natural instinct,' which is found in Ulpian.[15]

Let us return to Gratian's first definition which is the one by which he is remembered in the history of the natural law, the definition that was to prove such an embarrassment to the thinkers of the Middle Ages.[16] The definition is startling; but its dramatic appearance in the mid-twelfth century does not mean that it had no antecedents. This definition also has two elements; there is, first, the assertion that natural law is what is contained in the law and the gospel and, secondly, the suggestion that it is summarised in the precept (*Matthew* 7; 12) of doing to others as we would wish others to do to us together with the corresponding prohibition (*Tobit* 4; 15) of not doing to others what we would not wish to have done to ourselves.

With regard to the first element, one is immediately reminded of St. Paul's reference (in *Romans* 2; 14ff) to the "Gentiles who have not the Law (i.e. the Mosaic law)" and yet are bound by "the law written in their hearts"; they naturally know what is in

[14] *Decretum*, D.I, 7.

[15] Cf. J. Gaudemet, "La doctrine des sources du droit dans le Décret de Gratien" in *Revue de droit canonique*, 1 (1951), pp. 5–31. The question of the weight of the influence of Anselm of Laon's school is not yet settled (cf. D. Composta, *op. cit.*, p. 167; R. Weigand, *op. cit.*, p. 139, note 2); but there cannot be much doubt about that of Ivo of Chartres. Composta is surely right, *op. cit.*, p. 168, in saying that Gratian did not slavishly repeat what he found of Isidore in Ivo: "Graziano è agganciato alla secolare tradizione umanistica e cristiana; in questo filone aureo non vi è luogo per una passiva recezione delle dottrine trasmess, ma bensì per un abile ripensamento dell' insegnamento tradito; così (col Sejourné) Graziano sa modificare la definizione isidoriana e non ristagna il tesoro dottrinale dell' antichità."

[16] M. Villey, "Le droit naturel chez Gratien" in *Studia Gratiana*, 3 (1954), p. 85. "Parmi les innombrables définitions qui furent, en cours des siècles, proposés du droit naturel, celle-ci est justement célèbre." Villey goes on to point out that Gratian should be judged on his *Dicta*, which include the present definition (DD, 5, 6, 8, 9, 13, 20) rather than on the authorities he quotes, e.g. Isidore.

the law, their conscience bearing witness. This *locus classicus* provided a solid and well-recognised body of doctrine to which Gratian could appeal although, if truth be told, his definition appears to contradict the Pauline notion of a natural law *independent* of scripture. F.X. Arnold sees the special influence of St. Augustine, but expressed in imperfect terminology, in Gratian's definition. The passages he cites from Augustine, however, do not amount to much more than the suggestion that the fundamental precept of the natural law, or at least one fundamental precept, is that expressed in *Matthew* 7; 12, in brief, do as you would be done by.[17] Composta professes to have found a closer dependence lurking, so to speak, beneath one of Gratian's cross-references. It comes in that part of the *Decretum* where the question arises about the juridical capacity of clerics to possess property. Gratian refers to a passage in St. Augustine's commentary on John: "By what law do you defend the property (*villas*) of the Church? Human or divine? We have the divine law in the Scriptures; and the human in the legislation of kings."[18] Composta finds in the reference a confirmation of his view that Gratian was responsible only for a single definition of the natural law, contained in the written code of Scripture and containing the various prescriptions (including this one about property rights) that are universal and founded on nature. The quotation is made to carry a good deal of weight and it does seem a little far-fetched to discover in it the famous formula: *quod in lege et evangelio continetur.* On the other hand, Composta is clearly right – and here Weigand agrees – in asserting that there is no radical discrepancy between the two definitions of the natural law in the

[17] F. Arnold, "Die Rechtslehre des Magister Gratianus" in *Studia Gratiana,* 1 (1953), pp. 461–462, citing Augustine *Ep.* 157, 3, 15 (P. L., 33; 681): "Lex est enim in ratione hominis, qui iam utitur arbitrio libertatis naturaliter in corde conscripta, qua suggeritur, ne aliquid faciat quisque alteri, quod pati ipse non vult"; and *De ordine,* II, 8, 25 (P.L., 32; 1006): "In omni vero contractu atque conversationi cum hominibus satis est servare unum hoc vulgare proverbium; Nemini faciant quod pati nolunt"; *Enarr. in Ps. 118,* sermo 25, 4 (P.L., 37; 1574): "Nullus enim est qui faciat alteri iniuriam, nisi qui fieri nolit sibi; et in hoc transgreditur naturae legem, quam non sinitur ignorare, dum id quod facit non vult pati." J. Sauter, *Die philosophischen Grundlagen des Naturrechts,* p. 64 discusses these passages (some of which have already been quoted in Chapter III above) and adds a reference to *De doctr. christiana,* III, 14, 22 (P.L. 34; 74) in which Augustine states that the rule of doing as you would be done by cannot be corrupted by the customs of various races.

[18] D. Composta, "Il diritto naturale in Graziano" in *Studia Gratiana* 2 (1954), p. 171: "Quo iure defendis villas ecclesiae divino an humano? Divinum ius in scripturis habemus; humanum in legibus regum."

Decretum Gratiani.[19] It does not, however, follow, that Gratian made Isidore's definition his own in the sense that the identification of natural law and the Scriptures is his own.

Let us return, however, to the question of the origin of Gratian's own definition. The definition may be placed within the Augustinian tradition without our having to postulate Augustine as the direct source; Gratian's source may have been someone much closer. Rudolf Weigand, in his monumental study, having mentioned Holy Writ, Augustine and Isidore as sources, quotes a passage from Pope Urban II (1088–1099) giving an unusual view of law:

There are, he said, two laws, one public, the other private.... The private law is that which is written by the instinct of the Holy Spirit in the heart, as the Apostle said concerning some 'who have the law of God written in their hearts' and elsewhere 'When the gentiles have not the law, if they do naturally what is of the law, they are a law to themselves.... The private law is greater than the public. The Spirit is the law of God, and those who are led by the Spirit are led by the law of God.[20]

The question in discussion was that of the right of a priest to

[19] Weigand refers to Composta's study as 'eine überstarke harmonisierende Tendenz' (*op. cit.*, p. 138); and his own reconciliation of the two definitions is much more pragmatic: "Das bisher Skizzierte ist Gratians eigene und persönliche Auffassung vom Naturrecht. Diese hindert ihn jedoch nicht, auch Isidors Definitionen des Natur- und Völkerrechts in sein Dekret, das bekanntlich formal ein Lehrbuch, inhaltlich aber doch weitgehend ein Quellenwerk, eine Sammlung von 'gegensätzliche Canones' ist, aufzunehmen und damit als Textgrundlage der künftigen wissenschaftlichen Arbeit zur Verfügung zu stellen. Dass sich Gratians Isidors Ansicht nicht selbst zu eigen macht, geht nicht so sehr aus den Einleitungsworten zu D.I., c. 6 'est et *alia* divisio iuris' hervor, sondern aus seiner ganzen Darstellung, da er in seinen Dicta stets nur von der Naturrechtsauffassung spricht...."

[20] R. Weigand, *op. cit.*, p. 130, citing *Epistolae et Privilegia*, n. 278 (P.L., 151; 535): "Duae sunt, inquit, leges: una publica, altera privata ... Lex vero privata est, quae instinctu S. Spiritus in corde scribitur, sicut de quibusdam dicit Apostolus: 'qui habent legem Dei scriptum in cordibus suis' et alibi: 'Cum gentes legem non habeant si naturaliter ea quae legis sunt faciunt, ipsi sibi sunt lex.' ... Dignior est enim lex privata quam publica. Spiritus quidem Dei lex est, et qui Spiritu Dei aguntur lege Dei ducuntur." It is interesting to note that Ivo of Chartres (c. 1040–1116) begins his *Decretum* by referring to the rules in the Scriptures: "quaedam sic esse jussa ut observarentur, prohibita ne fierent. Ut est: Honora patrem et matrem, et Non moechaberis (Exod. xx; Ephes. vi) Horum autem quae jubendo et vetando scripta sunt alia sunt sacramentorum velata mysteriis.... Alia vero etiam nunc facienda sunt.... De his igitur quae ita sunt posita in litteris sacris, vel jubendo vel vetando, sive siniendo ut etiam nunc, id est tempore Novi Testamenti ad vitam piam exercendam moresque pertineant, hoc opus quod in manus sumpsi, componere aggressus sum; ut quantum Deus me adiuvat, omnia talia de canonicis libris colligam atque, ut facile inspici possint, in unum tanquam speculum congeram" (P.L., 161; 59–60).

follow a call to enter the cloister against the will of his bishop; and the appeal is to the law of the Spirit, which must prevail over the public or customary law, because it is God's law. Weigand sees here an exception due to the high regard the Middle Ages had for the cloistered life – the instinct to enter the cloister must come from God and the possibility of self-deception is hardly raised. It is not a sort of situation ethic before its time. The idea, however, was adopted by Gratian in the *Decretum*[21] and was to be subject of restrictive interpretations on the part of the decretists, anxious to avoid the possibility of misuse.

A closer approach to Gratian's definition, according to Lottin[22] is found in the teaching of the school of Anselm of Laon (d. 1117). This school, which dominated the theology of the early twelfth century, was particularly preoccupied with the natural law. The concept that emerged was a characteristically theological one. The natural law, the law of behaviour for humanity, is anterior to the Mosaic law (which became necessary precisely because men had neglected the law of their nature); it is the fruit of the *ratio naturalis* which can know God and discern the basic maxims, such as the prohibition of homicide and, in a general formula, the Golden Rule of not doing to others what you would not have done to yourself.[23] Still closer is the formulation found in Hugh of St. Victor (1096–1141) who, in his *De sacramentis*, elaborates on the content of the natural law; it comprises commands prohibitions and permissions – commanding what is essentially good, forbidding what is essentially evil and permitting what is good or evil according to circumstances.[24]

[21] C. 19, q. 2, c. 2.

[22] O. Lottin, *Le droit naturel chez saint Thomas d'Aquin et ses prédécesseurs*, 1931; *Id. Psychologie et morale aux XIIe et XIIIe siècles*, t. II, 1948, "La loi naturelle depuis le début du XIIe siècle jusqu'à saint Thomas d'Aquin," pp. 71–100 (which is a rehandling of the theme of the 1931 study).

[23] F. Bliemitzrieder, *Anselms von Laon Systematische Sentenzen*, Beiträge zur Geschichte der Philosophie des Mittelalters, 18, Münster, 1919, pp. 35–36: "Contra originale peccatum sunt inventa remedia et in naturali et in scripta lege et in tempore gratie. Naturalem autem legem naturalis ratio tenere persuadet, ut quod homo non occidatur; haud enim sua naturalis ratio unumquemque docet." And later, p. 79: "Lex naturalis hec est: quod tibi non vis fieri alii ne feceris." And see the other texts of the school of Anselm in Lottin *op. cit.*, p. 72 note 1 and in M. Villey, *op. cit.*, p. 92. (referring to F. Bliemitzrieder, *op. cit.*, pp. 35, 37, 38, 78 ff., 92, 94)

[24] *De sacramentis*, I, pars. 2 (P.L., 176; 341): "Tria sunt genera operum; quedam ita bona sunt ut nunquam licite preterire possunt; quaedam ita mala ut nunquam licite possint committi; quaedam autem media sunt quae pro tempore et loco agi possunt et praetermitti. Sola igitur quae sic se habent ut nunquam licite fieri possunt lex naturalis prohibuit; illa vero quae nunquam licite possunt praetermitti sola praecepit; media autem ad utrumlibet relinquens."

The summarising of the precepts of the natural law, in the words of *Matthew* 7; 12: "Do to others as you would have others do to you," is frequently mentioned in Hugh of St Victor's *De sacramentis.*[25] And Hugh is the most pronounced influence on Gratian. What these theologians, the school of Anselm and Hugh of St. Victor, did was to take a commonplace of Patristic theology – the idea of the natural law as a primitive law given to man and reiterated after the fall because of man's inability to obey or even to discover it – and to add the New Law (represented by the phrase of *Matthew* 7; 12) to the Old Law or the Decalogue. The Fathers normally gave the summary of the law of the New Testament from *Matthew* 22; 39 – the precept of loving God and loving one's neighbour, in which "is contained the Law and the prophets."[26] The theologians prefer the Golden Rule of *Matthew* 7; 12 (together with its negative formulation in *Tobit.* 4; 15). This appeal to different texts hardly constitutes an essential difference between the medieval theologians and the Fathers in the question of the natural law. In following the theologians Gratian touched a long tradition.[27]

So much for its origins; what must be said, now, about the meaning or interpretation of Gratian's natural law. The question here is this: Is the natural law, in Gratian's mind, to be identified with the revealed law of God or not? The fact that Gratian's definition has been an embarrassment for so long has led to a number of explanations. There seem to be three possibilities –

[25] S. Kuttner, "Zur Frage der theologischen Vorlagen Gratians" cited by M. Villey, "Le droit naturel chez Gratien" in *Studia Gratiana*, 3 (1954), p. 94.

[26] St. Augustine does cite *Matthew* 7; 12 in this context; but in texts that, as far as is known, were not accessible to Gratian. Cf. M. Villey, *op. cit.*, p. 93.

[27] A. Dihle, *Die Goldene Regel: Eine Einführung in die Geschichte der antiken und frühchristlichen Vulgärethik, Göttingen*, 1962. On p. 107 Dihle gives a list of 27 patristic texts giving the Golden Rule in either positive or negative form and occasionally both. See the entire section (e), Die Goldene Regel in der antiken und der christlichen Tradition, pp. 103–109; the following section (f), Die Goldene Regel und das Nächstenliebegebot, pp. 109–127, the last section in the book, discusses the relation between the Golden Rule and the precept about loving the neighbour – in Matthew 22; 39 (parallel passages in *Luke*, 10; 25, *Mark* 12; 31) and having its origin in *Leviticus*, 19; 18, F. Flückiger, *Geschichte des Natturrechts*, 1, p. 402, points out that the 'Golden Rule' is susceptible of many interpretations, ranging from the *lex talionis* 'an eye for an eye and a tooth for a tooth' to the naive egoism of prudential conduct; it can be understood in the sense of the precept of loving the neighbour; but the underlying ethical, subjectivism it contains reduces it to something like 'one is one's own neighbour' or 'one hand washes the other.' Further exploration in H. Welzel, *Naturrecht und materiale Gerechtigkeit*, p. 55 who mentions Scotus (*Ox. iv*, d. 21, qu. 2 n. 8) who turns the Golden Rule into a form of right reason.

either there is here a regrettable confusion between the natural law and the divine law;[28] or the two laws are kept totally distinct (in other words the definition does not mean what it says); or there is an acceptable meaning that Gratian, perhaps maladroitly, expressed. It is not to be assumed either that Gratian did not know what he was talking about, or that he was giving a wilfully perverse definition. The third possibility is the one that seems more likely. And, in fact it is confirmed in the *Decretum* itself where Gratian admits the obvious:

> The natural law is contained in the law and the gospel; but not all that is to be found in the law and the gospel is shown to belong to the natural law. There are certain moral precepts in the law such as: Thou shalt not kill etc.; certain mystical precepts, as those concerning sacrifice and others like them. The moral precepts belong to the natural law and so are seen to admit of no change.[29]

In other words, when Gratian says that the natural law is contained in the law and the gospel, 'contained' is the operative word. One may compare other words he uses to describe the relationship between natural law and the Scriptures – "comprehended in," or "coherent with." The matter seems obvious and the point would be hardly worth making were it not that Gratian's definition was so often, in his immediate successors, during the Middle Age at large and even in some contemporary scholars, interpreted as identifying the natural law and the divine law of the scriptures. The truth of the matter is, as Composta puts it, that the scriptures are the 'container' of the natural law, not its

[28] O. Lottin, *Le droit naturel chez saint Thomas d'Aquin et ses prédécesseurs*, p. 11: "Gratien ... soulignait une fâcheuse confusion. ..."; F. Flückiger, *Geschichte des Naturrechts*, I, pp. 401, 405–406: "Alles Recht steht unter dem göttlichen und natürlichen Gesetz. Dieses ist unveränderlich, es hat den Vorrang vor allen andern Gesetzen. ... Es ist enthalten im Gesetz des Alten und Neuen Testaments und stimmt also überein mit dem geoffenbarten Gesetz Gottes. ..."; F. Arnold, *op. cit.*, p. 461. The suggestion that the law in the definition is the Roman law hardly helps; cf. C. Leitmaier, "Das Privateigentum im Gratianischen Dekret" in *Studia Gratiana*, 2 (1954), p. 370.

[29] DG p.D. 6, c. 3: "In lege et evangelio naturale ius continetur; non tamen quecunque in lege et evangelio inveniuntur, naturali iure coherere probantur. Sunt enim in lege quedam moralia, ut: non occides et cetera, quedam mistica, utpote sacrifitiorum precepta, et alia his similia. Moralia mandata ad naturale ius spectant atque ideo nullam mutabilitatem recepisse monstrantur."

'content.'[30] The content of the natural law is approached by Gratian through his dependence on the Roman law ideas, for example the *naturalis instinctus* of Ulpian he found in Isidore, probably through the intermediary of Ivo of Chartres.

One need not follow Composta's assertion that this means that Gratian gives only one definition of the natural law – a single definition of which the formula referring to the scriptures and the formula referring to the natural instinct of all men are simply two stages. This seems an excessively harmonising interpretation.[31] The commonsense view, however, that Gratian is to be believed when he interpreted his own formulation, can be found in St. Thomas Aquinas;[32] and support can also be found for it in the Fathers.[33] It is also in some of the commentators on Gratian and it is well expressed in the seventeenth century by Suarez, writing at about the time Gratian's definition finally ceased to be influential.[34] Suarez suggests that the identification of the natural law

[30] D. Composta, "Il diritto naturale in Graziano" in *Studia Gratiana*, 2 (1954), p. 188: "Dunque la Rivelazione non è il contenuto, ma solo il contento del Diritto Naturale'; cf. *Id.*, *Natura e Ragione*, Zürich, 1971, pp. 50–53; R. Weigand, *Die Naturrechtslehre der Legisten und Dekretisten . . .*, p. 134, "Nach Gratian besteht aber keine volle, sondern nur eine teilweise inhaltliche Gleichheit zwischen Naturrecht und Hl. Schrift"; B. Tierney; "Natura idest Deus: A Case of Juristic Pantheism?" in *Journal of the History of Ideas*, 24 (1963), p. 311: "Natural law and divine law were not, then, really identical in Gratian's thought; rather the two categories overlapped."

[31] D. Composta, "Il diritto naturale in Graziano" in *Studia Gratiana*, 2 (1954), p. 170: "Nel *Decreto* Graziano non da due ma una sola definizione del diritto naturale. Le così dette due definizioni non sono che due momenti di un unico insegnamento"; *Id.*, *Natura e ragione*, p. 51: ". . . le due definizioni non si oppongono ma anzi si identificano, in quanto fanno parte di un unico insegnamento."

[32] 1–2ae, 94, 4 ad 1: "Ad primum ergo dicendum, quod verbum illud (scilicet Gratiani) non est intelligendum, quasi omnia quae in Lege et Evangelio continentur sint de lege naturae, cum multa tradantur ibi supra naturam; se ea quae sunt de lege naturae plenarie ibi traduntur. . . ."; cf. *In 4 Sent.*, d. 33, q. 1, a. 1 ad 4, where St. Thomas speaks of the natural law as being 'divine' in the sense that it arises "ex impressione et infusione superioris principii, scilicet Deus". St. Thomas is speaking of Gratian's natural law, – *quod in lege et evangelio continetur* – and mistakenly attributes it to Isidore. If the slip is Thomas's (and not simply a vagary of the transmission of his text) it is interesting; for the explanation of the definition seems to envisage, in fact, the content of the other definition in Gratian, the one he took from Isidore with its reference to the natural instinct of all men.

[33] D. Composta, *op. cit.*, pp. 51–52, citing Theodoret and Ambrose from O. Schilling, *Naturrecht und Staat nach der Lehre der alten Kirche*, Paderborn, 1914.

[34] F. Suarez, *De legibus ac Deo legislatore*, II, c. 7, 8–9. St. Thomas *In 4 Sent.*, d. 33, q. 1, a. 1 ad 4 and 1–2, 94, 4 and 1 and Torquemada are quoted.

with the divine positive law, an identification that, with St. Thomas, he rejects, is due not to Gratian himself, but to the *Glossa Ordinaria*, or commentary on the *Decretum*.[35] G. Fassò perhaps also exculpates Gratian. He says that the *Decretum* speaks not of determinate behaviour but of a formal norm of conduct, expressed in the Golden Rule, found in the Law and the gospel (and also in other religious and moral systems), to which behaviour must conform. Gratian, thus, gives a "most typical formulation of rational natural law" in which it is not so much a matter of reducing natural law to divine law but the reverse![36]

Before leaving Gratian's definition of the natural law there is one other matter that can be raised and briefly disposed of. It concerns the currency, apropos of the definition, of the phrase, *natura idest Deus*.[37] It arises more properly in the Glossators on the *Corpus Juris Civilis*; but it may be mentioned here as it does offer a possible interpretation of Gratian's definition. It may be viewed as an attempt to bring together the God (author of the Scriptures) of Gratian's personal definition and the *naturalis instinctus* of the so-called Isidorian definition, so that the whole could be inserted into the civil law, The Glossators knew something of Greek philosophy through the *Pandects* and this provided them with a way of inserting, with some subtlety, the idea of a natural law linked to the Scriptures into a legal system which takes no official cognizance of the Scriptures. The *natura idest Deus*, despite its pantheistic overtones, is simply the result of a slightly confused concordism rather than a heretical proposition for which currency was sought. W. Ullman suggested that it was a Stoic pantheism.[38] It was scarcely this in Gratian himself; for his sources were legal and theological, not philosophical. There were no pantheistic anticipations of the Renaissance views of nature in

[35] F. Suarez, *op. cit.*, n. 8: "Ad quod tacite respondens Glossa ibi dicit ius naturale vocari a Gratiano ius divinum, indicans comprehendere non solum ius divinum naturale set etiam positivum." The reference is given as Glos. Ord. Bartholomeia Brixiensis in Gratiani Decretum D. 1 c. 7 'Ius naturale ubi revera dicitur: 'Et omne ius divinum dicitur naturale ius' (*ibid.*, note 301).

[36] *Storia della filosofia del diritto*, I, p. 234.

[37] Cf. U. Gualazzini, "Natura idest Deus" in *Studia Gratiana*, 3 (1954), pp. 411–424.

[38] Cf. D. Composta, "Il diritto naturale in Graziano," p. 157.

the decretists.[39] The matter will recur when we consider the decretists and the glossators.

It can be said that Gratian posed a problem that still has not been altogether satisfactorily solved – that of the relation between the natural law and the revealed law of God. His terminology was defective, giving rise to misunderstandings that persist to this day (many of our contemporaries regard the natural law as somehow a Church preserve and, on the other hand, the Catholic Church claims to be an authentic interpreter of the natural law). Yet Gratian himself must be absolved from responsibility for most of these difficulties. His own view, despite his unhappy way of expressing it, was the relatively innocuous one that the Scriptures contain the natural law, without exhausting its provisions while, on the other hand, not all that the Scriptures contain can be said to be natural law.

The influence of Gratian's views might have been expected to be enduring; his *Decretum* after all, is possibly the most important document in the history of the canon law down to the codification of 1917. Among jurists, however, and theorists of the natural law his definition ceases to have much importance by the sixteenth century.[40] This was not merely a matter of its inherent ambiguity but – and perhaps particularly – because of its

[39] G. Fassò, "Dio e la natura presso i decretisti ed i glossatori" in *Diritto ecclesiastico* 67 (1956), 3–10; *La Legge della natura*, pp. 48–68; B. Tierney, "Natura idest Deus: a case of juristic pantheism?" in *Journal of the History of Ideas*, 24 (1963), 307–322. The orthodoxy of the phrase coming from Azo and brought into the *Glossa ordinaria* by Accursius, can be saved if nature is taken as *natura naturans* and not as *natura naturata.* Thus Tierney: "There was, however, yet another use of the word nature in XIIIth century scholasticism that does fit in perfectly with the Accursian gloss. That was the distinction between nature as *natura naturans* on the one hand, a creative first cause that could be identified with God, and nature as *natura naturata*, on the other, signifying the world of created beings. The idea of God as creative 'nature' is at least as old as Augustine (Ep. I, 18, 2; PL., 33; 85; *De Trin.*, XV, I, 1; P.L., 40: 1057).... The main conclusion is that the medieval jurists were neither pantheists nor so ignorant of accepted theological terminology as to stumble into a doctrinal error through inadvertence" (pp. 317, 321). Cf. R. Weigand, *op. cit.*, pp. 59–60.

[40] H. Rommen, *The Natural Law*, p. 65 "... Reformers, who belonged to the school of Occam ... saw the natural law exclusively in the words of Scripture. Indeed, with their doctrine of *natura deleta* they could not even attain to a moral law that is naturally good. Gratian's formula, *ius naturae quod in evangelio et lege* (Decalogue), which was now being misinterpreted, vanished." Rommen remarks that Ulpian's *quod natura omnia animalia docuit* also vanished at this time.

misuse in the voluntarist-intellectualist controversies from the fourteenth century onwards. Gratian's own justification of the definition is on the face of it a statement of voluntarism:

Since the natural law commands nothing other than what God wills to be and forbids nothing except what God prohibits and, finally, since in the canonical Scriptures nothing is found other than what is in the divine law – for divine laws agree with nature – it follows that whatever is contrary to the divine will or to the canon of Scripture, is by the same token against the natural law.[41]

The passage is in all conscience convoluted enough; and if voluntarists were to appeal to it, those who rejected voluntarism could not always be relied upon to put their finger on the ambiguity. Gratian, however, must not be asked to take all the blame for this.[42]

B. THE MEDIEVAL CIVILIANS

Before turning our attention to the important body of literature to which the *Decretum Gratiani* gave rise, we may consider briefly the writings due to the study of the Roman law, especially during the twelfth century. The glossators, or civilian lawyers, commenting upon the *Corpus Juris Civilis* of Justinian, and trying to adapt it to the greatly changed conditions of the Holy Roman Empire, were not less important than the decretists, that is the canon lawyers, commentators on the *Decretum* of Gratian; but they

[41] DGp D. 9, c. 11: "Cum ergo naturali iure nichil aliud precipiatur, quam quod Deus vult fieri, nichilque vetetur, quam quod Deus prohibet fieri; denique, cum in canonica scriptura nichil aliud, quam in divinis legibus inveniantur, divine vero leges natura consistant; patet quod quecumque divinae voluntati, seu canonicae scripturae contraria probantur, eadem et naturali iuri inveniuntur adversa. Unde quecumque divinae voluntati, seu canonice scripture, seu divinis legibus postponenda censentur, eisdem naturale ius preferri oportet."

[42] G. Fassò, *Storia della filosofia del diritto*, I, p. 234; M. Villey, "Le droit naturel chez Gratien" in *Studia Gratiana*, 3 (1955), p. 99: "Il se peut que l'influence de Gratien – le fait qu'il ait *juxtaposé* dans le *Décret* la vieille doctrine théologique de la loi naturelle et des textes de droit romain – ait historiquement servi de renaissance d'une théorie juridique du droit naturel. Les *juxtapositions* de Gratien sont à la source des *confusions* futures, sinon du patronage que les théologiens postérieurs ont accordé, peut-être inconsidérément, au droit naturel des juristes. Mais s'il y a confusion Gratien n'en est pas responsable. Au monisme, au systématisme de certains de ses successeurs, s'oppose la définition très ferme des quatre premiers mots du *Décret*, respirant combien plus la Cité de Dieu que les *Instituts*: *Humanum genus duobus regitur.*"

were less philosophical and, in fact, had less to say of importance for the doctrine of the natural law.

The most important figure in the beginning of the medieval study of Roman law is Irnerius (c. 1055–1130/38); and despite his commanding presence at the beginning of an important tradition – or perhaps because of it – he remains a shadowy figure.[43] With him the study of the Roman law emerges into the light. Whether, in fact, the Roman law was continuously studied in the early Middle Ages and Irnerius and the glossators on the *Corpus Juris Civilis* of Justinian simply entered into a field already tilled by pre-Bolognese writers, is a question that we need not try to solve.[44] Certainly Bologna in the twelfth century was the great law-school of Europe and Irnerius was its first great teacher. He and the early glossators confined themselves to brief glosses or explanations of the classical texts. In those texts, as we have seen, the problem of the natural law was already present. There were two focal points of discussion, (1) the actual definition of the natural law (the *Corpus Juris Civilis* had, it will be recalled, adopted Ulpian's definition of the natural law as what nature has taught all animals) and, (2) the divisions of law (where the main problem was the relationship between the natural law and the *jus gentium*).

The civilians have been much studied. Indeed this is one area where an interesting and important change of mind has been brought about by the advances of scholarship in recent years. A generation ago the great *History of Medieval Political Theory in the West* by R.W. and A.J. Carlyle[45] could suggest that, while the medieval canonists decided definitely in favour of a particular usage in the matter of defining the natural law, this was in contrast with the medieval civil lawyers. The contrast was doubly unfortunate; for, as we shall see, the canonists were the ones who were undecided, while there is reasonable unanimity among the civilians. When Carlyle was writing not many of the canonists' texts had been published;[46] nor was as much known about the civilians as is now available.

[43] R. Weigand, *Die Naturrechtslehre der Legisten und Dekretisten von Irnerius bis Accursius und von Gratian bis Johannes Teutonicus*, p. 17: "ähnlich wie Gratian tritt er (Irnerius) ganz hinter sein Werk zurück und wird nur durch es erkennbar."

[44] R. Weigand, *op. cit.*, p. 17 and Anhang II, pp. 453–460 for the literature on the question.

[45] 6 vols., Edinburgh, 1903–1936; Vol. II, p. 31.

[46] Gratian, Paucapalea, Rufinus and Stephen of Tournai, in fact.

Lottin, in 1931, published a revised version of his *Le droit naturel chez saint Thomas d'Aquin et ses prédécesseurs* in which he made a detailed study of twelfth and thirteenth century canonists and civilians and printed texts for the first time of some of them. The results of this investigation were to confirm that there was uncertainty among the canonists about defining the natural law – an uncertainty in part due to the strong civilian tradition that they, or the later among them, met in the cross-fertilising relationships between Roman and canon law in the late twelfth and early thirteenth centuries. And more recently the detailed study of Rudolf Weigand has afforded the grounds for making a fully-informed judgment on the contribution of both civilians and canonists to the question of the natural law.[47] In what follows, the references are to the texts published by Weigand.

Among the successors of Irnerius at Bologna Weigand considers some fourteen Roman lawyers, not all, obviously, of equal importance. They have in common that they gloss or comment upon the texts of Justinian and, consequently, have to face the problem of the natural law. It should be noted that they are primarily lawyers and have little interest or aptitude for philosophy.[48] In this they are unlike the canonists, whose formation would normally include philosophy and theology. The civilian glossators tend to be technicians of the law and to confine themselves to literal exposition of the text and to the solution of difficulties like that of reconciling the letter of the law with the dictates of equity. If they do rise above merely technical argument and exegesis of the law-texts, as in the question of natural law, this is because the question was inescapably posed in the texts themselves, because the Roman law posed the problem. Few of them, for instance, associate the natural law with the dictate of natural reason – a concept found in Cicero and made use of by the Fathers and one that is to reappear in the canonists. The Roman law glossators found Ulpian's definition of the natural law facing them in the Codex of Justinian and it was in terms of that definition that they tackled the problem.[49]

It is not true that the glossators abstained entirely from philosophical explanation. Their interpretation of the natural law

[47] R. Weigand, *op. cit.*, passim.

[48] G. Fassò, *Storia della filosofia del diritto*, I, p. 277: "I glossatori non sono e non vogliono essere filosofi...."

[49] G. Fassò, *op. cit.*, I, pp. 229–232.

taught by nature to all animals, for some of them at least, pointed in the direction of a 'cosmic' law of all creatures, of which Ulpian's *quod natura omnia animalia docuit* was one kind. So the author of the *Summa Vindobonensis*, once thought to be the work of Irnerius himself but now known to belong to the school of his pupil and successor, Bulgarus. This *Summa* defines the natural law as the condition imposed on created things by divine disposition, or instinct of nature, and not by any human agency.[50] The text goes on to say that all beings are to be taken as animals in this sense; to which a gloss was later added, by Martinus, to the effect that all are animals *quantum ad sensibilitatem non rationabilitatem.*[51] Martinus (c. 1100–1166/1178?) takes up the question of equity, the *fons et origo* of justice (as he expressed it).[52] His conception of equity, identified with God, really amounted to a hierarchical ordering of the senses of the natural law. He defined equity in Cicero's words (*Topics*, 4, 23). He went further than the text of Justinian (*Inst.* I, 2, 11) in connecting equity with God – he identified it with God – and this is the supreme category. Next comes the justice found in the permanent will of men; and finally law (*ius*) is defined as the expression of that will, whether in written or in customary precepts. With this background Martinus goes on to face the question of natural law in the following gloss. *Ius*, the *ars boni et equi*, is verified in natural law, *jus gentium* and civil law. For natural law he takes the definition of Ulpian, found in Justinian, seeing in it an expression of the divine will which has placed in nature the urge of the sexes to unite. The *jus gentium*, then, is said to be the disposition of reason, impressed by reason in the soul.[53] And when he returns to the natural law and to Ulpian's definition in

[50] R. Weigand, *op. cit.*, n. 26, p. 27:-"Ius naturale est conditio rebus creatis ab ipsa divina dispositione imposita, seu instinctu nature, non aliqua constitutione non enim ex hominum industria, sed ex ipsa divina dispositione est inductum. Est enim ius quod natura omnia docuit animalia, cuius iuris peritia omnia censentur animalia," p. 27.

[51] R. Weigand, *op. cit.*, note 11.

[52] R. Weigand, *op. cit.*, n. 34, p. 30: "Sed quia iustitie fons et origo est equitas, videamus prius quid sit equitas. . . nihil etiam aliud est equitas quam Deus, si talis equitas in voluntate hominis perpetua sit, iustitia dicitur, que talis voluntas redacta in preceptionem, sive scriptum, sive consuetudinarium ius dicitur."

[53] R. Weigand, *op. cit.*, n. 35, p. 32: "Ius enim naturale cum sit constitutio divine voluntatis potest dici ars boni et equi. A tali constitutione procedit coniugatio maris atque femine et multa alia que iura non dicuntur set effectus iuris. Item ius gentium cum sit constitutio rationis in natura in anima insite ars dicitur boni et equi. . . ."

particular, Martinus makes a most arresting admission, in which very few (certainly few of the civil jurists) were to follow him; he says that the natural law in animals is improperly called law; only in men is it properly law: *Ius vero quod est in brutis animalibus ut procreare filios et educare, non proprie in eis ius dici potest licet in nobis propter sensum rationalem ius proprie dici possit.*[54]

The jurist Rogerius (b. first quarter of 12th century, died c. 1170) brings us to another generation of glossators, or rather to the commentators on the Roman law. Rogerius was born in Piacenza. He studied and taught in Bologna but went, about 1162, to Montpellier and died there some eight years later. Roger understands the natural law in Ulpian's sense as common to all animals; but he says that there is also a natural law proper to man – to all men – and this is, in fact, the sense in which the *jus gentium* is called natural; and, finally, civil law is, in its way, natural when, for instance, it protects minors from injury caused by error or fraud. Here the conception seems to approach that of equity.[55]

With Placentinus, a pupil of Martinus and possibly of Rogerius,[56] we find further refinements. In his *Summa Institutionum*, when he discusses Ulpian's definition of the natural law, Placentinus makes an interesting suggestion. The meanings for the phrase *quod natura omnia animalia docuit* will depend upon the parsing of the *quod*. Taken as an accusative (as it usually is) and the word *natura* as nominative, the sense is that nature has taught all animals natural law. But, if the cases are reversed and *quod* becomes nominative, then the sense is that natural law is the nature that has taught all animals, namely by instinct. And Placentinus goes on at once to use the phase *natura idest Deus* to identify this nature. That phrase was to give rise to later misunderstandings and was ultimately given a pantheistic sense that was foreign to the mind of Placentinus and his followers.[57]

[54] R. Weigand, *op. cit.*, n. 37, p. 33.

[55] R. Weigand, *op. cit.*, n. 52, p. 39. According to Weigand, *op. cit.*, p. 51, Rogerius was the first of the civilians to set out the senses of natural law in hierarchical order.

[56] T. Gilby, *Principality and Polity*, p. 53 says that Placentinus "left Bologna in disapproval of its stringent spirit and founded the school of Montpellier."

[57] R. Weigand, *op. cit.*, n. 60, p. 43: "Ius naturale est quod natura etc. et si hoc nomen 'quod' erit accusativi casus et hoc nomen 'natura' erit nominativi casus, vel dic quod nomen hoc 'quod' sit casus nominativi, ut sic dicat 'quod docuit omnia animalia natura' id est per instinctum naturae. Natura id est Deus quia facit omnia nasci. . . ."

Another suggestion, to correct any impression that might still remain of the monolithic views of the medieval civilians of the 12th and 13th centuries, is found in Henry of Baila, a pupil of Martinus, who was active at Bologna in 1169 and 1170. He takes the Golden Rule, so popular with the canonists as a summary of the prescriptions of the natural law: Do as you would be done by; Do not to others what you would not have done to you. Henry takes it from the *Decretum Gratiani*, and it is not the only evidence of a cross-fertilisation between the civil law and the canon law, a cross-fertilisation that was, after all, only to be expected. Henry was also influenced by Rufinus, one of the earliest of the commentators on the *Decretum Gratiani* and, indeed, he refers explicitly to the *Decretum*. His verbal dependence upon the *Summa* of Rufinus is easily demonstrated by Weigand.[58] Another of the pupils of Martinus, the glossator Cyprianus (who came from Florence and taught in the second half of the twelfth century) also cites the *Decretum Gratiani*.[59]

Yet another view of the natural law is to be found in John Bassianus, who was the teacher of Azo. Bassianus distinguished between two natural laws, one defined after Ulpian in the *Corpus Juris Civilis* and indicating an instinct of nature as its source and another depending upon nature, meaning natural reason. This latter, however, he identifies with the *jus gentium* of the Code of Justinian. And for further discussion of meanings of natural law John Bassianus refers his hearers to "Ste," who can probably be identified as the canonist Stephen of Tournai.[60]

Azo and Accursius bring this succession of medieval glossators to an end. Azo was a pupil of John Bassianus and died about 1230, so that we are now into the thirteenth century. Azo gives five meanings for natural law.[61] The first is the natural law coming from a natural instinct and common to all animals, that is Ulpian's natural law *quod natura idest ipse Deus docuit omnia animalia*. He follows with the distinction made by Placentinus turning upon whether the word *quod* is made object or subject in the phrase: *quod natura omnia animalis docuit;* natural law is

[58] R. Weigand, *op. cit.*, n. 68, p. 47, where the phrases found verbatim in Rufinus are marked.

[59] R. Weigand, *op. cit.*, n. 70, p. 48.

[60] R. Weigand, *op. cit.*, p. 50, citing S. Kuttner, *Repertorium der Kanonistik*, 135 A 8.

[61] R. Weigand, *op. cit.*, p. 53: "In einer enzyklopädischen Weise führt Azo die ihm bekannten Bedeutungen des Naturrechts auf."

what nature has taught all animals or it is the nature that teaches all animals.

Then there are the natural law common to men (in this sense the *jus gentium* is said to be natural law), and the natural law contained in the Mosaic law and the gospel, as we read in the *Decretals.* Finally there is the natural law meaning what is most in accordance with equity in the regulations moderating the strict letter of the law; in this sense the natural law is taken over in the civil law. Elsewhere, in his *Summa* on the Codex, where he mentions offences like homicide, adultery, stealing and the like, Azo mentions too that they are prohibited by the natural law of the decalogue.[62] Yet despite all this he still thinks of the natural law as that common to all animals; this, for him as for the other jurists, is its primary meaning. He even tries to bring obligations, such as that of helping a fellow man, under this law[63] despite the fact that it patently does not apply to animals such as wolves, which are not notable for helping each other. Man, Azo can only suggest, is an animal *sui generis.*

Accursius, Azo's successor was born near Florence in 1184 or 1185, studied and taught in Bologna and died there about 1263. He was the author of the *Glossa ordinaria* or *Accursiana* on the *Corpus Juris Civilis* – an enormous work in which the glosses of his predecessors, especially Azo, appeared.[64] As Azo had done, he gives five meanings of natural law; but, at least in the glossa on the *Institutes,* the schema is very artificial; natural law is sometimes the same as *jus gentium,* sometimes it is the law of (keeping) pacts, sometimes the contrary (the breaking of pacts when equity demands it), and sometimes it is an instinct of nature as in the text of the Institutes. And Accursius adds Gratian's natural law as an afterthought.[65]

[62] R. Weigand, *op. cit.*, n. 82, p. 55: "Item si putat sibi licere impune occidere vel furtum committere vel rapinam vel adulterium, que etiam jure naturali decalogi prohibita sunt."

[63] R. Weigand, *op. cit.*, nn. 84–85, p. 56.

[64] T. Gilby, *Principality and Polity*, p. 49, points out that the authority of the *Glossa* was such that "it became almost axiomatic that a court would not recognise what the *Glossa* did not: *quidquid non agnoscit glossa non agnoscit curia.*"

[65] R. Weigand, *op. cit.*, nn. 86–87, p. 57: "Et nota quod quattuor modis ius naturale ponitur. Quandoque pro iure gentium... quandoque pro iure pactorum ... quandoque pro eius contrario, scilicet pro eo quod rescindit pacta, ut in restitutione minorum.... Secundum canones ius naturale dicitur quod in lege mosaica et Evangelio continetur ut in principio decretorum...."

In the glosses on the *Digest* the same approach is evident, with some minor modifications. In fact, the passing references to the natural law give the impression that the eclecticism has been self-defeating – for it can hardly be said that a clear image of the natural law emerges. And to add to the uncertainty, Accursius, like some of his predecessors, notably Placentinus and Azo, uses the phrase *idest Deus* as an expansion of *natura.* On the face of it this was pantheistic and was to be formally asserted in this sense much later. Accursius makes it clear that he understands God as creator of the world and in that sense the source of the natural law.[66] And in two other contexts Accursius, instead of God uses the philosophical term *natura naturans.*

With Azo and Accursius one sees the explicit influence of the canon lawyers' definition – natural law, according to Gratian, being what is found in the Law and the gospel. But, not surprisingly, the real meaning of natural law for the civilians, is that found in the Roman law, namely Ulpian's definition: *quod natura omnia animalia docuit.* This the civilians retained, despite the difficulties in understanding it; and from them it was to find its way into the canonists and, more importantly, into the theologians.

C. THE DECRETISTS

The *Decretum Gratiani,* like the *Corpus Juris Civilis,* soon began to be encrusted with glosses, explanations and commentaries. The glosses were at first short clarifications, written between the lines of the codex or, when they became less manageable, in the margins. They were labelled *authentic* when they depended upon the words of the law itself, parallel passages for example; *magistral* when they derived from the interpretations of the doctors of the law. As time went on the glosses became more abundant and took on more of the nature of a continuous commentary on the law. The glossators were sometimes anonymous, but more often they were identified by a special sign, such as an initial. Sometimes glosses were removed and substituted by others, leaving the present-day reader with a palimpsest, in which the original gloss can occasionally be recovered. The glosses were frequently put together into an *apparatus glossarum,* often by authors who also wrote *Summae* or treatises on the *Decretum.* The commonly

[66] R. Weigand, n. 93, p. 60: "Is est ab hoc iure naturali, scilicet Deo, qui primo Adam Eve coniunxit et in paradiso deliciarum posuit. Accur."

accepted *apparatus* on a given text was called the *Glossa ordinaria* and was cited in the schools and in the courts. Finally, the *Glossa ordinaria* itself became the subject of commentary.[67] It is clear that the process had disadvantages as well as advantages. One has only to look at some of the codices that have come down to us of the *Decretum Gratiani* to see how the short central columns of text are stifled by the copious interlinear and marginal commentary – and one can easily imagine the text's being forgotten! However on the positive side it must be allowed that the system ensured the preservation of the great variety of views on a topic like that of natural law.

This is an area in which much research has been done in the past twenty years; and once again the indispensable collection of texts is to be found in the work of Rudolf Weigand.[68] He studies the abundant literature in chronological order and according to school – the early and the later school of Bologna, the French and Rhenish *Summae*, the Anglo-Norman school etc. It is of interest to see what pattern, if any, emerges in the canonists' consideration of the natural law. One can straightaway expect that the difficulties of Gratian's definition will be explored; and one can expect to discover some influence of the civil law, which, as we have seen, had its own problems concerning the definition of the natural law. The civilians, who mean by natural law the definition of Ulpian, frequently take the specifically human natural law to be the *jus gentium*; and only the later among them take any account of the definition of Gratian. If they present the easier scene, the reason may well be, in part at least, that the civilian lawyers were less philosophically-minded than the canonists. Certain it is that the canonical development is much more complicated.[69] The canonists, besides being more aware of philosophical and theological considerations, dispose of a richer and more intractable source-material.[70] Gratian's own definition – natural law is what is contained in the Law and the gospel-looms large here.

The first of the commentators on the *Decretum Gratiani* in the

[67] S. Kuttner, "Prodromus Corporis Glossatorum" in *Repertorium der Kanonistik*, 1 (1937), pp. 1–58; A. Van Hove, *Commentarium Lovaniense in Codicem Iuris Canonici: Prolegomena*, I, t. 1, pp. 426–427.

[68] R. Weigand, *op. cit.*, II Teil, Kanonisches Recht, pp. 121–446.

[69] R. Weigand, *op. cit.*, pp. 443–446 (Schlusswort).

[70] R. Weigand, *op. cit.*, pp. 443–444: "Die Dekretisten sind wegen ihrer vielfältigeren und widersprüchlicheren Quellenlage in einer etwas anderen Ausgangsposition als die Legisten. . . ."

school of Bologna, Rolando Bandinelli (d. 1181), the later Pope Alexander III, in his *Stroma* simply summarises the first part of the Decretum, without comment. His contemporary Paucapalea, who wrote a Summa on the *Decretum* between 1140 and 1148, took up Gratian's definition and saw the natural law as part of the law that rules the church. He identified it with justice as defined by Gregory the Great[71] and related this identification to Isidore's statement that humankind is ruled by law and by custom; i.e. he takes Isidore's custom to mean the natural law. But he does not follow this with the consideration of Isidore's definition of natural law which one would naturally expect. In a word Paucapalea leaves the question of the exact definition of the natura law largely unclarified.

The influence of Paucapalea was great – the word '*palea*', meaning an authority inserted subsequently into the Decretum to explain or conform the *dicta* of Gratian, is due to Paucapalea, who was responsible for many such.[72] Wiegand quotes from a couple of anonymous *Summae* which derive from Paucapalea[73] one of which, the *Summa 'sicut vetus testamentum'*, is interesting for its effort to reconcile Gratian's definition with that of Ulpian and the Roman jurists, an effort that amounts, in fact, to an identification without any arguments to justify it.[74]

The most important, however, of the decretists, was Rufinus of Assisi (d. circa 1190) who wrote his *Summa* between 1157 and 1159. His approach to the natural law was to be taken up by many of his successors. He defines it was *vis quaedam humanae creaturae a natura insita ad faciendum bonum cavendumque contrarium;* and he divides its injunctions into *mandata, prohibitiones* and *demonstrationes.*[75] While he does not exactly reject Ulpian's

[71] R. Weigand, *op. cit.*, n. 230 p. 141: "Hoc ius (scil. naturale) a beato Gregorio iustitia appellari videtur, cum ait: Justitia est naturae tacita conventio in adiutorium multorum inventa. Ab hoc iure ut in libro Etymologiarum Ysidorus dicit, divinae leges a natura principium habuerunt, et humanae a moribus . . . dicit Ysidorus: Divinae leges natura, id est principium a naturali iure habent. . . ."

[72] A. Van Hove, *op. cit.*, pp. 341–342.

[73] R. Weigand, *op. cit.*, pp. 142–144.

[74] R. Weigand, *op. cit.*, n. 234, p. 143: ". . . ius nature tantum valet quantum ius divinum. . . . Naturale ius quod in lege et evangelio continetur . . . illud quodque unde descendit maris et femine coniugatio quod matrimonium appellatur, liberorum procreatio et educatio cuius pericia uidemus omnia animalia censeri. id est gubernari, ab exordio rationabillis creature cepit inicium et inter omnia primatum optinet; nullo enim uariatur tempore, set immutabile permanet."

[75] *Summa Magistri Rufini zum Decretum Gratiani*, ed. J.F. von Schulte, p. 4.

definition, Rufinus is careful to point out how 'what nature has taught all animals' can be restricted to the human species. Rufinus's achievement is that he was the first to see the need for such an interpretation – or at least the first to express clearly how such an interpretation might be justified. The natural law, for him, is human yet according to the nature that man shares with other animals.[76] Marriage, he points out is the union of the sexes, but not any union; the union that is proper to the human species of that of one man with one woman for life. This, it might be thought, is only a commonsense interpretation of Ulpian's definition; but not many showed such commonsense. We shall find this interpretation in St. Thomas Aquinas, exactly a century after Rufinus; and an overt rejection of Ulpian in Thomas's predecessor Albert the Great.[77] The phrase used by Rufinus is clearly reminiscent of Cicero's *ratio summa insita in natura* and his *quod... quaedam innata vis inseruit.* In general Rufinus's view must be counted within the rational tradition of natural law coming from the Stoics, through Cicero, to the Middle Ages.

Not alone did Rufinus get away from the artificiality of the *legistica traditio* of the natural law, but his suggestion that the natural law consisted in commands, prohibitions and counsels (*demonstrationes*) proved to be a very fruitful one; for, later on, the commands and prohibitions will be seen as the invariable core of natural law, the unchanging character belonging here above all, while the counsels cover the adaptation of the natural law to particular circumstances, which must change.[78] In elaborating upon how the law following upon the *nuda natura rerum* needs modifying by congruous order and decorum – so that, for example, the good to be achieved in the union of the sexes be not lustily, *passim et praecipitanter*, sought by man as by beast, but rather between such and such persons and in such and such conditions – Rufinus raises the question of the mutability of the natural law.[79] The law can be added to by good custom, as he has

[76] Cf. S. Ramirez, *El derecho de gentes*, pp. 36–37.

[77] *In 4 Sent.*, d. 33, q. 1, a. 1. Rufinus was not the only influence here, however. Among the theologians. Philip the Chancellor had distinguished between *natura ut natura* and *natura ut ratio* (and *ratio ut ratio*) in the context; and Albert the Great was still more forthright in saying that: *Natura omnia animalia hoc* (union of the sexes) *docet, sed diversimode secundum diversitatem specierum:* (*In 4 Sent*, d, 33A, a. 1 ad 4 (Borgnet, *Opera Omnia*, t. 30, p. 290).

[78] Cf. A.H. Chroust, "The Philosophy of Law from St. Augustine to St. Thomas Aquinas" in *The New Scholasticism*, 20 (1946), p. 37.

[79] *Summa magistri Rufini zum Decretum Gratiani*, pp. 4–5.

explained in the question of marriage; it cannot, however, be modified by subtraction, at least in the commands and prohibitions *quae derogationem nullam sentire queunt.* In the counsels, however that is where nature neither forbids nor commands, but simply points to goods such as personal liberty or common property, the civil law can take a hand. Here Rufinus touches upon two sensitive areas – both slavery and private property had been problems in the Roman law approach to the natural law. But the regulations of civil law in such matters, although they introduce a change in what the natural law counsels, may, in his rather picturesque phrase, constitute rivers of human justice flowing into the sea of natural law.[80]

Rufinus's was the outstanding influence in the decretists until Huguccio of Ferrara. This was due partly to his new technique (he imitated the analytical and exegetical technique of the Roman lawyers, although he seems not to have had much use for the Roman law itself). He glossed words and passages, noted cross-references, raised problems not raised in the text and dared to disagree with the Master on occasion. Even a cursory glance at Rufinus's *Summa* reveals qualities of style and exposition not usually found in medieval legal texts. Furthermore his authorities were not confined to the *Decretum* but included theologians like Hugh of St. Victor. Rufinus was in the tradition of Gratian for whom, as we have seen, theology and canon law were not yet mutually exclusive disciplines. And Rufinus is the first author known to have quoted Peter Lombard. Small wonder then, that his influence was great.

Stephen of Tournai (1128–1203) wrote a *Summa* on the *Decretum* about 1160 and was the first to set out clearly the various meanings of natural law. These meanings are four; (1) there is a sense in which natural law is common to man and animals (the natural law of Ulpian and the Roman jurists); (2) there is the natural law proper to man, termed *jus gentium* by the jurists and called natural because it comes from nature itself; (3) the divine law is also called natural, for our nature, that is God, teaches us through the law, the prophets and the gospel; and (4) there is a sense in which natural law includes both human and divine law and that common to all animals. And he adds Rufinus's meaning as an afterthought; in a fifth sense (5) natural law is that which is

[80] *Ibid.*, p. 5: "... et hunc in modum flumina honestatis humanae redeunt ad mare iuris naturalis, quod in primo homine perditum in lege mosaica revelatur, in evangelio perficitur, in moribus decoratur...."

proper to man and not to other animals and inclines them to seek the good and to avoid the evil. Stephen also adopts Rufinus's distinction of commands, prohibitions and counsels.

Stephen is clearly trying to harmonise a confused tradition. He uses his list of meanings in order to reconcile the various passages in which Gratian makes use of the term *ius naturale* – sometimes one meaning, sometimes another is intended. The method has certain advantages in removing apparent contradictions in the *Decretum.* And it allows Stephen to offer a subtle interpretation of Gratian's definition of natural law; the law is more than is found in Law and gospel; on the other hand, not all that is in Law and gospel is natural law; *si subtilius intueamur, nec solum nec totum.*[81]

This harmonising approach of Stephen of Tournai set a headline for many of the decretists in the second half of the twelfth century and into the thirteenth. The last representative of the early Bologna school is John Faventinus (d. 1187) who completed his *Summa* on the *Decretum* and wrote a series of glosses in the 70's of the twelfth century. He appears to make use of Rufinus[82] and insists that the canonists take a narrower view of the natural law, confining it to man, in contrast with the civil lawyers who speak of the natural law common to all animals. The harmonising tendency found in Stephen of Tournai is here too. John Faventinus begins his *Summa* by suggesting that Gratian, when he says that the human race is ruled by law and by customs, included in this bipartite division the tripartite division of the lawyers (and found also in Isidore).[83] This means that Gratian identifies natural

[81] R. Weigand, *op. cit.*, n. 244–246, p. 148: "Et notandum, ius naturale quatuor modis dici. Dicitur enim ius naturale, quod ab ipsa natura est introductum et non solum homini, sed etiam ceteris animalibus insitum.... Dicitur et ius naturale quandoque ius gentium, quod ab humana solum natura quasi cum ea incipiens traxit exordium. Ius etiam divinum dicitur naturale, quod summa natura nostra id est Deus nos docuit et per legem et prophetas et evangelium suum nobis obtulit. Dicitur etiam ius naturale quod simul comprehendit humanum et divinum et illud quod a natura omnibus est animalibus insitum.... Vel si quintam iuris naturalis acceptionem non abhorreas, intellige, hic dici ius naturale, quod hominibus tantum et non aliis animalibus a natura est insitum, scilicet ad faciendum bonum vitandumque contrarium. Quae quasi pars divini iuris est."

[82] R. Weigand, *op. cit.*, p. 152.

[83] R. Weigand, *op. cit.*, n. 251, p. 152: "Magister ergo ius dividens quod omnia iura continet tria membra que in legibus continentur bimembri divisione comprehendit, cum enim ibi dicatur ius aliud naturale, aliud gentium, aliud civile. Ius naturale similiter ponit; sub moribus vero ius gentium et civile includit, mores enim et a iure gentium initium et a civili confirmationem sumpserunt."

law with the *ius naturale* of the lawyers; and their *jus gentium* and *ius civile* are both put under '*mores*.' In practice Faventinus passes over the various senses of natural law in Stephen of Tournai in silence, with the exception of Stephen's interpretation of Gratian's definition; and his own notion of the natural law is very close to that of Rufinus, namely the rational inclination in man urging him to seek the good and avoid its contrary. In the foreword to his *Summa* John lists the six kinds of law, comparing them to the six wings of the cherubim before the throne of God. These are (1) the natural law; (2) the mosaic law; (3) the law of the prophets; (4) the law of the gospel; (5) the apostolic law; and (6) canon law. The first, namely natural law, was given by God in the beginning of creation according to the word: God made man and breathed into him the breath of life, namely the natural law.[84]

The first Bologna school of decretists, then, sets the lines for the development of the canon lawyers' approach to the natural law. From Paucapalea's literal following of the *Decretum* one comes to the more sophisticated approaches in Rufinus and in Stephen of Tournai, influenced by the Roman law and anxious to reconcile the conflicting definitions.

The pattern is repeated in the later decretists' schools. In the French and Rhenish school of the 1160's and the 1170's the various possible meanings of the natural law are juxtaposed, as they are in Stephen of Tournai.[85] However, where the Bolognese doctors generally settled for one meaning (and tried to show that this was Gratian's), the other schools were more welcoming to a variety of acceptable meanings. In the Summa of Odo of Dover and in the *Summa Monacensis* room is found for a natural law with a wider meaning even than that of Ulpian and the Roman law, a law that governs all creation, keeps the stars in their courses, brings waters back to their source, makes the magnet seek the iron. This first appears in Odo of Dover[86] and it

[84] R. Weigand, *op. cit.*, n. 254, p. 153.

[85] R. Weigand, *op. cit.*, pp. 154–173, listing the *Summa Parisiensis* (1160–70), the *Summa Coloniensis* (1169), the *Summa* of Odo of Dover (c. 1170), the *Summa Monacensis* (1175–8) and the *Summa* '*Inter cetera*' which is connected with the *Summa Monacensis*.

[86] R. Weigand, *op. cit.*, n. 269, p. 161: "Est itaque ius naturale in generaliore (!) significatione uis quedam insita creature a summa omnium natura id est a Deo. Quo iure stelle non deserunt cursus suos, atque redeunt ad fontes suos, ad anias attrahitur ferrum et similia."

reappears more succinctly in the *Summa Monacensis*.[87] It recalls the cosmic justice of Plato's *Timaeus.*

Another feature of these writers was the emphasis upon the natural law impressed on the heart of man and expressed in the Golden Rule of doing to others as you would have others do to you.[88] In the later writers of the school of Bologna, of whom the most important is Simon of Bisignano (who wrote his *Summa* on the *Decretum* between 1177 and 1179), one finds again a listing of meanings for natural law. In Simon himself, for instance, we find the suggestion that natural law is the same as *caritas*, which inclines a man to do good and to avoid evil. The view is admittedly not Simon's own; he found it in some of his contemporaries or predecessors. But he cannot accept it, since charity is found only in the good, whereas natural law is common to all. Others say that natural law is free will (*liberum arbitrium*) – an identification he also rejects, for the reason that free will is indifferent to good and evil, whereas natural law always prohibits evil. His own view is that natural law is the superior part of the soul, reason itself, called *synderesis*.[89] Here we have a terminology that will be current in the theologians of the early thirteenth century and a cataloguing of views that will still be canvassed in the time of St. Thomas in the mid-century.

With Sicard of Cremona (d. 1215), representing the French school, who wrote his *Summa* on the *Decretum* about 1179–1181, we again find the hierarchy of meanings for natural law: natural law as coming from divine nature and expressed in the Golden Rule; as coming from common nature of all animals; as coming from human nature. These derivations give, respectively, Gratian's natural law, Ulpian's natural law and Rufinus's natural law. In addition the *jus gentium*, Sicard points out, is in a sense natural law as coming from human nature, which accommodates the

[87] R. Weigand, *op. cit.*, n. 276, p. 163, *Summa Monacensis*. Ius naturale, id est iustitia naturalis.... Item ius naturale quandoque est uis cuilibet rei insita qua regitur.

[88] So, for instance, in the *Summa Coloniensis*; R. Weigand, *op. cit.*, pp. 157–160.

[89] R. Weigand, *op. cit.*, n. 293–295, p. 173: "Dicunt enim quidam quod ius naturale nichil aliud est quam caritas, per quam facit homo bonum uitatque contrarium. Set hoc stare non potest ideo, quia caritas in solis bonis est.... Ius vero naturale est commune omnium. Alii uero dicunt ius naturale esse liberum arbitrium. Set hoc similiter ex eo tollitur, quia libero arbitrio ad bonum et ad malum flectitur, ius vero naturale malum semper prohibet et detestatur. Nobis itaque uidetur quod ius naturale est superior pars anime, ipsa uidelicet ratio, que sinderesis appellatur...."

civilians' views. Furthermore the *ius divinum* can include the natural law (*a deo insitum*), as it does the Mosaic law (*a deo conditum*), the law of the gospel (*a deo editum*) and the canon law (*pro deo constitutum*).[90] In the same sense the *Summa 'Tractaturus Magister'* ranges the senses of natural law in order. The influence of Sicard and of Simon of Bisignano is seen in the pursuit of the question of the *uis insita* which Sicard and the others, following Rufinus, had spoken of; this *Summa* asks whether it may not be charity, urging to good, or *synderesis* of reason. The author excludes this latter with the interesting observation that reason *uses* natural law rather than *is* the natural law – a proposition all the more true if, as some do, one identifies reason with free will.[91] Finally the *Summa* arrives at what is perhaps an unexpected conclusion, namely that natural law is the collection of precepts, prohibitions and demonstrations placed in the human mind by God.[92] This suggestion, despite the terminology in which it is framed, seems extremely important and it has the great advantage of excluding the ambiguities and confusions characteristic of the writers of the half century subsequent to the *Summa*. The terminology comes from the tradition; but the idea seems new. The distinction of the natural law into commands, prohibitions and counsels, as we have seen, was Rufinus's; but the further, and important point, that behind these is to be seen a quality of mind arising out of them is a refinement that we do not find in Rufinus.

Next comes the Anglo-Norman school, represented by the *Summa Lipsiensis* and the authors dependent upon it. Here the

[90] R. Weigand, *op. cit.*, nn. 315–315, pp. 184–5: "Ius naturale dicitur a divina natura; hoc est quo quis iubetur alii facere etc. a communi natura; hoc est quod natura docuit omnia animalia; ab humana natura; hoc est quedam vis et potentia homini naturaliter insita ad faciendum bonum et uitandum contrarium. Ius etiam gentium potest dici naturale ab humana natura.... Ius divinum dicitur a deo insitum ut ius naturale, per deum conditum ut ius mosaycum, a deo editum ut ius euangelicum, pro deo constitutum ut ius canonicum."

[91] R. Weigand, *op. cit.*, n. 318, p. 187: "Si queritur de illa ui quid sit. Videtur quibusdam quod caritas.... Aliis quod sinderesis, scilicet superior pars rationis.... Sed potius uidetur ratio uti iure naturali quam ipsa esse ius naturale, maxime cum secundum quosdam nichil aliud sit ratio quam liberum arbitrium. Unde dicendum quod ius naturale est secundum istam acceptionem collectio praeceptorum, prohibitionum et demonstrationum humane menti a deo insitorum. (Non dico ipsa collecta sed qualitas quedam ex illis collectis surgens in anima, sicut scientia non dicitur ipsa scita sed qualitas ex illis proueniens)."

[92] R. Weigand lists two other anonymous *Summae* related to that of Sicard of Cremona – the *Summa 'Reverentia sacrorum Canonum,'* (1183–4), the *Summa 'Et est sciendum'* (1181–1185), *op. cit.*, pp. 188–195.

proliferation of senses of natural law is remarkable, six or seven meanings being distinguished. These are, in the main, the meanings that have already been met with in the tradition and in the canonical texts that have gone before. There is, inevitably, (1) the natural law that nature has taught all animals (Ulpian's Roman law definition); here described as an *instinctus* and *ordo* of nature; (2) natural law can mean what is left undetermined by divine command or prohibition; (3) or what is taught us by God, *summa natura*, in the law and the gospel; or (4) man's ability to discern good from evil; or (5) the judgment of reason (here the *Summa 'De iure canonico tractaturus'* cites Origen and Remigius on *Romans* 2; 14 concerning the gentiles who have the 'law written in their hearts'); (6) natural law is the observance of the divine commands – hence Hilary summarises it in the Golden Rule of not doing anything to another that we would not have done to ourselves; and finally (7) the natural law is the *karitas.*[93]

Honorius (1186–1190),[94] in close dependence upon the *Summa Lipsiensis*, stresses the importance of knowing the various senses of natural law in order to meet the difficulties of his subject-matter. And so he lists them. Likewise the *Distinctio 'Est ius naturale'* gives the same meanings and cites similar authorities – Origen, Hilary – as the *Summa Lipsiensis*. The number of senses of natural law is further increased by the author's identification of natural law with *jus gentium*, with the 'other law of the members' mentioned by St. Paul (*Rom.*, 7; 23) and with a kind of extra-predicamental (transcendental?) law of being or existence.[95]

Weigand finds the same list of meanings for natural law in a number of other canonical texts from the same school[96] showing the close dependence of the writers upon their model, the *Summa Lipsiensis*. Certain glosses in an Antwerp manuscript stress the

[93] R. Weigand, *op. cit.*, nn. 339–347, pp. 196–198.

[94] Honorius speaks of natural law in the first question of the third part of his *Summa quaestionum*, taken up with marriage-law. This is a context in which later theologians were frequently to discuss the natural law. Cf. R. Weigand, *op. cit.*, pp. 201–202, n. 351: "Sciendum est ergo varias esse acceptiones iuris naturalis quas qui ignorat de facili peralogicatur. vi. ergo gradus dicimus esse acceptiones iuris naturalis. . . ."

[95] R. Weigand, *op. cit.*, nn. 351–253, pp. 203–204: "Est ius naturale . . . (here he gives six meanings as in the Summa Lipsiensis). Quandoque ipsa sensualitas, unde Apostolus: Video aliam legem in membris meis repugnantem legi mentis mee; et in hoc sensu dicitur fornicatio procedere de lege naturali. Alii dixerunt ius naturale esse quiddam extra predicamentale habentem simul modum existendi per se ut essentiabile res et ens."

[96] R. Weigand, *op. cit.*, nn. 354–367, pp. 204–215.

distinction between the canonical concept of natural law (described, after Rufinus, as a *vis quedam* inserted in us by nature and inclining us to do the good and avoid the evil) and the lawyers' concept found in the Roman law definition, *quod natura omnia animalia docuit.* Another work of the same school makes an interesting distinction between the *lex naturalis* and the *ius naturale. Lex naturalis* is written by God in the heart of man; when the breath of life was breathed into man this was the natural law. When it was later confused and distorted by sin other laws, mosaic, prophetic, evangelical, apostolic, canonical and human, help to repair the situation (?). *Ius naturale,* on the other hand is given five meanings. Three of them depend upon the kind of 'nature' from which the law derives – the common nature of things, the nature of man, the *Summa natura* i.e. God (giving respectively, an enlarged natural law of animals and man, extended to include plants; a natural law in Rufinus's sense of the specificially human instinct of doing good and avoiding evil; and a natural law in Gratian's sense, found in the Scriptures). To these are added two further senses – natural law governs those things neither commanded nor forbidden by God or by law, what Paul has in mind when he says: All things are lawful to me; and, lastly, natural law may be taken in the sense of *jus gentium.*[97] Weigand remarks on the similarity with the views of the civil jurist Azo; but direct influence of Azo seems to be ruled out on chronological grounds.[98]

Finally, as representing not merely the Anglo-Norman school but also that of Bologna, we have Richard de Mores, known as Richardus Anglicus (1161–1242). He, too, follows the *Summa Lipsiensis* in listing the various meanings of the term natural law. Summarising the views of the school, Weigand notes that it is characterised by the multiplicity of meanings listed for natural law; this eclecticism was traditional in the school and the various meanings were well put together on the whole. An exception is one of the later *Summae,* belonging to some date after 1203, in which the opposite line is taken; the distinctions made in the school are stigmatised as useless and only one meaning is admit-

[97] R. Weigand, *op cit.,* nn. 358–359, pp. 208–210. Especially, n. 359: "Ius naturale a natura communi innatum. Ordo (et) instinctus nature secundum quem similia a similibus procreantur, procreata nutriuntur de quo dicitur insti, quod ius naturale est quod natura omnia animalia docuit. Hoc ius imitantur arbores et herbe ut insti. de iure naturali in princ.

[98] R. Weigand, *op. cit.,* p. 211.

ted, that proceeding from man's first and uncorrupted nature.[99] As Weigand remarks, this was not a very practical stance for a canonist, who had to explain the *Decretum Gratiani.*[100]

The succession of canonists and decretists closes with the later school of Bologna in the time of Huguccio of Ferrara and Alanus, in the last years of the twelfth century and with the works of the French school in the first decade of the thirteenth century. Here again there is cross-fertilization, for Huguccio depends upon the Anglo-Norman school. He lists the senses of the term natural law in the same way and shows the same accommodating attitude towards the various definitions in the tradition – Gratian's, Ulpian's and Rufinus's in particular.[101] In fact he begins with Rufinus's *uis anime* and goes on to mention the *naturale iudicium rationis* (for which the parallel can be found in the *Summa Lipsiensis* and in favour of which, like the *Summa Lipsiensis,* he adduces the authority of Origen and Hilary). He allows, however, that this is an improper sense of natural law, the judgment of reason being better described as an effect of natural law. He then mentions the *instinctus et ordo nature* by virtue of which like propagates like, looks after offspring, avoids disturbance and so on. This, he says, is *sensualitas,* and consequently the lawyers define natural law as "what nature has taught all animals." The fourth sense found by Huguccio makes the natural law a *ius divinum,* namely as contained in the mosaic law and in the gospel, and is a vindication of Gratian's definition. But here, too, he is temerarious enough to say that we are dealing with an improper use of the term. For this divine law is natural either in the sense that it comes from God, *summa natura* (instructing us through his law, prophets and gospel), or in the sense that natural reason (even if taught from without) urges us to the observance of what is contained in the divine law.[102] Having given these four senses of natural law, Huguccio goes on to take up the distinction made by Rufinus between precepts, prohibitions and demonstrations in

[99] R. Weigand, *op. cit.*, n. 367, pp. 214–215: "Hic notandum quod multi multas circa ius naturale inutiles proposuerunt distinctiones, plures vocabuli significationes assignando. Sufficit enim hec unica acceptio ut dicatur ius naturale quod procedit ex prima natura sine corruptione, secundum quod scilicet homo uiueret si Adam non peccasset. . . ."

[100] R. Weigand, *op. cit.*

[101] R. Weigand, *op. cit.*, nn. 368–377, pp. 215–221.

[102] R. Weigand, *op. cit.*, n. 371, p. 217: "Unde si audatia detur verbo, secure dico quod hoc ius improprie dicitur naturale, scilicet quia ad ea que in eo continentur naturale ius, scilicet ratio impellit et ad ea ex ratione quis tenetur."

the law, the precepts and prohibitions being self-explanatory, the demonstrations having to do with *quod convenit et expedit.*

Huguccio is also remarkable for a more penetrating analysis of Gratian's natural law than is to be found in his predecessors. He is very much aware of the importance of avoiding the loose use of terms and definitions.[103] In practice Huguccio recognises only two strict senses of natural law – those identifying it with the reason proper to man, on the one hand, and with the natural instinct of all living creatures on the other. As a commentator on the *Decretum Gratiani,* he identifies Gratian's natural law with the former of these senses – he can hardly, as Weigand remarks,[104] do otherwise. The result is that in Huguccio's view natural law subjectively consists in human reason and objectively in the legislative content of Old and New Testaments.

Huguccio's nuanced views were made use of by his successors to solve some of the difficulties that the traditional definitions posed; how, for example, fornication, which does seem to be what nature has taught all animals, is to be counted sin despite its being in accordance with natural law (in Ulpian's sense).[105]

Another writer of the school, the decretist Alanus, whose *Apparatus* of Glosses belongs to the turn of the twelfth century (1192–1205), in undertaking the familiar task of listing the meanings of the natural law, begins with what he calls the proper sense of the term, the cosmic law Plato "in the *Timaeus* calls natural justice."[106] Alanus is the author of what amounts to a tractate on the natural law – possibly an expansion of his introductory gloss on the *Decretum.*[107] In it he distinguishes three senses of natural

[103] R. Weigand, *op. cit.*, pp. 219–220, n. 375: "Et nota quod non omnia exempla iuris naturalis hic posita referantur ad eandem acceptionem iuris naturalis; ergo prudentis lectoris erit caute discernere quod exemplum ad quam acceptionem iuris naturalis referatur. Set ne ydiote animus in hoc confundetur, de quolibet diligenter assignabimus."

[104] R. Weigand, *op. cit.*, p. 221.

[105] This in the *Summa quaestionum 'Queritur utrum,'* R. Weigand, *op. cit.*, nn. 378–381, pp. 221–223: "Item ex sensualitate mouetur quis ad coitum illicitum, ergo ex instinctu nature, ergo de iure naturali, quia instinctus nature ius naturale est. . . . Set coitus illicitus est mortale peccatum, ergo qui facit contra illud bene facit."

[106] R. Weigand, *op. cit.*, nn. 386–396, pp. 225–230: "Hec appellatio ius naturale aliquando proprie accipitur et dicitur ius naturale ius quo reguntur omnes creature, quo scilicet deus fecit mundum, de quo iure dicitur Plato tractasse in thimeo et ibi appellatur iusticia naturalis, quo iure ascendunt leuia, ponderosa descendunt et ex similibus similia procreantur. Strictius . . . dicitur . . . ius naturale esse quod natura docuit omnia animalia. . . ."

[107] Text in R. Weigand, *op. cit.*, nn. 390–396, pp. 227–228.

law; one is Gratian's (what is found in the Law and the gospel), a second is natural equity and the third is that of Ulpian's definition (what nature has taught all animals). These senses, for Alanus, are not mutually exclusive but rather overlapping. He further distinguishes between simple natural law and relative, simple being that which does not depend upon any previous position of positive law (e.g. love God) and relative that which depends upon a previous disposition (as the right of inheritance depends upon the institution of private property).

It can be observed that the treatment of the natural law is becoming more sophisticated. The next representative of the later Bologna school studied by Weigand is William of Gascoigne.[108] Here, once again, we find the various meanings of natural law rehearsed – also beginning with the Platonic notion of divine law, but in a more developed way than Alanus. William speaks of the archetypal *nous* which can be none other than the word of God or the wisdom of the Father, which the jurists call 'nature.' He cites Plato in the second book of the *Timaeus* for the notion of the supreme *opifex* contemplating the eternal ideas and, as it were with a higher sight (*celsiori oculo*), the ideas of equity and the difference between good and evil....[109] Man is created, endowed with reason by God, who is Equity, and enabled to see right and wrong; but, dragged down by his human condition and the eye of his discretion darkened, man frequently, forgetful of his nature, looks at earthly rather than heavenly things and mistakes evil for good.[110] The metaphorical language is striking and marks a welcome change from the rather arid style of the other decretists. None of the others speaks, as does William, of man by reason of his original nature, longing to enter heaven through the door of equity.[111] When he comes to the different

[108] R. Weigand, *op. cit.*, nn. 397–402, pp. 230–237.

[109] R. Weigand, *op. cit.*, n. 397, p. 231: "Hunc itaque mundum archetipum phylosophi noym divinum nuncupauerunt, quam noym aliud quam uerbum dei vel sapientiam patris dicere non possumus, quam iuris consultus divinitus sibi inspirato.... naturam vocat.... Contemplans itaque ut ait Plato in secundo timei, ille summus opifex ydearum genera mundi intelligibilis et inter cetera quasi celsiori oculto ydeas equi et discretionis inter equum et iniquum attendens earum exempla tanquam principale merendi et demerendi fundamentum in existentiam curauit propagare."

[110] *R. Weigand, op. cit.*, n. 398, p. 232.

[111] R. Weigand, *op. cit.*: "Sic itaque humana anima, licet ex natura sue originis per equitatis ianuam celestem ingredi habitationem suspiraret, depressa tamen mole carnis lutea quasi nature sue inmemor potius terrena quam celestia cogitans oculo discretionis caligante frequenter iniquum pro equo comprehendit." It will be recalled that the civilian jurist Martinus also identified equity with God.

senses of natural law William does not differ greatly from the other members of the school except that his analysis is rather more philosophical. The meanings he expounds are one corresponding to the definition of Ulpian, one corresponding to the definition of Rufinus and a third corresponding to the definition of Gratian. Thus, despite the acuteness of the analysis, William comes back to the same data on the natural law as his predecessors.

The last part of Weigand's study of the decretists and canonists is taken up with the later works of the French and Bologna schools in the first two decades of the thirteenth century.[112] These may be noticed rather more summarily. There is the *Summa Duacensis*, written about 1200 in which the natural law appears first in the cosmic sense of the law of all creation; and the *Timaeus* of Plato is quoted. It will not be forgotten that Chartres was a centre of studies in the twelfth century in which the *Timaeus* was read with avidity.[113] Part of this general law is that which applies to all animals, viz. Ulpian's definition. To supplement this another natural law is required, a natural law proper to rational creatures: and this, in turn, needs to be supplemented by the natural law found in the Scriptures – so that a place is found for Gratian's definition. This central meaning, the natural law proper to man and reiterated in the Scriptures, is taken by the author of the *Summa Duacensis* in the sense of Rufinus; and, taken subjectively as man's reason, shows likewise the influence of Huguccio.[114]

Two other series of Glosses from the same school[115] also show this cross-fertilization. One, the Gloss–apparatus *Ecce vicit leo*, mentions six meanings of natural law but says that they can be reduced to four. The first is 'human reason' telling rational creatures what is right and wrong. In a second sense natural law is an instinct in all living creatures. This is natural law only in an extended sense because it is an impulse inclining the will rather than the giver of commands; it is called natural because nature is its origin. The third sense is Gratian's-what is found in Law and gospel. Finally, in a fourth and improper sense, civil law is said to be natural; what is meant is the *jus gentium*. The Gloss-apparatus

[112] R. Weigand *op. cit.*, nn. 403–439, pp. 238–259.

[113] Cf. M.D. Chenu, *L'éveil de la conscience dans la civilisation médiévale*, Montréal-Paris, 1969, p. 31.

[114] R. Weigand, *op. cit.*, nn. 403–412, pp. 238–242.

[115] The Gloss-apparatus *Ecce vicit leo* (1202–1210), and the Gloss-apparatus *Animal est substantia* (1206–1210), R. Weigand, *op. cit.*, 413–420a, pp. 242–246, and nn. 421–427b, pp. 246–250.

Animal est substantia (1206–1210) has only two meanings for natural law – a further reduction. One is the natural law common to men and animals (Ulpian) and the other that proper to man. The former, the author is careful to point out, is not really a law at all; it is simply an instinct that urges man in accordance with his animal nature. Who would want to say that a horse or an ass can sin?[116] The human natural law is a consequence of man's rationality. And all other meanings for natural law can be reduced to these two. And in another version of this Gloss-apparatus Gratian's definition is accommodated by appeal to the philosophical term *summa natura naturans*, i.e. God, who teaches us the contents of the *ius divinum*. The phrase *natura naturans* is not found elsewhere in the canonical writers of the time; it is used by the civilian Accursius.[117]

In general, then, the canonical teaching on the natural law in the France of the first decades of the 13th century shows a change of direction due, according to Weigand, to the influence of the Anglo-Norman school and also that of the Bologna school represented by Alanus.

Last of all, bringing to a close the canonical development that provided so much of the material for the theologians who were to discuss the natural law in the thirteenth century and after, comes the last series of Gloss-apparatuses of the Bologna school (1210–1220). Laurentius Hispanus (d. 1248) wrote his apparatus, the so-called *Glossa Palatina* about 1210. He speaks of a triple natural law – a *quoddam concretum* in every animal (i.e. Ulpian's definition) about which he does not propose to treat; another natural law which is *inspiratum*, namely natural equity which was in man before the fall; and, finally, the *jus gentium*. These meanings, it should be pointed out, are discussed in the context of private property; the underlying problem being: Is private property in accordance with the natural law? Weigand finds here the influence of the French school, namely the *Summa Duacensis*, in the terminology adopted by Laurentius.[118] When Laurentius faces the question of Gratian's definition, which does not really fit into his classification of meanings of natural law, he avoids difficulties by prescinding from the fact of inspiration and concentrates upon the content of the natural law, which is found in the Scriptures.[119] The revelation is incidental to the existence of the natural law.

[116] R. Weigand, *op. cit.*, n. 421, p. 246.

[117] R. Weigand, *op. cit.*, p. 248.

[118] R. Weigand, *op. cit.*, p. 252. The text of Laurentius is at nn. 428–429, pp. 251–252.

[119] R. Weigand, *op. cit.*, nn. 433–434, p. 254.

Johannes Teutonicus and Raymond of Peñafort, the later writers of the school of Bologna, are in their different ways, outstandingly important. John Zimeke, known as Johannes Teutonicus (d. 1245), wrote his work on the *Decretum* about 1215. His importance lies in that he was the author of the *Glossa ordinaria* on Gratian. This work may be regarded as a mosaic of the views of his predecessors, as the very name *Glossa ordinaria* suggests.[120] Here appears the hierarchy of natural laws, by now well established – a general natural law of all creation (*uis insita in rebus*); secondly, a natural law common to animals (*instinctus nature ex ratione proueniens*); thirdly, one proper to man (*instinctus nature ex ratione proueniens*); and, finally, a sense (to fit in Gratian's definition) in which natural law is taken to mean all natural precepts, such as those of the Decalogue.[121] And so the decretists' view of the matter was fixed in the *Glossa ordinaria.*

Lastly, with Raymond of Peñafort we meet a canonist who is at the same time a theologian. He treats of natural law in the first title of the first book of his *Summa iuris,* a manual written according to the order of the *Decretum* and dating to about 1220 when Raymond was professor at Bologna and had not yet become a Dominican.[122] He gives five meanings for natural law and follows John the Teuton very closely. Weigand shows the literal dependence by printing in a different typeface the passages in Raymond taken verbatim from John.[123] Once again it is a hierarchical classification, beginning with the widest sense of a natural law common to all living beings; then one common to man and animals; thirdly, one appertaining to man's reason; fourthly a natural law that is the equivalent of *ius divinum;* and, finally, a fifth sense in which natural law is identified with the *jus gentium.* This last, which Raymond adds to what he found in John, is said, following Isidore in the *Book of Etymologies,* to be common to almost all nations.

What general picture emerges from this study of the commentators on the *Decretum Gratiani?* One feature that strikes one is the contrast between the late Bologna school, which ends with four or five meanings for natural law and the late French school,

[120] Cf. A. Van Hove, *Commentarium Lovaniense in Codicem Iuris Canonici Prolegomena* I, t. 1, p. 430–431: "Prior redactor glossae ordinariae Decreti est Ioannes Teutonicus alias Zemeca, propositus Halbertstadiensis (+25 aprilis 1245 vel 1246) qui glossam absolvit post concilium Lateranense IV (1215). . . ."

[121] R. Weigand, *op. cit.*, nn. 435–437, 5p. 255–256; cf. O. Lottin, *Le droit naturel chez saint Thomas d'Aquin et ses prédécesseurs*, p. 23.

[122] A. Van Hove, *op. cit.*, p. 448.

[123] R. Weigand, *op. cit.*, nn. 438–439, pp. 256–258.

which, less expansively, gives only two. More importantly, a contrast appears between all these canonists and their contemporaries the civilians. The civil jurists, understandably, concentrated upon the definition of natural law they found in Ulpian: this is what they understand when they refer to 'the natural law' without qualification viz. Ulpian's *quod natura omnia animalia docuit.* They occasionally take the *jus gentium*, the law common to peoples, to be a natural law; and occasionally, too, they refer to Gratian and the Scriptures. In contrast, the decretists and canon lawyers, despite the handicap (for so it must appear) of having to start from a definition of natural law that identified it with the law of the Scriptures, have a much more philosophical and a much better-documented approach. The philosophy of the natural law is much better explored by them. The Golden Rule – do to others what you would have others do to you – provided an easy transition from a purely traditional or inspirational rule of conduct to something more like a philosophical notion. Rufinus, whose influence, in this matter, was paramount, produced the very useful terminology (the *vis nature*) to explain how there is a power in human nature enabling man to discriminate between good and evil. There were variations in the way in which this power or *vis anime* was explained, sometimes stressing the intellectual side sometimes the will. But, by and large, it provided the basis for a view of the natural law acceptable to the decretists and more popular with them even than the definition of Gratian himself. On the other hand Isidore's natural law found, as we have seen in Gratian's *Decretum*, (the law common to all nations and depending, not upon human enactment but upon a *naturalis instinctus*), was not taken up by the decretists. Remarkable, too, is the view found in the French school and also in Johannes Teutonicus and Raymond of Peñafort, which sees a general natural law of all creatures, divided into that common to animals and that proper to man. This general ordering of nature is not found in the civil lawyers.

In general, then, the contrast favours the canonists; and their views, more than those of the civilians, will be influential in the theological elaboration of the natural law in the great figures of the thirteenth century.[124]

[124] R. Weigand, *op. cit.*, p. 259: "Trotz der gegenseitigen Beeinflussung von Legistik und Kanonistik haben doch beide ihre ganz eigene Naturrechtsauffassung, die in der Kanonistik auf Grund des mannigfacheren Quellenmaterials viel bunter und unterschiedlicher ist als in der Legistik."

CHAPTER V

FRESH LINEAMENTS OF THE NATURAL LAW

The stage has now been set for the closer delineation of the natural law, the result of the efforts of the great scholastic theologians working on the rich material they found in the tradition. The elements in that tradition, as has been seen, were basically three: (1) a conception of the natural law, originally Stoic with a background in the pre-Socratics, Plato and Aristotle, translated into the Roman world, popularized by Cicero and finding its authoritative expression in the Roman law; (2) a conception of the natural law, complementing the preceding one, but tributary to St. Paul and the elaboration of his thought by the Fathers and ecclesiastical writers; and (3) the radical re-shaping of the Christian natural law in its identification, by Gratian and his followers, with what is found in the law and the gospel. The future history of the concept of natural law will be determined by the weaving together of these strands in the special environment of scholastic philosophy and theology. It is part of the thesis of this book that the profile that resulted in the work of St. Thomas Aquinas gets as close as is humanly possible to the natural law and that it has hardly been improved upon by his successors. To see this achievment in its context, we must first look – of necessity briefly and selectively – at some of his immediate forerunners.

A. SOME EARLY SCHOLASTIC THEOLOGIANS

We have seen how the medieval jurists, and particularly the canonists, tended to list the meanings of natural law. Some of these were, to say the least, difficult to reconcile. But the effort to harmonise the authorities was a factor in clarifying what natural law could mean. Ulpian's definition – natural law is what nature has taught all animals – was the one officially adopted in the *legistica traditio*[1] a fact which helps to explain its otherwise puzzling popularity with theologians, including St. Thomas. To prefer Ulpian was not to make an arbitrary choice among the available juristic texts; it was to take what the jurists themselves accepted. But, as we have seen, while the jurists were generally agreed on the matter, they were not unaware of the difficulties. Irnerius, the Father of the glossators of the Roman law, who taught at Bologna in the last decades of the eleventh century, has no explicit reference to Ulpian, either in the *Summa Codicis* or in the glosses on minor works attributed to him.[2] Nor do the Four Doctors of the following century (Bulgarus, Martin Gosia, James *de Boragine* and Hugh *de Porta Ravennate*) treat of the topic *ex professo.* A contemporary of theirs, however, Roger, wrote a treatise on the kinds of law, *De jure naturali, gentium et civili*, in which he recorded Ulpian's definition almost without comment.[3] The glossators confined themselves to the text of the *Corpus Juris Civilis* and, in time, were succeeded by the commentators who attacked the underlying problems.

Some – Roger, Azo, Accursius and others – take Ulpian's as the genuine natural law but interpret it in such a way that it is less a juridical conception, than an indication of the laws or patterns of behaviour discernible in the animal world. Azo defines it: *motus quidem instinctu nature proveniens quo singula animalia ad aliquid faciendum inducuntur.* This definition is accepted by most of the commentators, some adding the rider that it is really an improper sense of the term. Others, however, not merely accept Ulpian's natural law, but are prepared to accept some of its more paradoxical consequences. Marriage, for instance, presents a difficulty. The sexual inclination, common to man and animals, is equally the basis of marriage and fornication. Marriage is, of course, based upon consent, a rational act, and is, by the fact, removed from the ambit of the natural law conceived in Ulpian's terms. A way out of the difficulty, and perhaps as acceptable a meaning for Ulpian's definition as can be found in the cir-

[1] "Hoc autem ius legistica tradito generalissime definit, dicens: ius naturale est quod natura omnia animalia docuit" – Gloss of Faventinus cited in W. Ullman, *Medieval Papalism;* cf. J.M. Aubert, *Le droit romain dans l'oeuvre de saint Thomas*, p. 95.

[2] Cf. H. Kantorowicz, *Studies in the Glossators of the Roman Law*, pp. 35–37, 146–148.

[3] H. Kantorowicz, *op. cit.*, p. 275: "Dicitur 'ius naturale' quasi a natura animali, quod omnium animalium sit commune, ut in hoc titulo."

cumstances, is in the suggestion that the natural law has to do with *rational* nature but, in its strictest acceptation, concerns only those acts, such as procreation and the rearing of offspring, that are common to man and animals.[4]

At this stage the discussion has become rather unreal. A useful and probably unconscious *reductio ad absurdum* of Ulpian's definition and its acceptance by the jurists is provided in Odofredus's Gloss on the *Digest.* Odofredus accepts Ulpian's definition and agrees that the natural law applies to all animate nature. But this, for him, poses no more insuperable problem than that of determining whether partridge, pheasant and quail are subject to natural law (he says they are), or whether worms are bound by it, seeing that they are not born by the union of male and female but come to be out of the humidity of earth and air (here he is doubtful)![5] Later, the old Stoic question whether animals have rights, was thrashed out again.

It must not, of course, be forgotten that the jurists accepted definitions of the natural law other than Ulpian's. They speak of a specifically human natural law, a natural law sometimes also called *jus gentium* in the great commentaries of Accursius and Azo. The reconciliation of the two is described in a text of Cinus of Pistoia (1270–1336), Dante's friend and a poet of the *dolce stil nuovo* as well as a great civil lawyer.[6] These two definitions persist with the lawyers right through the twelfth and thirteenth centuries in an uneasy relationship. The question will serve an example of the fruitful antitheses that stimulated the theologians to reason about the true nature of natural law and, perhaps, to be less impressed by authorities.

The school of Anselm of Laon in the early years of the twelfth century has already been mentioned as a possible source for Gratian's ideas about the natural law; and likewise Hugh of St. Victor (1097–1141).[7] This concept of a natural law of human reason, at the same time somehow divine, was also shared by

[4] W. Onclin, "Le droit naturel selon les Romanistes des XIIe et XIIIe siècles" in *Miscellanea Moralia A. Janssen*, II, 329–338.

[5] G. Fassò, *Storia della filosofia del diritto*, I, p. 230.

[6] *De justitia et jure*, I, 10, 3, cited by W. Onclin, *op. cit.:* "Homo est creatus in duobus materiis, una scilicet quam communem habet cum ceteris animalibus ... et secundum hanc naturam describitur jus naturale in legibus; altera vero quam communem habet cum angelis, scilicet rationabilitatem, secundum quam jus definitur in canone."

[7] Supra, Chapter IV pp. 80–81; Hugo de D. Victore, *De sacramentis legis naturalis et scriptae* (P. L., 176; 39, 347–364).

Peter Abelard (1079–1142). Abelard's most considerable contribution to ethics was his insistence upon the interiority of moral life; the leitmotiv of his *Ethics* or *Scito teipsum* is that intention or consent, and not the external action, makes morality.[8] Yet Abelard is not a subjectivist because the law, which is obeyed or disobeyed, does properly command and prohibit; what he stresses is the need to make one's internal dispositions conform to the law. Elsewhere, in the *Commentary on Romans*, he speaks in familiar terms of the natural law, as pre-dating the mosaic law and he stresses its connection with natural reason. In the *Dialogus* he adopts the Ciceronian distinction between the *jus naturale*, prescribed by natural reason, and the *jus positivum*, set up by men. Despite the rationalism with which he is often credited, Abelard shared his contemporaries' inability to distinguish unequivocally between the natural law and the divine revealed law.[9]

About the middle of the twelfth century two texts of outstanding importance saw the light; one, the *Decretum* of Gratian, we have already considered; the other, Peter Lombard's *Book of Sentences* was of even more decisive influence. It was received as the theological text *par excellence* for four centuries and still attracted commentators at the time of the Reformation.[10] It was written about 1152.[11] Lombard, while he makes use of the *Decretum* of Gratian, is, in contrast very reticent about the natural law. He refers to it only in passing and in a context quite in keeping with the views of the school of Anselm of Laon: "Truth wrote in the heart of man that he should not do to others what he would not have done to himself, and this *precept of the*

[8] D.E. Luscombe (ed.), *Peter Abelard's Ethics*, especially pp. 4–36.

[9] *Expos. in Ep. Pauli ad Rom.*, I (P. L., 178; 814, 862); *Dialogus inter philosophum Judaeum et Christianum*, (P. L., 178; 1656); F. De Siano, "Of God and Man: Consequences of Abelard's Ethic" in *The Thomist*, 35 (1971), pp. 639, 652–654.

[10] F. Pollock, "The History of the Law of Nature" in *Jurisprudence and Legal Essays* (ed. A.L. Goodhart), p. 130, note 1, says "There is reason to believe that the *Decretum* was strongly influenced by Abelard" and quotes Thaner, *Abälard und das canonische Recht*, Graz, 1900. The suggestion does not appear to have been well-founded.

[11] F. Pelster, "Wann hat Petrus Lombardus die Libri IV Sententiarum vollendet?" in *Gregorianum* 2 (1921), pp. 387–392; D. Van den Eynde, "Nouvelles précisions chronologiques sur quelques oeuvres théologiques au XIIe siècle" in *Franciscan Studies* 13 (1953), pp. 71–118.

natural law, because of man's neglect, had to be reiterated in the Decalogue."[12] Peter Lombard refers again to the natural law in his *Collectanea* on the epistles of St Paul. He identifies the unwritten law which the gentiles have as the natural law, "by which one is aware of good and evil." He proceeds to list some of its precepts, such as not to injure another, not to take another's goods, to avoid fraud and perjury, not to undermine another's marriage and so on. It is summarised-and here he quotes St. Augustine-in the Golden Rule, which agrees with the gospel.[13] There is nothing original here; Lombard simply records the teaching of his time.

Lombard's relative reticence about the natural law was not to be shared by his commentators and successors at the turn of the century. The latter half of the twelfth century, as we have seen, witnessed a great deal of speculation about the natural law in the civilian jurists and the canon lawyers. The period helped to shape the theological treatise on the natural law which, well before the mid-thirteenth century, had become an integral part of moral theology. At first the natural law was treated, if at all, in a passing and incidental way by the theologians:

> Many Parisian summists, such as Martinus de Fugeriis, Peter of Capua, Martinus of Cremona, Praepositinus of Cremona, Simon of Tournai, Robert of Courçon, Petrus Cantor, Guido of Orchelles, Robert of Melun, Petrus Pictaviensis, have neglected to deal more thoroughly with the problems of natural law or even to dedicate a single separate chapter or *quaestio* to the nature of natural law.[14]

The honour of being the first to include a question *de jure naturali* in his *Summa* has been claimed for Stephen Langton (d.

[12] Petrus Lombardus, *Liber Sententiarum*, III, D. 37 (P. L., 192; 832). O. Lottin, *Psychologie et morale aux XIIe et XIIIe siècles*, II, p. 73, "nulle part il ne parle du droit naturel," appears to have overlooked this reference; he is more correct in *Le droit naturel chez saint Thomas d'Aquin et ses prédécesseurs*, p. 28, "nulle part il ne relève la moindre définition du *jus naturae*."

[13] *Collectanea in Epistolas Divi Pauli* (P. L., 191; 1345): "Etsi non habeat scriptam legem habet tamen naturalem, qua intelligit et sibi conscius est quid sit bonum, quidve malum. Lex enim naturalis est iniuriam nemini inferri. . . ."

[14] A.H. Chroust, "The Philosophy of Law from St. Augustine to St. Thomas Aquinas" in *The New Scholasticism*, 20 (1946), p. 39.

1228). What Langton actually says is, however, rather curtly dismissed by Lottin as hardly worth citing.[15]

The first to adopt the natural law fully into theology, giving it a question to itself in his *Summa aurea*, seems to have been William of Auxerre, writing about 1220. William had the advantage of being acquainted with the writings of the decretists. He finds inspiration, in particular, in the *Gloss* of John the Teuton when he points out that natural law can be taken in a wide or in a narrow sense. The wide sense proves to be that of Ulpian's definition – *quod natura omnia animalia docuit;* the strict sense is that which connects the natural law with natural reason which is intuitive or almost so. Elsewhere William adds a third sense – the widest of all – in which the natural law becomes synonymous with the harmony of creation. These general ideas of William's will recur in his successors. On more detailed points, too, his influence is felt. He insists, for example, that the natural law is the source and principle of all virtue; he is the first to essay the parallel between the first principles of the speculative and the practical intellect, a parallel that will figure in almost all discussions of natural law, *synderesis* and conscience henceforth; and he also insists upon the innateness of the natural law.[16]

As with the lawyers, the context is usually a list of the possible meanings of 'nature.' The theologians seem, on the whole, to be more discriminating and many of them express a more or less decided preference for a meaning of natural law connected with reason. So, for example, Philip the Chancellor (writing about 1233–1234) or the Dominican master Guerric of St. Quentin. In this category, also, must be placed Guerric's source, the author of an anonymous *Quaestio de lege naturali*, found in a Paris ms. and studied by Lottin.[17] Some theologians, however, appear embarrassed by the ingenuity required in order to reconcile the competing conceptions of natural law. Hugh of St. Cher, the first Dominican Cardinal, who had taught at Paris between 1230 and

[15] M. Grabmann, "Das Naturrecht der Scholastik von Gratian bis Thomas von Aquin" in *Mittelalterliches Geistesleben*, I, p. 68; E.E. Hölscher, *Vom römischen zum christlichen Naturrecht*, p. 63; O. Lottin, *Le droit naturel chez sàint Thomas d'Aquin et ses prédécesseurs*, p. 29: ". . . les quelques lignes qu'Etienne Langton consacre aux deux règles de droit naturel ne valent pas d'être citées." Cf. Id., in *Bulletin de théologie ancienne et médiévale*, 1930, n. 494; 1932, n. 1031. F. Flückiger, *Geschichte des Naturrechtes*, I, pp. 418–421, claims the honour for Hugh of St Victor.

[16] Texts in O. Lottin, *Psychologie et morale aux XII et XIII siècles*, II, pp. 75–76. Cf. A.H. Chroust, *op. cit.*, pp. 40–42.

[17] O. Lottin, *op. cit.*, II, pp. 77–82, 84–85; cf. pp. 138–157.

1235, is content to reproduce William of Auxerre's threefold division: *Ius naturale quoddam est speciale; quoddam universalius; quoddam universalissimum.* His predecessor, however, Roland of Cremona, the first Dominican professor at Paris, teaching about 1229–1230, had added a fourth member to the division of natural laws; the inclination towards good in all creatures is the generic natural law which is then specified in vegetative, animal and human nature.[18] The *jus specialius in animalibus* seems to be a general law of animal behaviour in virtue of which each animal joins with its like (Roland says that he finds this idea in Boethius) and there are also the more specific laws, like that which directs the spider to spin its web to catch the flies on which it feeds.[19]

Roland of Cremona was also responsible for an important distinction between primary, and invariable, precepts of the natural law and secondary precepts which may vary.[20] This distinction was to reappear in many of his successors and was to become part and parcel of natural law teaching. It is of some interest that the context in which Roland elaborates it, namely his discussion of whether or not monogamy is a rule of the natural law, is precisely the same as that in which Aquinas was also to distinguish between primary and secondary precepts of natural law.[21]

B. THE FRANCISCAN SCHOOL – AND ALBERT THE GREAT

Even more than the Dominicans the Franciscans at Paris were interested in the questions of law. The great achievement of the Franciscan school is the treatise on laws in the *Summa* commonly attributed to Alexander of Hales (d. 1245). The third part of this

[18] Text in O. Lottin, *Le droit naturel chez saint Thomas d'Aquin et ses prédécesseurs*, p. 115, Appendix VII. G. Graneris, *La filosofia del diritto*, p. 75, comments: "L'artifizio della nomenclatura rivela l'imbarazzo del teologo, che dovette sentirsi insodisfatto dell'opera sua, onde vorrebbe annullarla con questo commento; *aequivocatio est in jure*; cioè quell' elenco riposa su un equivoco."

[19] Text in O. Lottin, *op. cit.:* "Est aliud jus speciale magis in animalibus quod unumquodque animal coniungitur ad sibi simile, sicut dicit Boethius: et quaedam alia jura sunt specialia in animalibus sive natura ut quod aranea texit ut capiat muscas quas comedat."

[20] The text, from Bibl. Mazarine, Paris, Cod. 795, is referred to in A.H. Chroust, *op. cit.*, p. 43.

[21] *In 4 Sent.*, d. 33, q. 1, a. 1; cf. R. Armstrong, *Primary and Secondary Precepts in Thomistic Natural Law Teaching*, passim.

Summa fratris Alexandri seems to have been the work of Alexander's collaborator John of La Rochelle (d. 1245). The law-tract it contains is based upon certain *Quaestiones disputatae de legibus et praeceptis* (known as *Tractatus de legibus*) which may have been written by Alexander, as well as upon John of La Rochelle's own *Summa de praeceptis et consiliis.*[22]

In the treatise on the eternal law (for the elaboration of which the credit must go to the Franciscan school) the natural law, as indeed every law, is said to derive from the eternal law.[23] In fact there are said to be several kinds of natural law each derived in its own degree from the eternal law; there is the natural law limited to rational creation (the law of which St. Paul speaks in *Rom.*, 2;14) the natural law common to man and animal (Ulpian's definition, wrongly ascribed to St. Isidore) and the natural law that embraces all creation (and is described by St. Augustine). Here once again, are the meanings found in the *Glossa Ordinaria* of John the Teuton, in William of Auxerre and in Roland of Cremona,[24] and here too, one finds an ingenious reconciliation of the diverse definitions. There is *jus nativum* or the law of all living creatures, man and animal (Ulpian's *quod natura omnia animalia docuit*, once again mistakenly ascribed to Isidore); *jus humanum* or the specifically human natural law, and finally, *jus divinum* which orders man to the supernatural plane.

The great Franciscan preoccupation with the problem of law is not as remarkable in St. Bonaventure (1221–1275) as in, say, the *Summa fratris Alexandri*. Bonaventure has no special treatise on laws, yet law is prominent in his thought. The index to his *Opera Omnia* yields upwards to twenty discussions of the natural law in his various works. The fact of the matter, as J.F. Quinn points

[22] V. Doucet, *Prolegomena in librum III necnon in libros I et II in Summa Fratris Alexandri* (Quaracchi), t. 4, pp. CCCLXIX CCCVII; cf. also I. Brady, Law in the "*Summa fratris Alexandri*" in *Proceedings of the American Catholic Philosophical Association*, 24 (1950), pp. 133–136; F. Henquinet, "Ist der Traktat de legibus et praeceptis in der Summa Alexanders von Hales von Johannes von Rupella?" in *Franziskanische Studien*, 26 (1939), pp. 1–22, 234–258.

[23] *Summa fratris Alexandri*, lib. III, pars 2, Inquis. 1, c. 7, a. 4 (Quaracchi t. 4, n. 223, pp. 328–9): "Dicendum quod omnis lex naturalis est a lege aeterna, tamen secundum propinquinus et remotius, secundum quod naturae, in quibus est, se habent secundum propinquius et remotius ad Deum"; cf. A.H. Chroust. *op. cit.*, pp. 44–50.

[24] O. Lottin, *Psychologie et morale aux XIIe et XIIIe siècles*, II, p. 57, note 2: "Cette triple acception de la loi naturelle était courante à cette époque...."

out, is that the word 'law' had a number of senses for Bonaventure; it meant the written law of the Old Testament and it meant the threefold law of nature, of scripture and of grace. Law is interiorly imposed upon man since the institution of human nature; and it came exteriorly through the written law of Moses.

A great many of Bonaventure's texts on natural law are found in the above theological context. Not treating natural law for its own sake, he refers to it only in connexion with other problems. . . . To give a complete account of his understanding of natural law, therefore, it would be necessary to bring together all the texts where, handling particular problems, he either invokes or adverts to the law of nature.[25]

Taking in turn Bonaventure's conception of conscience, of *synderesis*, of freewill and of beatitude, Quinn disengages his fundamental conception of the natural law. We shall return to the questions of conscience and *synderesis* which are particularly enlightening. But for the moment we may concentrate upon Bonaventure's attitude towards the definitions of his predecessors.

With him the idea of order is capital. The world is, in a phrase he took from St. Augustine, *amplissima quaedam immensaque respublica.*[26] The doctrine of the eternal law, to which he makes few explicit references, is subsumed here. The natural law, too, is connected with the order of creatures and is, in fact the order God, in his wisdom, has established for all creatures. Thus Bonaventure regards Ulpian's definition as the best definition of the natural law.[27] His interpretation of this definition, *quod natura omnia animalia docuit*, is however, careful. He records, in fact, three definitions of the natural law (all of which he attributes to Isidore); there is Gratian's *quod in Lege et Evangelio continetur*,

[25] J.F. Quinn, "St. Bonaventure's Fundamental Conception of Natural Law" in *S. Bonaventura 1274–1974.* III, p. 572.

[26] Bonaventure, *Breviloquium*, I, 9 (*Opera Omnia*, Quaracchi, 1889, t. 5, p. 2176); cf. *De perfectione evangelica*, q. 4, a. 1 (Quaracchi, t. 5, p. 181): "Lex naturalis est impressio facta in anima a lege aeterna; lex autem aeterna est illa qua *incommutabili* permanente, cetera ordinantur. . . ."; cf. L. Baur, *Die Lehre vom Naturrecht bei Bonaventura*, p. 223.

[27] Bonaventure, *In IV. Sent.*, d. 33, a. 1, q. 1 (Quaracchi, t. 4, pp. 747–8): "Dicendum quod jus naturale tripliciter sumitur, scilicet communiter, proprie et magis proprie et secundum hoc tripliciter definitur ... Uno modo sic: Ius naturale est quod in Lege et Evangelio continetur. . . . Secundo modo dicitur proprie et sic definitur . . . jus naturale est quod est commune omnium nationum et hoc jus est quod dictat ratio recta. . . . Tertio modo dicitur jus naturale propriisime quod natura docuit omnia animalia."

Isidore's *quod est commune omnium nationum* and Ulpian's *quod natura omnia animalia docuit.*[28] The first of these is the common acceptance (*communiter*), the second more precise (*proprie*) and the third, Ulpian's the most exact (*propriissime*). Bonaventure does not give his reasons for this preference, which is a pity since he is going against the tradition of the decretists and theologians and following the civilians. His application of these notions of natural law is not much more enlightening. Fornication, he says is against the natural law in the first sense, since it is forbidden in the Law and the gospel; it is also against the natural law of the second definition, seeing that it is against right reason; but the natural law in Ulpian's definition has nothing to say to fornication, either by way of condemnation or approval, because animals propagate in different ways. Bonaventure does not appeal to Ulpian's definition of natural law in order to find a way around the difficulty of the polygamy of the Old Testament patriarchs (by suggesting that a plurality of mates is, after all, what nature has taught many animals). He says, on the contrary, that polygamy is against the animal nature of man which inclines him toward exclusiveness in marriage – and he concedes that God could and did dispense the patriarchs from this obligation. It seems then, that Bonaventure commends Ulpian's definition as the strictest but qualifies this acceptance somewhat in practice: for polygamy is certainly not taught by nature to all animals.[29]

Albert the Great (1206–1280) dealt expressly with the natural law more than once in his long career. In the *Summa de bono* (that is the third part of his *Summa de creaturis*) and in his *Commentary on the Nicomachean Ethics* of Aristotle his treatment is much the same and, in contrast with Bonaventure, includes a clear rejection of Ulpian. In the *Summa de bono*, written about 1242, he discusses the natural law in terminology

[28] *In IV Sent.*, d. 33, a. 1, q. 1 (*Opera Omnia*, Quaracchi, 1889, t. 4, p. 748).

[29] *In IV Sent.* d. 33, a. 1, q. 2 (*Opera omnia*, t. 4. pp. 749–750): "Si dicatur jus naturale quod natura imprensit animalibus, sic dicendum quod non omnibus, sed aliquibus animalibus brutis impressit; sed tamen in natura est aliquorum animalium irrationalium, et in nostra natura hoc natura plantavit"; cf. O. Lottin, *Psychologie et Morale aux XIIe et XIIIe siècles* p. 593: "A relever encore une thèse propre à Saint Bonaventure reprise par Saint Thomas; contrairement à toute la tradition scolaire, Bonaventure avait soutenu que, dans son sens le plus strict, le droit naturel est celui qui est commun à l'homme et à l'animal, *quod natura docuit omnia animalia*: on reconnaît la définition du jurisconsulte romain Ulpien. Il est remarquable que sur ce point Thomas d'Aquin abandonne son maître Albert et reprend pour son compte, presque dans ses derniers ouvrages, la conception de Bonaventure."

reminiscent of Philip the Chancellor; he speaks, for example of *natura ut ratio.* There is no room in his view for Ulpian's *quod natura omnia animalia docuit* – there can be no natural law common to man and brute. He begins his discussion by quoting Cicero's description of the natural law as implanted by some innate force – *quod non opinio genuit sed quaedam innata vis inseruit.* When enlarging upon this *quaedam innata vis,* in answering objections, he goes out of his way to say that he disagrees with the distinction in virtue of which natural law is understood in a number of ways, including one which would make it common to us and animals.[30] In the following article he discusses this distinction and is even more forthright. He begins by objecting to the enumeration of five meanings of natural law he finds in the decretists. The burden of his complaint is that these writers would make a natural law common to all creatures, animate and inanimate which, he says, is an absurdity; for there can be a natural law, in the proper sense, only for man. He suggests, a little sourly one suspects, that there is neither rhyme nor reason in this any more than in other distinctions made by the decretists.[31]

Further on Albert points out that the procreation and education of children are not the result of mere sensuality but of the sense-inclination *as found in man.* In a word he gives short shrift to Ulpian's definition. He appears even to grudge the admission that the tendencies of man's animal nature, as regulated by reason, properly form part of the natural law; and he has little patience with the ingenuity of the doctors who made distinctions to accomodate Ulpian.

Earlier, in the *De sacramentis* (which is the earliest part of the work known as the *Summa de creaturis*), in the context of matrimony where Albert, like his contemporaries, had to discuss the polygamy of the Old Testament patriarchs, there is a reference to animal nature in man. Albert here, too, clearly distinguishes between the nature man has in common with animals and needs only the difference beteween male and female for propagation,

[30] *Summa de bono,* Tractatus V, De iustitia, q. 1, a. 1 (*Opera Omnia,* XXVIII, Münster, 1951, pp. 265–6): "Non enim consentimus in distinctionem quam quidem posuerunt, scilicet quod ius naturale multis modis dicatur, et uno modo sit commune nobis cum brutis."

[31] *Ibid.,* q. 1 a. 2, pp. 268–269: "Non erit ius naturale nisi solius hominis. ... Haec distinctio nec artem nec rationem habet, sicut est mos decretistarum ponere distinctiones. ..."

and the nature (*ratio*) proper to man which demands that the act of propagation be reasonably accomplished.[32]

Some years later, between 1248 and 1252, when at Cologne he commented upon the *Ethics* of Aristotle and his commentary was written down by his pupil Thomas Aquinas, Albert's views had scarcely changed.[33] When he came to the celebrated passage in Book V, where Aristotle distinguishes between two kinds of political justice, one natural, the other legal, Albert, in common with the majority of commentators, takes it to refer to the natural law. He points out that natural law and natural justice belong to the specific nature of man, namely reason, and not to nature in general. In the latter context one could speak (as Plato does in the *Timaeus*) of natural, i.e. metaphysical or cosmic, justice. Again Albert explains that Aristotle's view is that natural law refers formally to the rational nature of man; only materially can one describe an act, such as sexual congress, as belonging to the animal nature of man.[34]

Finally there is Albert's *Ethica*, composed later than 1260.[35] Here Albert devotes his efforts to reconciling Aristotle's and Cicero's approaches to the natural law. He does not discuss Ulpian or the jurists directly; but when he comes to the innate force in nature, the *innata vis* of Cicero's conception of natural law, he takes care to point out that the nature in question cannot be the animal nature of man, but rather his rational nature. This precludes any real acceptance of Ulpian's definition and shows that Albert never wavered in his insistence upon the rational character of the natural law. It is curious that Thomas Aquinas, in

[32] *De sacramentis*, Tractatus IX, De matrimonio, (ed. A. Ohlmeyer, *Opera omnia*, XXVI, Münster, 1958, p. 165); the same teaching is found in Albert's *Commentary on the Sentences* (1244–1249), d. 33A, aa 1–3 (*Opera omnia*, ed. A. Borgnet, Paris, 1890–1899, XXX, pp. 289–296).

[33] A. Pelzer, "Le cours inédit d'Albert le Grand sur la Morale à Nicomaque recueilli et rédigé par S. Thomas d'Aquin" in *Etudes d'histoire littéraire sur la scolastique médiévale*, pp. 272–335.

[34] Cf. the passage quoted in G. Fassò, *La legge della ragione*, Appendice 19–20, pp. 268–269; G. Meersseman, "Le droit naturel chez S. Thomas d'Aquin et ses prédécesseurs" in *Angelicum*, 9 (1932), pp. 63–65.

[35] *Opera Omnia*, ed. A. Borgnet, VII. The relevant passages are cited in S. Ramirez, *El derecho de gentes*, pp. 56–61.

other matters the faithful follower of Albert, should still hanker after an acceptable meaning for Ulpian's definition.[36]

C. SCHOLASTIC TERMINOLOGY: *SYNDERESIS* AND CONSCIENCE

The terms *synderesis* and conscience have already been met with in the scholastic discussions of the nature of natural law. In fact those terms, particularly *synderesis*, may be said to have had an influence on the concept of natural law comparable to that of the definitions handed down in the tradition – Cicero's, Ulpian's, Gratian's and the rest. As the thirteenth century wears on one approaches a consensus not merely on the association of the natural law with reason, but upon the function of human reason in the knowing and expounding of the natural law and in its application to behaviour. In this matter, the theologians gave considerable attention to *synderesis* and to conscience discussing such questions as the indefectibility of *synderesis* or whether conscience is a *habitus* or an act; and some account of those discussions is required in order to appreciate the approach to the natural law.

(i) Synderesis: *The Word*

The word *synderesis* is hardly found in present-day moral theology. It made a sudden appearance in the thirteenth century, enjoyed its crowded hour of glorious life and faded away before the end of the century. It is a significant history.[37] The word itself is mysterious. It depends upon a passage in St Jerome's *Commentary on Ezechiel*, where he deals with the various interpretations of the prophet's vision of the four living creatures. A common interpretation, according to Jerome, sees in the man, the lion, the

[36] S. Ramirez, *op. cit.*, pp. 60–61; the comment of S. Cotta, *Il concetto di legge nella Summa Theologiae di S. Tommaso d'Aquino*, p. 64, is apposite: "il pensiero cristiano, sotto l'influenza di una gloriosa tradizione giuridica, non riesce a svincolarsene e in essa cerca di inserire, con risultati non molto coerenti e con visibile impaccio, quanto di nuovo il suo messaggio portava. E ciò vale, mi sembra, anchi per il S. Tommaso dei *Commenti* che non ha saputo valersi dell' intuizione pienamente chiarificatrice di Alberto Magno."

[37] I may be permitted to refer to my study: M.B. Crowe, "The Term *synderesis* and the Scholastics" in *Irish Theological Quarterly*, 23 (1956), pp. 151–164, 228–245.

ox and the eagle the three parts in the Platonic division of the soul, together with a fourth, superior and overseeing "above and outside these three, which the Greeks call *synteresis*."[38] The passage is interesting in itself, and fruitful, as the scholastic commentaries amply demonstrate. It is curious, therefore, that it should not have attracted attention in Jerome's time nor for centuries afterwards. Even the unusual word *synteresis* provokes no remark. Of the commentators on Ezechiel between the end of the fourth century, when Jerome wrote, and the last third of the twelfth century only Hrabanus Maurus seems to have preserved an echo of Jerome. Writing in 842, he quotes, with one significant omission and without comment, the passage concerning *synderesis*.[39] Others give entirely different explanations of Ezechiel's vision and make no reference at all to *synderesis* (or *synteresis*).[40] And the word is not found again until the late twelfth century.

Mid-twelfth century writers like Hugh of St. Victor, Peter Abelard and St. Bernard do not know the term. Peter Lombard, whose *Book of Sentences* belongs to the same period, refers rather gingerly to the passage in St. Jerome. He contrives to avoid the word *synderesis*, saying instead *scintilla rationis*.[41] This latter phrase was probably suggested by Jerome's *scintilla conscientiae;* but not necessarily for, as will be noted presently, the word *scintilla* has a classical pedigree that goes back far beyond St. Jerome.

The first reappearance of the word *synderesis* seems to have come in the *Sentences* of one Master Udo, written about 1160–5. It is found again in the *Sentences in five Books* of Peter of Poitiers, composed about 1170, and in the *Summa super Decretum* of Simon of Bisiniano, written 1177–9. Other canonists

[38] Hieronymus, *Comm. in Ezech.*, I, 1 (P. L., 25; 22): "Plerique, juxta Platonem, rationale animal et irascitivum et concupiscitivum . . . ad hominem et leonem ac vitulum referunt. . . . Quartamque ponunt quae super haec et extra haec tria est, quam Graeci vocant *synteresin*, quae scintilla conscientiae in Cain quoque pectore, postquam ejectus est de paradiso, non extinguitur, et qua victi voluptatibus, vel furore, ipsaque interdum rationis decepti similitudine nos peccare sentimus. Quam proprie aquilae deputant, non se miscentem tribus, sed tria errantia corrigentem. . . . Et tam hanc ipsam quoque conscientiam. . . . cernimus praecipitare apud quosdam et suum locum ammittere, qui ne pudorem quidem et verecundiam habent in delictis."

[39] Hrabanus Maurus, *Comm. in Ezech.*, I (P. L., 110; 508).

[40] J. de Blic, "Conscience ou synderèse?," in *Revue d'ascétique et de mystique*, 25 (1949), mentions St. Gregory, Rupert of Deutz, Richard of St. Victor and Peter the Chanter.

[41] *Liber Sententiarum*, III, d. 39, par. 3 (P. L., 192; 747).

and theologians contemporary with these either do not know the term or make no use of it. So, for example, the canonists Huguccio of Ferrara (d. 1210) and Sicard of Cremona and the theologians Simon of Tournai (d. 1201) and Prevostine of Cremona (d. 1231). In other words the term occurs sporadically. The canonists, in fact, never adopted it; and its popularity with the theologians was only assured after the year 1200.[42] The currency of the word *synderesis* from the beginning of the thirteenth century makes the silence of the preceding centuries the more surprising.

An even more curious feature of the history of *synderesis* is the fact that the word rests upon the single passage in St. Jerome's commentary already referred to. And it rests precariously, for there is good reason to suppose that Jerome did not use the word *synderesis* at all! As long ago as 1879 it was suggested, largely on *a priori* grounds, that the text of Jerome should have *syneidesis* in place of *synderesis.*[43] A sharp controversy followed, mainly in Germany; but it is only in quite recent years that the study of the manuscript tradition of Jerome's *Commentary* finally demolished the case for the authenticity of *synderesis* already seriously undermined. The arguments against *synderesis* are briefly these.[44]

(1) The word is exceedingly rare. Stephanus' *Thesaurus*, for instance, gives only four examples of its use – and in only one of these contexts does *synderesis* bear a meaning even approaching that demanded by the passage in St. Jerome. But Jerome says distinctly that his explanation that the eagle represents *synderesis* is a common one among the Greek interpreters of Ezechiel. *Syneidesis*, on the other hand, would fit such a statement admirably, for both the word and its Latin equivalent *conscientia* were widely current in ecclesiastical and profane writings in the early centuries of our era. Stephanus gives more than a score of

[42] O. Lottin, "Synderese et conscience aux XIIe et XIIIe siècles" in *Psychologie et morale aux XIIe et XIIIe siècles*, II, pp. 105–110.

[43] F. Nitzsch, "Uber die Entstehung der scholastischen Lehre von der Synderesis-ein historischer Beitrag zur Lehre vom Gewissen" in *Jahrbüch für protestantische Theologie*, 5 (1879), pp. 492–507. For other references to nineteenth century literature see M. B. Crowe, *op. cit.*, pp. 153–154.

[44] R. Leiber, "Name und Begriff der Synteresis" in *Philosophisches Jahrbuch*, 25 (1912), pp. 372–392; J. Hebing, "Über conscientia und conservatio im philosophischen Sinne bei Römern von Cicero bis Hieronymus," *ibid.*, 35 (1922), pp. 121–135, 215–231, 298–326; K. Schmeider, "Die Synderesis und die ethischen Werte," *ibid.*, 47 (1943), pp. 145–159, 297–307; M. Waldmann, "Synteresis oder Syneidesis – ein Beitrag zur Lehre vom Gewissen" in *Theologisches Quartalschrift*, 119 (1938), pp. 332–371; J. de Blic, *op. cit.*

instances of the use of *syneidesis* many of them from the New Testament.[45] *Syneidesis*, in fact, is an important Pauline term – one that in all likelihood, St. Paul knew to be familiar to his converts and therefore borrowed and developed for their instruction.

(2) St. Jerome's context seems to call for *syneidesis*. Some lines below the mention of *synderesis* he refers to *hanc ipsam conscientiam;* and the whole passage describes exactly what the Fathers, following St. Paul, understood by conscience. The argument is strengthened if it be true that Jerome's *Commentary* depends upon Origen (perhaps upon Origen's twenty-five book *Commentary on Ezechiel*). Jerome had already translated the homilies of Origen on Ezechiel before he wrote his own *Commentary*. And the substance of Jerome's teaching on the four living creatures in the prophet's vision is to be found in Origen's first *Homily on Ezechiel*, with the difference that for Origen the eagle signifies *spiritus praesidens animae*. Now, there is some evidence that for Origen *spiritus* in this sense is the exact equivalent of *syneidesis;* and, on the other hand, there is no evidence that he ever used the word *synderesis*.[46] For the phrase *spiritus praesidens animae* one may compare a Greek gloss on Ezechiel attributed to St. Gregory Nazianzen or, perhaps more significantly, the Stoic doctrine of the *hegemonikon* or principal part of the soul.[47]

(3) The manuscript tradition of Jerome's *Commentary* is practically unanimous in favour of *syneidesis*. This clinches the issue.

How, then, did *synderesis* come to be substituted for *syneidesis* in Jerome's *Commentary?* And when? It seems probable that *synderesis* somehow found its way into the *Glossa ordinaria* on Ezechiel.[48] The Glossator, writing at a date that we can only guess, may have followed a manuscript which had *synderesis* in place of *syneidesis;* or he may have taken his text from Hrabanus Maurus; or, least likely, he may have, consciously or unconsciously, substituted *synderesis* for *syneidesis* by association with *conservare* (*synterein*) and the early scholastic idea of a faculty preserved after original sin.[49] In any event, the *Glossa ordinaria*

[45] H. Stephanus, *Thesaurus linguae graecae*, t. 7, 1472, 1290–1291.

[46] Origenes, *Hom. in Ezech.*, I, 16 (P. G., 13; 681; cf. P. L. 25; 706–707). The Latin translation is all that remains of the greater part of this homily.

[47] Gregory in P. G. 36; 665; R. Leiber, *op. cit.*, pp. 378–379; J. De Blic, *op. cit.*, pp. 150–151.

[48] J. de Blic, "L'oeuvre exégétique de Walafrid Strabon à la Glossa Ordinaria," in *Recherches de théologie ancienne et médiévale*, 16 (1949), pp. 5–28.

[49] J. de Blic, "Conscience ou synderèse?" in *Revue d'ascétique et de mystique*, 25 (1949), p. 155.

was so widely accepted that it succeeded in giving currency to the false reading of Jerome. The tendency of a scribe who happened to see both would have been to correct Jerome by the *Glossa*, i.e. substitute *synderesis* for *syneidesis.* Peter Lombard's reluctance to use either term may even be due to his inability to decide which was the authentic one used by Jerome.

However, the question of origins is secondary. The fact is that *synderesis* is the term that came into the Schools and not *syneidesis* (which the scholastics never use). The doctrines we are about to examine briefly were not affected by the doubtful parentage of the term.[50]

(ii) *The Scholastic Doctrine of* Synderesis

Early scholastic references to *synderesis* have already been indicated. Stephen Langton was among the first to attempt a serious discussion of the term. For this theologian *synderesis* is part of the rational faculty. Godfrey of Poitiers has a similar treatment of the notion, to which he adds questions on merit and *synderesis* and on *synderesis* and sin. Alexander Neckham (d. 1217) discusses *synderesis* in connection with free-will. At first he appears to assimilate *synderesis* to the faculty of will. But he sees the difficulty that will is symbolised by the ox in Ezechiel's vision whereas the eagle is *synderesis.* His conclusion, then, is that synderesis is the *ratio superior* or, at least, the *scintilla rationis.*[51]

These terms, *ratio superior* and *scintilla rationis* require a word of explanation, for both will figure prominently in the discussions of synderesis.

The distinction between the *ratio superior* and the *ratio inferior* goes back to St. Augustine, although Augustine himself does not use precisely those terms. In the *De Trinitate,* when he is considering man as an image of the Blessed Trinity, he points out that reason has two parts; and elsewhere in the same work he refers to a *sublimior ratio.*[52] The parts are not quantitative in any sense, but represent two operations of the reason, one concerned with the life of contemplation, the other with the active life. The superior ought to direct the lower reason – otherwise the latter may become absorbed in material things. Only in the higher reason is there truly the image of God.

[50] R. Leiber. *op. cit.*, p. 373 quotes the remark of Hofman: "(Synderesis) ist mit einem Male in der Scholastik da, und niemand weiss, woher es kam, bürgt sich ein, und niemand fragt nach seinem Bürgerrecht!"

[51] O. Lottin, *op cit.*, II, 112–122 gives the texts.

[52] *De Trin.*, XII, 7, 12 (P. L., 42; 1007); cf. XII, 2, (P. L. 42; 999).

Augustine's sources in this matter are, in the main, Plato and the Platonic tradition. There is an obvious affinity between the doctrine of a higher and a lower reason, on the one hand, and Plato's picture of the soul with a place in two worlds, that of the ideas and that of sensation, on the other. The direct source of Augustine, however, is probably Plotinus.[53] Secondary sources may have been Manicheeism and Stoicism – and, in particular, the already mentioned Stoic doctrine of the *principale mentis humanae* (*hegemonikon*) attributed to Poseidonius.[54]

Neither in Boethius nor in the pseudo-Denis is there anything to correspond directly with the distinction suggested by St. Augustine. But, in the twelfth century, there appeared, in Gundissalinus's translation of Avicenna's *De anima*, a distinction between the two 'faces' of the soul.[55] In his own *De immortalitate animae* Gundissalinus retains these two 'faces,' using language which strongly resembles that of St. Augustine. William of Auvergne's *De immortalitate* elaborately paraphrases Gundissalinus's, and thus, perhaps, the distinction entered the schools. There cannot, however, be any certainty on such a question of sources.

Too many lines of thought converged in the 12th century to determine with any great precision the exact sources of these different distinctions between *ratio* and *intelligentia.* For our purpose their importance lies in this: the general distinction between the *ratio* as a faculty whose object was material, temporal things and the *intelligentia* as a faculty whose object was immaterial, eternal things very likely preserved and encouraged a tradition of thought similar to St. Augustine's doctrine of the lower and higher parts of the reason.[56]

Peter Lombard cites St. Augustine almost verbatim, and connects the lower reason with sensuality[57] and Lombard's text was

[53] R.W. Mulligan, "Ratio superior and ratio inferior – the Historical Background" in *The New Scholasticism*, 29 (1955), pp. 5–14.

[54] Cf. Tertullian, *De anima*, XV (P. L., 2; 670): "... sumus in anima gradus vitalis et sapientialis quod *hegemonikon* appellant, id est principale"; M. Waldmann, *op. cit.*, pp. 367–368; G. Verbeke, *L'évolution de la doctrine du pneuma du stoicisme à S. Augustin*, pp. 32–33.

[55] Text in R.W. Mulligan, *op. cit.*, p. 16: "faciem scilicet deorsum ad corpus ... faciem sursum versus principia altissima."

[56] R.W. Mulligan, *op. cit.*, pp. 22–23.

[57] *Liber Sentenriarum*, II, d. 24, par 13 (P. L., 192; 705). The *ratio superior* was regarded as active in repelling carnal thoughts; the dallying of the *ratio inferior* was, in effect, *delectatio morosa*, a term that has remained with moral theology. An unfortunate effect of Lombard's treatment was that the speculative activity of the two reasons was frequently ignored in the thirteenth century. Cf. R.W. Mulligan, *op. cit.*, p. 29.

an important factor when the late twelfth century theologians began to discuss the nature of *synderesis.* Philip the Chancellor and John of La Rochelle, to name two, quote Augustine (as Peter Lombard did) as the authority for the distinction between *ratio superior* and *ratio inferior.*

The term *scintilla* also has an interesting history. Literally it means a spark or particle of fire. In a transferred sense it can mean a fragment remaining of something that is compared with fire; or it can mean a germ. The transferred sense is of very respectable classical antiquity. Cicero, for example, speaks of the *scintillae* of virtue in children.[58] The word has obvious possibilities in discussions of *synderesis* and conscience. St. Jerome, as has been seen, had given the example in speaking of *scintilla conscientiae.* But it was not until the thirteenth century that the uncertainties of terminology involved between *synderesis,* conscience, *ratio superior* and *scintilla* were resolved. For St. Thomas the *scintilla conscientiae* is synderesis; not alone because it is the purest part of conscience but because it flies above the conscience as the spark does over the fire (and as, one recalls, the eagle does over the symbols of the faculties in the vision of Ezechiel).[59]

In parallel senses one also hears of *scintilla rationis* (in Peter Lombard, for example) and even *scintilla animae.* It was because of abuse of this latter term by the German mystics Suso and Eckhart that the nomenclature finally fell out of favour.[60]

(iii) Synderesis *and Conscience*

Let us return now to the scholastic discussions of *synderesis.* The first extended treatment of the term is found in William of Auxerre, the same who integrated the natural law into theology. For William *synderesis* is essentially rational and is, in fact, the *ratio superior.* Hugh of St. Cher and his followers merely repeat the views of William of Auxerre. Roland of Cremona also follows William but arrives at a different conclusion on the question of the fallibility of *synderesis.* William had conceded that *synderesis*

[58] *De fin.*, V, 43: "... in pueris virtutum quasi scintillas videmus"; cf. Forcellini, *Lexicon totius latinitatis,* t. 4, p. 253; J. de Blic, *op. cit.*, p. 148 note.

[59] *De veritate,* q. 17, a. 2 ad 3: "Sicut scintilla est illud quod purius est in igne, ita synderesis est id quod supremum in conscientiae judicio reperitur; et secundum hanc metaphoram synderesis scintilla conscientiae dicitur."

[60] H. Wilms, "De scintilla animae" in *Angelicum* 14 (1937), pp. 194–211; cf. M. Grabmann, "Die Lehre des hl. Thomas von der scintilla animae in ihrer Bedeutung für die deutsche Mystik im Predigerorden" in *Jahrbuch für Philosophie und spekulative Theologie,* 14 (1900), pp. 413–427.

could err. Roland denies it: *synderesis* for him is infallible; it is the *ratio inferior* that disobeys. This is no fault of *synderesis* – can we blame the abbot if the monks are recalcitrant? Meantime William of Auvergne, Bishop of Paris since 1228, was attacking these views of his contemporaries. For him *synderesis* is not a special faculty, nor is it the superior part of the reason. It is a function of this *ratio superior* inasmuch as it makes the natural law known – and this, he holds, is the only acceptable sense that can be given to an inerrant and universal *synderesis.*[61]

The most important of the early thirteenth century writers on *synderesis* was Philip, Chancellor of the University of Paris, who wrote about 1233–4. He virtually created the formal treatise on the subject; later writers like the author of the *Summa* attributed to Alexander of Hales, Odo Rigaldus, St. Albert the Great, Peter of Tarentaise and even St. Thomas Aquinas, did little more than discuss, and in the same order, the questions raised by Philip. To the questions on the inerrancy and indefectibility of *synderesis,* commonly discussed before his time, Philip prefaced two lengthy discussions of its nature. In the first of these he asked whether *synderesis* is properly a faculty or a *habitus,* and in the second he considered the relation between *synderesis* and the *ratio superior.*[62] Philip's answer to the first of these general problems is not very decisive – he finds that *synderesis* can best be described as a *potentia habitualis.* The second of the general problems, that of the relation between *synderesis* and reason, stimulates him to distinguish – with the object of reconciling the divergent authorities that faced him – four various senses of 'reason.' Further details of his conception of *synderesis* emerge when he comes to the question of the possibility of error in *synderesis.* Here the Chancellor squarely opposes, but without naming his opponent, the teaching of William of Auxerre. William had been impressed by the wholesale moral aberrations presented by history and experience; against this Philip stressed the indefectibility of *synderesis.*[63]

[61] Texts in O. Lottin, *op. cit.*, II, pp. 123–135.

[62] Texts in O. Lottin, *op. cit.*, II, pp. 140–142, 145–148.

[63] Texts and commentary in O. Lottin, *op. cit.*, II, pp. 148–157. The opposition between the views of William of Auxerre and Philip the Chancellor may be less marked than Lottin suggests. Each admitted variations in moral beliefs and practice and each postulated a *synderesis* that is above such variations. Philip's view has been compared with the doctrine of the *scintilla rationis* of Anselm of Laon and with the *jus naturale* of some of the decretists. Cf. F. Bliemitzrieder, *Anselms von Laon systematische Sentenzen*, pp. 35–36.

In the successors of Philip the Chancellor little that is novel appears, beyond a certain ringing of the changes on the concepts of *synderesis*, conscience, natural law and *habitus*. At least there is much to produce that impression.

Philip the Chancellor followed his treatise on *synderesis* with one on conscience. Conscience, he takes pains to point out, is not *synderesis* but the result of the application of *synderesis* to some matter provided by the reason. The close connection of *synderesis* and conscience was, of course, natural and inevitable. St. Jerome, in the text that dominated these scholastic discussions, had already referred to synderesis as *scintilla conscientiae*.

Among Philip the Chancellor's successors John of La Rochelle may be mentioned, the author of the third part of the *Summa fratris Alexandri* which contains the great achievement of the thirteenth century Franciscan school, the *Tractatus de legibus*. In his treatises on *synderesis* and conscience John of La Rochelle exemplifies the eclecticism so characteristic of these scholastic debates. *Synderesis* is the superior part of the reason, he says, repeating the view of William of Auxerre. His work on conscience, however, derives from the Chancellor, through the medium of an anonymous manuscript known as *Douai* 434. He gives three senses of the word "conscience," the first identifying it with *synderesis*, the second making it a *habitus naturalis dictandi bonum et malum*, and the third allowing it to be *opinio habita de agendis vel non agendis*.[64]

Alexander of Hales in his *Commentary on the Sentences* also depends upon Philip the Chancellor and upon the author of the manuscript *Douai 434*. He puts the question whether *synderesis* should be considered a faculty or a *habitus*. His answer is that, formally speaking, *synderesis* is a *habitus* (just as conscience, defined by St. John Damascene as *lex intellectus nostri*, is a *habitus*) while materially speaking it is a certain *judicatorium innatum* (a phrase which Alexander refers to St. Augustine in the *City of God* but which seems, in reality, to have come from St. Basil).[65] In the *Summa fratris Alexandri synderesis* and conscience are dealt with twice. In the first of these contexts the treatment of *synderesis* depends upon Philip the Chancellor, while that of

[64] Texts in O. Lottin, *op. cit.*, II, pp. 159–162, 167–171. On the *Summa fratris Alexandri* see supra note 22, p. 118

[65] *The Summa fratris Alexandri* (ed. Quaracchi, t. 2, n. 418, p. 492) ascribes the term *naturale judicatorium* to Basil; the original term was *kriterion physikon.* Cf. Basil, *Super princ. Proverb.*, (P. G., 31; 405); *In Hexaem.* hom. 7, n. 5 (P. G., 29: 158).

conscience depends upon a collection of questions by anonymous Franciscan masters. The second context is that of the influential law-tract already referred to; here the author sets down what he conceives to be the relations between natural law, *synderesis* and conscience – natural law is the primary rule, regulating reason through conscience and will through *synderesis.*[66]

Of the other pre-Thomistic theologians one may refer briefly to Walter of Château-Thierry and Odo Rigaldus. The former, who was Chancellor of the University of Paris from 1246 to 1249, in his verbose treatise distinguishes four possible meanings of conscience. The term may mean natural law, or *synderesis*, or a judgment of reason (i.e. of the *pars inferior rationis*) or, finally, a *habitus naturalis* of the superior part of the reason. Walter's treatise proves, in the event, to be a commentary on these four meanings with the aim of proving their substantial identity; the conclusion is that conscience is a faculty, endowed with a *habitus*, identical with *synderesis* but somehow having a different operation. Odo Rigaldus discusses the two common views of his time concerning the nature of *synderesis*, that of Philip the Chancellor (which made it a *potentia habitualis*) and that of the partisans of a *habitus innatus* (who brought *synderesis* into closer relation with natural law and with conscience). And Odo's conclusion, like that of Walter, is that the difference is only a matter of terminology.[67]

Enough has been said to suggest the extreme fluidity of opinion concerning the nature and relations of *synderesis*, conscience and natural law in the early thirteenth century theologians. In two immediate predecessors of St. Thomas, however, St. Bonaventure and St. Albert the Great, these questions are treated more on their merits and with less servility in the use of authorities and texts.

St. Bonaventure deals with *synderesis* and conscience in the second book of his *Commentary on the Sentences.* In the matter of conscience he takes his terms from the *Summa fratris Alexandri*, but his discussion is much more developed. In particular one notes the use of Aristotelian doctrines. When Bonaventure concludes that conscience is a *habitus* in the practical intellect, he

[66] Texts in O. Lottin, *op. cit.*, II, pp. 175–187; *Summa fratris Alexandri*, III, q. 27, memb. 2, a. 3 (ed. Quaracchi, t. 4, n. 245, p. 345): "Lex naturalis non est conscientia nec synderesis licet extendendo conveniant in hoc quod est regulare. Differunt tamen quoniam lex proprie est regula facultatis, et primo et per se; mediante autem conscientia est regula rationis, quoniam conscientia ex lege formatur; mediante vero synderesi, quae est scintilla conscientiae (?), est regula ipsius voluntatis. . . ."

[67] Texts in O. Lottin, *op. cit.*, II, pp. 187–196, 198–199.

uses, with express appeal to Aristotle, the distinction between the speculative and the practical intellect – *intellectus speculativus extensione fit practicus.*[68] And, when he asks himself whether this *habitus* is innate or acquired, he qualifies his conclusion in accordance with the Aristotelian epistemology. The *habitus* of first principles, practical as well as speculative, is innate; that is, we do not require any further light to see the evidence of these principles, but the terms involved must be acquired by experience. The *habitus* of conscience is, therefore, partly innate and partly acquired.[69]

The difficulty now is to find a place for *synderesis.* Bonaventure classifies the opinions he found in his predecessors. There are those who make *synderesis* a faculty, the *pars superior rationis.* (In this case conscience is a *habitus* informing the faculty, and natural law is the object of the information). And there are those who distinguish between the natural and the deliberate movements of the faculties, making *synderesis* a faculty concerning good and evil in general, conscience a *habitus* concerning good and evil in the particular, while natural law *indifferenter se habet ad utrumque.* Bonaventure's own view is that *synderesis* is the faculty of reason endowed with the habitual knowledge of first principles, which he calls *naturale quoddam pondus dirigens . . . in appetendis.*[70]

In St. Albert the Great the Aristotelian influence is even more marked than in Bonaventure. Albert passes in review the current authorities (who made *synderesis* a faculty, or a faculty endowed with a *habitus,* or the practical reason, or the sum of the faculties, or a remnant of original justice), before, himself, defining it as a faculty endowed with the *habitus* of the principles of natural law. Then, developing the parallel between the speculative and the practical reason, Albert identifies these principles of the natural law as the unlearned, innate source of our knowledge of the distinction between good and evil, together with the most general applications of that distinction.[71]

St. Albert's doctrine of *synderesis* is completed by his teaching on conscience. Here he makes what is, perhaps, his most striking innovation in these questions. Before his time conscience had

[68] *Nicomachean Ethics,* VI, 1–2, 1139 a 6 – b 14.

[69] *In 2 Sent.,* d. 39, a. 1, q. 2 (ed. Quaracchi, t. 2, pp. 901–904); J.F. Quinn, "St.Bonaventure's Fundamental Conception of Natural Law" in *S. Bonaventura* 1274–1974, III, pp. 572–580.

[70] *In 2 Sent.,* d. 39, a. 2, q. 1 (ed.Quaracchi, t. 2, p. 910); J.F. Quinn, *op. cit.,* pp. 580–584.

[71] *Summa de creaturis,* II, q. 71, a. 1 (*Opera omnia,* ed. Borgnet, t. 35, p. 593).

been identified, by various authors in turn, with the natural law, with *synderesis* and with free-will; and the resulting confusion was considerable. About the middle of the thirteenth century, when Albert was writing,[72] the majority of writers seem to have connected conscience with a *habitus* of some kind; conscience was a *habitus*, innate or acquired, or partly both, or even a faculty endowed with an innate *habitus*. There was, it is true, a certain foreshadowing of the identification of conscience with an *act* of the reason;[73] but it was left to St. Albert to ensure the acceptance of this view. The Aristotelian doctrine of the practical syllogism is laid under contribution, as also Aristotle's teaching on the relation between the speculative and the practical intellect.[74] The practical syllogism uses a major premiss, provided by *synderesis*, and a minor premiss, the work of reason (which brings the particular under the general rule laid down in the major premiss); and conscience draws the conclusion.[75] The same view is found, further developed, in the questions *De sinderesi* and *De conscientia* now attributed to Albert and in the *Summa theologiae* where, however, some vestiges of older views may be discerned.[76]

The idea of *synderesis* as the habitual knowledge of first moral principles, providing the major premiss of the practical syllogism

[72] The chronology of Albert's writings is a difficult and still unsettled question. The *Summa de creaturis* seems, however, to be an early work, 1240–1243, while the unfinished *Summa theologiae* (which shows the influence of Alexander of Hales but not of the *Summa theologiae* of St. Thomas) is a late work, 1270–1280. Cf. F. Van Steenberghen, *La philosophie au XIIIe siècle*, pp. 273–274.

[73] Texts in O. Lottin, *op. cit.*, II, pp. 166, 171, 173–174, 188–193, 196, 199–200 etc.

[74] Albert does not seem to have had the full text of the *Nicomachean Ethics* until about 1248 (the translation of Robert Grosseteste, which he used, was published in 1245?). Cf. A. Pelzer, "Le cours inédit d'Albert le Grand sur la Morale à Nicomaque, recueilli et rédigé par S. Thomas d'Aquin," in *Etudes d'histoire littéraire sur la scolastique médiévale*, pp. 272–235; F. Van Steenberghen, *op. cit.*, p. 278.

[75] *Summa de creaturis*, II, q. 72, a. 1 (*Opera omnia*, ed. Borgnet, t. 35, p. 599): "Dicimus quod conscientia conclusio est rationis practicae ex duobus praemissis, quorum major synderesis et minor rationis. . . . Major autem istius syllogismi est synderesis, cujus est inclinare in bonum per universales rationes boni. Minor vero est rationis cujus est conferre particulare ad universale. Conclusio autem est conscientiae."

[76] Cf. F.M. Henquinet, "Vingt-deux questions inédites d'Albert le Grand dans un manuscript à l'usage de S. Thomas d'Aquin" in *The New Scholasticism*, 9 (1935), pp. 312–322; Albert, *Summa theologiae*, II, tr. 16, q. 99, m. 3, a. 2, q. 1: Utrum conscientia sit eadem quod lex naturalis; Id. q. 2: Utrum conscientia sit semper in actu vel aliquando in habitu (*Opera omnia*, ed. Borgnet, t. 33, p. 244).

in which the actual drawing of the conclusion was the work of conscience, was an extremely important one. As has already been suggested, it went a good deal beyond the function Aristotle saw in the practical syllogism. In fact the practical syllogism, as Albert saw it, will play a vital part in the great natural law synthesis of St. Thomas Aquinas; and, perhaps ironically, *synderesis* itself will play a progressively less important part.

CHAPTER VI

AQUINAS FACES THE NATURAL LAW TRADITION

The complexity of the tradition, the variety of the strands to be woven together in the mid-thirteenth century, demanded a synthesist of genius. One such was found in St. Thomas Aquinas. Here there is no question of expounding once again his doctrine of the natural law – although some elements in such an exposition will be appealed to later in this book, as part of the argument that the profile of the natural law sketched by Aquinas can be restored and, indeed, must be, if the natural law is to continue to be man's moral court of appeal. At present it will be instructive to examine Aquinas's thought on the natural law with the aim of seeing what he made of the tradition. Such treatment will necessarily be selective. One may begin with an excellent example, both of his indebtedness and of his independence, in his approach to *synderesis.*

A. AQUINAS ON *SYNDERESIS*

In brief it can be said that *synderesis* is prominent in the early works of St. Thomas, as it had been in those of his predecessors, but plays a very minor role in his later works. On the other hand, his later thought, in the *Summa theologiae,* develops the idea of the first principles of the practical reason in terms of a philosophy of law, while the earlier works lack an analysis of the notion of law. The change seems to be significant.

The word *synderesis,* as we have seen, originated in a misreading of a passage in St. Jerome's *Commentary on Ezechiel,* but its illegitimate birth did not prevent its becoming the focus of an important body of moral teaching by the mid-thirteenth century. St. Thomas could not easily avoid it. He deals with it at some length in the *Commentary on the Sentences* and in the *De veritate.*

He argues in both works that *synderesis* is the *habitus* of first principles in the practical intellect. His conclusion makes some concessions to the controversies of the time. He concedes that synderesis may be a habit only, or it may be a faculty subject in us to an innate habit.[1] But the concessions are hardly warranted by the argument and they are soon tacitly abandoned. *Synderesis* is viewed in terms of the Aristotelian practical syllogism. This doctrine that the moral situation can be expressed in the form of a syllogism (or a sorites) had been used to good effect by St. Albert the Great when he said – and was, perhaps, the first to say – that conscience is neither a faculty nor a *habitus* but an act.[2] St. Thomas agrees that conscience is an act, the actual application of the principles known habitually in *synderesis; synderesis* and conscience, in his view, imply each other.[3]

In his early works St. Thomas proves the existence of *synderesis* in two ways. The first depends upon the analogy of reasoning with motion.[4] Every movement must proceed from an immovable mover. Everything that undergoes change must depend upon something that remains one and the same. Now reasoning is a sort of change, a movement from principles to conclusions. It must begin in knowledge *quae uniformitatem et quietem quamdam habeat.* Such knowledge is not arrived at by the normal discursive activity of the intellect but *subito intellectui offertur.* It is the knowledge of first self-evident principles, called in speculative matters *intellectus,* and in practical *synderesis.* Or more accurately, *synderesis* is the *habitus* of such first principles in the practical intellect.

The same argument, in essentials, is reproduced in the *De veritate.*[5]

The second argument for the existence of *synderesis* is much less Aristotelian. It is based upon the 'cosmic-continuity principle' found in the *Divine Names* of the pseudo-Denis the Areopagite.[6] The principle means that, in an ordered hierarchy of beings, adjacent members resemble each other in that the less perfect participates, in its less perfect way, in the perfection of the more perfect. Creation is just such an ordered hierarchy. No being,

[1] *In 2 Sent.,* d. 24, q. 2, a. 3.

[2] *Summa de creaturis,* II, q. 72, a. 1 (*Opera omnia,* ed. Borgnet, t. 35, p. 599).

[3] *In 2 Sent.,* d. 24, q. 2, a. 3; d. 39, q. 3, a. 1 ad 2; *De veritate,* q. 17, aa. 1–5.

[4] *In 2 Sent.,* d. 24, q. 2, a. 3.

[5] q. 16, a. 2.

[6] c. 7, n. 3 (ed. Pera, n. 324).

except God, is self-sufficient; all others are intermediate, links between lower and higher. So the pseudo-Denis accommodated to the Christian scheme of things the neo-Platonic idea that the cosmos is necessarily hierarchical, a pyramid whose apex is the One.

Man and angel are neighbours in the cosmic hierarchy. The continuity-principle suggests, then, that man at the highest point of his achievement, namely in his activity of knowing, should attain to something of the perfection of angelic knowledge. Because he is a rational nature, united to a body, man normally knows discursively; an angel knows intuitively.

The argument recurs, in greater detail, in the *De veritate*[7] Here St. Thomas shows the dependence of all subsequent discursive knowledge on the stable and certain apprehension of first principles.

Finally,[8] St. Thomas combines the two arguments, the neo-Platonic and that based upon the analogy of reasoning with motion. Discursive reasoning and intuitive apprehension are said to be related as coming-to-be and being or as motion and rest, in general, as imperfect to perfect acts of the same faculty of reason.

In the *Summa theologiae*, in which St. Thomas rehandles so many of the concepts found in his early works, one expects to find an extended discussion of *synderesis*. But the term, outside of the single laconic article devoted to it, is scarcely referred to.[9] In this article St. Thomas suggests, with the minimum of elaboration, that *synderesis* is not a special faculty, but rather a *habitus*. He rehearses briefly the familiar argument that reasoning, since it is a kind of motion, requires a fixed starting point. He omits entirely the argument from the neo-Platonic principle of continuity. The reason for the rejection is not any rejection of the principle of the pseudo-Denis; St. Thomas makes frequent use of that principle elsewhere in the *Summa*, and notably in the previous question.[10] The references to *synderesis* in connection with the natural law, where one would expect it to be highly relevant, are no more than passing references. And in one context St. Thomas speaks of "naturally known principles" of the practical reason in such a way

[7] q. 16, a. 1.

[8] *De verit.*, q. 15, a. 1.

[9] 1a, q. 79, a. 12. *Synderesis* is mentioned in 1a, q. 79, preamble; q. 79, a. 12 (18 times; q. 79, a. 13 (3 times); 1–2ae, q.94, a. 1, (3 times); 2–2ae, q. 47, a. 6 ad 1 et ad 3.

[10] 1a. q. 78, a. 2. See J. Durantel, *S. Thomas et le pseudo-Denys*, p. 189, n. 165 cited by J. Legrand, *L'univers et l'homme dans la philosophie de s. Thomas*, t. 1, p. 267, n. 1.

as to make it seem that he is deliberately avoiding the word *synderesis;* the term occurs only in the replies to the objections.[11] Something has clearly made St. Thomas lose interest in *synderesis.*

Before attempting to assign reasons for this loss of interest it will be profitable to examine a concept that acquires prominence with the decline of *synderesis;* law.

The word 'law' frequently appears in the works of St. Thomas; the natural law is discussed at some length in the *Commentary on the Sentences* and the *lex divina* in the *Contra Gentiles,* to take only two examples;[12] but what is not found in St. Thomas prior to the *Summa* is an analysis of the general notion of law. Aristotle in the *Nicomachean Ethics* had described law as a "rule proceeding from a sort of practical wisdom and reason" and so gave commentators an opportunity of discussing the nature of law.[13] It is curious that none of St. Thomas's predecessors, even of those who in the thirteenth century were writing *Tractatus de legibus,* should have made a study of the notion of law as such. St. Albert the Great did anticipate some of the elements of St. Thomas's handling of law[14] but the analysis that appears in *1-2ae, q. 90* is very largely St. Thomas's own. The definition of law to which it leads has passed firmly into the tradition: *Lex nihil aliud est quam ordinatio rationis ad bonum commune ab eo qui curam habet communitatis promulgata.*[15]

When he asks the question if there be such a thing as a natural law St. Thomas stresses the fact that rational creatures so participate in the eternal law that their participation is *aliquid rationis* and has the other qualities of law. And, in the later question devoted to the natural law, it transpires that this law consists of the first principles of the practical reason, together with the conclusions that can be drawn from them.[16] St. Thomas still thinks, with Aristotle, that the moral situation is represented by the practical syllogism. But, whereas he had formerly said that the major premiss of this syllogism is provided by *synderesis,* he now contents himself with saying that the major premiss is

[11] 1-2ae, q. 47, a. 6, ad 1 et ad 3.

[12] *In 4 Sent.,* d. 33, qq. 1,2; *Cont. gent.,* III, cc. 114–121.

[13] *Nic. Eth.,* X, 9, 1180 a 21.

[14] Cf. O. Lottin, "La loi en général; la définition thomiste et ses antécédents" in *Psychologie et morale aux XIIe et XIIIe siècles,* II, pp. 11–47.

[15] 1–2ae, q. 90, a. 4.

[16] 1–2ae, q. 91, a. 2; q. 94.

provided by the first principles (*quaedam praecepta communissima*) of the practical order. He only once says that the *habitus* of these principles is called *synderesis*, and that in the most perfunctory manner in the reply to an objection.[17] The *Summa* no longer says, as had the *Commentary on the Sentences*, *lex naturalis nominat ipsa universalia principa iuris, synderesis vero nominat habitum.*[18]

It is clear then, that, by the time he came to write his *Summa theologiae*, St. Thomas no longer regarded *synderesis* as a term of importance. At least that is true of him when he wrote the *Secunda Pars;* for it is possible that he was brief on the subject of *synderesis* in the *Prima Pars* because he then still had the intention of discusssing it fully in the 1–2ae. It would be tempting to think that the new factor in the situation, at the time of writing of the *Secunda Pars*, was St. Thomas's acquaintance with the complete text of the *Nicomachean Ethics* in the version (rather a revision of Grosseteste's translation) of William of Moerbeke. The Aristotelian practical syllogism, already well known to him, together with the elaboration of the concept of law as verified in the natural law, provided a terminology particularly apt to express what St. Thomas had to say about the first principles of the practical reason. In the *Commentary on the Sentences* he had spoken of *synderesis loco cuius Philosophus in VI Ethicorum ponit intellectum in operativis.*[19] But it is remarkable that, in the notes he took of St. Albert's lectures on the *Nicomachean Ethics*, neither *synderesis* nor conscience is discussed. In his own, late *Commentary on the Ethics* St. Thomas never mentions the word *synderesis.* Had he gradually become aware of the fact that, despite the doctrine of the practical syllogism, Aristotle has nothing to say about habitual knowledge of first practical principles? Such habitual knowledge would even be a superfluity in the Aristotelian system, in which the virtue of prudence is conceived as that concerned with particulars rather than with generalities.[20]

Again, it will have been noticed that *synderesis* appears in the early works of St. Thomas as a term with certain neo-Platonic overtones. One of the two arguments used to establish its existence is expressly neo-Platonic in its basis on the cosmic-

[17] *In 2 Sent.*, d. 24, q. 2, a. 4; 1–2ae, q. 94, a. 1 ad 2.

[18] *In 2 Sent.*, d. 24, q. 2, a. 4.

[19] *In 3 Sent.*, d. 33, q. 2, a. 4, sol. 4.

[20] O. Lottin, *op. cit.*, II, p. 218, note 1; Th. Deman, *La prudence* (*Somme théologique* ed. de la *Revue des jeunes*, II–IIae, q. 47–56), pp. 429–437.

continuity principle of the pseudo-Denis. And in the other argument, from the analogy between reasoning and motion, St. Thomas shows an anxiety to guard *synderesis* from any imputation of innate ideas. In short, *synderesis* could be regarded as a term with embarrassing associations, at least epistemologically; and, consequently, as a term for which St. Thomas would be glad to find a substitute. This is quite consistent with the retention of many neo-Platonic elements in the mature metaphysics of St. Thomas, elements more frequent and more important than at one time was thought; and, indeed, it is consistent with his retention of other phraseology more Platonic than Aristotelian in its epistemological associations. There is, for example, the illumination-theme of which St. Thomas makes use in his consideration of the natural law all through his career. He applies to the natural law the question and answer of the Psalmist: "Who shall show us good things? The light of your countenance is sealed upon us, O Lord,"[21] And, of course, there is the fundamental conception of the natural law as a *participation* of the eternal law.

Yet when all this is granted, it seems not too much to say that the eclipse of *synderesis* indicates an important evolution in the thought of St. Thomas. Not merely does it indicate an abandonment of a neo-Platonizing moral philosophy (if the term is not too strong) for one more consonant with Aristotelianism; it points to the central importance of the reasoning process in matters of natural law and underlines the conviction that the precepts of the natural law must be rational propositions. The acquisition and use of such propositions about morals can be quite well explained without having to appeal to the term *synderesis.*

B. AQUINAS AND THE DEFINITIONS OF THE NATURAL LAW

Is Aquinas as independent in his handling of his predecessors' definitions of the natural law as he is in his approach to *synderesis?* This is a large question and involves facing the entire cluster of concepts, of which *synderesis* is only one, connected with the natural law. Here it is argued that his thought on the natural law shows a development quite as remarkable as that evidenced by his approach to *synderesis.* To establish this conclusion it is, fortunately, not necessary to rehearse St. Thomas's synthesis of natural law teaching in its entirety. That, in any event, has been

[21] Ps. 4; 6–7; 1–2ae, q. 91, a. 2; *In S. Pauli ad Rom.*, II, lect. 3; *Opusc. de II praeceptis caritatis et X legis praeceptis*, c. 1.

the subject of numerous important studies. The argument can be selective, and may begin by concentrating upon his attitude towards the definitions of natural law presented to him by his predecessors and contemporaries and representing what we have seen to be a long and not uncomplicated tradition.

The picture that emerges is that of a number of relatively isolated discussions in the early works, giving way to the systematic treatment of the natural law in the *Summa theologiae* towards the end of his career. It comes as no surprise that in the earliest discussions of the theme, in the *Commentary on the Sentences* (1253–1255) and in the Disputed Question *De veritate* which immediately followed, a number of ideas of natural law should compete for his assent, ideas coming from predecessors like Albert the Great and supported by authorities like Cicero, Augustine, Ulpian or Gratian. He speaks, for example, of natural law as "the concept naturally impressed upon man," adding that it directs man's actions, both those that pertain to his generic (animal) nature, such as generation, eating and the like, as well as those that belong to his specific (human) nature, like reasoning and so on.[22] The reference to the generic nature seems clearly designed to accommodate Ulpian's definition–"natural law is what nature has taught all animals." But that the animal nature of man is a good deal less important than what specifies man as a rational being is also apparent – not merely from the development in the context but also from the concept of natural law that is made explicit in the cognate discussions of *synderesis* and conscience already noticed.[23] In the *Summa theologiae*[24] the natural law is firmly situated within the law-tract and tied to the preceding discussions of law in general and eternal law. Natural law, like any law "a work of mind for the common good coming from a legislative authority and promulgated," is properly defined as "the rational creature's participation in the eternal law." All this clearly marks a considerable advance. This broad outline, however, needs qualification. And one of the details that does quite fit is Ulpian's definition. For, agreeing somewhat uneasily with some of Aquinas's early formulations, it is impossible to reconcile with his mature thought on the essence of the natural law. Yet Ulpian

[22] *In 4 Sent.*, d. 33, q. 1, a. 1: "Lex ergo naturalis nihil est aliud quam conceptio homini naturaliter indita qua dirigitur ad convenienter agendum in actionibus propriis, sive competant ei ex natura generis ut generare, comedere et hujusmodi, sive ex natura speciei ut ratiocinari et similia."

[23] *In 2 Sent.*, d. 24, q. 2, a. 3; d. 39, q. 3, a. 1; *De verit.*, q. 16.

[24] 1-2ae, q. 90; q. 94.

remains in honour throughout Aquinas's career and the definition is even termed "the most proper definition" – a view in which Bonaventure, as has been seen, but almost no other thirteenth century scholastic, concurred. The matter deserves closer examination.

In the *Commentary on the Sentences* Aquinas, like any other commentator on Lombard, was faced with the problem of the natural law, notably in the discussion of marriage in Book IV, distinction 33. One of the questions raised was: It it against the natural law to have more than one wife? The question had a peculiar acuteness for a theologian, aware of the sacramental character of marriage but aware, too, of Old Testament practices, condoned if not actually approved, in the matter of polygamy and divorce. On the question of polygamy the conclusion reached by St. Thomas, is that polygamy is against the secondary precepts, although not against the primary precepts, of the natural law. This important distinction between primary and secondary precepts is destined to play a leading part in all subsequent discussions of the natural law. St. Thomas's authority is most often invoked for it – but he was not the originator of it, nor was his assigning of its basis free of ambiguity.[25] It is a distinction to which we shall return. For the present we may turn our attention to St. Thomas's conclusion that a plurality of wives is at least contrary to the secondary precepts of the natural law. An obvious objection is posed by Ulpian's definition – for nature has clearly not taught all animals that a plurality of mates is wrong. In replying to this objection St. Thomas sets out the three senses of natural law: (i) natural law is so called because "its principle is nature." It proceeds from, or is impressed by, nature. This meaning of the term is associated with Cicero's view that natural law is not generated by human opinion but implanted by an innate power (*quod non opinio genuit sed quaedam innata vis*

[25] A.H. Chroust, "The Philosophy of Law from St. Augustine to St. Thomas Aquinas" in *The New Scholasticism*, 20 (1946), p. 43 discusses the distinction in Roland of Cremona. See also the review of A. Cortesi's edition (Bergamo, 1962) of Book III of the *Summa* of Roland, in F. Van Steenberghen, *La bibliothèque du philosophe médiéviste*, pp. 86–89; Id, *La philosophie au XIIIe siècle*, pp. 157–158. O. Lottin, *Le droit naturel chez S. Thomas d'Aquin et ses prédécesseurs*, p. 76 had said: "La formule est une création de saint Thomas; elle n'apparaît pas, que nous sachions, chez ses prédécesseurs, mais elle ne laisse pas d'être quelque peu mystérieuse." This view needs to be qualified. Another possible source is William of Auvergne's distinction between precepts of the natural law *primae necessitatis* and precepts *secundae necessitatis;* cf. O. Lottin, *Psychologie et morale aux XIIe et XIIIe siècles*, II, p. 76.

inseruit); (ii) natural law, in a second sense "proceeds from an extrinsic principle which is above nature." In this sense, says St. Thomas, what is of divine law may be said to belong to the natural law, because it comes from and is infused by a higher principle, namely God. Thus he accommodates Gratian's definition (which, incidentally, he wrongly ascribes to Isidore) "natural law is what is contained in the law and the gospel." (iii) The third sense in which natural law can be understood is that upon which the objection depends. Natural law is so called "not merely because its principle is nature but also because it is concerned with the things of nature." Now, since nature is contrasted with reason, which is the distinguishing mark of man, it follows that the law which is proper to man, even though it be dictated by natural reason, is not the natural law in the strictest meaning of the term. That distinction must be reserved for the dictates of natural reason in matters common to man and animals alike. Hence Ulpian's definition.[26]

It is clear that, in this passage, St. Thomas is straining to give a tolerable meaning to some of the definitions that were firmly enshrined in the tradition coming down to him. The first, reminiscent of Cicero, really includes a whole series of definitions which are similar but not verbally identical; and it is hard to escape the impression that they represent the direction in which the thought of Aquinas is moving. The second definition – Gratian's – represents, as we have seen, a highly ambiguous formula. In the *Summa contra Gentiles* Aquinas will have a good deal to say about the 'divine law' (*lex divina*) which, at least in some of his statements, is taken to include the natural law; but the radical confusion between the natural law and the divine positive law is only removed finally in the *Summa theologiae*.[27] The difficulties surrounding St. Thomas's welcome for Ulpian's natural law seem more serious. He is concerned, as always, to find a tolerable meaning for a definition which came to him with a weight of authority behind it. He cannot reject it entirely; but in accepting it he must somehow change its sense. For a natural law genuinely common to man and animals is patently unreal – as many before him, and notably St. Albert the Great, had seen. By making it consist, instead, in the dictates of natural reason concerning that which man and animals have in common, namely sensitive nature,

[26] *In 4 Sent.*, d. 33, q. 1, a. 1 ad 4; J.M. Aubert, *Le droit romain dans l'oeuvre de saint Thomas*, p. 98, calls these respectively definition by intrinsic principle, by supreme extrinsic principle and by essence or content expressed.

[27] 1-2ae, q. 94, a. 4 ad 1.

St. Thomas gives the definition as acceptable a meaning as is, perhaps, possible. But the point of the objection he is answering is that a natural law common to man and animals does *not* prohibit polygamy. If he rejected such a natural law it would be understandable. But, having accepted it (in the sense just indicated) it is difficult to see why he felt obliged to concede that this natural law does not, in fact, forbid polygamy to man. In a similar context Albert had pointed out that nature teaches animals differently according to their different species inclining some to monogamous unions, others to polygamy.[28] St. Thomas is not at all unaware of this observation that polygamy may well be against what nature has taught some animals, since nature dictates to each animal in a way suitable to its species. In some species the care of both parents is required for the upbringing of the progeny and, in such cases, an instinct of nature sees to the preservation of a stable union of one male with one female. Elsewhere in the *Commentary on the Sentences*, when he asks the question whether marriage is natural[29] and when he discusses the natural law status of consanguinity as a marriage-impediment,[30] Thomas admirably develops this difference between the natural inclinations of the various species of animals. But in the present context, which cries out for a similar suggestion, he is content to forgo such a solution. At the very least the context is ambiguous.[31]

This point, whose importance is that it stresses a weakness in St. Thomas's thought on the natural law, may be put in the form of a dilemma. The natural dictate prescribing monogamy for the human race is essentially an animal instinct or it is not. If it is,

[28] *In 4 Sent.*, d. 33A, a. 1 ad 4 (*Opera omina* ed. Borgent, t. 30, p. 290): Natura omnia animalia hoc docet sed diversimode secundum diversitatem specierum."

[29] *In 4 Sent.*, d. 26, q. 1, a. 1 ad 1: "... Et sicut natura generis, quamvis sit una in omnibus animalibus, non tamen est eodem modo in omnibus; ita etiam non inclinat eodem modo in omnibus sed secundum quod unicuique competit...."

[30] *In 4Sent.*, d. 40, q. 1, a. 3 ad 3: "... Conjunctio maris et feminae dicitur esse de jure naturali quia natura hoc omnia animalia docuit; sed hanc conjunctionem diversa animalia diversimode docuit secundum diversas eorum conditiones..."

[31] *In 4 Sent.*, d, 33, q. 1, a 3 ad 4: cf. *Cont Gent.*, III, c. 124, n. 2; J. M. Aubert, *op. cit.*, pp. 98–99, seems to interpret St. Thomas too favourably here: "Le développement de l'article insère cette ... définition dans le même contexte idéologique que précédemment; la nature de l'homme est double, générique elle s'exprime dans la fin primaire du mariage; spécifique dans la fin secondaire. La bigamie ne s'opposant pas à la réalisation de la première, n'est pas contraire au droit naturel entendu au sens d'Ulpien; ce droit, tout en portant sur des inclinations communes à tout le règne animal, n'en est pas moins réglé par la raison; et sous cet aspect il est alors synonyme de loi naturelle, dont il exprime un des principes premiers."

then Ulpian's definition may be literally true – and, in any case, St. Thomas's interpretation of it is superfluous from the point of view of excluding polygamy. If, on the other hand, something other than a purely animal instinct is required to exclude polygamy in the case of man, then St. Thomas's interpretation of Ulpian is justified but his immediate concession that natural law – taken in this sense – does *not* forbid polygamy becomes difficult to understand. Why did St. Thomas give what may be a strained interpretation of *quod natura omnia animalia docuit* and then fail to use this interpretation to advantage? It appears not too much to say that the difficulty although not grave in itself, is yet symptomatic of St. Thomas's diffidence in handling what we have seen to be a formidable tradition.[32]

It has already been suggested that this formidable tradition made its impact even on the mature thought of St. Thomas, which might be supposed to have moved away from Ulpian's conception of the natural law. The contexts in which Ulpian's definition appears are well-known and have been much studied. Here it will suffice to indicate the problems they raise.

Ulpian makes his appearance in the *Summa theologiae*, an important appearance even though the part he plays is reduced. Thomas's mature thought on the natural law had moved further away from Ulpian. He, indeed, says as much in the article on the existence of a natural law, ending in the classical definition: Natural law is the rational creature's participation in the eternal law.[33] The third objection is a rather captious one, turning on the proposition that the freer a thing is the less it is under law. Men, being self-determining creatures, are, then freer than animals and

[32] G. Fassò, *La legge della ragione*, p. 80, points out with justice that St. Thomas's fascination for Ulpian's definition did not blind him to the fact that law is something exclusively rational. "Qualche passo di opere minori o giovanili potrebbe far pensare che l'Aquinate, per verità, si sia lasciato suggestionato dalla definizione di Ulpiano. Pero anche in esse la fondamentale distinzione tra esseri razionali ed esseri irrazionali – come destinatari della legge naturale – non manca mai." He cites in evidence St. Thomas's distinction between the natural law of man and the natural instinct of animals: *In* 4 *Sent.*, d. 33, q. 1, a. 1: "quia homo inter caetera animalia rationem finis cognoscit, et proportionem operis ad finem, ideo naturalis conceptio ei naturaliter indita, qua dirigitur ad operandum convenienter, lex naturalis vel ius naturale dicitur; in caeteris autem aestimatio naturalis vocatur. Bruta enim ex vi naturae impelluntur ad operandum convenientes actiones magis quam regulentur quasi proprio arbitrio agentia." Cf. S. Cotta, *Il concetto di legge nella Summa theologiae di s. Tommaso d'Aquino*, pp. 60–61.

[33] 1-2ae, q. 91, a. 2.

consequently less under law. This implication constitutes an objection to the conclusion of the article only on the assumption that animals are *not* under the natural law. And in his reply Aquinas concedes the point; and it seems decisive against Ulpian's definition:

Even irrational animals share in the eternal law in their own way, as also does the rational creature. But because the rational creature shares in it intellectually and rationally, therefore the participation of the eternal law in the rational creature is properly called a *law;* for law is a function of reason: but in the irrational creature it is not shared rationally; hence cannot be called a *law* except by a similitude.[34]

The same point is made in a later article in which Aquinas points out once again that law has to do with reason. A consequence is that man cannot impose a law upon irrational creatures, no matter how subject they are to him; "but on rational beings subject to him he can impose a law, inasmuch as by his precept or proclamation he impresses on their minds a rule, which is a principle of action... Hence in some way irrational creatures are subject to the eternal law, as being set in motion by divine providence; but not by any understanding of the divine precept, as rational creatures are."[35] The case against Ulpian's definition must seem to be closed. And if St. Thomas were entirely consistent it would be.

In *Prima-Secundae*, q. 94, art. *2* the question is raised whether the natural law contains several precepts or one only. St. Thomas's handling of the question has beeen justly called his "key-discussion of the natural law."[36] It begins with an exploration of what self-evidence might mean in relation to moral imperatives, continues with an appeal to the parallel between the activities of the speculative and the practical intellect and ends with an articulation of the precepts of the natural law following upon the different levels of natural tendency found in man. Man's

[34] *Ibid.*, ad 3: "Ad tertium dicundum quod etiam animalia irrationabilia participant rationem aeternam suo modo, sicut et rationalis creatura. Sed, quia rationalis creatura participat eam intellectualiter et rationaliter, ideo participatio legis aeternae in creatura rationali proprie lex vocatur; nam lex est aliquid rationis, ut supra dictum est, quaest. praec. art 1; in creatura autem irrationali non participatur rationaliter; unde non potest dici lex nisi per similitudinem."

[35] 1–2ae, q. 93, a. 5 "... Aliquo modo creaturae irrationales subduntur legi aeternae, inquantum moventur a divina providentia; non autem per intellectum divini praecepti, sicut creaturae rationales."

[36] By T. Gilby in his edition and translation of 1–2ae, qq. 90–97, *Law and Political Theory*, p. 78 note.

nature may be considered in the order of substance (with a tendency to persevere in being), in the order of animal life (with tendencies like those towards the coupling of male and female and the rearing of offspring) and in the order of reason (with tendencies to avoid ignorance, to cooperate with fellow-men and so on).[37] This classification is reminiscent of the triple acceptation of the *jus naturae* found in the *Glossa ordinaria* of Johannes Teutonicus on the *Digest.*[38] But it is curious that Ulpian whose authority, could appropriately have been invoked in the case of the tendencies related to the animal nature of man, is not mentioned[39] Is the passage a setting constructed for Ulpian's natural law? Or does the argument from silence indicate St. Thomas's basic rejection of Ulpian? There is here an ambivalence that is not remedied in the article under consideration.[40]

Ulpian, however, has not disappeared; in the very next question he makes an unmistakable return, albeit discreetly and anonymously. The logic of Isidore's division of human law is in question and, in particular, his putting of the *jus gentium* as a kind of human law 'used by nearly all peoples,'[41] Nowadays it would be regarded as misplaced ingenuity to attempt to introduce logical consistency into the divisions of Isidore. Further, to add a spice to the enterprise, the division of human laws into *jus gentium* and *jus civile* here attributed to Isidore by St. Thomas is not found formally in Isidore. An argument could even be made out that Isidore included *jus naturale* under human law for, shortly before the passage St. Thomas has in mind, he uses the phrase: *jus lex humana est.* The division found by St. Thomas seems to be a conflation of the two divisions in St. Isidore, the division of laws into divine and human and the classical trichotomy, *jus naturale, civile* and *gentium.* Now another of Isidore's *dicta* was that divine laws belonged to nature, human

[37] 1–2ae, q. 94, a. 2.

[38] J.M. Aubert, *op. cit.*, p. 101, note 1.

[39] T. Gilby, *op. cit.*, p. 82 note: "Ulpian's authority is not acknowledged here, though his sentiment is adopted, a sentiment more embarrassing to a lawyer than to an Aristotelean theologian...."

[40] There is a similar ambiguity in Gilby's note on the passage, *op. cit.*, p. 81: "The text here reads 'lex naturae,' not the more usual 'lex naturalis'; the terms are used synonymously, nevertheless the former, 'the law of nature,' more strongly suggests, though the point is not to be laboured, the non-moral and biological drives, here noticed, which underlie man's moral activity according to 'natural law' in the proper sense of the term."

[41] 1–2ae, q. 95, a. 4 ad 1.

laws to custom.[42] What easier, then, than to assimilate *jus naturale* to divine law and *jus gentium* (together with *jus civile*) to human law?[43]

When the objection is pressed that *jus gentium*, on Isidore's own showing (*quia eo omnes fere gentes utuntur*), belongs more to natural law than to human law, Ulpian comes to the rescue:

The *jus gentium* is indeed natural to man in the sense that he is reasonable, inasmuch as it is derived from the natural law by way of conclusion; and, not being far-removed, men readily agree about it. Nevertheless it is distinct from the natural law, most of all from the natural law common to all animals.[44]

The answer, while it meets the current difficulty, raises further problems. For, in arguing that the *jus gentium* consists of conclusions from principles of natural law, St. Thomas appears to have overlooked that he had already suggested, in the same question, that what follows as a conclusion from natural law is itself natural law.

Similar matters arise when we turn to the *Secunda-Secundae.* Here the topic is *jus*, the "object of justice." It is part of the discussion of the cardinal virtue of justice; and the viewpoint is, as might have been expected, different from that of the law-tract in the *Prima-Secundae.*[45]

Thomas asks whether the division of *jus* into *jus naturale* and *jus positivum* is exhaustive, and whether *jus gentium* and *jus naturale* are distinct or identical. The questions are connected; and the affirmative answer to the first leads on to the latter. And it is here that Ulpian's definition comes once more into play.[46]

Is the *jus gentium* better assimilated to natural law or to positive law? St. Thomas, in order to answer this question, examines the element of equivalence in *jus*, the object of justice. The equivalence may be in the very nature of a given

[42] *Etym.*, V, 2–4 (P.L., 82; 198–199): "Divinae (leges) naturae, humanae moribus constant."

[43] Cf. L. Clément, "Le jus gentium" in *Revue de l'Université d'Ottawa,* Section spéciale, 9–10 (1940), pp. 188–191.

[44] 1-2ae, q. 95, art 4 ad 1: "Jus gentium est quidem aliquo modo naturale homini, secundum quod est rationalis, inquantum derivatur a lege naturali per modum conclusionis quae non est multum remota a principiis. Unde de facili in hujusmodi homines consenserunt. Distinguitur tamen a lege naturali maximo ab eo quod est omnibus animalibus commune."

[45] 2–2ae, q. 57.

[46] 2–2ae, q. 57, aa. 2,3.

relationship – male is related to female for the purposes of generation or parent to child for the purposes of education. In such cases we have *jus naturale* absolutely speaking. But it may be that a relationship, of itself, does not give us enough information. Private property is an example: a field is no more mine than yours apart from outside considerations about efficient cultivation, peaceful possession, etc. Here we have *jus naturale*, but with a qualification. And the two kinds are reconciled for St. Thomas by the jurisconsults. He cites Ulpian for natural law in the absolute sense and Gaius for natural law in the qualified sense: Ulpian is not named explicitly, although Gaius is. But Ulpian's definition plays a critical role in solving the difficulty. Whether the solution, making the *jus gentium* a natural law peculiar to man, is consistent with the suggestion noticed in the *Prima-Secundae* that *jus gentium* belongs more to positive law, is another matter.

Further discussion of these terminological and other difficulties would require an examination of St. Thomas's handling of the two classical dispositions of the *jus gentium*, slavery and private property, and would be beyond the scope of the present study. It suffices to have indicated that, in the matter of definitions, St. Thomas has allowed himself to be swayed by the authority of the moment – Isidore or Ulpian – and has, in consequence, fallen into inconsistencies.[47]

One might ask, however, whether too much stress has not been laid upon some passing references in the *Summa* to Ulpian. Sergio Cotta, for one,[48] argues strongly and convincingly that St. Thomas's conception of the natural law in the *Summa theologiae* is irreconcilable with Ulpian's definition and rejects out of hand any concession to a law common to man and irrational creatures. It is easy, however, to overstate a good case. Ulpian plays a greater part in the mature thought of Aquinas than is suggested by

[47] Cf. J. Sauter, *Die philosophischen Grundlagen des Naturrechts*, p. 76: "Die römische Terminologie spielt ihm hier einen ganz bösen Streich." Efforts to explain away the inconsistencies are frequently weakened by the fact that they depend upon a much clearer distinction between *jus naturale* and *lex naturalis* than St. Thomas made in practice. Cf. B.C. Kuhlmann, *Der Gesetzbegriff beim hl. Thomas von Aquin im Lichte des Rechtsstudiums seiner Zeit*, p. 171, note 1; V. Cathrein, *Moralphilosophie* I, p. 524; J.M. Aubert, *Le droit romain dans l'oeuvre de saint Thomas*, pp. 99–108.

[48] *Il concetto di legge nella Summa theologiae de S. Tommaso d'Aquino*, pp. 64–75.

"occasional references to the formula of the Digest... heterogeneous elements, mechanically repeated."[49]

The point is that Aquinas felt a need, not altogether explained by his habit of deference to authorities, to make provision for Ulpian's definition. One cannot cavil at Cotta's general demonstration that this definition does not really accord with the notion of the natural law expounded in the *Summa theologiae.* But a consideration that should prevent too easy an acceptance of the suggestion that the references to Ulpian in the *Summa* are merely incidental is that, some years after the *Prima-Secundae*, when writing his *Commentary on the Ethics* of Aristotle, St. Thomas was still very far from rejecting Ulpian's definition.

Cotta's argument turns, in part, upon a chronology that cannot now be sustained. When he wrote he took it that the *Commentary on the Ethics* preceded the *Summa* (at least the *Prima-Secundae*);[50] at that time, indeed, a respectable body of scholarly opinion held for an early dating of the work, 1261–1264 (the pontificate of Urban IV) or even earlier.[51] Now the late date 1271–1272 is generally accepted, which means that the *Commentary on the Ethics* may be later even than the *Secunda-Secundae.*[52]

Aristotle's notice of 'natural justice' in the fifth Book of the *Nicomachean Ethics* provides St. Thomas, as it has done and to this day still does other commentators, with an occasion of discussing the natural law.

[49] *Ibid.*, p. 64: "... gli *occasionali* riferimenti alla formula del *Digesto* contenuti nella *Summa* mi sembra che debbano o esser considerati elementi eterogenei, quasi meccanicamente ripetuti, o vadano meglio intesi nel quadro generale del pensiero tomista...."

[50] *Ibid.*, pp. 64, 74.

[51] Cf. G. Verbeke, "La date du Commentaire de St. Thomas d'Aquin sur l'Ethique à Nicomaque" in *Revue philosophique de Louvain*, 47 (1949), pp. 203–220; *Id.*, "Authenticité et chronologie des écrits de S. Thomas d'Aquin" in *Revue philosophique de Louvain*, 48 (1950), p. 261; A. Mansion, "Autour de la date du commentaire de S. Thomas sur l'Ethique à Nicomaque" in *Revue philosophique de Louvain*, 50 (1952), p. 460.

[52] Cf. *Sententia Libri Ethicorum* (*Sancti Thomae de Aquino Opera Omnia*, v. XLVII (Romae, 1969) Praefatio, p. 201*: "... admirari enim solet de multitudine operum quae Thomas in parvo tempore confecit, praesertim cum *Sententiam Libri Ethicorum* Lutetiae Parisiorum circa annos 1271–1272 scripserit dum secundam partem Summae theologiae aliaque opera scribebat." The Leonine editors refer to R.A. Gauthier, "La date du commentaire de saint Thomas sur l'Ethique à Nicomaque" in *Recherches de théologie ancienne et médiévale*, 18 (1951), pp. 66–105.

Of political justice part is natural, part legal, – natural that which everywhere has the same force and does not exist by people's thinking this or that; legal that which is originally indifferent but when it has been laid down is not indifferent. . . .[53]

Aristotle's *dikaion physikon* was rendered *justum naturale* in the text used by St. Thomas, a revision of Robert Grosseteste's translation. The division of *justum politicum* into *justum naturale* and *justum legale* given by Aristotle is, according to St. Thomas, the same as the jurists' division of *jus naturale* and *jus positivum.* He goes on to explain the apparent discrepancy by adverting to the fact that *jus politicum* is taken in a different sense by Aristotle and the jurists; for Aristotle the *politicum justum* is divided into *naturale* and *legale;* for the jurists the *politicum* is divided against the *naturale.*

It is when Aquinas comes to consider the *justum naturale* at close quarters that he makes appeal to Ulpian (without naming him beyond saying that he is referring to the view of "the jurists"). There can be no doubt about his identifying the natural law with a series of rational principles, the kind of principles that can be related, in a reasoning process as premisses and conclusion, as the prohibition of stealing, for instance, follows as a conclusion from the prohibition of injuring others. These natural law judgments follow upon the inclinations of nature; and the nature of man is twofold. It is here that Ulpian is welcomed. The nature man shares with animals is the basis of the natural law as Ulpian defined it – *quod natura omnia animalia docuit.* The rational nature, proper to man, which enables him to distinguish rationally between good and evil, provides the basis for what the jurists called the *jus gentium.*[54] St. Thomas recognises that the

[53] *Nic Eth.*, V, 7, 1.134 b 18–21; S. Thomas, *In V Eth.*, lect. 12 *Sententia libri Ethicorum*, Romae, 1969, p. 304, 12–33.

[54] *Ibid.*, p. 305, 49–57; 57–75: "Est autem considerandum quod iustum naturale est ad quod hominem natura inclinat. Attenditur autem in homine duplex natura; una quidem secundum quod est animal, quae est sibi aliisque animalibus communis; alia autem est natura hominis quae est propria sibi in quantum est homo, prout scilicet secundum rationem discernit turpe et honestum. Iuristate autem illud tantum dicunt ius naturale quod consequitur inclinationem naturae communis homini et aliis animalibus, sicut coniunctio maris et feminae, educatio natorum et alia huiusmodi; illud autem ius quod consequitur propriam inclinationem naturae humanae, in quantum scilicet homo est rationale animal, vocant ius gentium quia eo omnes gentes utuntur, sicut quod pacta sint servanda, quod legati etiam apud hostes sint tuti, et alia huiusmodi. Utrumque autem horum comprehenditur sub iusto naturali, prout hic a Philosopho accipitur."

juristic definition of the natural law is restrictive – *Iuristae autem illud tantum dicunt ius naturale quod consequitur inclinationem naturae communis homini et aliis animalibus* – but he does make use of it, despite its incongruity with his general view.

It cannot pass unobserved that, in making the *jus gentium* consist of conclusions from principles of the natural law St. Thomas once again risks confusing the *jus gentium* and the *jus naturale.* Be that as it may, it remains true that, in his last important confrontation with the problem of defining the natural law, Aquinas is still surprisingly accommodating to the definition of Ulpian. He does not entirely accept it; rather in accepting it he changes and enlarges it; but he does feel the need to maintain it.[55]

To this consideration of St. Thomas's later thought on Ulpian's definition of the natural law one might add one or two vague passages in the *Commentary on the Politics* of Aristotle[56] There are no direct references to Ulpian's natural law. There is, however, the passage, apropos of Aristotle's saying that man is a political animal, in which St. Thomas enlarges upon the distinction between man and animals. Man's social or political nature is contrasted with the gregariousness of certain animals or with the organising capacity of bees. What really distinguishes man from the animals is his power of speech, the expression of thought; the voice of animals is sound without meaning. As example of the knowledge that man expresses in his speech St. Thomas adduces the distinction between good and evil, between just and unjust. This would seem to rule out any real acceptance of Ulpian's definition.[57]

[55] S. Cotta, *op. cit.*, pp. 61–62 admits as much: "Dunque i sudetti testi, lunghi dall' offrirci una univoca interpretazione naturalistica dello *ius naturale*, ci indicano invece come essa appaia insufficiente a S. Tommaso. Tuttavia non si può negare ch'egli, sia pure in parte, la mantenga e l'accetti, e quindi il problema, per quanto ridotto a proporzioni minori, rimane."

[56] The Thomistic text ends at *In III Pol.*, lectio 6, the completion being the work of Peter of Auvergne. The date has not yet been satisfactorily established, but there is fairly general agreement that St. Thomas began his commentary during his second Paris period, 1296–1272. On these matters cf. H.F. Dondaine, L.J. Bataillon, Préface, *Sententia Libri Politicorum* (*Opera Omnia,* t. XLVIII, Romae, 1971, pp. A5–A8).

[57] *In I Pol.*, lectio 1 (*Sententia Libri Politicorum*, Lib. 1, c. 1/b, 142–146, *Opera Omnia*, t. XLVIII, Romae, 1971, p. A79): "... locutio est propria hominibus, quia hoc est proprium eis in comparatione ad alia animalia, quod habeant cognitionem boni et mali, iusti et iniusti, et aliorum huiusmodique sermone significari possunt."

The same conclusion may be drawn, perhaps more vaguely, from those passages, further on in the *Commentary on the Politics*, in which St. Thomas puts as good a face as he can on Aristotle's doctrine of the natural slavery of some men. Speaking of the varieties of domination, he remarks that, despite their common nature, man is naturally master of the other animals. Domesticated animals are *digniora* than wild animals precisely because they participate in the rule of reason.[58] There is nothing here about a common law, based upon the common nature of man and animals; if anything the stress upon the rule of reason excludes it. Again, one might look to the following *lectio*, in which the issue of slavery is joined expressly in terms of natural and human law. In what reads like a piece of special pleading Aquinas concedes that slavery by conquest may be unjust (for the less wise may enslave their betters) and yet may be provided for in human law, on the ground that it places a premium upon valour, which is not without its use for the common good.[59] This recalls a controversy that was found already in the Roman law about the status of slavery and in which Ulpian's dictum that all men are by nature equal carried the implication that slavery must have been intoduced by the *jus gentium*.[60] But St. Thomas has nothing here to say about Ulpian's natural law.

It may be thought that undue attention has been given, in the preceding section, to the fate of Ulpian's definition in the works of St. Thomas. Why neglect Gratian's definition, which might be considered almost equally rebarbative? Above all, why not concentrate upon the 'Ciceronian' definition which, with its openness to reason, must be the one most attractive to the later thinking of Aquinas? In justification it may be said that St. Thomas's reaction to the Roman jurist's definition is instructive; for it shows him grappling with a very strong authority that he was unwilling to accept, yet loath to cast aside.

The picture might be completed, but hardly otherwise significantly altered, by a study of his use of Gratian. It is more important, however, to outline that Thomist 'rational' natural law, to

[58] *In 1 Pol.*, lect. 3 (*Sententia libri Politicorum*, I, 3, 178–185): "Similiter se habet in homine et aliis animalibus quod naturale et expediens est ut homo aliis dominetur; videmus enim quod animalia mansueta quibus homo dominatur, digniora sunt secundum naturam siluestribus in quantum participant aliqualiter regimine rationis."

[59] *In I Pol.*, lect. 4 (*Sententia libri Politicorum*, I, 4, 101–112).

[60] Cf. R. Voggensperger, *Der Begriff des 'ius naturale' im römischen Recht*, pp. 17–24.

which reference has been made and with which Ulpian's (and, indeed, Gratian's) natural law is found to be ultimately inconsistent. Here is not the place for an attempt at a complete exposition of St. Thomas's views on the natural law, with all their nuances; that effort has frequently been made and must continue to be made by each generation that endeavours to discern the profile of the natural law. The present aim is the more modest one of drawing attention to certain features of Aquinas's thought, particularly those that place him in the tradition, already millenary when he was writing, and those that show him open to development. Some of the salient points in his synthesis, and many of the capital texts, have already been considered. What remains to be said in this chapter may be broadly characterized as an account of the evolution of his thought towards the identification of the natural law with a series of rational principles. This will be more fully seen in the next chapter, concerned mainly with the synthesis in the *Summa Theologiae*, in which such matters as the distinction between the primary and secondary precepts of the natural law and the confronting of the major problems of the universality and possible variation of the natural law must find their place.

C. NATURAL LAW AND THE PRINCIPLES OF MORALITY

The identification of the primary precepts of the natural law with the first principles of morality in the *Summa theologiae* represents the result of an evolution in St. Thomas's thought. His first major discussion of the natural law, the discussion of the laws of marriage in the fourth book of the *Commentary on the Sentences*, offers a different view. The problem was posed by the polygamy of the patriarchs of the Old Testament and the Mosaic bill of divorce. How far are the unity and indissolubility of marriage to be considered requirements of the natural law? These problems were discussed by all Lombard's commentators and a variety of solution was offered. The underlying questions of the nature of the natural law, its immutability and dispensability, are the important ones; and the foundations for Aquinas's replies are deep-laid.

All beings, he says, have within themselves, by their very nature, principles which produce action and direct it to its proper end. In natural bodies, for example, there are the substantial forms. In cognitive beings the principles of operation are knowledge and appetite. In such beings, therefore, there must be a natural concept (*naturalis conceptio*), in the cognitive faculty and a natural inclination in the appetitive faculty.

Now, since man differs from other animals in his capacity of knowing the end *as such* and the relation of means to end, the 'natural concept', in his case, becomes the natural law.

Natural law, therefore, is none other than the concept naturally impressed upon man by which he is guided towards suitable action in the activities proper to him, whether they belong to his generic nature (such as reproduction, the use of food and so on) or his specific nature (reasoning and the like).[61]

The stress is upon the intrinsic character of the natural law, the extension to man of the intrinsic finality, or tendency to an end, that pervades all nature.

Finality in nature easily suggests its cause, divine providence. St. Thomas's handing of divine providence elsewhere in the *Commentary on the Sentences*[62] is closely parallel with his treatment of the natural law. There is the same contrast between animals – which are 'driven by a natural force', an *aestimatio naturalis*, rather than 'guided as free agents' – and men, who are directed by the natural law. In the article under consideration this alignment of human action, which is the work of the natural law, is said to depend upon a natural 'concept' in the cognitive faculty and a natural inclination in the appetitive faculty. But only the intellectual element appears in the definition of the natural law; St. Thomas has little to say at this stage about the appetitive element. In the latter part of this article, the definition is viewed in terms of the evident connexion between reason and human action, and we find that the primary precepts of the natural law, in questions of conduct, are like *communes conceptiones* in speculative matters and that secondary precepts are derived from the primary by way of conclusion (just as, in the province of the speculative reason, conclusions hold good in virtue of self-evident first principles).

The precepts of the natural law, are, then, rational judgments. But that law has just been defined *conceptio homini naturaliter indita*. There may be a difficulty here, for St. Thomas has already accepted an Aristotelian epistemology that has little room for innate ideas or 'impressed' judgments.

The truth is that there are two points of view here, not yet

[61] *In 4 Sent.*, d. 33, q. 1, a. 1.

[62] *In 1 Sent.*, d. 39, q. 2, a. 2.

perfectly reconciled. The teleological way of looking at the natural law is a heritage that came to St. Thomas through the Stoics, Cicero, Ulpian and theologians like Roland of Cremona: the idea that the natural law is a series of judgments of the practical reason is found, in varying degrees, in St. Augustine, Anselm of Laon, William of Auxerre, Alexander of Hales and St. Albert the Great. It is too soon in St. Thomas's career to expect the synthesis of these views. Rather, especially in a work that is a commentary, one should expect an eclectic tendency. And, in the latter connexion, we have seen St. Thomas's anxiety to find tolerable meanings for definitions of the natural law like Gratian's and Ulpian's.

Other references to the natural law in the *Commentary on the Sentences* are more incidental. Four may be mentioned briefly.

(1) THE NATURAL LAW, SYNDERESIS AND CONSCIENCE. Certain universal principles (*ipsa universalia principia juris*) constitute the natural law; *synderesis* is the habitual knowledge of those principles (or even the faculty of reason informed by such knowledge); conscience applies the principles to conduct by way of conclusion. The clarity of the foregoing distinction is, however, blurred when St. Thomas is led to refer to the natural law as *habitus principiorum juris.*[63] This recalls the well-known view of Alexander of Hales and St. Albert the Great that the natural law is a *habitus.*

(2) THE NATURAL OR INTERIOR LAW. This is "the light of reason by which we discern what ought to be done" and is contrasted with written or exterior law. Action in accordance with this light is right and whatever goes against it is unnatural and evil. This view of the natural law will be repeated by St. Thomas later; it is, perhaps, suggested by *Psalm* 4, 6-7: "Many say, Who sheweth us good things? (in St. Thomas's paraphrase, "Who will show us what we ought to do?") The *light* of thy countenance, O Lord, is signed upon us."[64]

(3) THE EXPRESSION OF THE ETERNAL LAW. Speaking of 'right reason' St. Thomas remarks that "since the natural law is that according to which reason is right reason, St. Augustine says that sin is defined as whatever is not in accordance with the eternal law, *of which the natural law is the expression.*"[65] the mention of

[63] *In 2 Sent.*, d. 24, q. 2, a. 4 and ad 5.

[64] *In 2 Sent.*, d. 42, q. 1, a. 4 ad 3.

[65] *Ibid.*, q. 2, a. 5.

the eternal law is noteworthy as standing practically alone in the works of St. Thomas prior to the *Summa*. Is it no more than a glancing reference, enlisting St. Augustine's definition of sin? Or does it point the way to developments that we shall find in the *Summa Theologiae?*

(4) THE NATURAL LAW AND THE TEN COMMANDMENTS. Peter Lombard appears to have used the term 'natural law' once only – in his discussion of the Decalogue. Truth wrote in the heart of man the precept: Do not to others what you would not have done to yourself. Man chose to ignore this precept of the natural law and, so, it had to be reiterated in the Decalogue. This view was not unknown among the Fathers and early scholastics. St. Thomas accepts it. He allows that the natural law is a work of reason, that its precepts are "written in everyone's practical intellect," where they resemble the first principles of the speculative reason inasmuch as they are readily known and are the source of other principles. But these primary precepts are identical with the Law given to Moses and all others may be reduced in some way to "these ten."[66]

The *Commentary on the Sentences*, then, as far as direct reference goes, presents the natural law in different contexts as a series of dictates of the practical reason, as a *habitus* of first practical principles, or as the light of reason itself.

So far the direct references. The related notion of *synderesis* in Aquinas has already been considered. It will be useful to look more closely at its correlative, conscience, also referred to, in passing, as the actual application of the principles of the natural law, known in *synderesis*.[67] It is a simpler notion than either natural law or *synderesis* – yet the confusion in its regard, in the contemporaries and predecessors of St. Thomas, appears, if anything to be greater. In the view he adopts St. Thomas once again follows an important innovation of St. Albert the Great, who as we have seen, in his early *Summa Theologica* makes conscience an act (while retaining some vestiges of the older views).[68] After he had become familiar with the full text of the *Nicomachean*

[66] *In 3 Sent.*, d. 37, q. 1, a. 1; cf. *ibid.*, aa. 2,3.

[67] *In 2 Sent.*, d. 24, a. 2, a. 4.

[68] *Summa theologica*, II, tr. 16, q. 99, n. 3, a. 2, q. 1 (*Opera omnia* ed. Borgnet, t. 33, p. 244) gives the doctrine of the practical syllogism; *ibid.*, q. 2 concludes that conscience is always an act in some sense. Nevertheless both here and in the previous article (*Ibid.*, a. 1: Borgnet, t. 33, pp. 240–242) he toys with the idea that conscience is a habit, in a sense innate and in another sense acquired.

Ethics, in the translation of Robert Grosseteste, Albert's identification of conscience as an act is clear and unequivocal.[69] It is here that the Aristotelian doctrine of the practical syllogism becomes relevant.

The syllogism consists of two premisses from which the third follows as conclusion. In practical matters the conclusion will be a particular judgment affecting the action in a particular situation. Universal principles (in the major premiss) are provided by *synderesis:* these are applied by being combined with other principles more immediately related to action (in the minor premiss); and the conclusion into which they issue is considered in the act of conscience. Thus, for example:

Major premiss (*synderesis*)	= All evil ought to be avoided.
Minor premiss (reason)	= Such and such an action is evil because forbidden by the law of God (superior reason); or because it is seen to be evil, unjust or wrong (inferior reason).
Conclusion (conscience)	= This particular action ought to be avoided.

The distinction between *ratio superior* and *ratio inferior* is found already in Peter Lombard, who cites St. Augustine.[70] It does not, in fact, appear to be of great importance. The inferior reason is that concerned with the conditions with which the moral philosopher has to deal.

Conscience can err precisely because it is an act of reason applying general knowledge to a particular case. It errs not because of any error in *synderesis* but because of an error in reason i.e. the major premiss of the practical syllogism is immune to error, but the minor premiss is not, nor is the actual process of drawing the conclusion. This is a view that St. Thomas will develop, without adding anything that is really new, in the second passage in which he considers conscience in the *Commentary on the Sentences.*

The function assigned to the natural law in St. Thomas's discussions of *synderesis* and conscience is consistent only with a view of its essence that would identify it as a series of rational

[69] *Cf.* O. Lottin, *Psychologie et morale aux XIIe et XIIIe siècles*, II, pp. 220–221.

[70] *Liber Sententiarum*, II, d. 24: "Rationis autem para superior aeternis rationibus conspiciendis vel consulendis adhaerescit; portio inferior ad temporalia gubernanda deflectitur"; cf. Augustine, *De Trin.*, XII, 7 (P.L., 42; 1003).

judgments. In other words, St. Thomas regards the natural law, in practice, as the means by which reason directs human action; there are in the practical reason certain fundamental and self-evident principles, the *habitus* of which is called *synderesis;* and these principles are the natural law. St. Thomas shows a tendency to confine the natural law to these principles – a tendency that was widespread, due to the influence of the twelfth century school of Anselm of Laon.[71] Be that, however, as it may be, it seems clear that, in the *Commentary on the Sentences*, St. Thomas has already made up his mind upon a whole series of questions (e.g. the function of reason in human action, the parallel between the speculative and the practical reason), that, in fact, determine his view of the natural law. Still, when he has to define the natural law, he is much less firm than one would expect; and, in particular when it is a question of considering the definitions of his predecessors, he shows a surprising readiness to welcome conceptions of the natural law that appear to have very little in common with each other or with that demanded by his own thought.

The *De Veritate*, St. Thomas's next major work after the *Commentary on the Sentences* has already been laid under contribution as indicating his views on *synderesis.* The related topic of conscience is also discussed here and the discussion leaves little doubt about the concept of natural law that was present to the mind of Thomas. Conscience is the *actual* application of first practical principles to a particular subject-matter.[72] This application is made syllogistically, because the judgment of synderesis is universal and cannot be applied to a particular action *nisi fiat assumptio alicujus particularis.*[73]

The application may be made: (a) to a matter of fact. In this case conscience is the judment whether an action has or has not taken place – a meaning of no ethical importance; (b) to a matter of right and wrong. This occurs in either of two ways, according as the matter is a future or a past action. With regard to the future, conscience decides whether or not an action ought to be done. With regard to the past, it examines an action and discovers whether it was rightly or wrongly done.

The double function of conscience in matters of right and wrong is important. St. Thomas compares it to the double function of

[71] Cf. O. Lottin, *Le droit naturel chez saint Thomas d'Aquin et ses prédécesseurs*, p. 98.

[72] *De verit.*, q. 17, a. 1.

[73] *De verit.*, q. 17, a. 2.

the speculative reason which proceeds from first principles to discover new knowledge (the *via inventionis*) and then judges this new knowledge by a return to first principles (the *via judicii*). Conscience in the latter sense is the practical reason making use of the criteria of morality, in a manner analogous to that of the speculative reason making use of the criteria of truth.

The practical intellect, no less than the speculative, is liable to error; and the discussion of error throws further light upon St. Thomas's thought on the natural law. Conscience, which is the application of practical knowledge to particular cases can err in two ways – by applying erroneous knowledge, and by wrongly applying true knowledge. In other words conscience may exemplify the material (false premiss) and formal (false reasoning) fallacies known to the logician. In the kind of practical syllogism being considered, the scope of material error is limited to the minor premiss. The major premiss of synderesis, as the *Commentary on the Sentences* had pointed out, is infallible.

There is an important qualification. There are some particular applications of practical knowledge in which conscience *cannot* err, namely when it is a question of the subject of one or other of the universal judments of *synderesis.* Here again emerges the parallel between the speculative and the practical reason. In the speculative reason there can be no error regarding the particular conclusions which come directly, and in the same terms, under the universal principles e.g. "*This* whole is greater than its part"; nor can conscience err regarding the proposition: "I ought not to love God" or "A certain particular evil ought to be done" (i.e. no conscience can accept these propositions as true). In speculative and practical cases alike, the major is a self-evident universal judgment and the minor is merely a particular application of it. An example is: Every whole is greater than its part: this is a whole: therefore it is greater than its part. A parallel practical example is: All evil ought to be avoided: this is an evil: therefore it ought to be avoided.[74]

The *De Veritate*, then, adds little directly to our knowledge of St. Thomas's thought on the natural law. Insofar as he defines the natural law, he does so in terms of its practical application. At times he appears to restrict it to the fundamental principles of *synderesis.* As against this, he refers to conclusions which "fall directly and in the same terms under the universal principles." Further he treats of "more particular principles" which emerge in

[74] *De verit.*, q. 17, a. 2.

the application of the principles of *synderesis*. These considerations seem to justify the inference that the natural law is concerned with more than the fundamental principles.

In the *De Veritate* the dependence of all subsequent practical knowledge on the habit of *synderesis* gets more emphasis than hitherto; as also does the position of intuitive apprehension at both terms of practical as well as speculative reasoning.

The *Summa contra Gentiles* contains no *ex professo* treatment of the natural law and it only once refers to the natural law in so many words. Its teaching, however, on matters like divine providence and the finality of creatures, points of contact between the natural law and St. Thomas's general system, is of importance Book III deals with "God, the end of creatures and their ruler"; and the phrase indicates the theological perspective of the long discussion of "divine law" (*lex divina*) that it includes. The term *lex divina* is ambiguous and can be confusing; one is inevitably reminded of Gratian's definition of the natural law as "what is contained in the Law and the gospel," a divine law in fact. Aquinas, although he frequently cites the Scriptures, does not identify the divine law with that of the Law and the gospel. He deals with the *lex divina* in much more general terms:

> Now the laws laid down ought to proceed on the basis of the dictate of nature if they are human laws, as, in the exact sciences, every human discovery takes its origin from principles naturally known; but, if they are divine laws, they not only develop the dictate of nature, but also make up the deficiency in what nature dictates, as dogmas divinely revealed surpass the capacity of the natural reason. . . .[75]

> This divine law is given to man as a help to the natural law. For example it is natural to all men to love their neighbour, in token of which there is a sort of natural instinct by which one man will help another in necessity–even a stranger–by calling him back from a wrong turn that he may have taken, lifting him up from a fall and the like: as though every man were kinsman and friend of every other man.[76]

[75] *Cont. Gent.*, III, c. 123:". . . leges autem positae oportet quod ex naturali instinctu procedant, si humanae sunt; sicut etiam in scientiis demonstrativis omnis humana inventio ex principiis naturaliter compertis initium sumit. Si autem divinae sunt, non solum instinctum naturae explicant, sed etiam defectum naturalis instinctus supplent; sicut ea quae divinitus revelantur superant naturalis rationis capacitatem."

[76] *Cont. Gent.*, III, c. 117: "Lex divina profertur homini in auxilium legis naturalis. Cujus signum est quod quodam naturali instinctu cuilibet homini, etiam ignoto, subvenit in necessitate, puta revocando ab errore viae, erigendo a casu, et aliis hujusmodi, ac si omnis homo omni homini esset naturaliter familiaris et amicus."

A great part of the discussion of the *lex divina* revolves about such "dictatecs of nature" or "natural instincts". Further, as will appear, the divine law is explicitly said to command what is in itself right; it cannot, therefore, be a purely positive law. Perhaps St. Thomas has in mind something not far removed from the natural law; many of his phrases and expressions might have been taken bodily from his treatment of the natural law in his other works.

The relations between divine providence, on the one hand, and rationality and freedom, on the other, form the prelude to the notion of law, in the *Summa contra Gentiles.*[77]

The providence which governs irrational creatures works through a blind, natural inclination. Something further is required for rational beings; and this further direction of human personal action is called 'law.' Again, since rational creatures are so subordinated to divine providence as to participate in it in some way, by directing their own actions, and, since actions are directed by law, it follows that God must have given laws to men. Law is, thus, a consequence of the rationality of creatures through which they participate, in a particular way, in divine providence. It is also connected with the freedom which follows from rationality – *illis danda est lex in quibus est agere et non agere.* Finally, law is concerned with action, which gets its meaning from the end. Hence all who are capable of receiving law receive it from that being by whom they are led to their end – as the journeyman-mason receives his rule from the master-builder, or the private soldier from his general. A rational creature attains its end in God and by God, and, therefore, its law is given to it by God.[78]

The divine law can now be defined as "that part of divine providence which is proposed to a rational creature." Its end is to subordinate man to God.[79] The intention of every legislator is to direct men to the end proper to him, by means of the law he imposes. Thus the general directs men to victory, the statesman to peace. The end intended by God is *Ipsemet Deus* and, so, this is also the end of his law. From the point of view of man, law also ordains to God because, as a participation of the divine providence, it must direct him to his end.[80]

[77] *Cont. Gent.*, III, cc. 111, 112, 113.

[78] *Cont. Gent.*, III, c. 114.

[79] *Cont. Gent.*, III, c. 115: "Lex ... est quaedam ratio divinae providentiae gubernentis rationali creaturae proposita"; c. 128: "Lex divina est quaedam ratio divinae providentiae ad homines gubernandos."

[80] St. Thomas argues also from the Aristotelian principle that every legislator's intention is to make good subjects; cf. *Nic. Eth.*, I, 13, 1102 a 10 ff.

Having established thus the existence of a divine law, St. Thomas turns to its precepts. Time and again he appeals to a 'natural instinct' or to an exigency of nature when he deals with them in detail. Particularly instructive is the close parallel between his treatment of the divine law as it governs marriage here and his discussion of the same subject, under the rubric of natural law, in the *Commentary on the Sentences.*[81] In general, the divine law prescribes that man "observe the order of reason in those things which are given over to his use." This general precept includes others, such as those commanding the love of God, belief in Him, love of one's neighbour, the use of sensible things in accordance with reason, the observing of the laws of marriage, etc.[82] And the climax of the whole discussion comes in a chapter which "contains the very pith and marrow of moral philosophy."[83] It is a chapter written to show that there is an objective scale of right and wrong independently of all law, a scale founded upon rational nature. And this is no more than a résumé of what St. Thomas had already said of the individual precepts of the divine law, namely, that what accords with reason is right and good and what does not accord with reason is evil. It is a distinction between good and evil that law may confirm but which is anterior to law; the law, therefore, of which St. Thomas has been speaking cannot be a purely positive law:

It appears from the foregoing that those things which are prescribed by the divine law are right not alone because they are established by law, but also by nature.[84]

To summarize, although he does not explicitly discuss the natural law and scarcely uses the term, the contribution of the *Contra Gentiles* to St. Thomas' thought on the natural law is not inconsiderable. The term of reference is divine providence; and the divine law is the result of the special relations between this divine providence and the rational creature which, because it is rational and free, must be governed in a special way. There is little in this that cannot be applied with perfect justice to the natural law. Further, the divine law is intimately connected with

[81] *Cont. Gent.*, III, cc. 122, 123, 124, 125; cf. *In 4 Sent.*, d. 33. qq. 1–3.

[82] *Cont. Gent.*, III, c. 128: "... secundum legem divinam homo inducitur ut ordinem rationis servet in omnibus quae in ejus usum venire possunt"; cf. cc. 116–118, 121, 122–125.

[83] J. Rickaby, *Of God and his Creatures* (translation of *Summa Contra Gentiles*), p. 292 note.

[84] *Cont. Gent.*, III, c. 129.

the finality of creatures in general, and of man in particular; this is an aspect of the natural law already sketched by St. Thomas in the *Commentary on the Sentences.* In the chapter just considered the foundation of the natural law in an objective scale of right and wrong, is very solidly laid. And, finally, St. Thomas stresses throughout his exposé the connection between the law he is dealing with and the inclinations of human nature. This too, relates to the teleological suggestion of the *Commentary on the Sentences.* If the intervening *De Veritate* dealt almost excusively with the rational aspect – the natural law as expressed in the first propositions of the practical reason – and if this latter aspect has not been remarked in the *Contra Gentiles* that is doubtless because St. Thomas's approach, as has been indicated, is a special one; he is dealing here with law within the context of the governance and finality of creatures.

It remains to be seen how these *disjecta membra* find their place in the synthetic view of the natural law which St. Thomas expounds in the *Summa Theologiae.*

CHAPTER VII

AQUINAS MAKES UP HIS MIND

We turn now to the 'final synthesis' of the *Summa Theologiae*; and may hope to look upon that familiar profile of the natural law with more critical eyes because of what we have seen of its background, immediate in Thomas's personal development and remote in the speculations and disagreements of his predecessors.

A. THE NOTION OF LAW

To begin with St. Thomas, in the *Summa Theologiae*, regards the natural law as genuinely satisfying the definition of law; he makes this clear not only by his inclusion of the natural law in the tract on laws but also by explicit statement.[1] It is important, then, to know what St. Thomas means by 'law.'

The notion is examined in its logical position of prominence at the head of the law-tract. Beginning with the provisional description of law as "a certain rule and measure of action by which one is induced to act or restrained from acting" one eventually arrives

[1] 1–2ae, q. 91, a. 2 ad 3. Whether or not it is convincing to speak of the natural law as a law in the sense in which human law is law is another matter and raises wider questions, not discussed here. It may, however, be suggested that for Aquinas the notion of law is analogical, not univocal. Cf. M.J. Adler, "A Question about Law" in *Essays in Thomism* (ed. R.E. Brennan); O. Lottin, "La valeur des formules de s. Thomas d'Aquin concernant la loi naturelle" in *Mélanges Maréchal*, II, pp. 345–357; J. Leclercq, *La philosophie morale de saint Thomas d'Aquin devant la pensée contemporaine*, pp. 386–388; D. O'Donoghue, "The Thomist Concept of Natural Law" in *Irish Theological Quarterly*, 22 (1955), pp. 90–92, 103–105; R. Stone, "Dr. Johnson: Philologist or Philosopher?" (on the definition of law) in *Cambridge Review*, Nov. 14, 1964, pp.114–121; S. Cotta, *Il concetto di legge nella Summa theologiae di S. Tommaso d'Aquino*, pp. 15–41.

at the formal definition:

> Law is nothing other than an ordination of reason for the common good by him who has the charge of the community and promulgated.[2]

This definition is the result of an effort of synthesis personal to St. Thomas; in this part of the law-tract his predecesors had given him very little to work on – some phrases of St. Augustine (following Cicero), some passages in the *Nicomachean Ethics* of Aristotle, St. Albert the Great's very tentative essay at defining law and not much more.

There are four qualities, then, that characterise the notion of law in general; it is a work of reason or mind, it is aimed at the common good, it proceeds from one having authority and it is promulgated. Of these qualities the fundamental one is the first, the dependence of law upon reason. And in the proof offered by St. Thomas two stages are noticed, the first, depending upon the fact that reason is the principle of human action, leading to the conclusion that law is *aliquid rationis;* the second, depending upon the parallel between the speculative and the practical intellect, leading to the identification of law with a universal proposition of the practical reason.[3]

Here we have not merely a confirmation of the assumption that Thomas was all along working towards the identification of the natural law with the first principles of the practical reason, but a valuable indication of the points at which the natural law joins his general system of thought. This view fits admirably with the place he accords to reason in human action.

In general, nature is the essence of anything considered as a principle of operation.[4] And, since the nature of man is distinctively rational, the actions proper to human nature will have reason as their principle. Such actions are, *by definition*, human actions.[5] Probing more deeply, it is seen that reason, as the principle of human action, is closely bound up with freewill. Human action is essentially free action, action over which the agent has control: and, conversely, control or *dominium sui actus* is possible only in an agent capable of selecting the ends of its action. In other words, rational agents, knowing the end, move themselves towards it; irrational agents not knowing the end as such,

[2] 1–2ae, q.90, a.4– "(lex) nihil est aliud quam rationis ordinatio ad bonum commune ab eo qui curam habet communitatis promulgata."

[3] 1–2ae, q. 90, a. 1.

[4] 1a, q. 29, a. 1 ad 4; *De ente et essentia*, c. 1; cf. also 3a, q. 2, a. 12.

[5] 1–2ae, q. 1, a. 1.

are moved to it by another. All this has been part of St. Thomas's thought since the *Commentary on the Sentences.*

Now, the self-motion of a rational agent towards its end is a function of freewill;[6] and the cause of freewill is, in turn, found in reason. It is because the reason can conceive the good in different ways, and is not confined to any single conception of it, that the will is free; for the will works upon the conception of the good presented to it by the reason. And, in the last analysis, the non-determination of the reason depends upon its power of neglecting an individual good, or of concentrating upon its 'non-good' aspect inasmuch as it falls short of the perfect good.[7] Already one notices how St. Thomas fits the concepts, with which he has been working all along, into the comprehensive system of the *Summa Theologiae.* The next step in his proof that law is a work of reason confirms this impression.

The now familiar parallel between the speculative and the practical intellect has its justification in the substantial unity and identity of the human intellect. The distinction between speculative and practical intellect is a notional one, *cum fundamento in re.* This is easily seen. Faculties are differentiated by the objects of their action – provided that the difference between the objects is not merely accidental. Colour, for example, does not provide a sufficient basis for a division of the genus animal into its species; an essential difference is required, something that touches an animal precisely as an animal – for example, a difference in the 'soul' which is sometimes found to be rational, sometimes not. Similarly with the sense-faculties; objects that differ only incidentally do not demand separate faculties for their appreciation. Sight is competent to deal with musicians, grammarians, men, stones, great and small objects etc. *as coloured.*

It is no more essential to an object of intellect (an 'intelligible') that it be related or not to action than it is to a coloured object that it be great or small. Intelligible objects, just as coloured objects, are apprehended by a single faculty; and for the same reason.[8] The basis, then, of the distinction between the speculative and the practical intellect is the presence or absence of an accidental relation to action in the intelligible object. In the *De Veritate,* speaking of the ideas in the mind of God, St. Thomas had said *practica addit super speculativam ordinem ad actum,*[9] and the

[6] 1–2ae, q. 1, a. 2.

[7] 1–2ae, q. 17, a. 1 ad 2: "Ex hoc enim voluntas libere potest ad diversa ferri quia ratio potest habere diversas conceptiones boni"; 1–2ae, q. 6, a. 2; q. 10, a. 2.

[8] 1a, q. 77, a. 3; q. 79, a. 11.

[9] *De verit.,* q. 3, a. 3 ad 6.

phrase may be applied to the intellect in the apprehension of its objects. The speculative intellect has as its object truth absolutely speaking, whereas the object of the practical intellect is truth as ordained or related to action. To the objection that it is not truth, but good that is related to action, St. Thomas replies that truth and goodness are in a sense mutually inclusive. Truth is a kind of good, although not considered as the object of appetite; good is a kind of truth although not considered as the object of intellect.[10]

There is nothing surprising in this view of the distinction between the speculative and the practical intellect; and St. Thomas's thought does not vary on the point. His view is no more than an expansion of the dicta of Aristotle – *intellectus speculativus extensione fit practicus* and *intellectus practicus differt a speculativo fine.* Its importance concerning the natural law will be thrown into greater relief presently. Meanwhile the position of will demands attention. It is clear from the long tradition we have examined that there was nothing like unanimity on the assigning of law (still less of natural law) exclusively to the faculty of intellect. Here one touches upon a major area of controversy: we shall see that the overshadowing of the natural law by the nominalism of the fourteenth century and afterwards in attributable to the exaltation of will at the expense of intellect. We shall find, too, that the greatest of St. Thomas's successors in the field of the philosophy of law – the one, in fact, who can dispute Aquinas's claim to be the greatest of the scholastic writers on these matters – Francisco Suarez (1548–1617), leans more than a little to the side of will.[11] Here, without engaging in the controversy, we may be content to try to see St. Thomas's view, which is considerably more nuanced that it is sometimes made to appear.

To an objection that law cannot be essentially an act of reason, because it moves to action, whereas to move to action is the property of will, St. Thomas replies that the reason gets its *vis movendi* from the will and that it is in virtue of an act of will regarding the end that reason can issue commands regarding the means. It is in this command of reason, presupposing an act of the

[10] 1a, q. 79, a. 11 ad 2: "Verum et bonum se invicem includunt. Nam verum est quoddam bonum alioquin non esset appetible; et bonum est quoddam verum alioquin non esset intelligibile"; cf. *De verit.*, q. 3, a. ad 9; and the more detailed discussion in *In 3 Sent.*, d. 23, q. 2, a. 3, quaestiuncula 2.

[11] T.E. Davitt, *The Nature of Law* discusses representative views, on the side of will Henry of Ghent, John Duns Scotus, William of Ockham, Gabriel Biel, Alphonse de Castro and Suarez and, on the side of intellect, Albert the Great, Thomas Aquinas, Cajetan, Soto, Medina and Bellarmine.

will, that law is found; the will of a legislator can only obtain the force of law when it is regulated by reason. This command is the act of *imperium*; and all now turns upon the proof that *imperium* is an act of reason.[12]

In the psychology of St. Thomas intellect and will are closely intertwined. Their close reciprocal causality, which runs right through St. Thomas's psychology of the human act, must be understood as the background to his discussion of the nature of *imperium*.[13] It is clear that intellect and will do interact as, for example, when one reasons about willing or wills to reason. An act of intellect may be preceded by an act of will and vice versa. And, since the effect of the previous act remains or carries over into the act that follows, there are some acts of the will which are such in virtue of a previous act of the intellect and, conversely, some acts of the intellect which are such in virtue of a previous act of the will. St. Thomas puts *imperium* in the latter category. In fact, if one examines his list of the elements in the moral act, (bearing upon end, means and execution, from the first apprehension of the end by the intellect down to the final act of its enjoyment by the will), one discovers a perfect alternation of acts of intellect and will.[14] This analysis, which St. Thomas claimed to have found in great part in St. John Damascene,[15] hardly commends itself to contemporary ideas of the psychology of the human act. It does, however, despite the dated terminology, contain some permanently valuable insights; and it was a psychology understandable to Thomas's contemporaries and successors for many centuries. It requires that *imperium* be an act of the intellect, following upon the will's choice of the means to be employed (*electio*) and preceding the will's active initiation of the employment of those means (*usus*).

Imperare, then, is an act of the intellect; it means to impose an order, whether this be done indicatively (*Hoc est tibi faciendum*) or imperatively (*Fac hoc*). To impose an order is a work of

[12] 1–2ae, q. 90, a. 1 ad 3: "Imperare est rationis ... ergo lex est aliquid rationis."

[13] 1–2ae, qq. 8–17.

[14] Cf. O. Lottin, *Psychologie et morale aux XIIe et XIIIe siècles*, II, pp. 38–41; V.J. Bourke, *St. Thomas and the Greek Moralists*, pp. 15–20.

[15] *De fide orthodoxa*, II, 22 (P.G., 94: 944–945). Damascené's word *hormè* seems to correspond with Thomas's *imperium*; it is rendered *impulsus* in Migne's *Patrologia graeca*, and *impetus* in the text of Burgundio of Pisa which was probably used by St. Thomas. Cf. O. Lottin, *op. cit.*, I, pp. 397–398; V.J. Bourke, *op. cit.*, pp. 17–20.

reason; but order can only be imposed when the will has made its choice.

Applying to law this teaching on the nature of *imperium* the part played by will becomes clear.[16] Law is essentially a work of reason – a universal principle of the practical reason. But this act of reason presupposes an act of the will in the leglislator. The act of will is necessary for the existence of law; but it does not formally constitute law.[17]

B. THE ETERNAL LAW

The concept of law in general is the first important preliminary to St. Thomas's consideration of the natural law in the *Summa*; a second and equally important preliminary notion is that of the eternal law, the archetype of law and the supreme norm of morality.

It was only in St. Thomas's own day that this latter notion was considered with any precision. Many of the early writers we have considered might be understood to refer indifferently to the natural law or to the eternal law. Even St. Augustine, to whom the treatises on eternal law are heavily indebted, does not always distinguish between eternal and natural law.[18] Some of the decretists and theologians who preceded St. Thomas spoke, it is true, of a natural law embracing all creation. But it cannot be claimed for any of them that he anticipated St. Thomas's eternal law.[19]

Nor did the immediate predecessors of St. Thomas make any great contribution to the literature on the subject. Only three treatises on the eternal law earlier than that in the *Prima-Secundae* have so far come to light – the treatise contained in the *Summa* attributed to Alexander of Hales; an anonymous manuscript, also of the Franciscan school, which is the source of the

[16] O. Lottin, *op. cit.*, II, pp. 38–47, III, p. 582, points out that St. Thomas nowhere formally identifies *ordinatio rationis* with *imperium*; that identification, which his system evidently demands, is found in his commentators, notably Gonet and Billuart.

[17] Cf. Cajetan, *In 1am–2ae*, q. 90, a. 1.

[18] Not all agree; cf. F. Senn, *De la justice et du droit*, p. 82, note 3.

[19] O. Lottin, *Le droit naturel chez saint Thomas d'Aquin et ses prédécesseurs*, pp. 19, 23, 33, 49 and Appendices VII, VIII; M. Grabmann, "Das Naturrecht der Scholastik von Gratian bis Thomas von Aquin" in *Mittelalterliches Geistesleben*, I, p. 74.

former; and the later and independent treatise of Peter of Tarentaise.[20]

A close parallel shows that St. Thomas must have been conversant with the Franciscan synthesis when he came to write the articles on the eternal law in the *Summa Theologiae.* Before then he only refers to the eternal law in a passing way. Once in the *Commentary on the Sentences,* as has been noticed, he makes the natural law the impression of the eternal law, in order to enlist St. Augustine's definition of sin. In the *De Veritate* he distinguishes between the eternal law and providence. In the *De Malo* he again refers to Augustine's definition of sin as "any word, deed, or desire contrary to the eternal law" but without pursuing this eternal law further. In fact he uses the term interchangeably with 'law of God', a looseness probably inherited from Peter Lombard who had misquoted St. Augustine to read "any word, deed, or desire contrary to the law of God."[21]

The eternal law is not mentioned in the *Summa contra Gentiles* although both "divine law" and providence are prominent there.[22] Nor is it mentioned in the *Prima Pars,* notwithstanding the fact that in the question on providence St. Thomas had made the pregnant distinction between the *ratio ordinis rerum provisarum in finem* and the *executio huius ordinis.*[23] It seems, then, probable, that St. Thomas became acquainted with the Franciscan account of the eternal law about the time of writing the *Prima-Secundae.*

St. Thomas's proof for the existence of the eternal law runs as follows. Law is a dictate of the practical reason by the governor of a perfect community; this is the very definition of law. The world – *tota communitas universi* – is governed by divine provi-

[26] O. Lottin, *Psychologie et morale auz XIIe et XIIIe siècles,* II, pp. 52–63, 67: "L'école franciscain a le mérite d'avoir créé le traité de la loi éternelle, en synthétisant les textes de saint Augustin. Le mérite de saint Thomas d'Aquin est d'avoir perfectionné la synthèse.... L'affinement des concepts qu'on a pu admirer chez saint Thomas n'a cependant pas altéré les grandes lignes de la synthèse franciscaine; le traité de saint Thomas sur la loi éternelle est un des chapitres de sa morale où s'est maintenu le plus fidèlement le génie de la pensée augustinienne"; cf. A. Bonucci, *La derogabilità del diritto naturale nella scolastica,* p. 125; W. Stockums, *Die Unveränderlichkeit des natürlichen Sittengesetzes in der scholastischen Ethik,* p. 30.

[21] *In 2 Sent.,* d. 42, q. 2, a. 5; *De verit.,* q. 5, a. 1 ad 6; *De malo,* q. 7, a. 1 obj. 1; q. 2, a. 1; Peter Lombard, *Liber Sententiarum,* II, d. 35, n. 1; Augustine, *Contra Faustum,* XXII, 27 (P.L., 42; 418).

[22] *Cont. Gent.,* III, cc. 64–130.

[23] 1a, q. 22, a. 3; q. 91, a. 1; q. 93, a. 1.

dence and the plan – *ratio* – of this government, as existing in God, the principle of the universe, satisfies the definition of law. And, since the Divine Reason is outside the limitations of time, the plan must be eternal. In other words, granted the definition of law and the fact of divine providence the existence of the eternal law follows at once.[24]

For the proof of the existence of divine providence one is referred to the *Prima Pars.*[25] And, in dealing with the qualities of the eternal law in the *Prima-Secundae*, St. Thomas follows closely the lines laid down in his articles on providence in the *Prima Pars.* So whatever in creation is necessary is subject to the eternal law as it is to providence; what is necessary as belonging to the Divine Essence, is really identical with the eternal law. Whatever in creation is contingent is subject to the eternal law, through the impression, by God, of an intrinsic principle of operation.[26] "Things human" come under the eternal law by participating in it just as other creatures do – *per modum actionis et passionis*; but they also participate in a manner proper to themselves, namely *per modum cognitionis.* In other words, man as a creature has a natural inclination towards what is in conformity with the natural law; and as a rational creature he knows the eternal law.

All other laws derive from the eternal law – here St. Thomas follows St. Augustine particularly closely. He uses the analogy of a series of dependant movers, each receiving its motion from the previous one and all depending upon the motion of the first in the series. So it is with rulers; petty kings depend on the High-King; or in matters of building, where the masons depend upon the master-architect. The eternal law is the *ratio gubernationis* in the supreme governor of the universe; the *rationes* of the subordinate governors must derive therefrom. The eternal law is the *summa ratio*, and all other laws insofar as they participate in right reason, i.e. insofar as they are laws at all, derive from it.[27] It is easy to see here St. Augustine's *lex moderatrix humanarum* systematised and developed by being brought into relation with St. Thomas's general concept of law.

From another point of view, too, God is seen to be the eternal legislator. He can legislate for all beings because he is their

[24] 1–2ae, q. 91, a. 1; q. 93, a. 1: "Lex aeterna nihil aliud est quam ratio divinae sapientiae secundum quam est directiva omnium actuum et motionum."

[25] 1a, q. 22, aa. 1–4.

[26] 1–2ae, q. 93, aa. 4,5.

[27] 1–2ae, q. 93, a. 3.

Creator and, in creating, can impress in their very natures the principles of their operations. Legislation involves control over the actions of the beings subordinated to it. And, since the nature of a given being is its principle of operation legislation means affecting the nature. That is why God is the universal legislator; he controls the natures of all beings. Man can legislate, on the contrary, only for those beings to whose nature he has a certain access, namely his fellow-man. This he does by impressing upon his subjects, that is making known to them, a practical proposition which becomes, for them, a principle of operation.[28] The point, although St. Thomas only makes it incidentally here, is worth noting for the confirmation it affords of his view that law is essentially a proposition, an item of practical knowledge.

C. THE NATURAL LAW AND ITS PRECEPTS.

St. Thomas's consideration of the eternal law to some extent anticipates what he has to say of the natural law in the *Summa Theologiae.* He has already remarked upon the special way in which rational creatures come under the eternal law. Now he goes further and says that the participation of rational creatures is such that, in them, it satisfies the definition of law; it is, in fact, the natural law. It is not a question of knowing the eternal law as it is in itself – that would require the Beatific Vision – but of knowing it, in a greater or less degree, in its effects.

When he considers in set terms the question of the existence of a natural law St. Thomas argues as follows. Law, a "rule or measure," can exist in either of two ways – *in regulante et mensurante* (where it always formally satisfies the definition of law, being a universal proposition of the practical reason ordered to action) or *in regulato et mensurato* (when it does not always satisfy the definition of law). The eternal law in God – *in regulante et mensurante* – is genuinely a law; is it also law in creatures, *in regulatis et mensuratis?* Once again the answer lies with the special position of rational creatures who come under divine providence in a "more excellent way," making provision for themselves and for other creatures. They participate in the eternal law "intellectually and rationally" and this participation, which is genuinely a law, is the natural law. Natural law may then

[28] 1–2ae, q. 93, aa. 4,5.

be defined as "the participation of the eternal law in a rational creature."[29]

It is clear, then, that the natural law is, in St. Thomas's view, a proposition or a series of propositions of the practical reason. This is confirmed when he has to answer the question: Is the natural law a *habitus* or not? The view that natural law is a *habitus*, as we have seen, had a considerable weight of tradition behind it. Consistently with his general notion of law, he concludes that the natural law is not a *habitus*. On the contrary it is the work of reason, just as a proposition is the work of reason, and must not be confounded with the process by which it is set up. But St. Thomas adds at once, with his usual deference to authority, that the natural law may loosely be termed a *habitus* because its precepts are not always under active consideration, but, like the first principles of the speculative intellect, are sometimes in the intellect *habitualiter tantum.*[30]

The comparison between the speculative and the practical intellect will have been noticed once again. Each proceeds from principles to conclusions, the speculative intellect from certain, naturally-known indemonstrable principles to a knowledge that is not "naturally impressed" but is the result of its own efforts, namely the conclusions of the sciences; the practical intellect from the precepts of the natural law to more particular dispositions.[31] There remains the further question why intellect, speculative or practical, should require first principles at all. It will be recalled, apropos of *synderesis*, that in the *Commentary on the Sentences* and in the *De Veritate* St. Thomas had used two arguments to prove the need for first principles, one depending upon the neo-Platonic principle of the perfect hierarchical continuity of creation, the other upon the principle that motion requires a fixed starting-point. The neo-Platonic argument is omitted in the *Summa* and the argument from the nature of motion is restated much as it is found in the *De Veritate.*[32]

Which are these principles? And how are they known? These questions are raised by St. Thomas in an article that has claims to be considered his greatest single contribution to the theory of the natural law. The key to the solution is familiar; the parallel between the speculative and the practical intellect, but here

[29] 1–2ae, q. 91, a. 2: "Lex naturalis nihil aliud est quam participatio legis aeternae in rationali creatura."

[30] 1–2ae, q. 94, a. 1.

[31] 1–2ae, q. 91, a. 3.

[32] Compare, however, 1a, q. 78, a. 2.

developed with a fecundity not found in the earlier works, The article begins:

> The precepts of the natural law are related to the practical intellect in the same away as the first principles of demonstration are related to the speculative intellect, for both are self-evident principles.[33]

There follows a discussion of the nature of self-evidence (*per se notitia*). Analytic propositions, whose predicate is contained in the notion of the subject, are self-evident. But such a proposition may not be universally self-evident; it will not be evident to one who does not have the necessary understanding of the terms. So the proposition that an angel is not circumscriptively localized is self-evident – but only to those who understand that an angel is not quantified; it is not self-evident to "the unlettered who do not grasp this." On the other hand propositions such as: 'The whole is greater than the part' or 'Equals of equals are themselves equals' are self-evident to all and sundry because the terms involved are known to all.[34]

Are the precepts of the natural law self-evident *secundum se* merely? Or, if they are evident *quoad nos*, are they evident only to the specialists or to everyone? In the present article St. Thomas does not answer these questions; he leaves the answers to be inferred from the comparison with the first principles of the speculative intellect. It will be easier to discover the answers when the precepts have been examined more closely.

The question St. Thomas has put himself is: Are the precepts of the natural law one or many? And his reply is that the precepts of the natural law are many, but reducible to a single fundamental precept: Do good and avoid evil.

There is a certain order to be observed in the objects of apprehension. What is first apprehended is being, the notion of which is included in all that a man apprehends. Hence the first indemonstrable principle, "that what is affirmed cannot at the same time be denied," is based upon the notions of being and of non-being. Upon it all other principles are founded. Just as being is what is first apprehended, simply speaking, so the good is what is first apprehended by the practical reason. Hence the first

[33] 1–2ae, q. 94, a. 2.

[34] *Ibid.*, cf. 1a, q. 2, a. 1, where such terms are said to be "quaedam communia-quae nullus ignorat, ut ens et non-ens, totum et pars et similia." The question of self-evidence is dealt with by St. Thomas in several works apropos of the ontological argument for God's existence: *In 1 Sent.*, d. 3, q. 1, a. 2; *De pot.*, q. 7, a. 2 ad 11; *Cont. Gent.* I, c. 11.

principle in the practical reason, based upon the notion of the good, is that good ought to be done and evil avoided. This is the "first precept of the law," and upon it are based all the other precepts of the natural law, namely "all those things which, according to the precepts of the natural law, ought to be done or avoided, practical reason naturally recognising them as human goods (and evils)."[35]

The doctrine of a fundamental precept of the natural law seems to be a real advance on St. Thomas's earlier works. There are, indeed, to be found traces of this way of thinking before the *Summa Theologiae*, but no clear statement. In the *Commentary, on the Sentences*, for example, the "primary and infallible measure" of human action is given, not as: *Bonum est faciendum et malum vitandum*, but as the Ten Commandments which express the intention of the Legislator and are "that in which the form of justice and of virtue in general consists."[36] And, in a passage where he does give a single fundamental precept, and even compares it with the principle of contradiction in speculative matters, the precept proves to be the injunction about loving one's neighbour.[37] Finally, in several passages which give examples of precepts of the natural law, *Malum est vitandum*[38] is mentioned as one among the others, without much indication that it is more important or more fundamental than those others.[39] The *Summa* sets the fundamental precept apart, quite unambiguously, as form and the foundation of all the rest.

Not alone is the fundamental precept the form of the rest, but without the other precepts it is itself otiose. "Do good and avoid evil" is a precept that obviously has to be supplemented by a knowledge of what, in fact, is good, what evil. St. Thomas had erected the general principle about doing good and avoiding evil upon man's general inclination towards good-in-general. Now man has also specific inclinations towards specific goods and these inclinations offer the foundation for the specific precepts of the natural law.

[35] 1–2ae, q. 94, a. 2.

[36] *In 3 Sent.*, d. 37, q. 1, a. 4, Sed contra.

[37] *Ibid.*, a. 2, quaestiuncula 2 ad 2.

[38] Despite appearances *Bonum est faciendum et malum vitandum* is a single precept; the good which ought to be done (i.e. is of obligation) is that whose omission is an evil; and the omision of evil is itself a good that ought to be done.

[39] *In 2 Sent.*, d. 24, q. 2, a. 3.

Since the good has the nature of an end, and evil is its contrary, it follows that the objects towards which man has a natural inclination are naturally apprehended by reason as goods and, consequently, as things which ought to be done, and their contraries as evils and to be avoided. Thus the order of the precepts of the natural law follows that of the natural inclinations. In the first place there is in man an inclination to good following the nature which he shares with all substances, inasmuch as every substance desires the preservation of its being according to its nature. Following this inclination those things are of the natural law which preserve the life of man and hinder what is contrary to it. Secondly, there is in man a more particular inclination which follows the nature which he shares with other animals. According to this, those things are said to be of the natural law which "nature has taught all animals" such as the union of male and female, the education of offspring and so on. Thirdly there is in man an inclination to good, which follows the rational nature which is proper to him. Thus man has a natural inclination to know the truth about God and to live in society. Following this, whatever regards such inclination belongs to the natural law e.g. that man should avoid ignorance, that he should not injure those with whom he ought to have intercourse and so on . . .[40]

In the interpretation of this celebrated passage there are certain points to be borne in mind. The first is that the specific precepts are not deduced from the fundamental precept about doing good and avoiding evil; goods and evils must be discovered independently of that principle (this is where the natural inclinations enter) and when identified they are related to the purely formal principle which tells what good and evil imply. The first principle is a mould into which propositions about good and evil are pressed; itself it gives no indication of content, any more than the principle of non-contradiction can give knowledge of the world or be a substitute for experience, even though it is conceded that experiential knowledge must have respect for the principle.[41]

Secondly, St. Thomas's division of natural inclinations into three kinds does not correspond with any real division in the nature of man. Man is not made up of three natures, substantial, sensitive and rational, successively superimposed one upon the other. The nature of man is one, and the single rational soul performs, *eminentiori modo,* the functions of man considered as a substance or as an animal. Reason, then, enters at all three levels of natural inclination.[42] In fact there is the appearance of a

[40] 1–2ae, q. 94, a. 2.

[41] On this topic see the excellent brief discussion in E. D'Arcy, *Conscience and its Right to Freedom*, pp. 49–55.

[42] 1a, q. 76, aa, 3,4; 1–2ae, q. 94, a. 4 ad 3; q. 100, a. 2 ad 1.

vicious circle here; the rational precepts of the natural law must follow the natural inclinations, but these inclinations must, themselves, be in accordance with reason.[43] That is a difficulty that St. Thomas does not face directly in the present article, but he proposes it in all its acuteness, following Aristotle, in his discussion of right reason in the *Commentary on the Ethics.*[44] It is a point that makes its appearance in the contemporary controversies about the natural law.

Finally, the division of man's natural inclinations into three groups cuts across the division, found in the *Commentary on the Sentences,* between primary and secondary precepts of the natural law. There are primary and secondary precepts belonging to each of the three grades of inclination.

D. PRIMARY AND SECONDARY PRECEPTS OF THE NATURAL LAW

St. Thomas's distinction between primary and secondary precepts of the natural law may now be profitably scrutinized, for there is an important shift in his thinking between the *Commentary on the Sentences* and the *Summa Theologiae.* In the *Commentary on the Sentences* the problem, it will be recalled, was the specific one of determining the status of polygamy vis-à-vis the natural law. It transpires that polygamy (rather polygyny) is against the secondary precepts, but not necessarily against the primary precepts. The primary precepts are said to be the equivalent, in matters of conduct, of the *communes conceptiones* in speculative matters. And, as in speculative matters conclusions hold good in virtue of the self-evident principles from which they derive, so in practical matters we may derive further principles from the primary principles. These further principles – or conclusions – are the secondary precepts of the natural law.[45] This distinction is of capital importance, and it is clear that St. Thomas regards it as a development of the concept of the natural law he had just outlined, for it

[43] 1–2ae q. 94, a.2: "Omnia illa ad quae homo habet naturalem inclinationem ratio naturaliter apprehendit ut bona et per consequens ut opere prosequenda, et contraria eorum ut mala et vitanda. Secundum igitur ordinem inclinationum naturalium est ordo praeceptorum legis naturae"; Ibid., ad 2 – "hujusmodi inclinationes . . . secundum quod regulantur ratione, pertinent ad legem naturalem."

[44] *In 6 Eth.*, lect. 2 (*Sententia libri Ethicorum*, Romae, 1969, VI, 2, p. 337).

[45] *In 4 Sent.*, d. 33, a. 1, a. 1.

depends upon an analysis of the natural ends of action. The principle is:

Everything that causes in an action a lack of proportion to the end is said to be against the law of nature.[46]

The distinction between primary and secondary precepts of the natural law will follow, therefore, the distinction between the primary and secondary ends or intentions of nature.[47] Examples of primary ends, ends primarily intended by nature, are in the use of food, bodily health; in marriage, the procreation and upbringing of children. Examples of secondary ends would be the becoming performance of one's functions,[48] as the purpose of eating, or the mutual assistance of the partners and the symbolism of Christ's union with His Church as the ends of marriage. Now the end of a given action may be hindered in either of two ways – by being totally excluded or by being made more difficult or less becoming of attainment. For example, over-much or excessively little in the matter of food entirely frustrates both primary and secondary natural ends of eating; whereas inordinateness with regard to the time of eating only makes those ends more difficult to secure. Those precepts of the natural law which forbid whatever totally impedes the primary end of nature now become the *primary precepts*: the other precepts (those which forbid whatever makes the attainment of the primary end of nature more difficult or less becoming, or whatever excludes the secondary end or hinders its attainment) are the *secondary precepts.*

The distinction is undoubtedly attractive; it has been welcomed into almost every treatise on the natural law since St. Thomas's time.[49] It does, indeed, seem reasonable to suppose that the natural law is more decided and unchangeable with regard to some matters than with regard to others. It is the kind of *practical* distinction that must follow the natural law if it is to be at all reasonable, the kind of distinction St. Thomas hints at in earlier

[46] *Ibid.*, "Omne autem illud quod actionem inconvenientem reddit fini quam natura ex opere aliquo intendit, contra legem naturae est."

[47] Cf. *In 4 Sent.*,d. 33, a. 2, a. 2, quaestiuncula 1.

[48] *In 4 Sent.*, d. 33, a. 1, a. 1: " . . . bona habitudo in negotiis exercendis."

[49] The distinction between the primary and the secondary ends of marriage seems recently, however, to have been given its quietus, doubtless because, at the end of its seven centuries' history, in contemporary controversies, it was made to bear far too much weight.

passages of his *Commentary on the Sentences.*[50] But to say, as he does here, that the primary and secondary precepts are related as principle and conclusion,[51] with the further implication – because of the parallel with first principles in the speculative reason – that the primary precepts are immediately or intuitively known (i.e. that they are self-evident) whereas the secondary precepts are known mediately and as the result of a reasoning – must appear to be something in the nature of an assumption. One looks in vain for a discussion of this identification, or for a recognition that it is an assumption. Elsewhere St. Thomas is content to use the parallel between the principles of the practical intellect and those of the speculative intellect in order to show that there are some precepts of the natural law that are self-evident, others that depend upon a reasoning process. But such a distinction implies a reference to something objective (such as the 'ends of nature') which will give a reason *why* some precepts should be known immediately, others only after a reasoning. This is a problem that St. Thomas hardly faces squarely, even later in the *Summa Theologiae.* The elements of the problem are clearly present in the *Commentary on the Sentences.*

As has already been seen, St. Thomas in proposing the distinction between primary and secondary precepts was not entirely innovating; there were foreshadowings of the distinction before his time. William of Auxerre had distinguished between natural law precepts of first and second necessity – and even between precepts of first, second, third and fourth degrees of necessity.[52] The same distinction appears in the *Summa* or *Liber quaestionum* of St. Thomas's fellow-Dominican and predecessor at Paris, Roland of Cremona, who applies it to the question of possible dispensations in the natural law. Roland's solution of the problem of the polygamy of the Old Testament patriarchs is very

[50] Cf. *In 2 sent.*, d. 24, q. 2, a. 4 ad 6 (distinction between the principles of the natural law and the conclusions contained in them); *In 3 Sent.*, d. 37, q. 1, a. 3 (distinction between laws which are 'impressed upon reason itself' and others 'directly and immediately reducible' to these); *Ibid.*, a. 4 ad 2 (distinction between what is 'always and in all places just' and what 'proceeds from this").

[51] O. Lottin calls it the contrast between the 'objective extension' and the 'logical extension' of the natural law; cf. *Principes de morale*, II, pp. 38–40.

[52] O. Lottin, *Le droit naturel chez saint Thomas d'Aquin et ses prédécesseurs*, pp. 37, 76; Id., *Psychologie et morale aux XIIIe et XIIIe siècles*, II, p. 76; M. Grabmann, "Das Naturrecht der Scholastik von Gratian bis Thomas von Aquin" in *Mittelalterliches Geistesleben*, I, p. 74.

similar to St. Thomas's.[53] The source of William of Auxerre and Roland of Cremona may well have been the distinction found in the decretists, following Rufinus[54] between *mandata et prohibitiones* (which deal with what is of strict necessity) and *demonstrationes* (which regard what is *conveniens*) – which distinction Rufinus and his followers may have derived, in turn, from Rolando Bandinelli.[55] Much further back there is the distinction, current among the Fathers, between primary and secondary precepts or, better, a primary and a secondary natural law. This however, is understood in reference to a doctrine of a state of nature, with its law, before the Fall and the state of fallen nature after original sin. Finally, that doctrine of the Fathers was, partly at least, the result of a borrowing from Stoic sources and an adaptation to Christianity. Cicero and Seneca in particular, have the notion of a primeval state of innocence (with its ideal natural law) which was replaced by a state of corrupted nature (with the actual natural law).[56]

Whatever the degree of St. Thomas's originality in the matter, the distinction between the primary and secondary precepts of the natural law offered, in the present context, the advantage of providing a justification for the conclusion that polygamy is contrary to the natural law only in an attenuated sense.[57] Perhaps it has too much the look of being constructed just for this purpose. At all events it is curious that St. Thomas does not later return to the distinction based upon the ends of nature. Whatever is the basis for the distinction between primary and secondary precepts in the *Summa* it is not this; or at least not explicitly. Unfortunately St. Thomas died before reaching the questions on marriage in the *Summa Theologiae* so that it will never be known how he would have treated the problem of polygamy in his later years. The account in the *Supplementum Tertiae Partis*[58] is, of course, taken from the *Commentary on the Sentences*; and its presence here probably explains in part the great authority enjoyed by the distinction in post-Thomistic writers. But St. Thomas

[53] *Summa Magistri Rolandi Cremonensis*, III (ed. A. Cortesi, Bergamo, 1962), q. 187, pp. 557–558.

[54] *Die Summa Decretorum des Magister Rufinus* (ed. Singer), p. 6.

[55] Cf. supra chapter IV, pp. 94–96.

[56] Cf. supra Chapter III, p. 58; J. Fuchs, *Natural Law-a Theological Investigation*, pp. 85–109.

[57] *In 4 Sent.*, d. 33, q. 1, a. 1: "...quodammodo contra legem naturae, quodammodo non est contra legem naturae".

[58] *Supplementum tertiae partis*, q. 65, a. 1.

himself may have realised that it raises as many problems as it solves and, therefore, abandoned it.

The *Prima-Secundae* does not repeat the distinction between primary and secondary precepts of the natural law found in the *Commentary on the Sentences*, but it has a distinction that bears it close resemblance. The basis of the distinction is no longer the ends or "intentions of nature" but takes us back to the question of the evidence of the natural law. In the law-tract St. Thomas gives slightly differing versions of this new distinction.

In the question on the natural law the distinction seems to run as follows:[59]

Primary common principles (*quaedam praecepta communissima*) are equally well-known to all men (a. 4) altogether immutable (a. 5), although concupiscence or passion may prevent their application in a given instance (a. 6).

The proximate conclusions from the foregoing principles (*quasi quaedam propriae conclusiones propinquae primis principiis* neither apply in all circumstances (aa. 4,5), nor, when they do apply, are always known (aa. 4,6).

The distinction is not as sharp as it seems.[60] When he deals with the moral precepts of the Old Law St. Thomas uses a threefold distinction:[61]

Principia prima naturaliter cognita or the absolutely primary precepts.

The proximate deductions from those principles, arrived at *statim cum modica consideratione.*

Other deductions which depend upon a more involved process of reasoning – the work of a specialist.

This version has found the favour of theologians and philosophers since St. Thomas. Both versions depend upon the rational character of the natural law and the function of reason in establishing its precepts, and they are strongly reminiscent of the early teaching on *synderesis* and conscience, for example in the *De Veritate.*

St. Thomas has surprisingly little to say about what precepts fall into these various categories. Even if one adds the contribution of various passages in his works other than the *Summa*, where he

[59] 1–2ae, q. 94.

[60] Cajetan, *Comm. in 1am–2ae*, q. 94 finds an ambiguity in St. Thomas's *prima praecepta*, sometimes primary without qualification, sometimes *prima in tali ordine.*

[61] 1–2ae, q. 100, aa. 1,3.

speaks of precepts "immediately known," "belonging to the habit of first practical principles," "naturally known and indemonstrable," "infallible" or "impressed as self-evident on the natural reason," the list is short and the examples given are never more than merely illustrative.[62] His real answer to the question: What are the precepts of the natural law?, is given in an article that has already been quoted. Speaking of the fundamental precept: *Bonum est faciendum et malum vitandum*, St. Thomas adds.

and on this are founded all the other precepts of the law of nature, so that all that the practical reason naturally recognises as human goods (or evils) belong to the natural law as things that ought to be done or avoided.[63]

In other words, just as the fundamental precept of all, *Bonum est faciendum et malum vitandum*, is based on the general tendency of human nature towards the good-in-general, so the other precepts are based upon the specific tendencies or inclinations of human nature towards particular goods; and, furthermore, the objects of these natural tendencies are *naturally* recognised as human goods. Now, for St. Thomas "natural knowledge" is the equivalent of self-evident knowledge or *per se notitia*.[64] So, there is here the possibility of a bridge between the distinction of primary and secondary precepts based on the ends of nature (*Commentary on the Sentences*), and the distinction of the precepts of the natural law that are naturally known from those that require a reasoning, more or less involved, for their recognition (*Summa*). Briefly, what is the primary intention of nature will also be intuitively known. And there the suggestion must be left.

E. THE VARIABILITY OF THE NATURAL LAW

Regarding the variability of the natural law, and the complexity of the field of human action which is its cause, the *Summa* resumes and systematizes the teaching of the earlier works.

The object of the practical intellect has not the necessary truth of the object of the speculative intellect – for human actions are

[62] *In 2 Sent.*, d. 24, q. 2, aa. 3,4; *De verit.*, q. 16, a. 1 ad 9; q. 17, a. 2; *Quodl. III*, a. 26.

[63] 1–2ae, q. 94, a. 2.

[64] *Cont. Gent.*, I, c. 10: "quae naturaliter sunt nota per se cognoscuntur; non enim ad ea cognoscenda inquisitionis studio pervenitur"; *In 1 Sent.*, d. 3, q. 2 ad 1; *In 4 Metaph.*, d. 3, q. 2 ad 1; *In 4 Metaph.*, lectio 6.

contingent. Thus, although the first principles of the practical intellect have a degree of necessity – *aliqua necessitas* – the further one descends to detail the more frequent will be the cases where the rule does not apply. The number of circumstances that must be taken into account precludes the rigid application of rule to each and every case. St. Thomas gives the well-tried example of the return of goods held in trust. Normally to return a deposit is to act in accordance with reason; but if the goods are sought for the purpose of rebellion against lawful authority it would be irrational to return them.[65]

The complexity of circumstances surrounding every human act is ineluctable and no legislation can meet every contingency. No human legislation can cater for all possibilities. Nor can the natural law. On one side there are its precepts and, on the other, the complexity and variability of moral life; and between the two a point-for-point correspondence cannot be established.[66]

This being so, it is little wonder that there should exist great differences between the morals of one society and another. St. Thomas instances the Germans in Caesar's *De bello gallico* who did not consider theft unlawful "although it expressly contradicts the natural law" and the morals castigated by St. Paul in the first chapter of his *Epistle to the Romans.* Such moral variations do not involve a denial of the natural law; they are due to the complexity with which the natural law is faced, to the corruption of human nature that takes advantage of that complexity and to the unequal development of reason which may prevent men from seeing clearly and, so, from acting rightly.[67]

There is room also for great divergence in the particular principles that men hold as self-evident. This is a consequence of the dependence of our knowledge of the natural law on the exercise of reason. The reasoning may be so simple and obvious that it becomes a process scarcely distinct from intuition. But what is thus evident to one, with a particular kind of education and cultural background, may not be so at all to one with a different background; or it may require a considerable effort of reasoning.[68]

[65] 1–2ae, q. 94, a. 4; cf. 2–2ae, q. 57, a. 2 ad 1.

[66] 1–2ae, q. 96, a. 6 ad 3.

[67] 1–2ae, q. 96, a. 4; J. Leclercq, *Les grandes lignes de la philosophie morale,* pp. 404–406.

[68] Cf. *Cont. Gent.*, c. 11; "Consuetudo autem, et praecipue quae est a puero, vim naturae obtinet; ex quo contingit ut ea quibus a pueritıa animus inbuitur, ita firmiter teneat ac si essent naturaliter et per se nota."

On this controversial matter of the reconciliation of the natural law with the patent variations in moral convictions and moral codes, whether one compares individuals, cultural situations or historical epochs, the views of St. Thomas have quite a contemporary ring. His system is far more flexible than the interpretations to which it has often been subjected. And, as the main argument of this book is that his views do have a highly important relevance to the contemporary moral scene, it will be in order to dilate somewhat upon the problem of natural law and moral variations. It is not, of course, the failure to observe the precepts of a natural law that is in question – the existence of a valid law is perfectly consistent with the disobedience of those subject to it. What does present a difficulty is that an allegedly natural law, said to be based upon human nature and consequently accessible to all men, should have been and should still be subject to such varying, not to say contradictory, interpretations. St. Thomas offers, broadly, three kinds of explanation:

When St. Thomas 'finds himself in the presence of different moralities, of contradictory laws, of diversely organized institutions,' he neither regards every variation as an anomaly nor attributes all divergences to the same cause. The explanations scattered through his works may be grouped under three heads: 1. the influence of the passions; 2. the unequal development of reason, of insight and of civilization; 3. the diversity of conditions, of situations, and of circumstances.[69]

The possibility of moral variations arising out of 'passion' does not require much elaboration. Human nature, whatever it is, is not exclusively rational; there is an affective and emotional side, not to speak of the bodily aspect, that must be taken into consideration when human behaviour is studied. For this reason Aristotle rejected the Socratic identification of virtue and knowledge and discussed at length the paradox of the incontinent man, the man who knows what is right and yet does the opposite. St. Paul put it more concretely, and in a theological setting: "the good which I will, I do not; but the evil which I will not, that I do ... but I see another law in my members, fighting against the law of my mind, and captivating me in the law of sin."[70] St. Thomas accepted the position; for him it was a patent fact that men acted sometimes out of passion and in spite of knowledge. He repeats the point more than once when speaking of the

[69] S. Deploige, *Le conflit de la morale et de la sociologie*, pp. 291–292.

[70] *Rom*, 7; 19–23; cf. Ovid, *Metamorph.* VII, 20: "Video meliora proboque, deteriora sequor."

natural law. We have already seen his reference to the Germans whom Caesar had accused of not regarding robbery as wrong. And even more striking is his insistence upon the necessity of moral precepts in the Old Law, brushing aside the objection that human reason ought to be able to discover these for itself:

> The habit of sinning blinds reason in particular cases; and concerning other moral precepts, which are as the conclusions drawn from the common principles of the natural law, the reason of many went astray in such wise that it recognised as licit what is in itself evil.[71]

Here the reference seems to be to something more than the ordinary influence of passion upon conduct; it is not the one gust of passion that extinguishes reason but the habitual bias that corrupts the objectivity of reason; what Plato calls "the lie in the soul." And St. Thomas allows it full scope.

The second factor explaining moral variations is the caducity of human reason. The individual reason is fallible; we all make mistakes, in our practical decisions as well as in our theoretical conclusions. St. Thomas seems to have accepted Aristotle's doctrine of the practical syllogism, moral decision being the conclusion drawn from moral premisses. He therefore mentions, side by side with the evil customs that corrupt good manners, the erroneous convictions that produce wrong conclusions: "the natural law can be blotted out from the hearts of men because of wrong convictions, in the same way that, in speculative matters, errors come about in necessary conclusion."[72] The deficiency of human reason, however, extends to more than simple error in the deductive process. There is the larger question of unequal development, not merely the difference between one individual and another, but, particularly, the differences between entire peoples at different stages of civilization. Jacques Maritain finds here the "law of the progress of moral conscience," which he considers to be a most important law in the philosophy of history. He speaks, of course, of progress in the knowledge of the moral law, which does not mean that men necessarily behave better. He gives as examples of this progress the present-day awareness that slavery is contrary to the dignity of the human person, that prisoners of war

[71] 1–2ae, q. 99, a. 2 ad 2. Cf. J.H. Newman, "Liberal Knowledge its own End" in *Scope and Nature of University Education*, Discourse IV, p. 112: "Quarry the granite rock with razors, or moor the vessel with a thread of silk; then may you hope with such keen and delicate instruments as human knowledge and human reason to contend against those giants, the passion and the pride of man."

[72] 1–2ae, q. 94, a. 6.

have rights, that child-labour is intolerable, that labour itself has its dignity, that authority does not need to be ruthless:

The sense of duty and obligation was always present, but the explicit knowledge of the various norms of natural law grows with time. And certain of these norms, like the law of monogamy, were known rather late in the history of mankind, so far as it is accessible to our investigation. Also, we may think that the knowledge of the precepts of the natural law in all of their precise aspects and requirements will continue to grow until the end of human history.[73]

This conception of progress and development in moral ideas is one that must be carefully distinguished from the view that moral ideas are simply products of evolution. This will be seen in its place. Meantime, the idea of growth points the way to the third of the factors that, in St. Thomas's view, makes for variation in morals – diversity of conditions, situations and circumstances.

This factor proves to be the most radical of all in explaining why men have so differed, and still differ, in their moral convictions as well as in their moral behaviour. For it goes deeper than the blinding of reason by passion or prejudice, deeper than the inadequacy of human reason faced with the complexity of some moral situations, right down to the nature of moral reasoning and to the essentials of the moral order. Moral decision, in fact, differs essentially from the conclusion drawn from speculative premisses – this is where the practical syllogism breaks down – and the principles of morality do not share the kind of universality and permanence characteristic of speculative assertions. St. Thomas accepted Aristotle's wise observation, at the beginning of the *Nicomachean Ethics*, that we should seek in each discussion only such precision as the subject-matter admits – "it is evidently equally foolish to accept probable reasoning from a mathematician and to demand from a rhetorician scientific proofs." With regard to "fine and just actions"

we must be content . . . in speaking of such subjects and with such premisses to indicate the truth roughly and in outline, and in speaking about things which are only for the most part true and with premisses of the same kind to reach conclusions that are no better.[74]

St. Thomas, in the *Summa Theologiae*, puts this view to work with interesting results. He is discussing the question whether the

[73] J. Maritain, *On the Philosophy of History*, pp. 82–83; cf. M. Ginsberg, *On the Diversity of Morals*, pp. 97–129 for a discussion of "variations due to differences of moral insight and general level of development, moral and intellectual."

[74] *Nic. Eth.*, I, 3, 1094 b 11–17; cf. II, 2, 1104 a 2–7.

natural law is the same for all men and he has, of course, to find an explanation for the evident discrepancies between men's views of that law. His argument turns upon the difference between speculative reasoning, which proceeds from firm principles to necessary conclusions, and practical reasoning which, while it may be sure of its principles – *si in communibus sit aliqua necessitas* – has to do with contingent human action. In speculative matters truth is the same for all, although perhaps not equally available to all since it may require effort or ability to see it; it is true, for all who are capable of understanding, that the angles of a triangle are together equal to two right angles. But in practical affairs one cannot always say that there is truth, if only one could discover it; the very truth may be different for one man and for another.[75]

It is right and true for all, without exception, that one should act in accordance with reason. From this it follows that goods held in trust should be returned when the owner claims them; and so it happens in the majority of cases. But the exceptional case may arise in which it would be harmful and, consequently, irrational to return the goods – if the goods were required by their owner *ad impugnandam patriam.*[76] In a word, the complexity of circumstances surrounding every human act is ineluctable and no law, not even the natural law, can cater for every contingency. The matter is plain in human law; no legislator can foresee all the possibilities his law may meet. If he tries to do so his law becomes a thicket of qualifying clauses and – worse still – the more conditions it includes the greater is the chance of one or other being unfulfilled and so rendering the law itself nugatory.[77]

St. Thomas, then, had a more flexible conception of the natural

[75] 1–2ae, q. 94, a. 4.

[76] Plato, *Republic,* I, 4331 C: "If we had been given weapons by a friend when he was of sound mind, and he went mad and reclaimed them, it would surely be universally admitted that it would not be right to give them back. Anyone who did so, and who was prepared to tell the whole truth to a man in that state, would not be just." A similar moral case is discussed in Xenophon, *Memorabilia,* IV, c. 2. But a more likely source for the scholastics is Cicero, *De officiis,* III, c. 26: "Si gladium quis apud te sana mente deposuerit, repetat insaniens, reddere peccatum sit, officium non reddere. Quid? Si is, qui apud te pecuniam deposuerit, bellum inferat patriae reddasne depositum? Non credo: facias enim contra rempublicam, quae debet esse carissima. Sic multa, quae honesta natura videntur esse, temporibus fiunt non honesta; facere promissa, stare conventis, reddere deposita commutata utilitate fiunt non honesta."

[77] 1–2*ae, q.* 96, *a.* 6 *ad* 3: "Nullius hominis possit omnes sapientia tanta est, ut singulares causas excogitare . . . et si posset legislator omnes casus considerare, non opporteret ut omnes exprimeret propter confusionem vitandam. . . ."

law than he is sometimes credited with. Passion and human fallibility as sources of moral diversity are compatible with a rigid view of human nature and of its law; but if differences in circumstances and situations can provoke differences in moral solutions it becomes less easy to be firm about nature and law. St. Thomas is, indeed, driven to say more than once in this connection: *Natura humana mutabilis est.* The phrase may epitomize his views on human nature and morality.[78]

Aristotle has been quoted on the uncertainty inescapable in moral propositions. One may conclude this already long section with a brief reference to St. Thomas's *Commentary on the Nicomachean Ethics,* a work that is now recognised to belong to the very end of his life. Aquinas takes Aristotle's point that there must be a variability in moral matters; he recognises that the moralist's terrain is a "shifting soil where the circumspection is indispensable and where advance is made gropingly."[79] Where Aristotle says:

> The whole account of matters of conduct must be given in outline and not precisely . . . the accounts we demand must be in accordance with the subject-matter; matters concerned with conduct and questions of what is good for us have no fixity . . . . The general account being of this nature, the account of particular cases is yet more lacking in exactness. . . .[80]

St. Thomas goes as far as to add that the causes of particular actions vary in infinite ways.[81] Such being the nature of the material which goes to make up human action it is obvious that the universality and immutability of morality, the province of the natural law, must be understood with certain reservations. And where Aristotle makes explicit mention of moral variations, as an objection to his theory of natural justice, his reply is rather laconic:

> It is evident which sort of things, among things capable of being otherwise, is by nature and which is not, but is legal and conventional, assuming that both are equally changeable.[82]

[78] 2–2ae, q. 57, a. 2; Cf. *Suppl. 3ae partis,* q. 41, a. 1 ad 3; *De malo,* q. 2, a. 4, ad 13; also M.B. Crowe, "Human Nature-Immutable or Mutable?" in *Irish Theological Quarterly,* 30 (1963), pp. 204–231.

[79] S. Deploige, *op. cit.,* p. 290.

[80] *Nic. Eth.,* II, 2, 1104 a 2–7.

[81] *In 2 Eth.,* lect. 2 (*Sententia libri Ethicorum,* Romae, 1969, II, 2, p. 81) "causae singularium operabilium variantur infinitis modis. . . ."; cf. *In* 2 *Eth.* lect. 8 in princ. (*Sententia libri Ethicorum,* II, 8, pp. 101–102): "Circa operationes universales sunt magis inanes et particulares sunt magis veri."

[82] *Nic. Eth.,* V, 7, 1134 b 30–32.

In expanding upon this, and within the limitations he set himself as a commentator anxious to elucidate Aristotle rather than to proffer his own views, St. Thomas repeats his views about the impossibility of universalizing moral judgements.[83]

If that last phrase appears startling and, at the least, to require qualification, it may be said that it is certainly more representative of St. Thomas's views than the complacent and rationalistic systems of deductive morality so often foisted upon him. But, before returning to this proposition, we must, in the chapters that follow, look at some significant features of the history of the natural law since St. Thomas.

[83] *In 5 Eth.*, lect. 12 (*Sententia libri Ethicorum*, V, 12 pp. 305–306).

CHAPTER VIII

THE BREAKING OF THE PROFILE AND ITS RE-MAKING

The profile of the natural law presented by St. Thomas Aquinas is not final; none is. But we have seen how painfully and painstakingly it was constructed, based upon the elements in a complex and age-long tradition and combining those elements in a new synthesis. It was not to be expected that this synthesis could remain unchanged – it must be adapted to new ages and new problems. It is the argument of this book that it is eminently capable of adaptation to the problems of our age, that it is still the best guide we have to morality. It must be seen, however, for what it is, with all its original flexibility and adaptability, and be purged of excrescences and misconceptions, the products of later ages. In this chapter and the following one we may take a selective look at the post-Thomistic history of the natural law in order to see how Thomas's concept was deformed and to discern how it may be recovered for our present instruction. There are two major turning-points in that history. The first, found in the nominalistic controversies from the fourteenth century down to and beyond the Reformation, will be the subject of this chapter; the second, the rise of the 'secular natural law' in the seventeenth and eighteenth centuries, will occupy the next chapter.

A. MODERATE NOMINALISM: SCOTUS

The contrast of views on the natural law between St. Thomas and his contemporary St. Bonaventure or, in general, between the Franciscan and the Dominican traditions in the matter, is hardly accentuated in the generation after Aquinas. One of Thomas's most distinguished pupils was his fellow-Dominican, Peter of Tarentaise, professor at Paris from 1259 to 1264 and probably again from 1267 to 1269, later Cardinal and finally (for the last months of his life, February–June 1276) Pope under the title of Innocent V. In his *Commentary on the Sentences* (1257–1259) Peter, discussing polygamy, concedes that there is a sense in which the natural law may be said to be common to all animals – for man shares a nature with all animals. The same view is found in his later *Quaestiones disputatae super praecepta* where he allows that fornication is not against the natural law common to all animals, while it is, of course, contrary to the specifically human natural law.[1] The division that governs these admissions is set out earlier in the same work. There are three kinds of law according as they regulate inanimate, animal or rational nature; but natural law, in the proper sense, applies only to rational nature. Specifically, apropos of fornication, Peter distinguishes the double nature in man, again confines natural law to the rational nature and excludes, for practical purposes, the animal nature.[2]

Giles of Rome (1247–1316), likewise a disciple of St. Thomas, in a well-known passage, in the *De regimine principum* distinguishes between the meanings of natural law – that common to all beings (in the sense in which Plato, in the *Timaeus*, speaks of a harmony between the parts of the universe); that common to all animals (the *ius animalium*, which is how Giles describes Ulpian's natural law); and that proper to man (called *ius gentium* by Giles and defined in the terms suggested by the Roman jurisconsult Gaius).[3]

As for the tradition in which Bonaventure stood, one may consider his pupil Matthew of Aquasparta (1240?–1302). Matthew having taught at Paris, Bologna and Rome, became, like

[1] *In IV Sent.*, d. 33, q. 1, a. 1 cited by O. Lottin, *Psychologie et morale aux XIIe et XIIIe siècles*, p. 92–93. Lottin also cites, *ibid.*, an anonymous *Commentary on the Sentences* in a Basle University ms. and some marginal comments on Peter of Tarentaise's *Commentary* in an Avignon ms. (Bâle Univ. B, VIII, 5; Avignon 288) for the same views.

[2] Ms. Arras 873, cited by Lottin, *op. cit.:* "Contra ius naturale illud dicitur esse quod est contra instinctum et dictamen naturae. Instinctus uero naturae duplex est; unus nature generalis qui est communis nobis et brutis; et hic est preter rationem et discretionem; alter uero specialis qui est proprius nobis, et hic est cum ratione et discretione...."

[3] III, Pars. ii, c. 25; cf. G. Fassò, *Storia della filosofia del diritto*, I, pp. 271–272; F. Pollock, "The History of the Law of Nature" in *Jurisprudence and Legal Essays* (ed. A. L. Goodhart), p. 128). Fassò is a little sanguine in his comment, *op. cit.*: "E manifesto presso Egidio Romano la coscienza dell' impossibilità di ridurre l'uno all'altro questi vari modi di concepire l'ordine giuridico, e altresì quella della destinazione puramente umana di uni di essi, quello posto della ragione. Evidentemente dopo San Tommaso, la vecchia confusione delle varie versione del diritto naturale non è più possible...."

his master, Minister-General of the Franciscans and a Cardinal. In his *Quaestiones disputatae*[4] it is clear that, in clear contrast with his master Bonaventure, Matthew has no use for a natural law common to all animals. He nowhere in these *Quaestiones* names Ulpian; but, following John of La Rochelle in the *Summa fratris Alexandri*, he argues for the existence of a natural law on the grounds that rational creatures require a law even more than irrational creatures, for rational creatures can err whereas irrational creatures cannot. Now irrational creatures *are* regulated by law, for example sun, moon and stars and the sense-creation (*animantia*). But Matthew, while prepared to turn Ulpian's definition of the natural law to the advantage of his argument, is by no means committed to the view that there is a natural law common to all animals; all he asserts, on what he believed to be the authority of Isidore, is that irrational creation is regulated by law.

Matthew's own arguments for the existence of a natural law, twenty-three arguments and seven 'proofs,' directed towards showing that the natural law is a law of reason, quite explicitly reject any reduction of the natural law to the irrational impulses in man: *non sic loquimur de lege naturali.*

There is, as yet, no radical break with the thirteenth century acceptance of the natural law, whether in the modality of Aquinas or of others. The break comes with John Duns Scotus (1266–1308) and his voluntarism was a reaction against the intellectualism of his thirteenth century predecessors and showed the way to the extreme or exaggerated voluntarism of later thinkers, particularly William of Ockham (1295–1350). This is the broad outline of a picture whose details are by no means clear.

The division between those who held that law is essentially an act of reason and those who held that it is essentially an act of will is already found in the thirteenth century; but the lines were not as clearly drawn as they were to be in the later Middle Ages. One might debate whether the concept of a natural law is really consistent only with an intellectualist approach to the nature of law. But be that as it may, it is clear that fourteenth century nominalism, drawing its inspiration from the voluntarism of John Duns Scotus, amounted to a denial of the kind of natural law asserted by Albert the Great, St. Thomas Aquinas and other intellectualists of the preceding century. The *quaedam prohibita quia mala* adage sufficiently characterises the intellectualist position. It is in the nature of things that some actions are evil; reason

[4] Fr Matthaei ab Aquasparta Quaestiones disputatae (ed. C. Piana, Quaracchi, 1959), *De legibus*, q. 2, De lege naturali, pp. 451–476.

can identify them but their malice is not dependent upon judgment or will, even those of God. God can no more alter this state of things than He can square the circle or make $2+2=5$. Defective human knowledge of such objective standards of good and evil is, of course, another matter.

That Scotus has something in common with both intellectualist and voluntarist approaches to morality is clear enough from his own statements. The formulae he uses on occasion in connexion with the problems of good and evil have always, in fact, presented something of a difficulty – his insistence, for example, on 'right reason' as the standard of right and wrong seems difficult to reconcile with his view that law is essentially a work of will.[5] Some see here, a trifle optimistically, a basic agreement between Scotus and Aquinas.[6] The truth, no doubt, lies somewhere between the extremes of agreement and irreconcilability.

Given the general trend of his metaphysics to emphasise the individual rather than the universal, it was perhaps to be expected that Scotus would not give any technical definition of 'nature' or of 'human nature.' He was not, of course, nominalist to the extent of denying a common human nature – a view later associated with Ockham.[7] But he was impressed by the ambiguity of the word 'nature.'[8] His conception of human nature, above all in the context of natural law, must be gleaned from his general metaphysical position, and particularly from his teaching on the relationship of intellect and will.

The question: Which is the nobler faculty, intellect or will? is almost as old as philosophy – as may be concluded from the

[5] *Ox.*, I, d. 17, qq. 1–2, n. 3: "convenientia actus ad rationem rectam est qua posita actus est bonus, et qua non posita, quibuscumque aliis conveniat, non est bonus...."; *Ox*, *Prol.*, q. 4, n. 5: "electio recta necessario requirit rationem rectam...."; cf. G. Stratenwerth, *Die Naturrechtslehre des Johannes Duns Scotus*, pp. 30–31; G. Budzik, *De conceptu legis ad mentem Joannis Duns Scoti*, passim.

[6] E.g. E. Piernikarczyk, "Das Naturrecht bei Johannes Duns Scotus" in *Philosophisches Jahrbuch*, 43 (1930), pp. 67–91: "...formaler Unterschied aber materiale Übereinstimmung" (p. 85). Contrast C.R.S. Harris, *Duns Scotus*, II, p. 331: "a latent contradiction in Scotus' thought... nor can we find any satisfactory solution to the antinomy."

[7] E. Gilson, *Jean Duns Scot: Introduction à ses positions fondamentales*, pp. 605–610. Cf. *Ox.*, II, d. 3, q. 1, n. 7: "natura est indifferens ad unitatem singularem"; G. Stratenwerth, *op. cit.*, p. 66; C.R.S. Harris, *op. cit.*, II, pp. 9–13.

[8] E.g. *Par.*, IV, d. 43, q. 4, scol. 1, nn. 2–5: "naturale est aequivocum et non uno modo dictum. Hoc apparet ex pluralitate illorum, quibus opponitur. Nam naturale uno modo opponitur libero ... secundo modo naturale opponitur supernaturali ... tertio modo naturale opponitur violento."

authorities quoted on either side in the thirteenth and fourteenth century controversies. Indeed when Scotus opposed the intellectualist view of Albert the Great, Thomas Aquinas, Godfrey of Fontaines and others and asserted instead the primacy of will, he could claim to represent the traditional opinion going back to St. Augustine and, beyond him, to the neo-Platonists and their predecessors. For Augustine will played a great part, even in the epistemological process itself.[9] The rediscovery of Aristotle's works, and of the Arab commentaries on them, in the thirteenth century, did much to provoke the great controversy. For Aristotle and his followers intellect predominated and the will was in a distinctly subordinate position, dependent upon intellect for its information. Certain expressions of this viewpoint seemed to rule out freedom. The Averroistic disputes, culminating in the condemnations of 1277, underlined the importance of the issue. Scotus, and some of his contemporaries, reacted against 'Greek necessitarianism' and stressed the fundamental character of liberty in God and man. There was a sense in which, for the intellectualist, nature was the opposite of freedom. This, quite apart from the recent condemnations of an excessive intellectualism bordering upon necessitarianism, was found unacceptable by thinkers like Henry of Ghent and Duns Scotus.

The specific question: *Utra potentia sit nobilior, intellectus vel voluntas?* allowed Scotus to set out his view of freedom, especially God's freedom in the creative act.[10] He rejected the dependence of will upon intellect as tantamount to a denial of the originality of God's will and an invasion of the divine freedom. The repercussions of this view, upon moral philosophy generally and upon the notion of the natural law in particular, were enormous. What can the nature of man be in this perspective of divine freedom? And in what sense, if at all, can this nature be said to give rise to a natural law?

For Scotus, God's will is supremely indifferent. Will, in general, cannot be determined by intellect, even by knowledge of the supreme good.[11] To say that God's will depends upon an object,

[9] Cf. E. Gibson, *Introduction à l'etude de saint Augustin*, pp. 312–314; G. Stratenwerth, *op. cit.*, pp. 5, 21–30; A.H. Chroust, "Hugo Grotius and the Scholastic Natural Law Tradition" in *The New Scholasticism*, 17 (1943), pp. 101–112.

[10] *Ox.*, IV, d. 49, q. ex latere post q. 4.

[11] *Ox.*, I, d. 1, q. 4: "... nihil voluntas necessario vult, et ideo non oportet quod necessario velit illud ratione cuius omnia alia vult, si quid esset tale." And in the context of natural law cf. *Ox.*, III, d. 37, q. un: "... voluntas divina in nihil aliud a se tendit nisi contingenter."

even an object presented by the divine intellect (as the intellectualist view requires), would be to take from the originality of the divine choice. The sole limitation upon what God wills is the principle of non-contradiction; and to be incapable of willing what is contradictory is, in reality, no limitation. Now God, in fact, chose to create man. Of the infinite number of possible combinations of simple ideas He chose to give reality to that one which constitutes human nature. He might have chosen otherwise. There can be nothing in the idea of human nature to render it necessary that God should have created man. This is common ground between intellectualists and voluntarists, as also is the assertion that God could have as easily created another nature in the place of man. None of this amounts to an attribution of arbitrariness or irrationality to God; if it did then Thomists no less than Scotists would have to answer for it. Scotus can still say that God wills all that He wills *rationabilissime*, *ordinatissime* and that His will is the *prima rectitudo*, the *prima regula omnium agibilium et omnium actionum.*[12] The real divergence between the Scotist and the Thomist views comes in the problem of deciding whether God, having created the human nature He did, is now bound by that nature, or whether He is free to impose any law, or no law, upon man. The dichotomy is clear between, on the one hand, the doctrine of a natural law settled by the nature of man, which God has freely created and which God Himself cannot, without contradiction, depart from and, on the other hand, the view that God's will must, even in this sphere, remain independent. The former, intellectualist view was put forward moderately enough by St. Thomas and was to receive its apotheosis in the rationalist eighteenth century; the latter, voluntarist view was exaggerated in fourteenth century Ockhamism which, in turn, paved the way for the exaltation of personal judgment at the time of the Reformation.

Where exactly Scotus stands on the question is not altogether clear. The celebrated distinction between the *potentia absoluta* and the *potentia ordinata* of God, a distinction much used by later nominalists, does not settle the question. If one says that God, of His absolute power could impose any law, whereas *de potentia ordinata* He is bound to respect the order of the natures He has chosen to create (i.e. to impose only what suits that order), a

[12] *Ox.*, III, d. 32, q. un, n. 6; *Par.*, III, d. 7, q. 4, n. 4; *Par.*, IV, d. 46, q. 4, n. 8. Cf. E. Piernikarczyk, *op. cit.*, p. 72, quoting E. Longpré, *La philosophie du B. Duns Scot.*

great deal depends upon where the stress is laid. To see where Scotus laid it let us turn to his conception of law.[13]

For Scotus law is essentially an act of will; here he takes issue fairly with the intellectualist view making law a work of reason. St. Thomas, for example argues that the lawgiver's act of *imperium* is an act of reason presupposing an act of will; for Scotus the lawgiver lays down imperatively what must be done – and this is an act of will, preceded, it may be, by an act of intellect that points out *ostensive* what may or may not be done.[14]

How does the natural law fit this concept of law? Suppose that some kinds of action can, by comparison with human nature, be pronounced good (because suitable to that nature) and others evil (because unsuitable). Could God, having once created that nature, fail to impose the law of seeking the good and avoiding the evil? That is how the intellectualist sees the problem. And there is no doubt about his answer: God must, under penalty of self-contradiction, impose the natural law. But if law is a matter of will rather than reason and if will, further, must be radically free, then the problem takes on another aspect. In this case human nature provides a *lex mere indicans*, which falls short of the true concept of law; the scale of good and evil, determined by comparison with human nature must wait upon God's will which, by imposing it, makes it a *lex obstringens.* The question remains: Might God refrain from that will-act? And to this the Scotist answer is that *de potentia absoluta* He could: but *de potentia ordinata* He cannot but will what accords with the natures He has created and with the rules of justice and wisdom He has established.[15] God's will, it must be recalled, cannot be limited according to Scotus by anything outside itself; another way of putting this is to say that any limitation upon the *potentia absoluta* of God is a contradiction in terms. The law of contradiction itself is the only limit – and it is not really a limit – upon God's will.

This, although it may look like it, is not necessarily an extreme voluntarism. Scotus has always suffered from having the views of later voluntarists ascribed to him. A fairer deduction from his general principles is that there is a natural law that cannot be altered even by God, but that this natural law is much less

[13] Cf. E. Gilson. *Jean Duns Scot: Introduction à ses positions fondamentales,* pp. 611–612; H.A. Oberman, *Harvest of Medieval Theology*, pp. 30–38.

[14] *Summa*, 1–2, q. 90, a. 1; q. 17, a. 1; G. Stratenwerth, *op. cit.*, p. 26, note 92 draws attention unconvincingly to a passage, 1–2, q. 71, a. 6 ad 2, in which St. Thomas appears to say that *imperium* is an act of will.

[15] *Ox.*, I, d. 44, q. 1, n. 2; E. Gilson, *op. cit.*, pp. 611–612.

extensive than is often thought. One should conclude, therefore, not that there is no natural law, but that the natural law is confined to those matters which God, under penalty of self-contradiction, must impose upon man. That this was Scotus's view can easily be shown from his examination of the content of the natural law.

For Scotus there are two ways in which a precept may belong to the natural law, as a first, self-evident, practical principle or as a necessary consequence of such a principle. *Haec dicuntur esse strictissime de lege naturae.* Such are the principles concerned with the very notion of good and the nature of God – in practice, since Scotus is discussing the Decalogue, the Commandments of the First Table. These not even God can relax; they are as fixed as the divine nature.[16] But there is also a wide sense in which precepts can be said to belong to the natural law, as neither self-evidently part of the natural law nor necessarily deducible from it, but yet eminently congruous with its provisions. This is the status of the Commandments of the Second Table, *multum consona illi legi* (*naturae*). These have to do directly with human nature – and not with the divine nature – and consequently God can dispense in them.[17] Scotus was impressed, as were his contemporaries, by certain Old Testament incidents – the command to Abraham to slay Isaac, the polygamy of the Patriarchs, the spoliation of the Egyptians, the fornication of Hosea – that seemed to confirm the possibility of dispensation. Intellectualists, like St. Thomas, who held that the whole of the Decalogue belonged to the natural law, held perforce that these were *dispensationes improprie dictae*, God having so altered the matter that the precept no longer applied.[18] Scotus, with equal logic and perhaps more realism, having decided precisely what he means by dispensation, concludes that, since these precepts have in fact been relaxed, they cannot belong to the natural law. But he had a

[16] *Ox.*, III, d. 37, q. un.; "Utrum omnia praecepta Decalogi sint de lege naturae"; *Par.*, IV, d. 17, q. un.

[17] Cf. *Ox.*, d. 26, q. un., n. 7: "Propriisime de lege naturae est principium practicum per se notum et conclusio demonstrative descendens ex tali principio; secundario autem de lege naturae est verum evidenter consonum talibus principiis et conclusionibus licet non necessario sequens..."; R. Prentice, "The Contingent Element governing the Natural Law on the last Seven Precepts of the Decalogue according to Duns Scotus" in *Antonianum*, 42 (1967), pp. 259–292.

[18] *Summa*, 1–2, q. 94, a. 5 ad 2; q. 100, a. 8 ad 3 etc.; cf. W. Stockums, *Die Unveränderlichkeit des natürlichen Sittengesetzes in der scholastischen Ethik*, Freiburg 1911, pp. 84–90.

much more metaphysical reason for this conclusion in the absolute indeterminability of the divine will by anything outside itself. To hold that human nature can determine God's will is, according to Scotus, to fall into the error of the philosophers.

Does not all this amount to a moral positivism, mitigated it is admitted, but still undermining the natural law and preparing the way for the extreme views that followed? But appearances may be deceptive. There is, beside the differences, an unexpected similarity between Scotus and the intellectualists that should give us pause. They agree, for instance, that the natural law cannot admit of dispensation. Scotus draws the conclusion that the Commandments of the Second Table are not strictly natural law; while Aquinas says that they have not, strictly speaking, been dispensed. To suggest that there is here no more than a disagreement about the extent of the natural law would be to underestimate the difference between the voluntarist and the intellectualist approach – but the view has its attraction.[19] Further, some surprising parallels between Scotus's and Aquinas's handling of the problem of dispensation can be drawn.

It may be urged that this similarity, mainly terminological, is no more than may be expected when two writers address themselves to the same subject, albeit from different standpoints. There are, however, weightier reasons for assimilating Duns Scotus more to his thirteenth century opponents than to his fourteenth century followers. They can only be indicated summarily here. In the first place Scotus is far more moderate and conservative on the Decalogue than might appear. The first three Commandments, concerned with God, are absolutely indispensable. The famous question *de odio Dei*, which was to become the touchstone of moral nominalism, could have little meaning for him; and the view of Ockham and others, that God could command a man to hate Him and the man could meritoriously obey, could not be farther from the mind of Scotus.[20] Secondly, Scotus distinguishes clearly and explicitly between those precepts of the Second Table of the law which are *consona legi naturae* and the divine positive

[19] E. Gilson, *op. cit.*, pp. 613–614, points out that one should not hasten to label Scotus a voluntarist simply because he subjects part of the Decalogue to God's will: "La discussion entre scotistes et thomistes ne peut porter que sur ce qui, *en fait*, est inclus dans la loi naturelle; quant à la notion même qu'ils ont de cette loi, elle n'est pas moins intellectualiste chez Duns Scot que chez Thomas d'Aquin."

[20] Cf. H.A. Oberman, *op. cit.*, p. 92.

law. The ceremonial ordinances of the Old Testament are instances of divine positive law; there is, of course, no incongruity between these and the law of nature, since they are ordered by God; but neither would their opposites be incongruous with the natural law. In this respect they differ from the precepts of the Second Table which are seen to be reasonable and good and so congruous with the natural law as to be evidently preferable to their opposites. The distinction, when it comes to a matter of dispensation, may be a fine one; but it is a distinction that Scotus does make.[21] And, finally, Scotus is clear that only God can dispense in the precepts of the Decalogue. These considerations remove his teaching from the category of the thoroughgoing nominalism and positivism of the Ockhamists. It is unfair to regard him as doing no more than open the way to the disintegration of scholastic thought.

Scotus, then, was not just a half-hearted positivist who did not dare to draw all the logical conclusions from his principles. He was saved by his realism in metaphysics from the consequences of extreme voluntarism. His basic position – bearing in mind that he was much more preoccupied with the problems of salvation and supernatural merit than with those of natural morality – has its own impressive logic.[22] His consistency in referring all reality, including all law, to the divine will is far from a manifesto of nominalism. It is not the natural law of a St. Thomas; but it is a consistent and measured voluntarism.

B. NOMINALIST DEVELOPMENTS: WILLIAM OF OCKHAM, GREGORY OF RIMINI

If Scotus's nominalism was moderate, although it undermined the basis of the natural law, it was so in comparison with the

[21] *Par.*, IV, d. 17, q. un., n. 4: "Alia autem sunt extra ista, quae sic demonstrative concluduntur ex eis, quae multum sunt consona illis principiis practicis; quia ab omnibus sunt visa multum rationabilia et bona et ab omnibus juste servanda, licet non possint ex eis demonstrari sicut priora, et quatenus consona talibus principiis dicuntur de lege naturae, licet non simpliciter, quia non simpliciter sequuntur ex eis sed ex iure positivo. Alia vero sunt adhuc talibus principiis consona sed ita quod etiam eorum opposita sunt ita eis consona, sicut illa; et ita stare possunt cum eis; cuiusmodi sunt caeremonialia et consuetudines quae mere sunt de iure positivo tantum. . . ."

[22] J. Sauter, *Die philosophischen Grundlagen des Naturrechts*, p. 84; E. Gilson, *op. cit.*, p. 609; S. Rehrl, "Grundlegung der Moral bei Johannes Duns Scotus" in *Salzburger Jahrbuch für Philosophie und Psychologie*, 3 (1959), pp. 137–228.

exaggerations that were given currency by William of Ockham (c. 1290–1350). Whether or not these exaggerations are to be taken at their face value is a question that is not yet or easily settled;[23] indeed a whole generation of scholars has now been concerned nor merely with the re-interpretation of Ockham but with the re-assessment of the entire movement labelled 'nominalism.' Something of this must be considered presently; but for the moment we may record the radical views which that stormy petrel of the fourteenth century passed on to his successors. Ockham, more than Scotus, took the voluntarism of the Franciscan tradition to its ultimate consequences. Man is free, even to will or not his own happiness; he is free even in the face of the judgment of his own intellect. This stress gives an authoritarian character to Ockham's ethics. Nothing is good or evil in itself; the distinction between good and evil is due to God's decree, which might as easily have been reversed. We cannot know morality for certain by inspecting human nature, for this would be inconsistent with the Divine liberty and omnipotence. Our created wills are subject to moral obligation, expressed as dependence upon God. The whole moral law becomes contingent, the precepts of the First as well as of the Second Table of the Decalogue; positivism or moral nominalism, sweeps away the natural law. This extreme view found expression in what became the touchstone of nominalistic controversy, the famous question *de odio Dei;* could God command a man to hate Him? and would this hate then become an act of virtue? Ockham's affirmative answer passed to his fourteenth and fifteenth century successors, Peter d'Ailly (1350–1420), John Gerson (1364–1429) Gabriel Biel (c. 1425–1495) and many others. At least this is the usual picture of Ockham and his influence.

This picture has been re-touched in various ways by recent scholars[24] and in particular, Ockham's attitude towards the natural law has been the subject of some very interesting re-interpretations. One of the starting-points for fresh interpretations has been the interesting fact that Ockham makes appeal to

[23] E. Bonke, "Doctrina nominalistica de fundamento ordinis moralis apud Gulielmum de Ockham et Gabrielem Biel" in *Collectanea Franciscana*, 14 (1944), pp. 60–70.

[24] Cf. W. Kölmel, "Das Naturrecht bei Wilhelm Ockham" in *Franziskanische Studien*, 35 (1953), pp. 39–85; H.A. Oberman, *The Harvest of Medieval Theology*, chapters 2–4; F. Oakley, "Medieval Theories of Natural Law: William of Ockham and the Significance of the Voluntarist Tradition" in *Natural Law Forum*, 6 (1961), pp. 65, etc.

the natural law in his political writings but does not mention the term in his ethical and theological writings.[25] There was, of course, a well-marked division in his career between his early logical and theological works, for which he came under suspicion (he was summoned to Avignon to answer for their orthodoxy) and the writings of his later political involvement when, with Marsiglio of Padua and John of Jandun, he took the side of Ludwig of Bavaria when that Emperor entered Rome and deposed the Pope. *Tu me defendas gladio,* Ockham is supposed to have said, *ego te defendam calamo.*

In the *Dialogus de imperio at pontificia potestate* Ockham distinguishes three kinds of natural law. The first is the natural law consisting in conformity with right reason; the second has to do with the 'state of nature' or natural equity or justice before the coming to be of civic society; and the third is the *jus gentium.*[26] McDonnell argues that the first of these, the natural law connected with right reason, has its analogue in the earlier philosophical and theological works, in passages where Ockham deals with practical reason and prudence – for example in the *Commentary on the Sentences.* But why, one might ask, did not Ockham use the term natural law in those contexts? McDonnell suggests two reasons: (1) the idea of 'nature' posed problems for Ockham who found it a limitation upon freedom; and (2) Ockham propounded a personalist ethics in which 'nature' could only figure as an unnecessary link between God and man. E. Bonke, in his well-documented survey of Ockham's (and Biel's) views on the basis of the moral order, arrives at a parallel conclusion. Some of the more exaggerated expressions of moral nominalism are indubitably found in Ockham, but they are capable of a more benign interpretation than they have always had. Even the famous passages about the possible reversal of the precepts of the Decalogue or about the *odium Dei* do not, according to Bonke, entirely exclude an intellectual element; good and evil, for Ockham are not absolute but relative, not by way of relation of means to end but rather by relation of the human will to right reason and to the will and command of God.[27]

Issues, however, much wider than the partial rehabilitation of William of Ockham arise. The term 'nominalism' has for so long

[25] K. McDonnell, "Does William of Ockham have a Theory of Natural Law?" in *Franciscan Studies,* 34 (1974), pp. 383–392.

[26] Pars. III, tr. 2, lib. 3, c. 6; cf. W. Kölmel, *op. cit.*, pp. 55–64.

[27] E. Bonke, *op. cit.*, pp. 60–70.

been used as a pejorative description of the philosophy and theology of the fourteenth and fifteenth centuries that it is now impossible to get away from it. The word was originally taken in the narrow epistemological sense of the denial of extra-mental reality to concepts; this was then broadened to include the consequent denial of metaphysics and the making of moral principles to depend solely upon the omnipotent and arbitrary will of God. Whether this is a just assessment, either of the period or of some of its representatives, is precisely what is now called in question.[28] An excellent example of the matter in dispute is the case of Gregory of Rimini (d. 1358), long known as the 'standard-bearer of nominalism.' The phrase, *antesignanus nominalistarum*, is due to the anti-scholastic Johannes Thurmayr of Abensburg (Aventinus). Thurmayr was appointed historiographer of his native Bavaria in 1517; but his annals were not published until 1554, at Ingolstadt. In describing the quarrel between fourteenth century realists and nominalists he names, as the standard-bearers of the nominalist party, William of Ockham, Marsilius of Heidelberg, John Buridan and Gregory of Rimini.[29] Damasus Trapp argues very convincingly that Gregory would have been much more accurately described as the standard-bearer *against* the nominalists. It is a case of giving a dog a bad name. And it was a slander that was made plausible because of the almost universally accepted picture of the fourteenth century and its quarrels. The qualification 'nominalist,' as we have seen, was taken in an extended sense to include extreme voluntarism in theology. It is

[28] Philotheus Boehner, *Collected Articles on Ockham*, St. Bonaventure, 1958, argued that Ockham was not a nominalist but a "realistic conceptualist." Cf. W.J. Courtenay, "Nominalism in Late Medieval Thought" in *Theological Studies*, 33 (1972), pp. 718–721: "For Boehner the radical nominalists were found among some of Ockham's disciples (for whom he was not responsible), such as Robert Holcot."

[29] For this passage in the *Annalium Boiorum libri septem* and for the details about Aventius cf. D. Trapp, "Augustinian Theology of the 14th Century; Notes on Editions, Marginalia, Opinions and Book-Lore" in *Augustiniana*, 6 (1956), pp. 182–184. Trapp's summary is that "the light weight of Aventinus' historical erudition and competence is counterbalanced by nothing but a heavy dosis of anti-scholastic animosity. The passage quoted was dragged in by Aventinus for emotional reasons. ... But Aventinus achieved his purpose of blackening the record of Gregory in a way beyond his fondest expectations. He is even used by Ueberweg's *Grundriss* II (1928) 589 to give a 'competent' evaluation of Gregory."

important to note, however, that the history of the controversies was written by the victorious party; a case, in fact, of *vae victis.* Trapp, who has probably done more than anyone else to secure the rehabilitation of Gregory of Rimini,[30] rather than speak of essentialists versus nominalists, prefers to describe the parties as *antiqui* and *moderni.* The history of the fourteenth century was written by the victorious *antiqui* and "from the fifteenth century down to our own days the research in fourteenth century theology has suffered from the incubus of nominalism."[31] Other scholars, while willing to retain the label 'nominalism' for William of Ockham and his followers like Peter d'Ailly and, a century later, Gabriel Biel, agree that the term requires much more careful definition than it has usually been given.[32]

One of the beneficiaries of this new look at fourteenth century nominalism is Gregory of Rimini. He can no longer be classed automatically with the nominalists.[33] Important points of disagreement between him and Ockham had, indeed, long been noticed. J.W. O'Malley, in speaking of Gregory's handling of authorities, remarks on the rough treatment he reserves for the philosophers who held opinions he believed to be false, and the only slightly less rough treatment he gave to the *doctores*

[30] D. Trapp, "Augustinian Theology of the 14th Century: Notes on Editions, Marginalia, Opinions and Book-Lore" in *Augustiniana,* 6 (1956), pp. 146–274; "Peter Ceffons of Clairvaux" in *Recherches de théologie ancienne et médiévale,* 24 (1956), pp. 101–154; "Gregory of Rimini, Manuscripts Editions and Additions" in *Augustiniana,* 8 (1958), pp. 425–443; "Gregorio de Rimini y el nominalismo" in *Augustinianum,* 4 (1964), pp. 5–20.

[31] *Augustiniana,* 6 (1956), p. 186. For a useful corrective cf. E. Bonke, *op. cit.,* pp. 57–83.

[32] So, for example, Paul Vignaux, "Nominalisme" in *Dictionnaire de théologie catholique,* t. 11, Paris, 1930, 717–784 and more recently H.A. Oberman, *The Harvest of Medieval Theology.* For a survey of this and other literature see W.J. Courtenay, "Current Theology: Nominalism and late Medieval Thought: A Bibliographical Essay" in *Theological Studies,* 33 (1972), pp. 716–734.

[33] Leibniz, for instance, held that the sect of the nominalists, said to have begun with Roscelin, and after suffering eclipse for many years, was suddenly revived by William of Ockham, "a man of highest genius and of outstanding erudition for his time. In agreement with him were Gregory of Rimini, Gabriel Biel and the majority of the Augustinian Order." Cf. *Dissertatio de Stilo Nizolii* paraphrased by A. Maurer, "The Unity of a Science; St. Thomas and the Nominalists" in *St. Thomas Aquinas 1274–1974 Commemorative Studies,* Toronto, 1974, II, pp. 270–271.

moderni.[34] In dealing with the question of the unity of a science A. Maurer, having remarked that Gregory parts company on the question with his nominalist contemporary (Ockham), goes on to say:

> This is but one indication that what goes by the name of fourteenth century nominalism was really a complex of many doctrines which, though they have common features, are really quite different[35]

Even when one allows that the history of the fourteenth century nominalist controversies may have been written with bias, one wonders why the bias has not been exposed before now and why Gregory is still so commonly listed with the nominalists. Trapp, in his detailed study of the fourteenth century, remarks upon the different style of theology it evinces as compared with the thirteenth century; more positive, historico-critical, exact in quotation, more interested in the individual (which includes an interest in individual conscience), more interested in moral theology than in dogmatic and expressing itself in new literary forms.[36] And his case for Gregory of Rimini is that his chances of getting a fair hearing were greatly compromised by the strong possibility that he was in the bad books of both *antiqui* and *moderni.* He may have been one of the inquisitors involved in condemning the Ockhamists, John of Mirecourt and Nicholas of Autrecourt, in 1347[37] in which case he would have fallen out with the extremists among the *moderni.* At the same time he incurred the jealousy of the *antiqui* because he was himself an outstanding *modernus.* It is a good, but not unanswerable case. All turns upon the fact or otherwise of Gregory's playing a part in the condemnation of John of Mirecourt and Nicholas of Autrecourt in 1347 – and this has not been proved. Trapp's thesis has been challenged by W.J.

[34] "A Note on Gregory of Rimini: Church, Scripture, Tradition" in *Augustinianum,* 5 (1965), pp. 365–378 at p. 374.

[35] *Op. cip.*, p. 287.

[36] "Augustinian theology of the 14th century: Notes on Editions, Marginalia Opinions and Book-lore," in *Augustiniana,* 6 (1956), pp. 146–151.

[37] D. Trapp, "Peter Ceffons of Clairvaux" in *Recherches de théologie ancienne et médiévale,* 24 (1957), pp. 101–54. Cepons refers intemperately to the inquisitors as "three foreign wrinkled old hags," *tres vetulae rugosae;* Peter of Ceffons, *Epistula introductoria,* n. 135, ed. D. Trapp, *op. cit.*, note (59), p. 138. There is a denunciation in similar terms in the text of Ceffons's *Commentary, id.*, pp. 149–152.

Courtenay.[38] In general, however, Trapp has little difficulty in showing that Gregory opposes Ockham on a number of questions and that, in different ways and on different topics, he rejects the theses frequently associated with 'nominalism,' as we have seen.[39] He also stresses the close dependence of Gregory upon Augustine and the exactitude with which he documents his dependence, especially on topics like those of grace and predestination. Heiko Oberman, who like Courtenay has some reserves about Trapp's characterisation of the *via moderna*, allows that Gregory of Rimini represents a right-wing tendency within the nominalist development of the fourteenth century.[40]

This may be exemplified by a passage in Gregory's *Commentary on the Second Book of the Sentences* where he discusses the nature and causes of sin. Now the classical definition of sin was that of St. Augustine, in the *Contra Faustum* ("any act, saying or desire against the eternal law"); and Gregory compares it with another description of sin ("actual sin seems to me to be nothing other than voluntary action against right reason. . . .") with which his discussion begins.[41] The phrases are, he says, equivalent; for Augustine goes on to explain that the eternal law is "the divine

[38] "John of Mirecourt and Gregory of Rimini on Whether God can Undo the Past" in *Recherches de théologie ancienne et médiévale*, 39 (1972), pp. 224–256; 40 (1973), pp. 147–174. Courtenay points out – and Trapp agrees – that the general picture of Ockhamism, built upon slender evidence, has persisted in text-books and elsewhere long after the evidence for it has been overturned. He is not convinced, however, that Gregory of Rimini can be placed among the major figures in the condemnation of John of Mirecourt – for Mirecourt was condemned, *inter alia*, for the proposition that God can undo the past, a proposition he did *not* hold, whereas Gregory did! Also "seeing the number of times the inquisitors misinterpreted the thought and intention of Mirecourt, it seems unlikely that they would have among their number anyone so gifted and critical as Gregory." Further, as regards the 1347 condemnation, "Gregory had every reason to feel as uncomfortable as Mirecourt, if not more so." Cf. especially *id.*, pp. 154–165.

[39] Cf. J.W. O'Malley, *op. cit.*

[40] "Some Notes on the Theology of Nominalism" in *Harvard Theological Review*, 53 (1960), pp. 47–76.

[41] Gregorius Ariminensis, *In secundum Sententiarum*, d. 34, q. 1, art. 2 (ed. Paulus de Genezano, Venice, 1503, 107–108): ". . . videtur mihi posse dici quod peccatum actuale non est aliud quam voluntarie committere aliquid vel ommittere contra rectam rationem. . . huic descriptioni convertibilis est et consona descriptio Augustini qui (*Contra Faustum* 22) deffiniens peccatum ait peccatum est factum vel dictum vel concupitum aliquid contra aeternam legem . . . lex vero eterna est ratio divina vel voluntas dei ordinem naturalem conservari iubens perturbari vetans. . . ."

reason or will of God commanding the preservation of the natural order and forbidding its disturbance." What is against the eternal law is against right reason; and if one prefers to use the phrase 'right reason,' rather than 'divine reason,' in this context this is to guard against the mistake of thinking that sin is sin because it is contrary to divine reason as divine, rather than contrary to divine reason as right reason. And the point is hammered home in a famous hypothesis, which will later be used to effect by Hugo Grotius:

> If, *per impossibile*, the divine reason, or God himself did not exist, or that that reason were mistaken, still if one were to act against right reason, angelic, human or any other if such there be, he would sin.[42]

On the face of it, this is an essentialist view, surprising in one usually described as a nominalist. The balance is redressed, further on in the discussion, when Gregory comes to make a distinction, between an indicative or ostensive law on the one hand and a prescriptive or preceptive law on the other. Gregory is meeting the objection, based upon texts of Augustine and Ambrose, that God's prohibition is what makes sinful actions sinful. "Prohibition," he says, "may be understood in either of two ways – as may precept and law – in the indicative or in the imperative mode." An indicative law, precept or prohibition, points to something that is to be done or avoided and goes no further; an imperative law, precept or prohibition, imposes the doing or the avoidance of the act in question.[43] Gregory appeals to the authority of Hugh of St. Victor;[44] but it is difficult to avoid the impression that he is pushing the text of Hugh rather hard.

[42] Gregorius Ariminensis, *op. cit.:* "Nam si per impossibile ratio divina sive Deus ipse non esset, aut ratio illa esset errans, adhuc, si quis ageret contra rectam rationem angelicam vel humanam aut aliam aliquam si qua esset, peccaret."

[43] Gregorius Ariminensis, *op. cit.:* "... prohibitio potest dupliciter accipi et similiter praeceptum et lex.... Indicativa est illa qua tantummodo significat aliquid non esse agendum seu aliud aliquid ex quo sequiter ipsum agendum non esse sicut cum significatur aliquid esse iniustum aut pravum seu vituperatione vel poena dignum.... Imperativam dico illam qua imperatur alicui aliquid agere vel non agere; et hoc exprimitur per verbum imperativi modi vel aliud eius vice...."

[44] Hugh of St. Victor, *De sacramentis Christianae fidei,* I, c. 7, (P.L., 176; 268): "In praecepto naturae tria sunt, praeceptio, prohibitio et concessio; praeceptum autem naturae nos nihil aliud intelligimus quam ipsam discretionem naturalem quae intrinsecus inspirata est, ut per eam homo erudiretur de his quae sibi vel appetenda vel fugienda fuerunt. Quasi enim quoddam praeceptum dare erat discretionem et intelligentiam agendi cordis hominis aspirare. Quid ergo

The upshot is that Gregory can conclude that sin is such by reason of God's prohibition (God's indicative *and* imperative law) but that in the absence of God's imperative law and even on the hypothesis that God did not exist, sin would still be against right reason. Thus he purports to reconcile the essentialist view (the distinction between good and evil is in the nature of things) and the voluntarist (God's will is what determines good and evil). It is an important and influential suggestion.

Gabriel Biel, more than a century later, reproduces the argumentation of Gregory of Rimini in a passage that shows a remarkable verbal dependence upon his model. Is it not strange that a doctrine, that seems quite clearly to be anti-Ockhamist and anti-nominalist, should be propagated by two writers who are regarded as leading nominalists? Biel, in particular, was identified with Ockhamism in the fifteenth century; his epitome of Ockham *On the Sentences* was so popular that the Ockhamists at Erfurt and Wittenberg were known as *Gabrielistae.*[45] It can hardly now come as a surprise to find that scholars are discovering that Biel does not fit the stereotype of nominalism any more than Gregory. The major contribution to this re-assessment has been that of Heiko

---

cognitio faciendorum fuit nisi quaedam ad cor hominis facta preceptio? Et quid rursus cognitio vitandorum fuit nisi quaedam prohibitio? Quid vero cognitio eorum quae media fuerunt estimanda nisi quaedam concessio?" The distinction that Hugh had made, in the passage preceding this one cited by Gregory, was between the *praeceptum naturae* and the *praeceptum disciplinae;* and there is undoubtedly a resemblance to Gregory's *lex indicativa* and *lex praeceptiva;* but perhaps not more than a resemblance.

[45] F.C. Copleston, *History of Philosophy*, London, vol. III, 1953, p. 150: "Biel's work was a methodical and clear exposition of Ockhamism and, though he did not pretend to be more than a follower and exponent of Ockham, he exercised a considerable influence. Indeed the Ockhamists at the Universities of Erfurt and Wittenburg were known as Gabrielistae. It is, perhaps, interesting to note that Biel did not interpret Ockham's moral theory as meaning that there is no natural moral order." On the latter point see E. Bonke, "Doctrina nominalistica de fundamento ordinis moralis apud Gulielmum de Ockham et Gabrielem Biel" in *Collectanea Franciscana*, 14 (1944), pp. 57–83. The passages from Gregory of Rimini (and Gabriel Biel) are reproduced in G. Fassò, *La legge della regione*, pp. 276–284; an excerpt from the Biel text (*In II Librum Sententiarum*, Tübingen, 1501, dist. 35, quaest. 1, art. 1, litt. D) is in Corpus Hispanorum de Pace, Vol. XIII, p. 80, note 199. Otto Gierke had noticed the similarity between Biel and Gregory; cf. Giorgio Del Vecchio, cited in J. St. Leger, *The 'Etiamsi Daremus' of Hugo Grotius*, pp. 55–56. G. Fassò, *Storia della filosofia del diritto,* II, p. 16 draws attention to precedents for the distinction between indicative and prescriptive law in the Stoics, in Marsilius of Padua and in Albert the Great.

Oberman.[46] Already in 1960 he had suggested that the nominalist development should be seen in four schools: (1) a left-wing school, represented by the English Ockhamists Holcot and Woodham; (2) a Paris 'synthesising' school, represented by Peter of Candia; (3) a right-wing nominalism taking an Augustinian stance, in contrast with contemporary Pelagian trends, and represented by Gregory of Rimini and Henry of Oyta; and finally (4) a conciliatory school, representing, incidentally, the mainstream of the Ockhamist tradition and associated with Gerson and Biel. Apropos of these thinkers Oberman says:

(Gerson and Biel) have both done much to make Nominalistic theology acceptable; Gerson by including mystical warmth in his theological formulations, Biel by neutralising the extreme positions of the left-wing. The text-books of Biel especially brought the *via moderna* to many German Universities.[47]

The picture is not different in Oberman's book on Biel. One of the conclusions of this extremely well-documented survey of late nominalism is that the traditional assertion, that the thirteenth century synthesis of faith and reason disintegrated in the later Middle Ages and was replaced by a radical divorce of faith and reason (the stereotype once more) is certainly not verified in Gabriel Biel. Oberman devotes a good deal of attention to Biel's sermons; but his conclusion about Biela's 'Catholicity' is based upon the scientific works also.[48] On the specific question of the moral order the views of Biel were nuanced. The fact is that some of his expressions were such as to lead some scholars to assert that he held a doctrine on the natural law practically indistinguishable from that of St. Thomas Aquinas.[49] This is clearly an exaggeration; but it is instructive that the texts should be capable of this interpretation. On the famous question *de odio Dei* (Could God command a man to hate Him?) Oberman remarks that Biel follows John Duns Scotus and Gregory of Rimini "and his position on this issue can be characterized as a more or less

[46] *The Harvest of Medieval Theology; Gabriel Biel and Late Medieval Nominalism.* Also E. Bonke, "Doctrina nominalistica de fundamento ordinis moralis apud Gulielmum de Ockham et Gabrielem Biel" in *Collectanea Franciscana*, 14 (1944), pp. 57–83.

[47] "Some Notes on the Theology of Nominalism; with Attention to its Relation to the Renaissance" in *Harvard Theological Review*, 53 (1960), p. 55.

[48] *The Harvest of Medieval Theology*, p. 88.

[49] *Ibid.*, p. 106: Oberman rejects the interpretation of G. Ott, "Recht und Gesetz bei Gabriel Biel: Ein Beitrag zur spätmittelalterlichen Rechtslehre" in *Zeitschrift der Savigny; Stiftung für Rechtsgeschichte* 69(1952), 251–296.

open departure from Occam."[50] Biel's assertions of the moral order as being unchangeable, or even independent of God, must be taken in their nominalist context. God is beyond human intelligence and we cannot say that it would have been impossible for Him to have decided in favour of a natural law different from the present one. But *de facto* (or *stante lege*, or *de potentia Dei ordinata;* these phrases are, in the context, roughly equivalent) the natural law is, for Biel, the direct extension of the eternal law and is as unchangeable.[51]

All human justice consists in conformity to the will of God as known through his *voluntas signi.* This is the ultimate norm and basic rule for man's moral behaviour. For this norm Biel uses the term eternal law: because of its conformity with this eternal law, natural law is right: and all other righteousness in man's laws is derived from this eternal law. There is nothing unusual or original in this construction: Biel could have found these thoughts in Duns Scotus' works and actually did find them in Gregory of Rimini. . . .

Natural law according to Biel has an immanent rationality which enables man in principle to reach the right conclusion as to his temporal felicity. . . . It is quite evident that the often-repeated charges – despotism, decisionism, positivism and ethical relativism – made against the ethics of nominalism, here represented in Biel's ethics, are absolutely without foundation.[52]

An interesting by-product of this process of re-assessment of medieval nominalism in morals is that it can now be argued, without paradox, that Hugo Grotius's 'impious hypothesis' ("even if there were no God"), which is something like the charter of seventeenth and eighteenth century rationalism, should count amongst its ancestors the nominalists, Gregory of Rimini and Gabriel Biel, no less than the recongnised essentialist, Gabriel Vazquez. As the re-interpretation, not only of Gregory and of Biel, but of the entire nominalistic scene in the fourteenth and fifteenth centuries, proceeds it may be seen that the hypothesis of God's non-existence, as a way of underlining the immutability of the moral order, is even a continuous strand linking the thirteenth and the seventeenth centuries. This, in

[50] *Ibid.*, p. 95. Cf. E. Bonke, "Doctrina nominalistica de fundamento ordinis moralis apud Gulielmum de Ockham et Gabrielem Biel" in *Collectanea Franciscana*, 14 (1944), pp. 57–83. Bonke's remark, *op. cit.*, p. 77, is apposite: "Ambiguitas terminorum est una ex characteristicis philosophiae et theologiae nominalisticae."

[51] H.A. Oberman, *The Harvest of Medieval Theology*, p. 100.

[52] H.A. Oberman, *op. cit.*, pp. 104, 110.

broad terms, is the argument of Guido Fassò in his book *La legge della ragione*. It does seem safe to assert that there is nothing like the radical discontinuity that was formerly thought to exist between Grotius in his *Etiamsi daremus* and his predecessors; the hypothesis no longer protrudes like an intellectualist good deed in the naughty world of nominalism! Before coming to Grotius and the Age of Reason, however, it remains to look briefiy at the re-making of the medieval profile of natural law in the later scholastics.

C. THE REFORMATION AND THE SCHOLASTIC SILVER AGE

Closer study of the opposition between the *antiqui* and the *moderni* from the fourteenth century onwards cannot but be enlightening for the understanding of the opposition between Catholic and Protestant thinkers from the time of the Reformation in the sixteenth century. For, even if there is more continuity than one suspected between intellectualism and voluntarism, there is still a fundamental difference, touching the basis of moral philosophy, which was hardly nearer resolution two centuries after the death of Ockham. It seems broadly true that the Reformers took the voluntarist or Ockhamist line on the precepts of morality, while the Catholic writers tended towards the objectivist or intellectualist view. This, like most generalisations, has to be handled with caution. Martin Luther, it is well-known, was a pupil of Gabriel Biel's follower Bartholomaeus Arnoldi von Usingen;[53] but it would be too much to say that Luther adopted the views of Biel, the foremost exponent of Ockhamism of his time. It is true, however, that the voluntarism in much Reform theology presented an uncongenial setting for anything like the classical thirteenth century concept of a natural law;[54] and in fact

[53] H.A. Oberman, *op. cit.*, pp. 4, 178; A Truyol y Serra, *Historia de là filosofia del derecho y del estado de los origenes a la baja edad media*, pp. 380, 399; P. Simoniti, "Ueber die *Responsio contra* Apologiam Melanchthonis: Ein wiedergefundenes Werk des Augustiner Eremiten Bartholomaéus Arnoldi von Usingen," in *Augustiniana*, 25 (1975), pp. 48–57. Luther is said to have been able to quote Biel from memory. Cf. J.E. Biechler, "Gabriel Biel on *Liberum Arbitrium:* Prelude to Luther's *De Servo Arbitrio*" in *The Thomist*, 34 (1970), 114–127.

[54] A.P. d'Entrèves, *Natural Law*, p. 70: "(Thomistic natural law) was out of place in the Reformers' theology and actually they found little or no room for it."

the natural law was disparaged in favour of the Bible as the expression of the legislative will of God:

> ... if Christ be the only source of ethics, what place is left for natural law, unless perchance for the non-Christian? The neo-orthodox tend to exclude from Luther's thinking not only the natural law, but all law, claiming that his ethic was entirely spontaneous and unstructured.[55]

Yet–and this is a dilemma that contemporary situationism in ethics has also failed to resolve–some way must be found of formulating the moral requirements of the law of the Gospel. Far from being inconsistent, the Sermon on the Mount and the Decalogue are complementary; to contrast true morality with legalism is to fail to do justice to either of the terms of the comparison. Once this has been accepted the apparent inconsistencies in the early Reformers' references to the natural law can be understood.

Martin Luther reacted against the subtleties of the decadent scholasticism in which he had been educated. This alone would have been enough to make him suspicious of the elaboration of the term 'nature' in the sphere of morality by scholastic theologians. Much more basically, however, his views concerning the total corruption of human nature and man's radical incapacity for morally good action, effectively deprived the natural law of its traditional rôle. But yet Luther cannot help slipping back into the older terminology. It may be that anything less than a complete antinomianism must involve some recourse to a criterion like that of 'nature.'[56] Reformation theology was not antinomian.[57] But it is understandable that the Reformers would be cautious in their approach to 'nature.'[58] The Reformation has been seen to mark a

[55] R.H. Bainton, *Studies on the Reformation*, p. 114; cf. G. Graneris, *La filosofia del diritto nella sua storia e nei suoi problemi:* "... il protestantesimo primitivo non si stacco con un taglio netto delle tradizioni giusnaturalistiche cristiane. Tuttavia va osservato che non si strinse alle tradizioni migliori, ma a quelle più sospette, vogliamo dire a quelle che fanno capo ad Occam."

[56] Cf. A. Verdross, *Abendländische Rechtsphilosophie*, pp. 82–83; J.M. Aubert, *Loi de Dieu lois des hommes*, pp. 108–109.

[57] Cf. G. Söhngen, *Grundfragen einer Rechtstheologie*, pp. 102–103: "... die reformatorische Lehre von Gesetz und Evangelium nicht die Lehre von einem gesetzlosen Evangelium und werklosen Glauben ist. Die reformatorische Lehre ist von Haus aus nicht antinomisch, nicht gesetzes- und werkfeindlich, die Gesetzlosigkeit und Werkfeindlichkeit liegt auch nicht in der inneren Folgerichtigkeit der reformatorischen/Lehre, sondern ist ein massives Missverstandnis der reformatorischen Lehre. ..."

[58] Cf. H. Steubing, *Naturrecht und natürliche Theologie im Protestantismus*, pp. 11–13.

return to the rigid alternatives described by St. Augustine as the City of Man and the City of God.[59] In fact, Luther does make a distinction between two kinds of natural law, a temporal and profane law corresponding with fallen nature and another and superior law corresponding with nature as redeemed, the law of man without God in his heart and the law of man recaptured by the Spirit of God. This distinction, added to the fact that Luther trained in the law and was prepared to teach it at Erfurt, goes some way towards explaining the otherwise surprising abundance of texts in which he might have been expounding a Thomistic natural law.[60] One should not, however, be misled by the occurrence of the terms *natürliches Gesetz* or *lex naturae*; it does not at all follow that Luther espoused the conventional view of the natural law.[61]

Was it Luther's profane natural law that found its expression in Grotius and subsequently in the natural law of the Age of Reason? On the face of it this cannot be ruled out.[62] Yet as an explanation of Grotius's initiative and of the widespread influence of his views it is not altogether satisfactory. For, in fact, as far as the *Etiamsi* hypothesis goes Grotius's sources are much more likely to be found among the scholastic writers on the natural law than among his co-religionists.

For scholasticism had been rejuvenated in the work of the great fifteenth and sixteenth century commentators on St. Thomas, most of them Spanish. The way was shown by Cajetan (Tommaso

[59] A. P. d'Entrèves, *Natural Law*, pp. 70, 36–37.

[60] Cf. F.X. Arnold, *Zur Frage des Naturrechts bei Martin Luther*, passim.

[61] The controversy is an old one. The view that Luther accepted the natural law was expresed by Ernst Troeltsch and Max Weber and was rejected by Karl Holl in *Der Neubau der Sittlichkeit*, 1919 (Gesammelte Aufsätze, Tübingen, 1948, I, p. 249) cited by R.R. Calmerer, "The Natural Law; a Theologian's View" in *Colloquy on Law and Theology*, St. Louis, 1962. Luther's exegesis of St. Paul's reference to natural law in *Romans* 2; 14 is conventional. Cf. *Martin Luthers Werke*, Weimarer Ausgabe, Bd. 56, 1938, p. 23, Bd. 57, 1939, pp. 26–27; see, however, the important qualifications in S.E. Ozment, *Homo Spiritualis*, pp. 189–208.

[62] Cf. J.M. Aubert, *Loi de Dieu lois des hommes*, p. 109: "En prolongement de l'idée luthérienne d'un droit naturel sécularisé, le Protestantisme des XVIIe et XVIIIe siècles s'intéressa assez largement au droit naturel, mais en le laïcisant et le faisant passer dans le droit positif...." The views of the other important Reformers – Melanchthon, Zwingli, Calvin – on the natural law were less radical than those of Luther, either in allowing that human nature is not totally corrupted by sin (Melanchthon) or in taking a more positive approach to the world (Calvin). Cf. A. Verdross, *Abendländische Rechtsphilosophie*, pp. 84–85; J.M. Aubert, *Loi de Dieu lois des hommes*, p. 109.

de Vio: 1468–1534) and Ferrariensis (Francisco de Silvestris of Ferrara: 1480–1566) and was followed by a succession of important writers like Melchior Cano (1509–1560), Domingo de Soto (1494–1560), Bartolome de Medina (1527–1581), Domingo Bañez (1528–1604), Luis de Molina (1536–1600) and Gabriel Vazquez (c. 1551–1604). In the context of the philosophy of law the most important were Francisco de Vitoria (1483?–1546) and Francisco Suarez (1548–1617).

Francisco de Vitoria, having become a Dominican in 1504, was sent to study at Paris, where he had as teacher the Scot John Mair (or Major), a follower of Ockham; but he also came under the influence of the Renaissance humanism. He spent sixteen years at Paris before returning to Spain to lecture at Valladolid (1523–1526) and Salamanca (1526–1546). He revitalized the scholasticism of his day; and it would not be unfair to describe his achievement as the re-thinking of the principles of the natural law in the light of the new conditions of the sixteenth century. The old problems of law and sovereignty had been transformed, above all by the Spanish discovery and conquest of the New World. As part of his professorial duty at Salamanca, Vitoria had each year to deliver a formal lecture on a topic of public concern. Thirteen of these *Relectiones* survive; two of them are capital documents in the history of natural law, the *De Indis Prior vel de Indis recenter inventis* and the *De Indis posterior seu de jure belli Hispanorum in barbaros.* In these works he stressed the moral basis of international law and insisted upon the overriding requirements of justice, especially in matters of conquest and subjection. He exposed the illegitimate claims of his countrymen to dominion over the inhabitants of the New World, claims based upon a variety of considerations – the Imperial power, the temporal power of the Pope, the fact of discovery, the paganism of the Indians who must be evangelized, their moral turpitude etc. A century and a half later Dr Samuel Johnson was impressed by the situation: "I love the University of Salamancha," he said, "for when the Spaniards were in doubt as to the lawfulness of their conquering America, the University of Salamancha gave it as their opinion that it was not lawful."[63] Vitoria's work – which also examines the legitimate claims of the *conquistadores* – is a prime, if often unacknowledged, source of modern international law.[64] In addition to his *Relectiones* Victoria pronounced on matters of the

[63] James Boswell, *The Life of Samuel Johnson*, aet. 1763.

[64] H. Muñoz, *Vitoria and the Conquest of America*, passim; B. Hamilton, *Political Thought in 16th Century Spain*, passim.

natural law in his commentary on the *Summa Theologiae* of St. Thomas;[65] one of his innovations at Salamanca had been to take the *Summa* and not St. Thomas's *Commentary on the Sentences* as his text.

More important even than Vitoria in the philosophy of law was Suarez. During his active life he held a number of important professorships, at Segovia, Valladolid, Rome (the *Collegium Romanum*, where his teaching fell under some suspicion), Alcalà and Coimbra. At Coimbra he lectured, apart from other subjects, on law. The result, his *De legibus ac de Deo legislatore*, which saw the light in 1612, is probably the greatest scholastic contribution to the philosophy of law. Like Vitoria, Suarez sets out to re-think the classical scholastic natural law in the changed conditions of his time. In his notion of law he combines, as far as possible, the intellectualism of Aquinas and the voluntarism of Scotus – for the centuries' long controversy between the two schools was one of the factors in the situation he wished to take account of. He derives the natural law from the eternal law and includes in it not alone the primary principles of the moral order, but all their necessary conclusions. He attaches human law to the natural law as the ground of its validity. He further refines the notion of *jus gentium* found in Vitoria. And like Vitoria he is a prime source for modern international law.

In his approach to the natural law one sees Suarez's advantage of being able to pluck the fruit of almost four centuries' speculation about law since the time of St. Thomas, speculation stimulated and illuminated by the enormous developments in social and, above all, political life. Suarez's work is basically a commentary on Aquinas (*Summa Theologiae*, 1–2, 90–108), a commentary that, if it runs to prolixity, covers every thinkable legal topic and, in addition, is extremely well documented.

In the second book (*De legibus*, II, c. 5) Suarez discusses the *ratio formalis* of the natural law. Is it human rational nature as such (with which actions may be found to conform or not to conform)? Or is it rather rational nature understood as the faculty

[65] V. Beltran de Heredia, *Francisco de Vitoria, Comentario al Tratado de la Ley*, Madrid, 1952. Vitoria's commentary was the model for that of his younger contemporary Domingo de Soto; cf. F. Puy-L. Nuñez, *Domingo de Soto De Legibus*, Granada, 1965. This is simply one of a long series of commentaries culminating in the great treatise of Suarez, *De legibus*.

capable of judging such conformity or want of conformity? It is much more than a *lis de verbis*, even though justification for each of the two views can be sought in St. Thomas.[66] Suarez names Gabriel Vazquez as an upholder of the first view – human nature is in such wise the foundation of morality that some actions are intrinsically, in their nature, evil; their malice in no way depends upon an extrinsic prohibition, not even upon the judgment or will of God; other actions, on the contrary, are intrinsically good and their goodness does not depend upon any external cause (ibid., n. 2). While conceding that it has some truth, Suarez rejects this view, his fundamental reason being that the concept of law, for him, includes that of the lawgiver imposing it; to assert that human nature as such *is* the natural law would be, in effect, to deny that the natural law is truly a law (nn. 5–6). Human nature may be the foundation of the natural law, the basis for the distinction between right and wrong; but if it is identified with the natural law absurd results follow – such as that God would be bound by the natural law (n. 7). Suarez is attacking not only Vazquez but his other Jesuit colleagues Molina and Lessius. He concludes that the natural law cannot be identified with human nature, even though human nature may be said to be the measure of good and evil.

Nor, on the other hand, can the natural law be identified with a power or faculty of rational nature; nor with 'right reason' (n. 9). A further question touches on whether the natural law should be said to consist in a *habitus* or an act of reason; otherwise put, in the light of reason itself or in an activity of reason (n. 13). Suarez's own view is that it all depends upon how one defines law (n. 14); and in the following chapter (c. 6) he comes to this issue.

What constitutes a genuine law? Suarez now introduces a distinction of capital importance, that between an indicative law and a prescriptive law (*lex indicativa, lex praescriptiva*). It was not a novelty; the distinction, as we have seen, was common coin in the intellectualist-voluntarist controversies since the fourteenth

[66] This is confirmed by the fact that a closely similar controversy separated thomists in the 1920's; this was the debate as to whether the 'ratio' said by Thomas to be the norm of morality should be understood as 'reason, the specific form of human nature' or 'reason, the faculty or act of judging.' For a brief summary see O. Lottin, *Principes de morale*, II, pp. 118–125.

century.[67] In Suarez's mind only the *lex praeceptiva*, because it cannot exist apart from a *praecipiens* or legislator whose will it imposes, is truly a law. If the natural law, or its dictates, can be said to be independent of all will, even the Divine will, then we are not talking about a law at all (n. 1) – *non est verum praeceptum, ergo nec vera lex.* The distinction is crucial and in his exploration of it, citing his authorities, Suarez refers to the theologians who, while saying that human nature is the natural law, avoid the difficulty of denying that it is a law by calling it a *lex indicativa.* The passage must be quoted:

In this matter the first view is that the natural law is not properly a prescriptive law, for it is not the expression of the will of any superior but rather a law indicating what is to be done and what avoided, what is by its nature intrinsically good and necessary and what intrinsically evil. Thus many distinguish between two kinds of law, one indicative, the other prescriptive, and say that the natural law is law in the former sense and not in the latter. So Gregory (of Rimini), who cites Hugh of St. Victor. Gabriel (Biel), (Jacques) Almain and (Antonio de) Cordova follow the same opinion.

Consequently these authors appear to concede that the natural law does not come from God as a legislator, for it does not depend upon God's will so that in virtue of it God does not comport Himself as a superior commanding or forbidding. Gregory, whom the others follow, even says that even if God did not exist or did not make use of reason, or did not judge rightly of things, as long as there was in man the same dictate of right reason – saying, for example, that it is wrong to lie – that dictate would have the same character of law that it now possesses, because it would be a law manifesting the evil that resides intrinsically in the act.

The second view, diametrically opposed to the first, is that the natural law consists entirely in the divine command or prohibition, proceeding from the will of God as author and governor of nature.... Thus

[67] Cf. O. Gierke, *Political Theories of the Middle Ages*, (translation by F.W. Maitland), p. 172, n. 256: "The Realists explained the *lex naturalis* as an intellectual act independent of will – as a mere *lex indicativa*, in which God was not a lawgiver but a teacher working by means of Reason – in short as the dictate of Reason as to what is right, grounded in the Being of God, but unalterable even by Him.... The opposite opinion, proceeding from pure Nominalism, saw in the law of nature a mere Divine command, which was right and binding merely because God was the lawgiver. So Ockham, Gerson, d'Ailly. The prevailing opinion was of a mediating kind, though it inclined to the principle of Realism. It regarded the substance of the natural law as a judgment necessarily flowing from the Divine Being and unalterably determined by that nature of things which is compised in God; howbeit the binding force of this law, but only its binding force was traced to God's will. Thus Aquinas, Caietanus, Soto, Suarez."

Ockham, who says that no act is evil except insofar as it is forbidden by God, and which cannot become good if commanded by God and vice versa. Hence he assumes that the entire natural law consists in divine precepts given by God which He can abolish or change.... And Gerson inclines to this view.... And Peter d'Ailly defends this view where he says that the divine will is the first law and that, therefore, it could create men having the use of reason but without any law. Similarly Andrew of Novocastro....[68]

Suarez goes on to find this view foreshadowed in Anselm's *Proslogion* and in a work attributed to St. Cyprian, *De singularitate clericorum*, as well as in Hugh of St. Victor.[69] The passage is a fair summary of the controversy that had divided theologians since the fourteenth century – and not merely of the two extremes that opposed each other, broadly one might say Thomists and Ockhamists, but of the compromise view, turning on the distinction between a *lex indicativa* and a *lex praeceptiva*, associated with Gregory of Rimini and his followers. None of the views adduced satisfies Suarez, who sets out (n. 5) to expound a *via media*, which he believes to be the view of St. Thomas and common among theologians. The detail of the long discussion that follows need not concern us, beyond noting the three propositions that epitomize Suarez's view:

(1) the natural law is not merely indicative or ostensive; it is a genuinely prescriptive law, expressing the will of God (otherwise contravention of the law would not be going against God's will).

(2) precept and prohibition, on the other hand, do not constitute the totality of goodness or malice in observance or transgression of the law; God's will, in a word, presupposes an objective goodness or malice in the actions concerned and adds the special obligation of divine law (n. 11). Suarez quotes a wide range of authorities for this view, ranging from Augustine to Scotus, Durandus, Gabriel Biel, Cajetan, Soto and others.

(3) the natural law is truly a law and God is its legislator (n. 13).

In the subsequent sections (nn. 14–25) of this same chapter 6 of Book II Suarez refines his view, exploring an hypothesis of Bartholomé de Medina. Medina asks whether, assuming that God has not forbidden or commanded what is of the natural law, lying would nevertheless be evil and respecting one's parents good. In his handling of this problem, – which we need not pursue – Suarez

[68] *De legibus ac Deo legislatore*, II, c. 6, nn. 3–4 (ed. L. Pereña-V. Abril, Corpus Hispanorum de Pace, vol. XIII, Madrid, 1974, pp. 79–83).

[69] *De legibus ac Deo legislatore*, II, c. 6, n. 4.

examines the nerve-points of the nominalist-realist controversies, the question *de odio Dei* (Could God command a man to hate God?) and the distinction between God's *potentia absoluta* and His *potentia ordinata* (nn. 15, 20). The true reply (*vera responsio*, n. 23) is a reconciliation of opposites: God cannot but prohibit what is intrinsically evil; and yet the Divine liberty is not thereby excluded.

The genesis of Suarez's view has recently been studied and the stages in his development identified, by the team of Spanish scholars engaged in bringing out the critical edition of the *De legibus ac Deo legislatore.*[70] P. Suñer distinguishes and documents four stages in Suarez's advance from an initial post-Tridentine anti-voluntarist view (in his teaching at the Collegium Romanum, 1581–1582) through a difficult and doubtful period at Alcalà (1593) to the first drafts of the *De legibus* (1601–1603), and finally, to the nuanced and definitive synthesis of the *De legibus* (1612).[71] And with regard to the sources, which Suarez usually takes care to acknowledge, there is the list of the books, property of the University of Coimbra, which Suarez was allowed to keep in his room, 1603–1608.[72] One detail of interest touching the citation of authorities is that Gabriel Vazquez, one of Suarez's prime sources in the matter, had died in 1604; by the fact, as Pereña points out[73] the censure was lifted in virtue of which the General of the Order had forbidden these two distinguished Jesuits to attack, or even to quote, each other.[74]

Suarez's views on the nature of the natural law and the basis of morality, nuanced views to which no summary can do justice, are a notable landmark in the return to the concept of the natural moral law. It is not suggested that the scholastic revival was the only defence of the natural law against the nominalism of the fourteenth and fifteenth centuries. A history of the concept would demonstrate otherwise; but that cannot be attempted here. It may, however, be useful, to conclude the present chapter with

[70] Francisco Suarez, *De legibus*, Edición crítica bilingüe, L. Pereña, V. Abril, P. Suñer et al. edd., Corpus Hispanorum de Pace, Vol XI sqq., Madrid, 1971.

[71] "Teocentrismo de la ley natural" in Corpus Hispanorum de Pace, Vol. XIII, Madrid, 1974, pp. xxxviii-lv.

[72] Corpus Hispanorum de Pace, Vol. XI, Appendice IV, pp. 167–183.

[73] Corpus Hispanorum de Pace, Vol. XIII, p. xxvi.

[74] In *De legibus ac Deo legislatore*, II, c. 5, 2, for example, Suarez quotes Vazquez by name, whereas in the draft of 1602, in the corresponding passage, Vazquez's name appears only in the margin of the ms. Cf. Corpus Hispanorum de Pace, Vol. XIII, pp. 59–60.

one or two soundings in English legal history, not since the Reformation noticeable for a deference towards natural law.[75]

One may begin with an elder contemporary of St. Thomas, Henry Bracton whose massive *De legibus et consuetudinibus Angliae* written about 1250, has been called (by Maitland) "the crown and flower of English medieval jurisprudence."[76] The Introduction defines a number of general terms, including natural law. Bracton gives, as the first sense of natural law, a "certain instinctive impulse by which individual living things are led to act in certain ways." Thus, he says: *Ius naturale est quod natura, id est ipse Deus, docuit omnia animalia.* He goes on, then, to parse the words of the definition. But the discussion ends with another definition, which associates the natural law with the will and the reason of man.[77] This is the approach found in those other great English lawyers, Sir John Fortescue (1396–1470) author of *De laudibus legum Angliae* and of Christopher St. Germain, who, in 1523, wrote his *Doctor and Student or Dialogue between a Doctor of Divinity and a Student in the Laws of England.*[78] It is also the view of Sir Edward Coke (1552–1634), Lord Chief Justice under James I, amongst whose dicta were the following: "the law of nature is part of the law of England," "the law of nature was before any judicial or municipal law" and "the law of nature is immutable."[79] Coke has been quoted as saying that "God at the time of creation of the nature of man infused into his heart (natural law) for his preservation and direction; and this is *lex naturae*, the moral law . . (Moses was) the first reporter or writer of law (and Aristotle) nature's secretary."[80] Such views were still to be found in William Blackstone's (1723–1780) *Commentaries on the Laws of England* despite the evergrowing insistence upon the supremacy of Parliament.[81]

Of much greater moment in the present context is "that learned and judicious divine" Richard Hooker (1554–1645). Of

[75] See the gloss in Bracton: "In Anglia minus curetur de jure naturali quam in aliqua regione de mundo," cited by B. McCabe, "Francis Bacon and the Natural Law Tradition" in *Natural Law Forum*, 9 (1964), p. 120.

[76] G.E. Woodbine (ed.), *Bracton on the Laws and Customs of England*, with translation, revisions and notes by S.E. Thorne, I–II, Harvard, 1968.

[77] G.E. Woodbine, *op. cit.*, pp. 26–27.

[78] Cf. J.C.H. Wu, *Fountain of Justice*, pp. 78–85.

[79] J.C.H. Wu, *op. cit.*, pp. 91–93; G.H. Sabine, *History of Political Theory*, pp. 383–386.

[80] B. McCabe, *op. cit.*, p. 117.

[81] Cf. W. Friedmann, *Legal Theory*, p. 84.

him Pollock said: "An English reader in search of a general explanation of the Law of Nature as understood down to the Renaissance might, indeed, do well enough to take Hooker for his guide."[82] The judgment is all the more intriguing in that Hooker's considerable debt to St. Thomas is well-known. Page after page of the first book of *The Laws of Ecclesiastical Polity* paraphrases St. Thomas's views on law in the *Prima-Secundae;* and it is perfectly clear that for Hooker the natural law is the law of reason.[83]

One cannot be complacent, however, with insistence upon the law of reason as sufficient defence for the natural law or sufficient guarantee that it will not be misconceived. In fact, as the next chapter will indicate, the greater danger to the profile of the natural law in modern times was presented, not by the nominalist attack upon reason, but by the rationalist hypertrophy of reason following upon Grotius.

[82] P. Surlis, "Natural Law in Richard Hooker" in *Irish Theological Quarterly*, 35 (1968), pp. 173–185.

[83] P. Munz, *The Place of Hooker in the History of Thought*, especially ch. 2 'Hooker and St. Thomas', [pp. 29–67 and Appendix A, "Hooker's Debt to St. Thomas,"] pp. 175–193 in which Hooker and Aquinas are set in parallel columns.

CHAPTER IX

THE FALSE FACE OF THE NATURAL LAW

It has already been suggested that, in the history of the concept of the natural law since the thirteenth century, the rationalist natural law of the seventeenth and eighteenth centuries presents an important turning-point. For a number of reasons, not least because it is closer to our time, the natural law of the Age of Reason has usurped the attention of historians of thought and has tended to obscure their vision of the natural law of the scholastic revival of the sixteenth and seventeenth centuries and, possibly even more so, their vision of the natural law of the High Scholasticism of the thirteenth century. More serious still, the rationalist natural law proved extremely vulnerable to criticism, particularly from the historical schools of the nineteenth century; and the impression is sometimes conveyed that refutations of this natural law amount to disposing of the concept purely and simply. Nothing could be further from the truth. To see that such is the case, we must briefly examine the rationalists' natural law.

A. HUGO GROTIUS AND THE 'IMPIOUS HYPOTHESIS'

Hugo Grotius (Huig de Groot, 1538–1645) published in 1625 his epoch-making *De jure belli et pacis.* It may be described as a watershed in the history of ideas, ushering in the secularization of the natural law.[1] In the *Prolegomena* to his work (n. 11) Grotius emitted the celebrated hypothesis:

What we have been saying (viz. about the natural law) would have a degree of validity even if we should concede that which cannot be

[1] The phrase may be due to Otto von Gierke cf. *Natural Law and the Theory of Society*, 1500–1800, translated by E. Barker, I, p. 36: "It was a definite epoch in the history of thought when Grotius proceeded to elaborate a purely secular philosophy of law...." Whether in fact this was Grotius's intention or was rather an interpretation fostered by his successors is not easily decided.

conceded without the utmost wickedness, that there is no God, or that the affairs of men are of no concern to him.[2]

Was this 'impious hypothesis' as it has been called a device to take the natural law out of the theological controversies of the age? This was the century of the Thirty Years' War (1618–1648); and Grotius himself had suffered greatly from the religious intolerance of the time. Furthermore, current conceptions of the natural law were divided more or less according to the religious differences between Protestant and Catholic. It is not implausible to think of Grotius as wishing a plague on both their houses. The reality, as might have been anticipated, is more complex.

To begin with, Grotius was and remained a theologian. He had no intention of divorcing the natural law from theology, still less of constructing an atheistic or agnostic ethic. To establish this, one need look no further than the very next section in the *Prolegomena* (n. 12):

> Herein, then, is another source of law besides the source in nature, that is, the free will of God, to which beyond all cavil our reason tells us we must render obedience.

And, in the body of the work, Grotius defines the natural law in entirely traditional terms:

> Natural law is 'the dictate of right reason indicating that an act, according as it conforms to or is in disagreement with nature, individual and social, is either morally wicked or morally necessary and in consequence such an act is commanded or forbidden by God, the author of nature.[3]

Grotius's other writings leave no doubt about the matter.[4] But if

[2] "... etiamsi daremus, quod sine summo scelere dari nequit, non esse Deum, aut non curari ab eo negotia humana." The translation in the text is that of Francis W. Kelsey in *Hugo Grotius Prolegomena to the Law of War and Peace* (reprinted from the edition in the Carnegie Endowment for Peace series 'Classics in International Law'), p. 9. H. von Cocceji (1644–1719), follower of Pufendorf and professor at Heidelberg, writes of the *Etiamsi daremus*, "Pugnat haec sententia cum pietate, quod hominem subiciat alii causae quam Deo"; *Hugonis Grotii De Jure Belli et Pacis*, Lausanne, 1751, cited by J. St. Leger, *The 'Etiamsi Daremus' of Hugo Grotius, p.* 44 *and note.*

[3] *De Jure Belli et Pacis*, I, c. 1, n. 10: "Ius naturale est dictamen rectae rationis indicans alicui actui, ex eius convenientia aut disconvenientia cum ipsa natura naturali ac sociali inesse moralem turpitudinem aut necessitatem moralem, ac consequenter ab auctore naturae Deo talem actum aut praecipi aut vetari."

[4] Cf. in particular the *De Imperio Summarum Potestatum circa Sacra* cited in A.H. Chroust, "Hugo Grotius and the Scholastic Natural Law Tradition" in *The New Scholasticism*, 17 (1943), pp. 101–133 at pp. 125–133.

the hypothesis was not intended to remove the natural law from all theological contamination, the question remains whether or not it is more than a rhetorical flourish. Herein lies the relevance of the background to Grotius's work, not merely the immediate background of post-Reformation controversy about the natural law but, more particularly, the wider background of the nominalistic controversies, stemming from Scotus and Ockham.

It has already been argued that the sources of Grotius's hypothesis are likely to be found among the representatives of scholasticism. But there is someting of paradox in the fact that, while Grotius's *Etiamsi* has all the looks of an intellectualist proclamation, his models seem to have been in the main voluntarist; and the hypothesis was exploited by successors like Pufendorf, who were also mostly voluntarist. Grotius could not, of course, have foreseen these subsequent developments; but he may have had some misgivings about his sources. It is interesting to note that in his earlier writings he was voluntarist – in the *De jure praedae*, for instance, written 1604–1606 – whereas by the time of the publication of the *De jure belli et pacis* in 1625 he had adopted an extreme intellectualist position.[5] There is some circumstantial evidence of a direct influence of Suarez here. Briefly, a passage inserted by Grotius at some stage in the composition of the *De jure praedae* seems to show a remarkable familiarity with Suarez's *De legibus ac Deo legislatore;*[6] it adopts Suarez's understanding of the *jus gentium*, which understanding Grotius reiterates in the *De jure belli et pacis* twenty years later. Suarez, as we have seen, was not an intellectualist in philosophy of law; but he had also rejected extreme voluntarism. If one were to characterize his position one would say that it was an attempt to harmonize the competing views.[7] A reading of the *De legibus* might well have influenced Grotius towards intellectualism. Nor would Grotius necessarily have stated his debt, if debt there was; his

[5] G. Fassò, *La legge della ragione*, pp. 161–164; cf. J. St. Leger, *The 'Etiamsi Daremus' of Hugo Grotius*, pp. 29–30, 137–140, citing notably J. Basdevant, "Hugo Grotius" in *Les fondateurs du droit international*, Paris, 1904, pp. 125–127 and G. Ambrosetti, *I presupposti teologici e speculativi delle concezioni giuridiche de Grozio*, Bologna, 1955.

[6] J. St. Leger, *op. cit.*, pp. 99–103.

[7] Cf. T. E. Davitt, *The Nature of Law*, pp. 86–108, 219–299. Davitt notes (p. 87, note 2; pp. 92–93, note 19) that Suarez, too, changed his mind on this matter; in his early works he was intellectualist and in the later *De legibus* took the voluntarist view of the essence of law.

reticence in this regard with reference to Suarez has been remarked.[8]

The extent and the detail of such debts cannot always be ascertained, above all when it is a matter of views which had become a commonplace of legal philosophy.[9] The divergence of views in Grotius's commentators is interesting. Already, in the generations following him, in early commentators and popularizers like Pufendorf, Barbeyrac, Heineke and others, there was criticism of Grotius for his excessive dependence upon the scholastics. There is less agreement, however, on the identification of the scholastics suggested as the origin of the *Etiamsi daremus.* Pufendorf, who condemned the hypothesis as absurd, attributes it to the scholastics Zentgravius, Suarez, Vazquez and Durandus and holds Vazquez particularly responsible. Of more recent scholars, Otto Gierke attributed it to Hugh of St. Victor, Gabriel Biel and Almain – names, he says, found in Suarez's *De legibus* (II, 6, 3) where all the older opinions are reviewed.[10] Johann Sauter, who characterizes the hypothesis as an expression of *Wertobjectivismus,* sees it in a line of descent from Vazquez – who depends upon Gregory of Valentia (sic) and Hugh of St. Victor – to Arriaga, Grotius, Christian Wolff and down to Nicolai Hartmann in the twentieth century.[11] A.H. Chroust mentions not merely Gregory of Valentia (sic), Vazquez and Arriaga (relying

[8] Different explanations for this lack of candour have been suggested; for indications cf. J. St. Leger, *The 'Etiamsi Daremus' of Hugo Grotius,* pp. 106–110; A. Nussbaum, *A Concise History of the Law of Nations,* revised edition, New York, 1954, Appendix II, "J.B. Scott on the Superiority of the Scholastics over Hugo Grotius"; J. Muldoon, "The Contribution of the Medieval Canon Lawyers to the Formation of International Law" in *Traditio,* 28 (1972), pp. 483–497.

[9] "Grotius n'est pas surgi de rien; mais il baigne dans un milieu de riche culture juridique, qui se développe sans heurt sur la tradition médiévale . . .": M. Villey, "Abrégé du droit naturel classique" in *Archives de philosophie du droit,* 6 (1961), p. 76, citing P. Ottenwalder, *Zur Naturrechtslehre des Hugo Grotius*; G. Ambrosetti, *Il diritto naturale della riforma cattolica*; E. Reibstein, *Die Anfänge des neueren Natur- und Völkerrechts*; *Id., Johannes Althusius als Fortsetzer der Schule von Salamanca*; See especially J. St. Leger, *op. cit.,* pp. 45–57.

[10] S. Pufendorf, *Spicilegium controversiarum,* I, 1, 6, 13; O. Gierke, *Johannes Althusius und die Entwicklung der naturrechtlichen Staatstheorien,* pp. 73–75: cited in J. St. Leger, *The 'Etiamsi Daremus' of Hugo Grotius,* pp. 47–48, 51.

[11] *Die philosophischen Grundlagen des Naturrechts,* pp. 86–87.

upon Sauter), but also Molina and even St. Thomas.[12] H. Rommen mentions Vazquez's doctrine of the *lex indicans* (as opposed to the lex *praecipiens*).[13] Giorgio Del Vecchio cites Suarez and points out that the passage from Gabriel Biel adduced by Gierke is actually attributed by Biel to Gregory of Rimini; Del Vecchio also draws attention to a passage in which John Duns Scotus, almost four centuries before, appears to have anticipated Grotius's hypothesis.[14] In the course of a lengthy discussion of Grotius's sources Guido Fassò, although he regards the question of verbal dependence as of secondary importance, adds some interesting suggestions.[15] Formulae implying the hypothesis of God's non-existence are certainly found in scholasticism and, more generally, in the tradition of rationalism in morals. Thus not only Gregory of Rimini and Gabriel Vazquez but other scholastics, from the fourteenth to the seventeenth century might have been the source of Grotius's *Etiamsi daremus.* Robert Bellarmine, for one, emits a very similar hypothesis in the *Controversies;*

If (*per impossibile*) law did not come from God, it would still bind under pain of fault; just as if (*per impossibile*) there existed a man not created by God, he would still be rational.[16]

[12] "Hugo Grotius and the Scholastic Natural Law Tradition" in *The New Scholasticism,* 17 (1943), pp. 111–116. The confusion of Gregory of Rimini (+1358) with Gregory of Valencia (1549(?)–1603) is in Sauter. G. Fassò remarks upon another confusion, between Gabriel Vazquez (1551–1604) and Fernando Vazquez de Menchaca (1512–1569) a jurist much-quoted by Grotius; cf. *La legge della ragione,* p. 149. Arriaga appears to have published his *Disputationes theologicae* in 1644, almost twenty years after Grotius's *De jure belli et pacis.*

[13] *The Natural Law,* 1947, p. 71.

[14] "Si per impossibile poneretur alius Deus, qui non creasset nos. . . ." *Reportata Parisiensia,* III, D. 27, q. un. n. 6; cf. J. St. Leger, *op. cit.,* pp. 55–56, citing G. Del Vecchio, *Lezioni di filosofia del diritto,* 10th ed., Milano, 1958, p. 40, note 1; G. Stratenwerth, *Die Naturrechtslehre des Johannes Duns Scotus,* p. 43; H. Welzel, *Naturrecht und materiale Gerechtigkeit,* p. 94, calls it "Das Gedankenexperiment, Gott wegzudenken und an seine Stelle etwas anderes zu setzen."

[15] *La legge della ragione,* pp. 128–160: "La questione dei precedenti dell' ipotesi ateistica groziana non ha sostanzialmente grande importanza" (p. 134). . . . :" "La ricerca, o, come qualcuno l'ha chiamato, la 'caccia' ai precedenti delle' atteggiamento di Grozio può apparire oziosa. . . ." (p. 146).

[16] *De membris Ecclesiae militantis,* III, 11 cited by Fassò, *op. cit.,* p. 135n: "Si (per impossibile) esset lex non a Deo, adhuc obligaret ad culpam, sicut si (per impossibile) homo existeret non factus a Deo, adhuc esset rationalis."

Again, Gabriel Biel, to whom in this matter Gierke called attention in the last century, repeats almost word for word the text of Gregory of Rimini.[17] But why confine the search to the scholastic tradition? The entire Stoic-Ciceronian tradition, developed by the Church Fathers and the scholastics, can provide models. In this tradition one must place St. Thomas Aquinas, no less than Melanchthon, and such various authorities as St. John Chrysostom, Pelagius, Rufinus, Peter Abelard.[18] Of particular interest is the passage from the *Meditations* of Marcus Aurelius (VI, 44) because, not alone in his hypothesis about the non-existence of God but also in his definition of the natural law, Grotius seems to use the very phraseology of the Stoic Emperor.[19] Finally, with regard to possible sources within the Protestant tradition, Fassò argues that the writers usually mentioned – Johannes Oldendorp, Nicholaus Hemming and Benedikt Winkler – derive, not from the Ockhamist Luther nor from the voluntarist Calvin, but from the one who has been called the 'Protestant scholastic,' Melanchthon.[20]

[17] *In II Sent.*, d. 35, q. unica, a. 1: "... si per impossibile Deus non esset qui est ratio divina, aut ratio illa divina esset errans, adhuc si quis ageret contra rectam rationem angelicam vel humanam, aut aliam aliquam, si qua esset, peccaret. Et si nulla penitus esset recta ratio: adhuc si quis ageret contra id, quod dictaret ratio recta, si aliqua esset, peccaret. Haec Gregorius (viz. of Rimini), dist. XXXIV, art. II" (Text in G. Fassò, *La legge della ragione, Appendice*, pp. 283–284).

[18] G. Fassò, *op. cit.*, pp. 37–40, 56–59.

[19] Pufendorf had already noted the resemblance in his *De jure naturae et gentium*, II, c. 3, n. 19 (Oxford, 1934, photographic reproduction of edition of Amsterdam, 1688): "Neque enim adstipulari possum Grotio, qui in Prolegomenis autumat jura naturalia locum aliquem habitura etiamsi daremus, quod sine summo scelere dari nequit, non esse Deum aut non curari ab eo negotia humana. Nam si vel maxime quis impiam istam ac absurdam hypothesin fingeret, ac genus humanam ex se scilicet ortum conciperet vita tamen rationis dictata, tunc nullo modo possent habere vim legis, quippe quae necessario superiorem ponit.... Videtur autem Grotii sententia expressa ex illa M. Antinini 1. VI, n. 44: Si nulla re nostra consilia Dii ineunt, quod tamen impium est credere, quidniegomet consulam? Mihi autem deliberatio competit de eo quod conducat mihi. Conducit vero unicuique quod est constitutionis et naturae ipsius consentaneum. Porro natura mea rationalis et civilis est...." The text of Marcus Aurelius appears to have been first translated from Greek into Latin by Guilelmus Xylander in 1558. It is a text not easily come by today. It would be interesting to know if this is the version quoted by Pufendorf who, in any event "in the matter of quotations from other works... often took considerable liberties with the text" (Translators' Preface to the above-named edition, p. 63a).

[20] Cf. G. Fassò, *La legge della ragione*, pp. 154, 159–160, citing P. Ottenwalder, *Zur Naturrechtslehre des Hugo Grotius.*

B. NATURAL LAW IN THE AGE OF REASON

Perhaps history has accorded more importance to Grotius's hypothesis of God's non-existence than he did himself. Be that as it may, the influence of the voluminous *De jure belli et pacis*, far the greatest part of it taken up with international law (or, as it was then known, *jus gentium*), was enormous. If the legal philosophy behind Grotius's discussion of the burning juridicial problems of his day is pithily expressed in the *Etiamsi daremus* with which he begins, it was taken up enthusiastically by his successors. And it is scarcely too much to say that, in those followers, the hypothesis with its implications became a kind of standard of rationalism in law and morals.

Grotius's most influential follower was Samuel Pufendorf (1632–1694); through him may be traced Grotius's influence upon Locke, Rousseau, Thomasius, Wolff, Barbeyrac, Burlamaqui, Blackstone and Montesquieu – a list whose variety is a tribute to Grotius's universality and Pufendorf's versatility.[21] These writers, however, are in varying degrees voluntarist; and Pufendorf expressly rejects the *Etiamsi daremus* as an absurd hypothesis of the scholastics.[22] How, then, one might well ask, has Grotius maintained his reputation as the father of the school of natural law? This question raises very wide issues indeed which cannot be explored here. Two points, nevertheless, may be made.

Firstly, even if it were clear that, by this hypothesis of God's non-existence, Grotius meant to withdraw the field of natural law from theology – and we have seen that this is, at the very least, debatable – it would not follow that his system stood or fell with the validity of the hypothesis. What is true of Suarez is true, *mutatis mutandis*, of Grotius, namely that great parts of his system of political theory and jurisprudence can be detached from his theology – or philosophy of moral obligation – without serious mutilation.[23] Otto Gierke, in the last century, made a suggestion along these lines, which deserves fuller development today. Having referred to the realist-nominalist controversy about the origin of the *jus naturale*, whether in the will or the being of God,

[21] Cf. L. Krieger, *The Politics of Discretion; Pufendorf and the Acceptance of Natural Law*, pp. 225–266.

[22] Cf. J. St Leger, *op. cit.*, pp. 41–44; cf. H. Welzel, *Die Naturrechtslehre Samuel Pufendorfs*, pp. 9–10.

[23] The remark is made about Suarez and theology by G.H. Sabine, *History of Political Theory*, p. 354.

he remarks:

> The appeal to Divine Authority in order to secure a legal validity for the Law of Nature resulted in little more than the provision of a formal basis for it; and those who never introduced the name of God at all were able to secure the same result almost equally well (by contenting themselves with human reason as the formal basis of natural law).

And in a footnote to this passage he writes:

> When as in Grotius . . . and his precursors . . . the assumption was made that there would be a Natural Law even if God did not exist, or if He were unjust, the logical consequence of that assumption was the abandoning of any idea that it was derived from the nature or will of God; and this is what we find in Thomasius. . . . After Locke in England and Rousseau and his successors in France had contented themselves with merely invoking 'the order of nature,' the connexion of Natural Law with the idea of God tended also to disappear among German thinkers.[24]

Pufendorf's natural law theory depended upon a notion of *socialitas*[25] and this is adumbrated in Grotius's definition of the natural law as "the dictate of right reason indicating that an act, according as it conforms to or is in disagreement with nature, individual and social, is either morally wicked or morally necessary. . . ."[26] It is seen, then, that the question of the foundation of the natural law in the intellect or the will of God can become a marginal one and disagreement between Grotius and his successors becomes, on this point, unimportant.

Secondly it may be recalled that the Age of Natural Law was also the Age of Reason and that, once preoccupations about realism and voluntarism had been, so to speak, placed between parentheses, the widely-accepted framework for the exposition of legal and philosophical ideas was one into which Grotius's hypothesis fitted easily. Grotius's suggestion that there would still be a natural law even if there were no God was acceptable to thinkers whose methodology was open to the seduction of mathematical models. Mathematics, after all, does not in any readily acceptable sense depend upon the will of God; and if mathematical reasoning is the ideal, even in the moral and legal

[24] *Natural Law and the Theory of Society, 1500–1800* (translated by Ernest Barker), Cambridge, 1950, p. 99 and note 11, p. 289.

[25] Cf. H. Welzel, *Die Socialitas als oberstes Prinzip der Naturrechtslehre Samuel Pufendorfs; Id., Die Naturrechtslehre Samuel Pufendorfs*, pp. 31–51.

[26] *De Jure Belli et Pacis*, I, c. 1, n. 10.

sciences, then a point of departure that stresses the independence enjoyed by basic principles must be an advantage.

The ideal of mathematical certainty exercised a great attraction over the writers and thinkers of the seventeenth and eighteenth centuries. Aristotle's warning, in the *Nicomachean Ethics*,[27] that in any study we should look only for the kind of certainty that the subject-matter admits, was largely ignored. Perhaps it was to have been expected in thinkers like Descartes, Spinoza and Leibniz, who were mathematicians. Spinoza wrote an *Ethica more geometrico demonstrata.* The teacher of Leibniz and of Pufendorf, Erhard Weigel (1625–1699) was the author of *Ethica Euclidea* and *Idea Matheseos Universae.* Leibniz believed that political problems were amenable to mathematical methods of proof – in 1617 he published a work purporting to demonstrate to Louis XIV that that monarch should despatch his armies from the Low Countries to Egypt to break the power of the Turk; and in 1699 he published his *Specimen demonstrationum politicarum pro eligendo rege Polonorum.* His efforts to construct a *scientia universalis* are well-known. His 'logic of life' implied that all ideas could be represented by symbols and that consequently

> if controversies were to arise there would be no more need of disputation between two philosophers than between two accountants. For it would suffice for them to sit down to their slates and to say to each other (with a friend to witness if they like): 'Let us calculate'[28]

Pufendorf, also under the influence of Weigel, speaks of the possibility of a certain science of 'moral beings.'[29] The same ambition of finding a certain method in moral matters is expressed by Pufendorf's contemporary, John Locke – although Locke does enter a caveat very like Aristotle's in the first chapter of his *Essay Concerning the Human Understanding.*[30] Similarly David

[27] I, 3, 1094 b 11–31.

[28] Cited by L.I. Bredvold, *The Brave New World of the Enlightenment* cf. a letter of Leibniz to Van Velthuysen quoted in S. Gagner, *Studien zur Ideengeschichte der Gesetzgebung*, Uppsala, 1960, p. 111 n., in which Leibniz speaks of Euclidean methods in jurisprudence; cf. also A.H. Chroust, "Hugo Grotius and the Scholastic Natural Law Tradition," in *The New Scholasticism*, 17 (1943), pp. 101–133 et p. 122 and note 72.

[29] About which M. Villey remarks "je ne vois pas que dans la mise en oeuvre il garde longtemps l'illusion d'arriver, par cette méthode, à des conclusions substantielles." Cf. "Les fondateurs de l'école de droit naturel moderne" in *Archives de philosophie du droit*, 6 (1961), p. 88.

[30] Book I, ch. 2, n. 1; Book III, ch. II, n. 16; Book IV, ch. 3, nn. 18–18; ch. 4, nn. 7–9; ch. 12, n. 8. The warning against expecting too much from mathematical methods is in Book I, ch. I. See also the passage from Locke's Journal cited in P. Laslett, *Locke's Two Treatises*, pp. 84–85.

Hume, who like Locke represents the English empirical development as opposed to the Continental rationalism issuing from Descartes, makes a bow in the direction of mathematical reasoning. His great work, the *Treatise of Human Nature* carries the sub-title "An Attempt to Introduce the Experimental Method of Reasoning into Moral Subjects." Less than twenty years before, another moralist, Francis Hutcheson, described his *Enquiry into the Origin of our Ideas of Beauty and Virtue* (1725) as including an effort to "introduce a mathematical calculation into subjects of morality."[31]

The medievals, too, hankered after this *ignis fatuus.* Oxford, in particular had its philosophers and theologians who also distinguished themselves in mathematics. P. Vignaux refers to the "immense fecundity of this discipline as a principle of universal explanation and a way to certitude" and instances Adam Marsh and Robert Grosseteste. And Roger Bacon summed it up by saying that only in mathematics could agreement be found: *excluso mathematicae beneficio, tot sint dubitationes, tot opiniones, tot errores.*[32]

The difference between these medieval aspirants after mathematical certitude in other fields and their seventeenth and eighteenth century successors was that the latter had before their eyes the palpable results of the application of mathematical methods. Isaac Newton's *Naturalis Philosophiae Principia Mathematica* – the title is significant – epitomized the spirit of the age; it was published in 1687.[33] The laicisation of the natural law, believed to flow from Grotius's hypothesis, fitted comfortably with that *Zeitgeist.*[34] It was a *Zeitgeist* that Pufendorf caught when

[31] Which prompted Laurence Sterne's remark that Hutcheson "plus's and minus's you to heaven or hell by algebraic quotations – so that none but an expert mathematician can ever be able to settle his accounts with St. Peter, except perhaps St. Matthew, who had been an officer in the customs, must be called in to audit them." Cf. W.R. Scott, *Francis Hutcheson,* p. 32 note.

[32] *Philosophie au moyen-âge,* p. 98. On this entire question see the interesting essay by L.I. Bredvold, "The Invention of the Ethical Calculus" in *The Seventeenth Century; Studies in the History of English Literature and Thought,* by R.F. Jones and others, Stanford, 1951, pp. 165–180. Bredvold refers to Descartes, Hobbes, Cumberland, Spinoza, Christian Wolff, Weigel, Leibniz, Samuel Clarke, John Craig, Hutcheson, Fontenelle, Locke, William Godwin and others.

[33] In 1699 John Craig published a *Theologiae Christianae Principia Mathematica.*

[34] L.I. Bredvold, *op. cit.,* p. 175: "The Utopianism of the age might be defined as the aspiration of every radical thinker to be the Newton of Ethics or the Newton of Politics."

he said:

It seemed worth making the effort to prove that what is handed down on this matter does by no means all rest upon vacillating opinions, but flows clearly enough from fixed and first principles.

Now, the knowledge which considers what is upright and what is base in human actions, the principal portion of which we have undertaken to present, rests entirely upon grounds so secure, that from it can be deduced genuine demonstrations which are capable of producing a solid science. So certainly can its conclusions be derived from distinct principles, that no further ground is left for doubt.[35]

Here we can place a finger upon the cause of aberrations like the suggestions that the constitution of the Holy Roman Empire and the postal system belonged to the natural law, as did the jury system (with a definite number of jurors). K.D.A. Roeder cites as elementary contraventions of the law of nature: to enter unbidden, to make journeys troublesome and the stiff leather stocks worn by soldiers. The concept of nature giving rise to a comprehensive system of legal rules stretching to the minutest detail was, indeed, absurd. And it was the source of further absurdities such as the case of the disturbed New Englander, recounted in Carl Van Doren's *The Great Rehearsal*, who objected to the two-year senatorial term, proposed by the Constitutional Convention, on the ground that a one-year term was a 'dictate of the law of nature; spring comes once a year, and so should a batch of new senators.'[36]

It is easy to single out such absurdities. But, needless to say, there was a great deal more to the seventeenth and eighteenth century rationalist systems of natural law. The treatises *De jure naturae et gentium* that proliferated in the generations succeeding Pufendorf were grandiose philosophical and juridical monuments. And, while the natural law philosophy in them was totally destroyed by the historical criticism of the nineteenth century, he would be a confident historian who easily permits himself a smile at their expense. For we may reject the concept of human nature typical of the Age of Reason; but how are we to know that what we put in its place is not equally limited, the limitations this time being those of our own age? That is a matter to which we shall

[35] S. Pufendorf, *Elementorum jurisprudentiae universalis*, II, xxix: *De jure naturae et gentium*, II, 25, cited by L. Krieger, *op. cit.*, p. 39.

[36] *Grundzügen des Naturrechts*, 1863, II, 82, 91, 98, cited by A. Ross, *On Law and Justice.*, p. 247; cf. H. Romman, *Natural Law*, pp. 107, 107, 227. J.C. Murray, *We Hold These Truths*, p. 302 cites Van Doren's book.

have to return in the final chapter. Meanwhile we may draw attention once again to the fact that the grounds for rejecting the rationalist natural law are not, and should not be taken as, grounds for the abandonment of the natural law as such.

C. ANOTHER FACE OF NATURAL LAW: HUMAN RIGHTS

There is another side to natural law thinking in the seventeenth and eighteenth centuries and one that our present age finds much more congenial. While being dismissive of the rationalist systems of natural law, one speaks appreciatively of the age of human rights, associated with the names of John Locke (1632–1704) and of Jean-Jacques Rousseau (1712–1778), to whom so much of the contemporary insistence on the rights of man can be traced. It should not, however, be thought that these rights are a modern discovery. They are as old as the natural law itself; they have simply been given a new emphasis. To put the matter in a nutshell, rights, no less than the duties whose correlative they are, depend upon law; civic rights upon civil law and natural rights upon natural law. Rights and duties might be called the obverse and the reverse of the moral coinage. To use a metaphor attributed to Lamennais, they are "like two palm-trees, which fructify only if planted one beside the other."[37]

Expressed more technically, right and duty are the two *termini* of the relation created by law. Perhaps it is only human that men should be vastly more interested in rights than in duties. Yet rights could not survive without duties. My right to life or liberty or property, if it is to mean anything, must mean that others have a duty to refrain from molesting me in these matters. If children have the right to nurture, support and education, then someone, parent or guardian, must have a duty to provide these things. Or, again, my right to life goes with my duty or preserving my life; my right of property is correlated with my duty of using my goods well. These are commonplaces of the philosophy and theology of rights – and the principle that rights are correlated with duties is a useful corrective of the more exaggerated insistence on human rights in the Rousseauistic literature of the eighteenth century.

This kind of analysis may appear irrelevant. For one may ask what those realities of the moral order, rights and duties, have to do with the Rights of Man before which modern democratic man stands in such awe. Edmund Burke, speaking of the French

[37] "Le droit et le devoir sont comme deux palmiers qui ne portent fruit s'ils ne croissent à côté l'un de l'autre."

Revolution, said that the revolutionaries had "made and recorded a sort of institute and digest of anarchy called the Rights of Man."[38] This was an understandable opinion in face of the excesses committed by the revolutionaries; and Burke was not the only one to recoil from them. "Liberty," said Madame Roland on the step of the guillotine, "what crimes are committed in thy name!" To understand such paradoxes one must know something of the history of human rights and realize that they were not a discovery of the Age of Reason.

Ancient and medieval times knew human rights, perhaps often had their attention drawn to them because of ostentatious violation. Roman citizen-rights were a very real thing; when St. Paul, a "citizen of no mean city" appealed to Caesar, the governor Portius Festus had no option: "Hast thou appealed to Caesar? To Caesar shalt thou go."[39] The same Roman law, admittedly, refused citizen-rights to slaves and barbarians. But in time citizenship began to be extended, as we have seen, to the subject-races. And, more importantly, the idea of the essential equality of all men gained ground, stimulated by Stoic ideas of citizenship of the world – the "city of Zeus" as Marcus Aurelius called it – and, above all, by the Christian teaching on the dignity and vocation of the human person. Human rights were known and recognized, even if not given practical effect, for centuries. It is against such background that one must consider such phenomena as slavery, or feudal and military service, or the neglect or violation of individual rights by unscrupulous princes.

As for the medieval theologians, was it not Lord Acton who called St. Thomas Aquinas "the first Whig"?

It is a striking phrase and one still often finds it quoted in textbooks and in candidates' answers to questions about Aquinas in examinations in the history of political thought. But it is not a remark that stands up to much reflection. Aquinas believed assuredly in freedom and natural rights and government by consent; but there is no clear evidence that he thought men had a right to rebellion; he explicitly rejected the theory of the social contract; and as for the 'natural right' that interested the Whig theorists most – the right to property–Aquinas denied that it was, strictly speaking, a natural right at all.[40]

[38] From a speech on the Army estimates, cited in A.E. Doolan, *Order and Law*, p. 85; cf. R.R. Fennessy, *Burke, Paine and the Rights of Man*, chapters 3–4.

[39] *Acts*, 25; 12.

[40] M. Cranston, "St. Thomas Aquinas as a Political Philosopher" in *History Today*, May, 1964, pp. 313–314.

One could quarrel with several of the statements in this passage, but hardly with its recognition that St. Thomas believed in freedom and natural rights. He found room in his philosophy for "four species of law" – the phrase is Ernest Barker's[41] – "all hung by golden chains to God." Of these the natural law may be fairly said to dominate his political philosophy; and natural law generates natural rights and natural duties. The lack of practical recognition afforded to natural rights by the rulers of the time no more destroys them than mathematical obtuseness or wilful miscalculation puts the two-times-table in jeopardy; human rights, indeed, are seen in all their majesty when they are violated.

The Silver Age scholastics, mainly the Spaniards of the sixteenth and seventeenth centuries, Vitoria, Cano, Medina, Soto, Molina, Suarez and a host of others, can be said to have learnt well the lessons of their predecessors of the High Scholasticism of the thirteenth century. The last thing of which they can be accused is the neglect of human rights. Vitoria's *Relectio* on the newly-discovered Indies, a seminal text of modern international law, was a defence of the Indians' rights against the Spanish *conquistadores.* Nor was the protest altogether ineffective for, less than twenty years later, in 1550, the Emperor Charles V suspended the conquests and set up a Commission of theologians to examine their liceity.

Side by side with the achievement of these "ecclesiastical writers on natural law" (as Otto Gierke called them) went the development of the "secular natural law," the myriad systems of natural rights and natural law that saw the light in the seventeenth and eighteenth centuries. Samuel Pufendorf, the first to occupy a special Chair of Natural Law, (at Heidelberg)[42] published in 1673 a work entitled *De Officio Hominis et Civis*, an abridgement of his *De Jure Naturali et Gentium*, in which many of the natural rights of Rousseau and of 1789 were anticipated. It was not left, therefore, for Rousseau and the eighteenth century to discover natural rights; on the contrary

> We can hardly even understand Rousseau, the great popularizer (as we may call him without offence) of natural-law speculation, until we get back to his sources. He was not the inventor of the *personne morale*, or

[41] Introduction to O. Gierke, *Natural Law and Theory of Society 1500–1800*, p. xxxviii.

[42] Or so Putendorf claimed. In reality it was a chair of international law and philology. Cf. L. Krieger, *The Politics of Discretion; Pufendorf and the Acceptance of Natural Law*, p. 19.

its *volonté générale.* They were as old as Pufendorf, and even older. 'Style is the man,' and style is fame; but the scholar must go behind the stylist to those who dug the quarry, and hewed the stone, upon which the stylist drew. Even Kant and Fichte, who were thinkers rather than stylists, drew generously upon the great quarry of Natural Law for their ideas.[43]

John Locke (1632–1704) is the author of two works either of which would have ensured him a place in the history of the natural law. In his *Second Treatise of Civil Government* he makes man's natural rights depend upon a "law of nature," a law whose writ ran already in the "state of nature," before men had contracted to found civil society. In the *Essay concerning the Human Understanding* he discusses the epistemological problem of alleged innate practical principles. It is curious – and an anomaly that has puzzled many critics – that in neither work does he submit this notion of a law of nature to proper examination. Considerable interest, therefore, attended the discovery, after almost two and a half centuries, of nine *Essays on the Law of Nature*, written by Locke, in Latin, in the early 1660's.[44]

The question is raised of Locke's indebtedness to scholasticism.[45] When the subject is the natural law the source-problem becomes peculiarly intractable. So many of the ideas and arguments used were commonplaces of the tradition that, apart from exceptional evidence of a turn of phrase or sequence of thought, one cannot trace them with any confidence to one author rather than to another. Locke had already made the acquaintance of scholastic philosophy as an undergraduate, when he complained of its futility, before he wrote the *Essays on the Law of Nature.* Von Leyden suggests[46] that Locke was directly acquainted with the *Summa Theologiae* of St. Thomas Aquinas. He maintains that a number of arguments in the *Essays on the Law of Nature*, especially in the seventh, are traceable to definite passages in the *Summa;* that the opening paragraph of the first essay, where Locke discusses man's nature and his relation to God and the universe, and also the way in which he formulates the titles of his essays, "betrays Thomist influence." We have seen that it was a

[43] E. Barker, *op. cit.*, p. xiii.

[44] W. von Leyden (ed.), *John Locke: Essays on the Law of Nature*, Oxford, 1954.

[45] Cf. W. Küppers, *John Locke und die Scholastik;* E. Krakowski, *Les sources médiévales de la philosophie de Locke;* A. Tellkamp, *Das Verhältnis Lockes zur Scholastik.*

[46] W. von Leyden, *op. cit.*, p. 36.

great question in the Schools whether law is essentially an act of reason or of will. To some extent the controversy was a technical one, a question of deciding the relative rôles of these two higher faculties, generally agreed to be both necessary in law-making. But as will happen in controversy the points of difference were exaggerated and the struggle became one between the rule of law and arbitrariness, between the limitation of sovereignty and the view represented in the Roman law maxim: *Quod principi placuit legis habet vigorem.* It is curious to find Locke, the champion of toleration and the rights of man, ranged on the side of the partisans of will. His thought on the matter, it will be seen, conceals an unresolved dualism. His express statements are voluntarist, but his incidental phraseology often betrays an intellectualist point of view.

In *the Essays on the Law of Nature* Locke has not much to say about law in general. But what he does say is clearly on the voluntarist side. He cannot conceive of obligation, the effect of law, as being formally constituted otherwise than by the *will* of the legislator, the expression of which is law.[47] The natural law is defined as the ordination of the divine will, known by the light of nature, indicating what agrees or disagrees with rational nature and, by the fact, commanding or forbidding.[48] The terms in which the definition is couched are familiar and might have come from any scholastic text. Elsewhere Locke points out that the natural law differs from the divine positive law only in the method of its promulgation; each is the expression of the divine will.[49] Yet there is more to the definition of the natural law than the expression of God's will. The conception of *convenientia*, conformity with rational nature, although common in works on the natural law, does not readily fit the voluntarist theory. But that Locke does not wish to depart from voluntarism is shown by his next sentence. "Some," he says, (he seems to mean Grotius), "have not rightly understood the natural law, calling it a *dictatum rationis.*"[50] His main reason for rejecting this conception seems to be based upon a misunderstanding of what is meant by a *dictatum rationis;* "reason," he says, "does not so much establish and pronounce this law of nature as search for it and discover it as a law enacted

[47] W. von Leyden, *op. cit.*, p. 184.

[48] W. von Leyden, *op. cit.*, p. 100: "ordinatio voluntatis divinae lumine naturae cognoscibilis, quid cum natura rationali conveniens vel disconveniens sit indicans, eoque ipso jubens aut prohibens."

[49] W. von Leyden, *op. cit.*, p. 188.

[50] W. von Leyden, *op. cit.*, p. 110.

by a superior power and implanted in our hearts." Admittedly the natural law cannot be the work of an autonomous human reason; but why should it not be a work of divine reason, discovered and reiterated by human reason–a possibility that Locke does not entertain? It seems not unfair to suggest that the first a good case for voluntarism. It is interesting to notice that the first of the five arguments to prove the existence of the natural law, that Locke has just defined, should begin with an appeal to the authority of Aristotle who said: "the special function of man is the active exercise of the mind's faculties in accordance with rational principle."[51]

Locke's preoccupation, for most of the *Essays on the Law of Nature*, is with the problem of how men know the natural law. It is in the long discussions that fill these essays that his latent rationalism comes to the surface. When he lists the possible ways in which man, by the unaided use of his faculties, might come to the knowledge of the natural law, he omits reason. But he feels the need of justifying the omission, since the natural law "is most often called right reason itself and the dictate of right reason."[52] His justification is that he is here investigating the "first principles and the sources of all kinds of knowledge, the way in which primary notions enter the mind." Such principles are not provided by reason; they are the matter upon which reason works. Locke argues that first practical principles are the expression of the will of the lawgiver; but he has slipped somewhat into the manner of expression of those who hold that the first principles of the practical reason are precepts of the natural law, basically because they are *ordinationes rationis.* There are only three ways in which such principles could be acquired, by 'inscription,' by 'hearsay' or from sense-experience. Locke rejects the first of these, remarking that to speak of innate practical principles is to take the easy view, and to render superfluous the demonstration that man can know the natural law by the 'light of nature.' He devotes an entire essay, the third, to a polemic against an innate natural law.[53] In it he makes great play with the difficulty presented by the enormous variations in moral matters that even a superficial knowledge of history and anthropology evidences. Any natural law theory has to account for these variations, and Locke's explanation is that there are degrees of knowledge of the

[51] *Nic. Eth.*, I, 7, 1098 a 7.

[52] W. von Leyden, *op. cit.*, p. 124.

[53] W. von Leyden, *op. cit.*, pp. 136–145; cf. the *Essay concerning Human Understanding*, Book I, ch. 3, 'No innate practical principles.'

natural law, that the knowledge of the natural law is capable of development. Again one has the impression that he is really thinking of the natural law in rationalist, rather than voluntarist, terms. His final argument against an innate natural law is that there are no innate speculative first principles; why, then, should there be innate practical principles? The parallel between the first principles of speculative and practical intellect was a favourite with St. Thomas Aquinas, who would certainly accept this argument of Locke's.

Finally, Locke is left with sense-experience – or rather, as it transpires, sense-experience elaborated by reason – as the source of our knowledge of the natural law. He devotes another entire essay, the fourth, to this subject.[54] There is no question of our being able to see or touch or otherwise "read off" the natural law in sensation. But we can perceive the world by the senses and, from the design apparent in it, reason can conclude to the existence of God, creator of the universe and author of universal law. Not all men make this discovery of the supreme lawgiver; just as not all discover the veins of gold and silver buried in the earth.[55] But those who do, learn the precepts of the natural law partly from "the end of all things," partly from "man's own constitution and the faculties with which he is equipped."[56] Man is urged "by a certain propensity of nature" to praise and honour God, to live in society etc. Locke here projected, but never wrote, a further essay: *An ex inclinatione Hominum naturali potest cognosci Lex Naturae? Negatur.* It is a pity. For in drawing out fully his thought on the relation of the natural law with the inclinations of nature he might have been led to modify his views.

In his sixth and seventh essays Locke discusses the obligation of the natural law.[57] He is dealing, he says, with "no private or positive law created according to circumstances and for an immediate convenience." Rather is it "a fixed and permanent rule of morals, which reason itself pronounces, and which persists, being a fact so firmly rooted in the soil of human nature."[58] Human nature must be changed before this law can be either altered or annulled. Not that God could not have fashioned man differently. But having constituted man as He did, certain duties

[54] W. von Leyden, *op. cit.*, pp. 146–158.
[55] W. von Leyden, *op. cit.*, p. 134.
[56] W. von Leyden, *op. cit.*, p. 156.
[57] W. von Leyden, *op. cit.*, pp. 180–203.
[58] W. von Leyden, *op. cit.*, p. 198.

arise of necessity and cannot be otherwise than they are. Locke goes even further in his rejection of arbitrariness; it seems to him that the duties appropriate to rational nature follow from the constitution of that nature in the same way as it follows from the nature of a triangle that its angles should equal two right angles, although, through laziness or thoughtlessness, men frequently do not advert to these plain truths.[59]

It cannot be surprising, then, that his later works should show a considerable departure from the expressed voluntarism of the *Essays on the Law of Nature.* The *Second Treatise of Civil Government* insists that the law of nature is the law of reason.[60] In the *Essay concerning the Human Understanding* the problem is complicated by Locke's identification of good and evil with pleasure and pain. Yet Locke is still convinced that morality might be mathematically demonstrable; the existence of "a Supreme Being, infinite in power, goodness and wisdom, whose workmanship we are and on whom we depend; and the idea of ourselves as understanding rational beings being such as are clear in us, would, I suppose, if duly considered and pursued afford such foundations of our duty and rules of action as might place morality amongst the sciences capable of demonstration."[61]

The doctrines of the *Second Treatise of Civil Government* reappear in such important places as the American Declaration of Independence. Locke is the source of a most important tradition of political thought; his *Treatise,* in Sir Frederick Pollock's well-known judgment, is "probably the most important contribution ever made to English constitutional law by an author who was not a lawyer by profession." But we may not assume that, because he stands at the head of a tradition, Locke spun a system of the gossamer of his own speculations uninfluenced by what went before. No one really innovates in philosophy, no one begins with a *tabula rasa* and perhaps least of all those who profess to begin from nothing, or almost nothing (like Descartes) or preserve mental hygiene (as Comte put it) by not reading the speculations of others! Locke had the experience of the 'Glorious Revolution' of 1688, of which he became the apologist; and, more significantly, he had a wide acquaintance with English post-scholastic writers on the natural law, as shown from his early Latin *Essays on the Law of Nature.*

[59] W. von Leyden, *op. cit.*, pp. 198–201.

[60] Ch. II, par. 6 and 11.

[61] Book IV, ch. 3.

Locke had argued in the *Second Treatise* that man brings into civic society certain basic rights he already enjoyed in the condition of nature, the rights of life, liberty and estate, which the state, the result of the social compact, cannot abolish but must protect and enforce. This was the doctrine that had such an influence upon modern constitutional history. It is reflected most dramatically in the American Declaration of Independence (4th July, 1776) and in the Constitution of the United States of America (adopted on 17th September, 1787) with its nine early Amendments (ratified on 15th December, 1791).[62] Jean-Jacques Rousseau, beginning from principles very different from those of Locke, arrived at conclusions not so dissimilar. If Locke was the ideological father of the American Revolution, Rousseau was the ideological progenitor of the French Revolution. Locke said in the *Second Treatise:*

> The State of Nature has a Law of Nature to govern it, which obliges every one; and Reason, which is that Law, teaches all mankind, who will but consult it, that being all equal and independent, no one ought to harm another in his Life, Liberty or Possessions.[63]

Rousseau's view of the natural law was very different. In the Preface to *The Origin of Inequality* he wrote of the natural law:

> We cannot see without surprise and disgust how little agreement there is between the different authors who have treated this great subject. Among the more important writers there are scarcely two of the same mind about it. . . . The Roman jurists subjected man and other animals indiscriminately to the same natural law. . . . The moderns understanding by the term 'law' merely a rule prescribed to a moral being, . . . confine the jurisdiction of natural law to man, as the only animal endowed with reason. But defining this law, each after his own fashion they have established it on such metaphysical principles that there are very few persons among us capable of comprehending them, much less of discovering them for ourselves. So that the definitions of these learned men, all differing in everything else, agree only in this, that it is impossible to comprehend the law of nature, and consequently to obey it, without being a very subtle casuist and a profound metaphysician.

In the *Contrat Social* he argued for the foundation of morality and the distinction of right and wrong in the conventional character of society. At the same time, as a moralist, he had to seek a basis for his denunciations of the immorality of the society he

[62] Cf. Roscoe Pound, "The Revival of Natural Law" in *Notre Dame Lawyer,* 17 (1942), pp. 328–352.

[63] *Second Treatise of Civil Government,* ch. 2.

lived in. And, while there are passages like those just cited, in which he rejects the natural law, there are others in which Rousseau, not greatly noted for his consistency as a thinker, appears to adopt the natural law as that basis.[64] His attitude has been summarised as follows:

There is a natural law which man can grasp independently of any knowledge of God. It is natural in the sense that in a given set of circumstances man by a combination of simple reason and conscience can know what is right and wrong, just and unjust. However its obligatory character is conditional. In the one case it depends on the ascertainable fact of human enforcement, and in the other, on a strong inner faith in the existence of God. If both of those faiths are in vain, the whole question of natural law becomes at best academic, and the ideal of moral freedom quixotic.[65]

It is, however, through his inspiration of the 'Principles of '89' that Rousseau is best remembered. The famous opening phrase of the *Social Contract* – "Man is born free, and everywhere he is in chains" – was the programme in the name of which the French revolutionaries overthrew the *ancien régime*. But it is often forgotten that the doctrine of natural law enshrined in that programme was not, for Rousseau, a doctrine of imprescriptible individual rights; rather it conferred absolute and inalienable authority on the people as a whole "regarded for this purpose as constituting a somewhat vague and mystically conceived entity, the general will (*Volonté générale*) which differed from the mere sum of the individual wills of the citizens."[66]

The French Revolution produced the *Declaration of the Rights of Man and Citizen*; and after it there came a positive cascade of declarations – the Declaration of '89 was placed at the head of the Constitution of 1791; a Declaration of the Rights of Man was adopted by the Convention of 29 May, 1793; another, voted on 23 June, was placed at the head of the Constitution of 24 June, 1793; a Declaration of the Rights of Man and Citizen appeared, inevitably, in the Constitution of 5 Fructidor III (22 August, 1795); and one might add the later constitutional documents of 1814, 1815 (two), 1848, 1852.[67] France was, indeed, a special

[64] Cf. J.B. Noone "Rousseau's Theory of Natural Law as Conditional" in *Journal of the History of Ideas*, 33 (1972), pp. 23–42.

[65] J.B. Noone, *op. cit.*, p. 42.

[66] Cf. D. Lloyd, *The Idea of Law*, p. 85.

[67] J. Darmor, "A travers les grandes déclarations" in *Revue de l'action populaire*, janvier, 1964, p. 21.

case. But similar things were happening elsewhere. The nineteenth century saw a spate of constitution-making; and the recipe almost invariably included a greater or less infusion of natural rights. The original eighteenth-century rights of man were a programme, embraced with enthusiasm, claims for liberty of conscience, worship, speech, assembly and so on against absolutism. The nineteenth century added the economic and social rights and, not content with stating them, tried to make them effective. And this, it transpired, was an exceedingly difficult task. Abraham Lincoln may be taken to represent the measured view of human rights:

I think the authors of that notable instrument (the *Declaration of Independence*) intended to include *all* men, but they did not intend to declare all men equal *in all respects.* They did not mean to say that all were equal in colour, size, intellect, moral development or social capacity. They defined with tolerable distinctness in what respects they did consider all men created equal – 'with certain inalienable rights, among which are life, liberty and the pursuit of happiness.' This they said, and this they meant. They did not mean to assert the obvious untruth that all were then actually enjoying that equality, nor yet that they were about to confer it immediately upon them. In fact, they had no power to confer such a boon. They meant simply to declare the right, so that the enforcement of it might follow as fast as circumstances should permit.[68]

A very different point of view was taken by Jeremy Bentham for whom natural rights were, in a celebrated phrase, "nonsense upon stilts," the sole function of an alleged natural right being "to enlist sympathy in the attaining of some political right." When a man is shown to have no political right the natural right is a "sort of thread he clings by." Sir Frederick Pollock has remarked that "if Bentham had known what the Law of Nature was really like in the Middle Ages, he would have had to speak of it with more respect."[69] But Bentham's view is still widely current although not always expressed with his trenchancy.

Not to labour the point, the doctrine of natural rights in many ways played, in the nineteenth century, the part played by the natural law doctrine of former ages. That part might be described as the placing of a curb upon the exercise of power in the political

[68] *Speeches and Letters of Abraham Lincoln,* London, 1907; p. 66 "Speech on the Dred Scott Decision, Springfield, Illinois, 26 June, 1857."

[69] J. Bentham, *General View of a Complete Code of Laws,* ch. 2 (*Works,* ed. Bowring, vol. III, p. 157 ff); *Pannomial Fragments,* ch. 1 (*Works,* pp. 211 ff.); F. Pollock, 'History of the Law of Nature' in *Jurisprudence and Legal Essays,* ed. A.L. Goodhart, p. 135.

sphere (this is the particular force of the teaching on human rights) and the setting of objective standards of good and evil for individual conduct. There is here an additional reason for not taking at its face value the nineteenth century's rejection of the natural law, the refutation by positivists in the wake of Auguste Comte (1798–1857), by Utilitarians like Jeremy Bentham (1748–1832) and John Stuart Mill (1806–1873) or by the schools of historical jurisprudence, Friederich Carl von Savigny (1779–1861) and Georg Friederich Puchta (1798–1846) in Germany and Henry Sumner Maine (1822–1888) in England. For the doctrine survived under another face, that of natural rights; and that it is alive and well, although by no means undisputed, may be gleaned from the contemporary preoccupation with documents, in the direct line of descent from Locke and Rousseau, the declarations already referred to[70] and their updating in texts like those of Roosevelt's 'Four Freedoms' of 1941, the United Nation's *Universal Declaration of Human Rights* of 1948 or the Council of Europe's *Convention on Human Rights* of 1950 or Pope John XXIII's Encyclical *Pacem in Terris* of 1963. The key to the understanding of this situation is well-expressed by A.P. d'Entrèves: "In my opinion," he says, "what really calls for attention on the part of the modern student is the function of natural law rather than the doctrine itself, the issues that lay behind it rather than the controversies about its essence."[71]

[70] A. Aulard-B. Mirkine-Guetzévitch, *Les déclarations des droits de l'homme;* this study, published in Paris in 1929, gives one hundred and forty texts.

[71] *Natural Law*, p. 18.

CHAPTER X

NATURAL LAW: A TWENTIETH-CENTURY PROFILE?

What has gone before is not a history of the natural law, but simply the consideration of selected developments within that history. The pattern, however, is not significantly altered, it would appear, in a complete history; and certain statements can be made with confidence. It can be said that the natural law, as an idea, is almost as old as philosophy itself. Since the Greeks first began to philosophize it has appeared in every age and can be described as a sort of recurring decimal in the history of thought. It has, of course, had its great moments and its moments of eclipse, its flowering times and barren times, catabolic and anabolic periods. It has been declared dead, never to rise again from its ashes; but it has risen livelier than ever and buried its undertakers. It is commonplace to observe that the funeral orations for the natural law have always been premature.[1] There is, indeed, no doubt of the revival of interest in the natural law in our time. Some, however, compare it with the interest of anatomists in a cadaver – and we have here, perhaps, part of the secret of the vitality of the concept; for the natural law requires to be justified anew in every age. It is not enough that there should be many upholders of the natural law in our day; what is required is that the concept should be shown to be sound and relevant in the conditions of our century. And that will certainly prove no light task. For side by side with the revival of interest in the natural law one must place the acutely critical approach of so many of our contemporaries. The same critic who said that the natural law was like a cadaver studied by anatomists, Norberto Bobbio, has pointed out that philosophers tend to say that the natural law is

[1] 'Leichenreden sind zu früh gehalten worden:' cf. supra, Introduction, p. ix, note 1.

not natural and lawyers tend to say that it is not a law. Most of the contemporary attacks upon the natural law can be put under one or other of those rubrics, which in all truth cover a very wide field.[2]

It is the argument of this chapter – emerging from what has gone before in the rest of the book – that there is a common ground between many of the contemporary attackers and upholders of the natural law. This is no more paradoxical than the cyclic character of natural law history itself; in that sense it can be said to emerge from the history. What is agreed upon is a set of features constituting the natural law's contemporary profile. It is no more final or definitive than any other in the history of the concept; but it is a valid likeness and is adapted to our age.

A. NATURAL LAW EMERGING FROM ECLIPSE

In view of what was said in the last chapter, about the stress upon human rights during the nineteenth century while the formal doctrine of a natural law was very much on retreat, it is no surprise that our age's interest in the natural law should first of all be found in the area of rights. The point need not be made again, beyond the reminder that the dominating values of our everyday life, the values taken for granted like the dignity of the human person, the importance of personal freedom, the equality of citizens before the law, toleration, the citizen's right to participate in the building of the state, the importance of the common good, the public administration of justice and so on, were brought to the fore by the natural law theories at the end of the eighteenth century.[3] On the other hand the revived natural law of the twentieth century "which today dominates the greater part of legal philosophy, is not a revival of the eighteenth century rationalist systems, but a thread of scholasticism that has been picked up again"[4]

[2] "Les critiques anciennes et récentes du droit naturel peuvent être partagées en deux groupes, suivant qu'elles visent le substantif ou l'adjectif, c'est-à-dire qu'ils aient nié que le droit naturel soit un droit, ou que le droit soit naturel. Ce sont surtout les juristes qui se sont consacrés à la première critique, et les philosophes à la seconde": "Quelques arguments contre le droit naturel" in *Le droit naturel* Annales de philosophie politique, III, p. 175.

[3] H. Welzel, *Naturrecht und materiale Gerechtigkeit*, p. 236.

[4] Cf. A. Ross, *On Law and Justice*, p. 255; C.J. Friederich, *The Philosophy of Law in Historical Perspective*, p. 179.

At this point the historian of the natural law would pause to consider the various important thinkers, philosophers and jurists, who overtly or covertly accepted a doctrine of natural law. The list would include not only scholastic philosophers expressly propounding a natural law, like Theodor Meyer (1821–1913). G. von Hertling (1843–1919) Viktor Cathrein (1845–1931) Jacques Leclercq (1891–1971) or Johannes Messner (b. 1891) but also jurists like Louis Le Fur (1870–1943) or Jean Dabin (b. 1889) who accepted it in their fashion or like Leon Duguit (1859–1928) or François Geny (1861–1938) who reject it, but whose systems, nevertheless, contain elements or principles or appeals to a higher law which at least place them outside the category of pure positivism. The scholastic natural law theorists are exploiting a tradition that we have seen in the Middle Ages and at the time of the Counter-Reformation, a tradition that survived, in the work of thinkers like Taparelli d'Azeglio (1793–1862), right through the nineteenth century. The jurists had seen that positivism (taking that term to mean that the validity of a law is independent of its content) has its limitations.[5]

More systematically, the natural law revival might be placed under definite headings, neo-Kantian, neo-positivist, sociologial, neo-Thomist.[6] Labels, especially in such matters, have a limited value and are rejected by many of those to whom it is proposed to apply them. Yet, if not positively misleading, they can be instructive in the enterprise of surveying contemporary attitudes towards the natural law.

The best-known representative of the neo-Kantian natural law is Hans Kelsen (1881–1973) whose formalistic Kantian conception of the juridical led him to a 'normative' (later called 'pure') concept of law. This pure theory of law (*reine Rechtslehre*), independent of all sociological content and all ideology, is really a logical structure of law. Kelsen wants no part in the farce "whereby various proponents of natural law demand opposite things as required by natural law."[7] The most important neo-Kantian in this respect is Rudolf Stammler (1856–1938), whom it is also difficult to see as an upholder of natural law. He, too, speaks of the *idea of law* as a fundamental criterion, a way of judging all positive human law. No content can be deduced from

[5] C.J. Friederich, *op. cit.*, ch. XIX, pp. 178–188; H. Rommen, *Natural Law*, ch. VII, pp. 135–158.

[6] G.E. Langemeijer, "Philosophie du droit," in *Philosophy in the Mid-Century*, II, p. 103; D. Lloyd, *The Idea of Law*, p. 88.

[7] W. Luijpen, *Phenomenology of Natural Law*, pp. 21–25.

this *Grundgedanke.* In this connection Stammler is the author of the celebrated formula: "Natural law with variable content" (*Naturrecht mit wechselndem Inhalt*) The third and most objective of the neo-Kantian legal philosophers is Giorgio Del Vecchio (1878–1970). From an early preoccupation with the pure form of justice he came, at the end of his long and prolific career, to insist more and more upon a natural law in opposition to the positive law of the state.

Of neo-positivism perhaps the most influential example is H.L.A. Hart's 'minimum content' theory of natural law, as explained in chapter 9 of his book *The Concept of Law* where he discusses law and morals.

Having examined some of the difficulties and interpretations of natural law, Hart proceeds from 'the contingent fact that most men most of the time wish to live.' This implies certain rules of conduct which any social organisation must conform to if it is to be viable i.e. a minimum content of natural law. Hart gives as his sources for this empirical version of natural law Hobbes, *Leviathan* (chapters 14 and 15) and Hume, *Treatise of Human Nature* (Book III, part 2).

Its content is formulated in a series of truisms, reasons why, given survival as an aim, law should have some specific content. These rules have to do with (1) human vulnerability; (2) the approximate equality of men; (3) limited altruism (men are neither devils nor angels); (4) the limited resources of the world; (5) the limited understanding and strength of will of men. These rules provide a basis for the criticism of existing law. Hart believes it pointless to say of a given law that it is simply not law; on the other hand he is critical of the positivist hypothesis that 'law may have any content.' One may sometimes have to say: 'This is law but it is too iniquitous to obey or to apply.'[8]

While this is not a natural law theory in the usual sense, one is tempted to reflect that a rose by any other name would smell as sweet. And the phraseology used by Hart, in discussing the function of sanction in a legal system, a page or two later, does nothing to banish the temptation:

> We can say that, given the setting of natural facts and aims which makes sanctions both possible and necessary in a municipal system, this is a *natural necessity;* and some such phrase is needed also to convey the status of the minimum forms of protection for persons, property and promises, which are similarly indispensable features of municipal law. It

[8] H.L.A. Hart, *The Concept of Law*, pp. 190–194 and note, p. 254.

is in this form that we should reply to the positivist thesis that 'law may have any content.' For it is a truth of some importance that for the adequate description, not only of law but of many other social institutions, a place must be reserved, besides definitions and ordinary statements of fact, for a third category of statements; those the truth of which is contingent on human beings and the world they live in retaining the salient characteristics which they have.[9]

To such more or less theoretical considerations may be added the more practical argument that the twentieth century, with its wars and its genocides, crimes against humanity and against peace, has seen such abuses of power and of the trappings of legality that the poverty of positivism becomes evident; there must be something beyond the positive law to which appeal can be made. For this reason the Nuremberg War Crimes trials are taken by many for, if not an open avowal of the natural law, an expression of customary international law. Here perhaps the most dramatic example is that of the German jurist Gustav Radbruch (1878–1949). Radbruch's professedly positivist approach to law, in his *Rechtsphilosophie*,[10] had formed several generations of German jurists, in the pre-war period and well into the Hitler era, with the result, as has been said, of delivering the German judiciary bound hand and foot into the toils of Nazism. After the war, however, Radbruch published a celebrated article in which, impressed by the enormities that had been perpetrated with the trappings of legality, he saw the need to qualify his former views and to move towards something like a concept of natural law.[11]

It would be much too simple a view to see in the natural law the only answer to the excesses of totalitarianism or the only defence against their repetition. It has, indeed, been argued that

[9] H.L.A. Hart, *op. cit.*, p. 195; cf. I.T. Ramsey, "Towards a Rehabilitation of Natural Law" in *Christian Ethics and Contemporary Philosophy*, pp. 382–396; A.P.d'Entrèves, *Natural Law*, Appendix C "A Core of Good Sense: On Hart's Theory of Natural Law." pp. 185–203.

[10] The 3rd, 1932, edition, translated by K. Wilk as *Legal Philosophy*, in *20th Century Legal Philosophies*, vol. IV, Harvard, 1950, pp. 47–224; the 4th German edition appeared in Stuttgart, 1950 and the 5th (edited by E. Wolf after the author's death) in 1956, also at Stuttgart.

[11] "Die Erneuerung des Rechts" in *Die Wandlung*, 2(1947), pp. 8–16, reprinted in W. Maihofer (ed.) *Naturrecht oder Rechtspositivismus*, Darmstadt, 1972, pp. 1–10; cf. L.R. Ward, "Natural Law in Contemporary Legal Philosophy" in *Proceedings of the American Catholic Philosophical Association*, 1959, p. 141; R.D. Lumb, "Law, Reason and Will" in *Philosophical Studies*, 10 (1960), pp. 186–189. Z.U. Tjong, "Über die Wendung zum Naturrecht bei Gustav Radbruch" in *Archiv für Rechts- und Sozialphilosophie*, 56 (1970), pp. 245–262.

the doctrine of natural law has contributed to the rise of Nazism.[12] This, however, is an extreme view. There can be hardly any doubt that, in the immediate post-war period, legal positivism was considered by many to have been seriously undermined, "an hypothesis wrecked by the gruesome reality of history."[13] It was an opportunity readily taken by the already-established and greatly differing currents of thought favouring the natural law, not merely neo-Kantian and neo-positivist, as we have seen, but also sociological and neo-scholastic. The euphoria generated by the United Nations' *Universal Declaration of Human Rights* in 1948 and the progressive de-colonisation of much of Africa and Asia in the 1950's, contributed to the favourable atmosphere for natural law thinking – an atmosphere that has since given way to one of disillusion and a renewed appreciation of old difficulties against the natural law with the addition of new ones. We shall return to this question. Meanwhile we may continue with the list of contemporary approaches to the natural law.

The sociological approach to the natural law is usually associated with the name of Roscoe Pound (1870–1964), to whose thought the pragmatism of William James (1842–1910) and John Dewey (1859–1962) made considerable contributions. Pound's early thought was historicist and critical of previous theories of law, on the ground that they neglected the fact that law is determined by historical needs. The function of a philosophy of law is to discover how law may serve the needs of the community and it is summed up in the phrase, which has since been given a much more sinister connotation; 'social engineering.' Towards the end of his life Pound abandoned this predominantly relativist approach, because he believed that relativism paved the way for political absolutism; law – he used the term 'natural law' – presents the most effective obstacle to absolutism.[14]

"Among modern sociologists, the reputation of natural law is not high. The phrase conjures up a world of absolutisms, of theological fiat, of fuzzy, unoperational 'mystical' ideas, of thinking uninformed by history and by the variety of human situations." So Philip Selznick begins his essay on "Natural Law and Sociology," which turns out to be a plea for cooperation, for "sociology should have a ready affinity for the philosophy of

[12] So, for example, L.C. Midgley, *Beyond Human Nature: The Contemporary Debate over Moral Natural Law*, pp. 53–63.

[13] W. Luijpen, *op. cit.*, p. 27.

[14] R. Pound, *Justice according to Law*, 1951; "The Revival of Natural Law" in *Notre-Dame Lawyer*, 17 (1942), pp. 287–372.

natural law."[15] The bad name the natural law has with sociologists is easily documented.[16] Erich Fechner, for instance, summarizes his case against the natural law by saying that sociology has simply removed the basis upon which it was built; as present day man can no longer bow to instinct or to the image of the gods or the heroes of the past or the universal and convincing rules of revealed religion, he must in future look, for the regulation of his life, to the model uncovered by sociological investigation.[17] The same point – that norms depend upon cultural situations, or rather cannot be formulated or understood outside of such situations – and that those situations are studied by the sociologist, is made by Franz Böckle.[18]

What is true of the sociologist is true also of the anthropologist. The anthropologist studies the moral ideas of a given culture and raises the difficulty, thought to be fatal to the idea of a natural law, of their transfer to another culture. There is here a serious difficulty; but hardly fatal to a properly-nuanced concept of the natural law. For one of the benefits of the advances in studies, such as those of the anthropologists, has been to make it very unlikely that a modern proponent of a natural moral law would fall into the mistake of taking for eternal and universal what is, in fact, temporal and culturally-conditioned. And even the specific problem of the transfer of ideas across cultural barriers is capable of solution, as may be seen, for example, in a recent discussion of ideas of E.E. Evans-Pritchard and Alasdair Mac Intyre by Peter Winch.[19] And an even more optimistic view of the relationship between such studies and the natural law is argued by Philip Selznick in the article already referred to. The obstacles to the natural law on the part of sociology are seen as (1) the insistence

[15] In J. Cogley and others, *Natural Law and Modern Society*, pp. 154–193 (also in *Natural Law Forum*, 6 (1961), pp. 84–108).

[16] Cf. A. Laun, *Die naturrechtliche Begründung der Ethik in der neueren katholischen Moraltheologie*, p. 22, citing G. Meyer, R. Hofmann and J.G. Ziegler; D. Composta, *Natura e ragione*, pp. 11–13 casts a very wide net to include F.X. Kaufmann, J. Dabin, N. Bobbio, G. Fassò, P. Piovani, J.T.C. Arntz and even Jacques Leclercq.

[17] E. Fechner, "Die Bedeutung der Gesellschaftswissenschaft für die Grundfrage des Rechts" in W. Maihofer (ed.) *Naturrecht oder Rechtspositivismus*, pp. 257–280.

[18] In *Das Naturrecht im Disput*, p. 10; cf. B. B. Hamilton, "A Developing Concept of Natural Law" in *The Month*, 236 (1975), pp. 196–200.

[19] P. Winch, *Ethics and Action*, London, 1972, pp. 8–49 "Understanding a Primitive Society"; pp. 50–72, "Nature and Convention"; pp. 73–89, "Human Nature."

that facts and values be not confused; and (2) the moral relativism implied in sociological studies. With regard to the first of these, Selznick argues that the separation of fact and value, itself a useful principle in its place, has been taken to unreasonable lengths in excluding the study of moral ideas, such as that of a natural law. And, with regard to the second, he points out that

> radical conclusions regarding human nature and moral relativism are neither well-grounded in theory nor truly supported by the empirical evidence. In particular, the argument from cultural diversity is at best inconclusive.[20]

B. RE-SHAPING THE FEATURES OF THOMISTIC NATURAL LAW

The rapid survey in the previous section should not convey the impression that everyone nowadays accepts the natural law. A recent writer, Bernice Hamilton, speaking of the insights suggested by modern writers on natural law, remarks that "one curious result has been a tendency to identify nearly everyone – from Rousseau to Karl Marx-as natural-law thinkers, in the rather newer sense that they believe in an ideal of the truly human person, the fully human being (whose pattern for Christian natural-law thinkers is, of course, Christ)." A very different way of looking at the same situation would be to say, with Alf Ross, that "like a harlot, the natural law is at the disposal of everyone."[21] The contrast underlines again, if need were, the contradictions in the history of natural law. It is time, however, to address ourselves to the problem of discovering which features in the Thomistic profile of the natural law can be retained in the present age. It will not be an operation, useful though that be, like Paul Ramsey's, who in his book *Nine Modern Moralists* finds a thread of natural law running through the thought of Tillich, Marx, H.Richard Niebuhr, Dostoevski, Reinhold Niebuhr, Maritain, Sartre, Brunner and Cahn.[22] It will be, instead, a critical look at some attitudes towards the natural law and some reflections on the difficulties and responses they imply.

It is worth pointing out at the outset that the rigid demarcation between the natural law and theology is no longer to be found. The breach was there at the beginning of the seventeenth century,

[20] P. Selznick, *op. cit.*, p. 168.
[21] B. Hamilton, *op. cit.*, p. 198; A. Ross, *op. cit.*, p. 261.
[22] Cf. A. Ross, *op. cit.*, Introduction, pp. 1–9.

when Alberico Gentili at Oxford could provide the motto, in 1612 – *silete theologi in munere alieno* – under which the natural law of the Age of Reason, the age of Grotius and of Putendorf, was to develop. This natural law, independent of religious and confessional differences, issued, three and a half centuries later, in the break-down of law in the totalitarian regimes we have seen. Jurists and natural law thinkers need no longer feel compromised if they enter into dialogue with theologians.[23] In fact contemporary discussion about the natural law is largely in the context of theology. This does not mean that the natural law as a philosophical concept has been abandoned; on the contrary, when theology makes use of it there is all the greater need for clarification and for the facing of difficulties. It has already been suggested that both supporters and attackers of the natural law today have something in common. Many Catholic moral theologians are profoundly dissatisfied with the natural law as it has been expounded by their predecessors.[24] Charles E. Curran, in a recent survey of Catholic moral theology classifies the reactions of the moralists in three broad categories:

> There are some who reject any change in the methodology or the practical conclusions of the manuals of moral theology. . . . Some have abandoned the concept of natural law altogether and adopted newer and different methodologies; while others, retaining the concept of natural law, have tried to show how the manuals departed from the true natural law approach of the past as seen now in better appreciation of the exact position adopted by Aquinas and not the one espoused by later scholastics.[25]

The first and diminishing category need not, perhaps, detain us; the writers in the other two categories, however, will repay study if we want to understand the case for or against the natural law in the presentday world. At first sight the authors mentioned by Curran do not appear to have much more in common than their rejection of the 'manualist' conception of natural law. Those who reject the natural law as the basis for ethics differ on what is to

[23] H. Welzel, *op. cit.*, pp. 110–247.

[24] Cf. E. McDonagh, "Moral Theology and the Need for Renewal" in *Moral Theology Renewed*, pp. 13–30; Id. *Invitation and Response*, p. vii: "The developments which have taken place over the past fifteen years in the discipline known as 'moral theology' within the Roman Catholic Church are at least so far-reaching as to make the manuals in near-universal use even ten years ago almost entirely irrelevant now."

[25] "Catholic Moral Theology Today" in *New Perspectives in Moral Theology*, p. 6. This essay appeared in slightly different form as "Moral Theology: The Present State of the Discipline" in *Theological Studies*, 34 (1973), pp. 446–467.

replace it – a 'love-ethic,' a 'morality without anthropology,' a morality 'based upon phenomenology' etc.; and those who claim to return to the pristine notion add to the variety by the kaleidoscope of opinions they identify as misconceptions needing correction:

... abstractionism (which undertakes 'to pull all its moral precepts like so many magician's rabbits out of the metaphysical hat of an abstract human 'essence'); intuitionism (which regards *all* natural imperatives as self-evident); legalism (which reduces the natural law to a detailed code 'nicely drawn up with the aid of deductive logic alone, absolutely normative in all possible circumstances, ready for automatic application'), immobilism (which denies the historicity of the human person); biologism (which confuses brute facticity with the normatively natural); rationalism (an 'alleged deafness to the resonances of intersubjectivity).[26]

The attack upon the natural law, with all its contemporary insights and new terminology, adds little that is specifically new to old arguments, founded upon the ambiguity of 'nature' and of 'law' and upon the evident fact of moral variations. The rehabilitation of the natural law, on the other hand, stresses the historicity of human nature and human existence and rejects the naiveté of moral formulations in the past that failed to account for, or worse still, excluded, this dimension of the human. Let us look, in turn, at the landmarks of this middle ground between supporters and opponents of the natural law.

(i) *The Ambiguity of 'Nature'*

It is by now a commonplace to note that the word "nature" is one of the most ambiguous of philosophical terms. Lalande's standard *Vocabulaire technique et critique de la philosophie* lists some eleven meanings for 'nature' and thirteen for 'naturel.'[27]

[26] R. McCormick, "Human Significance and Christian Significance" in G.H. Outka and P. Ramsey (eds.) *Norm and Context in Christian Ethics*, p. 239. McCormick refers to J.C. Murray's *We Hold These Truths: Catholic Reflections. on the American Proposition*, pp. 295–296 and to Murray's remark (*op. cit.*, p. 298): "I list these misunderstandings of natural law only to make the point that those who dislike the doctrine, for one reason or another, seem forever to be at work, as it were, burying the wrong corpse. For my part, I would not at all mind standing with them, tearless, at the grave of any of the shallow and distorted theories that they mistake for the doctrine of natural law."

[27] 8me édition, revue et augmentée, pp. 667–673; cf. J.C. Piguet, *Le vocabulaire intellectuel*, p. 67. Having given nine senses of "nature" Piguet concludes – "L'emploi des termes 'nature' et 'naturel' exige les plus grandes précautions." Cf. also P. Foulquié-R. Saint-Jean. *Dictionnaire de la langue philosophique*, s.v. 'Nature'.

Raimundo Paniker, in 1931, recorded no less than twenty meanings for 'nature,' meanings discussed and tabulated more recently by Philippe Delhaye.[28] In the context of natural law alone Erich Wolf listed nine meanings for 'nature.'[29] But almost any book on the natural law can provide a similar exposure of the ambiguities in the term. More often than not it is taken for granted that this effectively disposes of any idea of an unchanging natural law. Norberto Bobbio, for one, has pointed out that 'nature' is such an equivocal term that diametrically opposed laws have been thought natural and that a new *Praise of Folly* might be written by simply listing the institutions – slavery or liberty, private property or communism, polygamy or monogamy and so on – said to be "in conformity with nature."

This fundamental ambiguity helps to explain why, despite a good deal of neo-Kantian, sociological and neo-scholastic support for sundry variants of the natural law, there is a general impression that the concept has lost whatever validity it ever had and has no place in the twentieth century. The reasons for the rejection are as often implied as expressed. Some of them may be seen in the clash between the competing philosophies of our time.

Let us take first the obvious lines of criticism of the natural law on philosophical grounds. Existentialism, particularly in the version proposed by Jean-Paul Sartre, is unfriendly towards the natural law. The concept of human nature, upon which the natural law depends, has no place in his view of the world; and he and many of his contemporaries find it impossible to accept an invariable and universal standard of morality such as human nature is held to afford. This is clear from the treatment of subjectivity and freedom in Sartre's major philosophical work, *Being and Nothingness;* and the issue is hardly affected by the failure of Sartre to produce the promised work on ethics.[30] In an early and well-known essay on *Existentialism and Humanism* – a popular exposition which does not agree in every detail with *Being and Nothingness* and seems to have been later disowned by Sartre himself – the matter is put beyond doubt. The classical metaphysics, Sartre argues, has been vitiated by *une vision technique du monde*, by the assumption that there is a God, artificer of

[28] R. Paniker *El concepto de naturaleza-análisis historico y metafísco de un concepto*, passim; Philippe Delhaye, *Permanence du droit naturel*, Introduction, pp. 9–21.

[29] *Das Problem der Naturrechtslehre.*

[30] Francis Jeanson, *Le problème moral et la pensée de Sartre*, has provided the nearest approach to this.

the universe, whose divine ideas define the things in the universe, much in the way in which the exemplar idea in the mind of a manufacturer of paper-knives defines the article he makes. There is, in fact, no God; there is no divine idea which defines human nature; man first exists and then only is defined by what he makes himself.[31] This same paradox, characteristic of existentialism, that the nature of man is, so to speak, not to have a nature, can be found also in other writers like Gabriel Marcel or Maurice Merleau-Ponty.[32]

Human nature has hardly fared better with the logical positivists. A.J. Ayer, for instance, began his *Language, Truth and Logic* with a chapter on 'The Elimination of Metaphysics' and followed it with a later one entitled 'Critique of Ethics and Theology.'[33] Between them these two chapters were thought to have disposed of human nature as a metaphysical concept and to have shown that statements about it, being neither tautologies nor empirically verifiable, were, strictly speaking, meaningless. Ayer has since abandoned this extreme view, in which the only function left to ethical terms and propositions is that of expressing emotion. It is a theory that can claim a respectable background in empiricism going back to David Hume. But the prejudice against metaphysics has scarcely been abandoned; and many contemporaries who might not accept the variety of logical positivism found in the early A.J. Ayer would still reject a natural law.

Other considerations of a more pragmatic kind also contribute to the general hostility of the climate of thought in the twentieth century towards natural law. An obvious one, not peculiar to our time but taking a new urgency from contemporary studies, is the discrepancy between the claims of an unvarying natural law and the phenomenon of the widely divergent moral codes and practices of different peoples and different periods. John Locke began his *Essay on Human Understanding* with a polemic against innate ideas; and amongst innate ideas he included innate moral ideas. The natural law is not to be identified necessarily with a doctrine of innate moral ideas. But the arguments used by Locke can be used against the natural law. The argument from moral variations so emphasized by modern writers basing themselves upon anthropological, ethnological and other data, was anticipated by

[31] *L'existentialisme est un humanisme* (1947), p. 22.

[32] Cf. P. Foulquié-R. Saint-Jean, *Dictionnaire de la langue philosophique*, s.v. 'Nature.'

[33] Chapter I and chapter 6.

Locke:

> He that will carefully peruse the history of mankind, and look abroad into the several tribes of man, and with indifference survey their actions, will be able to satisfy himself that there is scarce that principle of morality to be named or rule of virtue to be thought upon . . . which is not, somewhere or other, slighted and condemned by the general fashion of whole societies of men, governed by practical opinions and rules of living quite the opposite to others.[34]

The same argument is found in a passage in the *Pensées* of Pascal in which morality appears to be a matter of latitude and longitude; all depends upon whether one lives on this or the other side of the Pyrenees:

> Why do you kill me? Is it not because you live across the water? My friend, if you were to live on this side I should be an assassin and it would be unjust to kill you in this fashion; but because you live on the other side I am a brave man and this is just.[35]

The problem of moral variations – not simply the fact that many do not observe the moral law but that they formulate, in good faith, moral or natural laws totally at variance with each other – is one that any natural law theory must meet.

This leads on to a connected problem, that of the natural law in the context of the evolutionary theory of our time. Scientific humanism accounts for a good deal of the climate of opinion inimical to the natural law, particularly when it is associated, as in the case of Sir Julian Huxley, with the idea of bio-cultural evolution. Such a viewpoint has little use for an unchanging human nature, and none for stable and unchanging principles of morality based upon such a nature. The natural law is easily relegated to the realm of mythology, with theology and the supernatural; it is by definition beyond the only sphere that counts, the human.

The idea of 'human nature' can also, paradoxically, be criticized from a Christian and theological point of view, although the consequence of denying the natural law seems rarely to have been drawn. *Nature pura*, it has been pointed out, never existed as such; it is an abstraction of the philosophers. Man was created in a supernatural state, fell below that state by the original sin and was later redeemed. These are facts, known admittedly only through Revelation; but facts may not be neglected.

[34] Book I, ch. iii, n. 10; cf. *ibid.*, n. 9.

[35] Ed. V. Giraud, Paris, 1943, nn. 293–294.

The current defence of the natural law accepts much of this critique of 'nature' – and blames eighteenth century rationalism for having imported a rigidity and an unreality into what had been a much more flexible concept in the great scholastic treatises on the natural law. This acceptance of the basic insights of contemporary thought, critical of any "unchanging, static schematizations" or any "abstract, individualistic concept of man," is neither recent nor confined to Catholic theologians defending a new kind of natural law.[36] It will be instructive to examine some of the rubrics under which this discussion of human nature is carried on.

(1) '*Biological*' *Human Nature*

A widespread criticism of neo-scholastic conceptions of natural law has been that they are based on a physical or biological idea of human nature, or that they assign a biological or physical structure to certain human actions independently of the function of reason. Hans Küng, in his book *Infallible?*, makes the point with some trenchancy:

> They (the majority on the Papal Commission on birth control) found that the Encyclical's (*Humanae Vitae*) arguments based on natural law were not convincing, that its concept of what is natural is naive, is static, narrow and completely unhistorical, that it ignores man's historicity, that it dissects him in the light of an abstract conception of his nature, that the restriction of the concepts of nature and natural law to the physical and biological sphere is a regression to the long obsolete Aristotelian, Stoic and medieval idea; that the distinction between natural and artificial is arbitrary (and becomes a matter for the microscope and of milligrams).[37]

This criticism makes a number of points, the most notable, particularly as it regards the contraception controversy, being that human nature is unduly restricted to the biological dimension of man's being. It recalls the definition of the jurist Ulpian – "natural law is what nature has taught all animals."[38] Contemporary writers are not inclined to take Ulpian's definition at its

[36] W. Pannenberg, "Toward a Theology of Law" in *Anglican Theological Review*, 55 (1973), pp. 395–420, at. pp. 398, 399; cf. L.C. Midgley, *op. cit.*, Part III, "Protestant and Catholic Views on Natural Law Compared," pp. 53–77. Midgley traces a development of Maritain's views in this matter; and Maritain was influenced by Yves Simon. See Simon's posthumous work (ed. V. Kuic) *The Tradition of Natural Law: A Philosopher's Reflections.*

[37] H. Küng, *Infallible? An Enquiry*, New York, 1971, p. 35.

[38] Ulpianus, *Liber I Institutionum*; *Corpus Iuris Civilis*, Inst. I, 1; Dig., 1, 1, 3: "Jus naturale est quod natura omnia animalia docuit."

face value – nor, as we have seen, were the medievals unaware of the paradox it presents. But something of its influence can be detected in some now discredited natural law arguments, as, for instance, the one based upon the supposition that every frustration of a natural function is wrong.

We have observed how St. Thomas, like his contemporaries, was impressed by the authority of Ulpian's definition, featuring prominently in the *Corpus Juris* of Justinian. But his bias is certainly towards a natural law of reason, not a biological natural law; and there is, in the last resort, something a little puzzling in his deference towards Ulpian.[39] His contemporaries and successors were faced with some of the awkward consequences of the definition – how to explain, for example, that marriage relations are 'natural' whereas fornication is 'unnatural.' But, even though Ulpian has hardly been taken seriously since the seventeenth century, this does not mean that what John Courtney Murray has described as "the particularly gross and gratuitous misinterpretation" which "imputes to natural law theory a confusion of the 'primordial', in a biological sense, with the 'natural' ", has been altogether abandoned.[40]

If natural law is seen as the quest for an objective or ontological basis for morals, there will always be a danger of taking what is close to hand, namely the physical nature of man or the biological structure of certain of his acts, and making an absolute of what should be seen to be, in an important sense, relative. The contraception controversies of recent years have simply drawn attention to the danger. This ever-present danger is only avoided by appeal to some other criterion, which allows us to say which of the features of man's physical nature are important for morals and which are not, which biological structures in his actions impose an obligation and which do not. Tertullian, arguing from the premiss that what God had not created must not be produced by man, concluded that purple or blue sheep were wrong! And elsewhere he condemned the use of floral garlands on the ground

[39] C.E. Curran, *New Perspectives in Moral Theology*, p. 7 criticises J.M. Aubert's interpretation of St. Thomas as one-sided "for he fails to appreciate that Thomas did employ Ulpian's understanding of natural law as that which is common to man and all the animals." This does justice neither to Aquinas nor to Aubert. Cf. M.B. Crowe, "St. Thomas and Ulpian's Natural Law" in *St. Thomas Aquinas Commemorative Studies*, I, pp. 261–282.

[40] *We Hold These Truths*, p. 296. E. McDonagh, *Invitation and Response*, p. 23, in outlining the dangers inherent in describing morality in ontological terms, refers to the misunderstanding of "extending the being too far, to include, for example, biological elements in an undifferentiated way."

that what was created to be looked at and to give fragrance was being put to another and unnatural use.[41] It is easy to see the absurdity of such conclusions; but it is not so easy to provide the criterion that will enable us to distinguish between the structures that are ethically relevant and those that are not.

It may be thought that too much importance is being given to refuting a conception of natural law that has such obvious limitations. The matter, however, is not as simple as might appear. Recently a much more sophisticated notion of natural law, linking it to the 'natural inclinations' in man, has attracted support; but it looks as though the arguments against the 'biological' natural law militate against this too.

The question of the natural inclinations was raised by J.T. Arntz in his study of the development of natural law thinking within Thomism.[42] He distinguishes between the material and the formal aspects of the natural law in St. Thomas. The formal aspect is the rational one; St. Thomas's answer to the question: What for man are the precepts of the natural law? is that its first principles are known by reason, although non-discursively. The material aspect is given in *Summa theologiae*, 1–2, 94, 2– "All that towards which man has a natural inclination, reason naturally apprehends as good . . . the order of the precepts of the natural law follows that of the natural inclinations." The passage is, of course, the *locus classicus* – and it has been variously seen as epitomizing St. Thomas's thought on the natural law or as the source of all the conflicting interpretations of his thought. Arntz remarks that the passage makes more sense for the historical than for the systematic thinker. Historically, Thomas is seen to be reconciling, as was his wont, schemata of his predecessors; in this case that of Johannes Teutonicus, the canonist, who brought the natural inclinations into relationship with the natural law and William of Auxerre, the theologian, who insisted upon the universality of the natural law. Thomas's listing of the inclinations that man has as substance, as animal and as rational makes the most of both; and it has the additional advantage of accommodating Ulpian's definition. For the systematic thinker, however, there are some unresolved difficulties. What exactly are these *inclinationes naturales?* Are they to be taken at the level of psychology? Or is

[41] A. Laun, *Die naturrechtliche Begründung der Ethik in der neueren katholischen Moraltheologie*, pp. 69–70; cf. Ph. Delhaye, *Permanence du droit naturel*, p. 123.

[42] J.T. Arntz, "Die Entwicklung des Naturrechtlichen Denkens innerhalb des Thomismus" in F. Böckle (ed.) *Das Naturrecht im Disput*, pp. 87–120.

locus classicus

there an underlying metaphysical reality? And, if so, are the inclinations themselves normative, or do they point to something else which, *solitarie sumptum* (Cajetan's phrase adopted by Arntz) may be good, but whose opposite in given circumstances may be – even must be – chosen.[43] It is, as Arntz points out, a capital question; for upon the answer to it depends the characterisation of the natural law as essentially reason or essentially (biological, physical) nature. One view makes reason merely record and follow the order of nature – not at all an impossible view but one unlikely to have been St. Thomas's; the alternative is to see in the natural inclinations a field into which man's reason introduces an order.[44]

In his study of the mistaken interpretations of St. Thomas[45] Arntz discovers four competing conceptions of the natural law, linking it respectively with the order in the cosmos (Ulpian), with the psycho-physical nature of man (the moralists of the late nineteenth and early twentieth centuries), with the metaphysical nature of man (Gabriel Vazquez) or with *ratio ut natura* (William of Auxerre and St. Thomas). The last he believes to be the correct view; and the misinterpretations of Thomas start with Vitoria.

Franz Böckle takes up the issue of the natural inclinations, as used by the moral theologians of this century in their arguments about the natural law, and as they appear in documents of the Church magisterium. The adjectives 'natural' and 'unnatural' as applied to human actions refer to a biological structure, to an "inner-organic teleology" or an "immanent natural teleology" which ultimately go back to a physiological-biological understanding of human nature. Böckle recognises the core of truth here; but insists that it cannot be the entire truth. Man's essence includes his body – man is not man without a body – and the bodily structure may not be arbitrarily treated. On the other hand this bodily structure does not of itself provide the ethical norm; that involves man's understanding of himself, in his individual and

[43] J.T. Arntz, *op. cit.*, pp. 97–100, "Die Rolle der inclinationes naturales"; cf. Cajetan, *Comm. in* 1–2*ae*, *q.* 39, *a.*1.

[44] It should be pointed out that 1–2ae, q. 94, a. 2 is not the only discussion of the natural inclinations in St. Thomas. Cf. *In* 2 *Sent.*, d. 42, q. 2, a. 5; *Summa contra Gentiles*, III, c. 129; *Sententia libri Ethicorum*, V, 12; VI, 2 (Romae, 1969, pp. 303–307, 336–338).

[45] J.T. Arntz, *op. cit.*, pp. 100–120, "Die Fehlwege in der späteren Interpretation des hl. Thomas."

social nature.[46] It amounts to saying that there is no ethical norm, fully written out in nature and available for our inspection; for man himself has a share in the writing. This is not to say that a general pattern of man's moral conduct may not be derived from observation of "existential human ends," the "ends inherent in the tendencies and propensities of human nature."[47] But it remains true that the genuinely natural tendencies (and ends) must be identified; and some solution must be found for the cases of conflict, or apparent conflict, between natural ends.

An excellent example of the traditional treatment of the natural inclinations is found in Johannes Messner's *Social Ethics*[48] – detailed, persuasive and, one may say, optimistic.

> Man proceeds to the understanding of his own nature and its specific functions in the same way that he learns to understand the nature and functions of other things, namely, by the apprehension of the ends inherent in their tendencies and propensities.[49]

This does not require a detailed knowledge of the mode of working of all the functions in man but only of the essentials of his biological and spiritual nature. Messner's list of the existential ends of man is very comprehensive – self-preservation, bodily integrity, social respect, personal honour, self-perfection spiritually and physically, development of man's faculties, provision for one's economic welfare, including necessary property and income, enlargement of experience, knowledge and receptivity of the values of beauty, self-propagation, benevolent interest in the spiritual and material well-being of one's fellow-man, social fellowship, the establishing of peace and order, control of the forces of nature, knowledge and worship of the Creator and the ultimate fulfilment of oneself in union with Him.[50] And towards the end of the discussion there is the significant phrase: "it is well to mention

[46] F. Böckle in *Das Naturrecht im Disput*, pp. 121–150, "Rückblick und Ausblick."

[47] F. Böckle, *op. cit.*, pp. 139–140: "Der Mensch ist Mensch nur im Leib. Darum darf er auch die leiblichen Strukturen nicht ungestraft willkürlich missachten. Aber diesen Strukturen *an sich* kommt keine ethische Normkraft zu, Sittliche Norm ist in jedem Fall nur das Verständnis dieser Wirklichkeit und ihre Sinngebung durch den Menschen"; cf. W. Pannenberg, "Toward a Theology of Law" in *Anglican Theological Review*, 55 (1973), p. 408; W. Luijpen, *Phenomenology of Natural law*, pp. 98–100.

[48] J. Messner, translation of his *Naturrecht*, St. Louis-London, 1949, pp. 19–27.

[49] J. Messner, *op. cit.*, p. 19.

[50] J. Messner, *op. cit.*, p. 21.

that our discussion will show the impossibility of ultimate conflict between existential ends and thus between actual duties and rights."[51]

More recent writers are more aware of the difficulties in establishing the foundation of morality on the natural inclinations – more aware, perhaps, of the difficulty already seen by St. Thomas but unnoticed by some of his modern followers. Germain Grisez, for instance, having said that empirical enquiry, mainly by psychologists, has come to a remarkable consensus on what are the natural inclinations, gives this list

> the tendency to preserve life, especially by food-seeking and by self-defensive behaviour; the tendency to mate and to raise his children; the tendency to seek certain experiences which are enjoyed for their own sake; the tendency to develop skills and to exercise them in play and the fine arts; the tendency to explore and question; the tendency to seek out the company of other men and to try to gain their approval; the tendency to try to establish good relationships with unknown higher powers; and the tendency to use intelligence in guiding action.[52]

The ends of these tendencies are goods and apprehended as such by the practical reason which, in its first principle underlying all human action, tells us that good must be done and evil avoided. Grisez pays a great deal of attention to the notion of practical reason – which, indeed, is an inescapable one in the present context. But one feels that, like Messner, he is optimistic about man's ability to identify the natural tendencies and about the absence of conflict (although he allows that man must choose between the goods indicated by the natural tendencies) between them.[53]

Probably the most ambitious effort to rehabilitate the natural inclinations in the context of natural law is that of Dario Composta.[54] His book is divided into three parts. The first part studies

[51] J. Messner, *op. cit.*, p. 26.

[52] *Contraception and the Natural Law*, p. 64.

[53] See also G. Grisez, "The First Principle of Practical Reason: A commentary on the *Summa theologiae*, 1–2, question 94, article 2" in *Natural Law Forum* 10 (1965), pp. 168–196 and reprinted in abridged form in A. Kenny (ed.) *Aquinas: A Collection of Critical Essays*, pp. 340–382. The relation between the first principle of the practical reason and other principles is discussed by E. D'Arcy, *Conscience and its Right to Freedom*, pp. 49–71.

[54] D. Composta, *Natura e ragione: studio sulle inclinazioni naturali in rapporto al diritto naturale.*

the natural inclinations from the historical point of view, in the Greeks, particularly Aristotle and the Stoics, in Christian thought from the Fathers down to the Silver Age of scholasticism, and in the natural law theorists of the seventeenth and eighteenth centuries. The second part is a psychological study of which the argument is that psychology alone cannot explain human inclinations: the fact that man's tendencies, instincts, drives, impulses escape psychological explanation is either acknowledged expressly or is deducible from the uncertainties, obscurities and contradictions in the various explanations proposed. The third part of the work is a systematic study of human inclinations in relation to the natural law. Composta's basic position is that the natural law is known through the natural inclinations and is based ontologically upon them.

An important part of his case is that the only appropriate methodology for the study of the natural inclinations is philosophical. He calls it, perhaps a little unfortunately, "the classical metaphysical method" – for he concedes that the charge most frequently laid against this method is that it is "naturalistic and too much linked to biology."[55] He explains the method, however, as "inductive-ontological"; it is inductive in that it is based upon the concrete, existential experience of the human individual; and ontological in that the entirety of the real basis for inclinations and not merely part (such as consciousness, or structure or other aspects studied by methods that are psychological or purely empirical) is taken.

In the event the "classical metaphysical method" is used to face the two main problems concerning the natural inclinations, the gnoseological (how are they identified?) and the metaphysical (what is their ontological standing?). Composta's argument is wide-ranging and offers many valuable clarifications. Particularly valuable is his discussion of the three basic inclinations, as listed by Aquinas in the *Summa Theologiae* 1–2ae, q. 94, a. 2, towards life, towards propagation and towards rationality.[56] But it cannot be said that he has solved the central issue of what, in the last analysis, constitutes a natural inclination. Is an inclination natural because reasonable or reasonable because natural? His concluding phrase about a reciprocal dynamic irradiation of reason and

[55] D. Composta, *op. cit.*, pp. 191–199.
[56] D. Composta, *op. cit.*, pp. 218–243.

nature[57] looks very like having it both ways. To have recognised the danger of biologism is, unfortunately, no guarantee of having escaped it.

(2) *'Metaphysical' Human Nature*

If 'biological' human nature runs into difficulties as the basis for the natural law, the same may be said, and with much more justice, of 'metaphysical' human nature. This is a label of convenience under which may be grouped various conceptions of nature attacked in contemporary discussions of the natural law. The notorious ambiguity of the word 'nature,' in general and in the context of natural law, forms the background to these attacks. As a broad generalisation it may be said that, from a variety of standpoints, contemporary writers reject the so-called 'Platonic essence' thought to lie behind formulations of a natural moral law.

(I) *Science and human nature.* For over a century the theory of evolution has been undermining the idea of an unchangeable human nature; and the process is accentuated in the sophisticated variation of the theory propounded by the late Julian Huxley and the many scientific humanists who follow him. In this version man now finds himself able to understand and to control the evolutionary process.[58] The ethical question, of course, is: in what direction, to what end, shall the evolutionary process be directed? And the answer cannot be a natural law answer; for human nature itself is being re-shaped. Those who are supporters of a theory of natural law must, therefore, look farther afield for their criterion. And such may be found; but not in a concept of human nature made familiar by modern positive science. For the moment it will suffice to point out that it is not merely the theory of evolution, and its modern corollaries, that present the difficulty; modern

[57] D. Composta, *op. cit.*, p. 244: "Una conclusione ovvia emerge dal nostro discorso: il diritto naturale è una irradiazione dinamica della natura sulla ragione e, viceversa, una irradiazione illuminante della ragione sulla natura." Cf. F. Hammer, "Bemerkungen zur Sexualanthropologie des Thomas von Aquin" in *Zeitschrift für katholische Theologie*, 98 (1976), pp. 1–8, especially p. 8 for an interesting reflection on St. Thomas's text on the specifically human inclinations "quorum proprium est excogitare aliquid ut bonum et conveniens, praeter id quod natura requirit" (1–2, 30, 3). On the logical problem of the natural inclinations see P.J. McGrath, "Natural Law and Moral Argument" in J.P. Mackey (ed.) *Morals, Law & Authority*, pp. 67–68.

[58] See for example J. Huxley, *Evolution in Action*, pp. 141–161.

science and technology appear to be radically opposed to anything like the traditional concept of a natural moral law.

The scientist takes the view that "human nature will continue to evolve mostly through the mass effect of applied science in transforming human subjectivity."[59] P. Heelan, from whom this sentence is taken, had begun his article by distinguishing between the two meanings of nature "sedimented in common usage: one opposes it to the man-made; the other opposes it to mind or spirit, the domain of meaning, culture and values." The former meaning is Aristotelian-Christian and the latter is born of the scientific movement of the fifteenth and sixteenth centuries issuing in the progressive mathematicising and geometricising of nature. The alliance of the traditional concept of natural law with the former meaning of nature puts it at a disadvantage vis-à-vis modern science. The difficulty is felt in its acuteness when one contemplates the possibilities now opened before mankind by science and technology; or, to use more moral terms, when one looks at the rate at which science-fiction becomes fact before our eyes and without, in many cases, any reference to the ethical issues involved. Such issues range from nuclear and other kinds of environmental pollution to interference in the human genetic process. Ultimately man is regarded as the subject, not of philosophical, but of bio-technical and anthropological study.[60] This is a factor that the moralist and the theologian cannot neglect.

(II) *Phenomenology and human nature.* William Luijpen's *Phenomenology of Natural Law*[61] opens with a chapter on the difficulties facing the latterday defender of the natural law, "The Ever-Recurring Dilemma." It is, however, in a later chapter, "The Thomistic Doctrine of the Natural Law," that the fullest expression of the difficulties is to be found; for, in underlining what he sees as the defects of the Thomistic presentation of the natural law, Luijpen indicates the demands made by

[59] P. Heelan, "Nature and its Transformations" in *Theological Studies*, 33 (1972), p. 502.

[60] Cf. N. Hurley, "The Natural Law and Man's Open-ended Nature" in *New Catholic World*, 216 (1973), Nov.–Dec., pp. 259–263; also A,G,M. Van Melsen, "Natur und Moral" in F. Böckle (ed.) *Das Naturrecht im Disput*, pp. 77–78; also K.M. Weber, "Ethische Probleme der Biotechnik und Anthropotechnik" in *Artzt und Christ*, 2 (1965), p. 231 and L. Strauss, *Natural Right and History* quoted by D. Composta, *Natura e ragione*, pp. 10–11.

[61] Pittsburgh, 1967.

phenomenology on the elaboration of the concept. He speaks, it should be said at once, of Thomism and not of St. Thomas himself, whom, indeed, he exonerates from the excesses of some of his followers.

The criticism begins from the suggestion that the Thomistic doctrine of natural law overrates the possibility of talking about God and notably forgets God's transcendence in the detail of what is said to be His law. This raises the question about the need for God in a theory of natural law. One must agree with Luijpen's rejection of the *deus ex machina*, God as a way out of a philosophical impasse.[62] Luijpen's own view is that Thomistic ethics is perfectly capable of being truly philosophical even if it speaks of God, that to speak of God as the legislator of the natural law is not to renounce speculation about that law – quite the contrary. It is, however, true that some Thomists have misused a terminology, that needs careful weighing:

If we look now at the way in which Thomism bases the natural law on God, we are struck by the reckless abandon with which the necessary terms are used. According to Bender, who is a Thomist, 'God has given wings to swallows,' He 'wills that animals eat,' He has 'given all kinds of things to man'; God 'made birds and wanted them to fly'; He has inserted the natural law into man's life because He wanted man to have means at his disposal' to reach his ends; 'in God's mind there exists a plan that expresses the order of all things to their end'; and 'all things tend to their own actions and ends through an imprint of God's Eternal Law.' When this author wants to state clearly that God orientates actions to an end but Himself is in no way oriented to anything else as His end, he says that God's purposive action is not 'as the action of Peter who eats to remain healthy' but is 'as the action of Peter who *makes* his horse eat in order that it remain healthy.'

Such a way of speaking about God is naive to the point of being scandalous. If one cannot *unqualifiedly* say that God 'is' then likewise one cannot blandly assert that 'God directs creatures and their actions to an end to be attained '*just as* Peter directs his horse to the eating of its food.'[63]

Luijpen makes no allowance for pedagogic necessities; but it must be confessed that sound doctrine easily becomes impoverished when it is filtered into text-books. His criticism here is well-based. And the difficulty runs deeper than the unfortunate

[62] W. Luijpen, *op. cit.*, p. 92: "Erich Fechner . . . rejects the Thomistic theory of the natural law because a philosopher, he thinks, should not cover up the fact that he is caught in a philosophical *cul de sac* by seeking a theological exit."

[63] W. Luijpen, *op. cit.*, p. 97.

terminology in which the doctrine is expressed. For the question really is whether the purpose of nature is written in nature in such a way that man can read it there.

Some, like Sartre, as we have noted, cut this Gordian knot; if one does not accept the existence of God, the Divine artificer, the trace of whose finger may be sought in His creation, there is little more to be said on this question. But one may well accept that God does exist and is the Creator without having to sustain that the purpose of creation is written in a discernible way in creatures. It is certainly not written in detail sufficient to settle the cases of moral controversy. It may be true that, in many cases, the purpose of nature may be read with some assurance – as the purpose of eating is to sustain life or that of sexual relations to propagate the species. But the question immediately arises as to whether there are not other purposes too, the companionship at a meal, the expression of mutual love in sexual relations; and the further question whether these purposes should not be achieved, in given circumstances, even at the expense of the former. That the question arises is clear from the most cursory acquaintance with current controversy about contraception; and the point is that it is not settled by mere inspection of 'nature.' Luijpen reinforces the point by reminding of the many and contradictory things advocated, in the past, on the basis of 'nature's intentions.' Slavery is a case among many. Statements in St. Thomas, and in the theologians at the time of the conquest of America by the Spaniards, make curious reading in our age of human freedoms. Another example is the justification of the existing social and economic order in the nineteenth century (the age of Marx), as the *natural* order. Or, in its time, feudalism. Or the marriage patterns, such as polygamy, opposed in the name of *natural* monogamy. To arrive at the truth in such questions requires much more than the search for something already inscribed in nature.[64]

But to return to the phenomenological objection, Luijpen argues that when a Thomist proponent of natural law appeals to

[64] There is no difficulty in adding to Luijpen's list of contradictory, and often absurd moral judgements said to be dictated by nature. Cf.A. Ross, *On Law and Justice*, p. 247; N. Bobbio, "Quelques arguments contre le droit naturel" in *Annales de philosophie politique*, III, pp. 181–183. Luijpen takes some of his examples from A.M. Knoll, *Katholische Kirche und scholastisches Naturrecht*, of which he says: "Full of rancour as it is, a work of August Knoll presents us with an imposing and well-documented list of examples which one cannot simply disregard as irrelevant" (p. 94). See also A. Laun, *Die naturrechtliche Begründung der Ethik in der neueren katholischen Moraltheologie*, p. 22, note 28 for the condemnations of vaccination and street-lighting as unnatural!

'nature' and the 'natural' he may well be mistaken – for the reading of nature is not a simple procedure – and, if mistaken, his doctrine becomes a camouflaged legal positivism. Here the divergent meanings for 'nature' have full scope; not merely institutions like private property or community of possessions, but man's nakedness (for nature has not clothed him),[65] the orientation of the sexual act to procreation, the 'natural' authority of husband over wife.... The list is disparate, deliberately so; and while items in it can be disputed, and Luijpen may be accused of unfairness in his presentation, there is certainly a case to be met. It is arguable that upholders of the natural law appeal to a radically unverifiable concept and that, insofar as it can be verified, it refers to time- and culture-conditioned features of human existence rather than to the timeless and unconditioned aspects it claims to represent.

Here is the kernel of the phenomenological distrust of the nature law. Natural law is vitiated by a basic failure to take account of the fact that man's nature is affected by his existence, that history is present in the kind of being a human is, that

> It is utterly foreign to man's real essence to represent matters as if the man who lived half a million years ago was merely a primitive edition of the cultured man of the twentieth century. Today's civilized man is the result of a long intersubjective history, of which positive anthropology and ethnology show us the origin.[66]

Precisely because this historicity of man is not taken account of, the norms of natural law are invested with characters of universality and immutability; and the difficulty arising from the observable departures from these standards is ingeniously explained as defective knowledge of human nature and not as resulting from "a different mode of being of that nature and its orientations."[67] In a word, the objection to the 'Thomistic' natural law is that it is 'objectivist.' There is an objectivism that needs to be asserted in order to avoid failing into arbitrariness; but excessive stress loses sight of the fact that human knowledge is a mixture of the objective and the subjective and that emphasis on the objective truth 'out there' leads, in the last resort, to a Platonic doctrine of essences and, in morals – more dangerously – to the impression of being in possession of absolute truth; the situation in which, in the words of Merleau-Ponty, "I piously kill my opponents."[68]

[65] St. Thomas, *Summa theologiae*, 1–2ae, q. 94, a. 5, ad 3.

[66] W. Luijpen, *op. cit.*, p. 101.

[67] W. Luijpen, *op. cit.*, p. 102.

[68] W. Luijpen, *op. cit.*, pp. 103–111; M. Merleau-Ponty, *Sens et non-sens*, p. 189

(III) *Theology and human nature.* The phenomenological considerations just outlined underlie a good deal of the current theological speculation about human nature and natural law. It has more than once been observed that many of the presentday difficulties in theology are fundamentally philosophical; in which context it is of interest to recall Karl Rahner's saying that the natural law calls the whole of philosophy in question.[69]

The phenomenologist's point that the classical doctrine of natural law is based upon an unhistorical and indefensible conception of human nature is taken by Charles Curran. Speaking of changing theological methodology, he contrasts the "abstract, *a priori* and a-historical world-view" with "the historical, the contingent, the personal and the existential" and traces the defects of the "classical" natural law to the preponderance of the former view in moral theology of the past:

> A classicist methodology tends to favour the existence of absolute, abstract, universal norms in moral theology.... A more historically conscious methodology will not be able to seek the absolute certitude of unchanging universal essences. A change in methodology will have to reflect the best aspects of both approaches, but the greater importance attached to a historically conscious methodology will necessarily mean less emphasis on the existence of absolute norms which are binding in all circumstances.[70]

John Macquarrie expresses the same view: "The traditional moral theology was too strongly tied to the notion of a fixed, essential human nature, set in the midst of a static, hierarchically ordered universe." Moral theology and natural law must consider "the man of the modern age, caught up in rapid change" and must bow to the fact that, since man's understanding of himself is part of his existence, "the existent man himself changes too."[71] And, not to multiply authorities, the view is repeated in Wolfhart Pannenberg and others.[72]

[69] "Mit Recht bemerkt Rahner, dass das Naturrecht die ganze Philosophie ins Spiel bringt". Cf. A. Laun, *op. cit.*, p. 22 citing K. Rahner, "Bemerkungen über das Naturgesetz und seine Erkennbarkeit" in *Orientierung* 19 (1955), p. 239.

[70] "Absolute Norms in Moral Theology" in G. H. Outka and P. Ramsey, *Norm and Context in Christian Ethics*, pp. 139–173; cf. pp. 168–169.

[71] *Three Issues in Ethics*, pp. 42–45.

[72] "Toward a Theology of Law" in *Anglican Theological* Review, 55 (1973), pp. 395–420; cf. p. 407: "A theology of law . . . cannot proceed by deducing the fundamental contents of law from certain principles, not even from specifically theological principles. . . . A theology of law is in its proper province only when the foundations of law appear within the horizon of history . . . only the narration of human history expresses the closest approximation of what man is *in concreto*." Cf. N.H.G. Robinson, *The Groundwork of Christian Ethics*, Appendix B, especially pp. 302–307.

The dissatisfaction with the "moral theology of the manuals" is, however, older than these expressions of it. Nor should it be thought that this new chapter in the history of moral theology is negative in character, based upon criticism of what has gone before. It can be said that the progressive isolation of moral theology from dogmatic and its too close alliance with canon law helped to limit its perspectives and make of it a study of sin rather than a study of virtue. It is no accident that words like 'casuistry' and 'legalism' have today an almost inescapably pejorative connotation. It would be too much to say that all the manuals of a generation ago were excessively preoccupied with legalities and prohibitions. But, on the whole, they cannot be said to have done justice by a noble discipline. The great scholastic moral theologians would have had little use for some of the pettifogging discussion of minutiae that passed for moral theology within living memory. There were, of course, the exceptions; the moral theologies, for instance, based upon the plan of the virtues rather than upon the schema of the Ten Commandments and the precepts of the Church. And, on the other hand, one is well aware that there must be legislation, even in morals; that Christ came, not to destroy the Decalogue, but to fulfil' and that, as well as the Sermon on the Mount, there is needed, if the Church is to survive and to function as a society, a body of legislation to protect Revelation and the sacramental order. Yet, all this being understood, moral theology failed.

The failure was seen by authors like Tillman, Mersch, Leclercq and others in the 1930's and 1940's.[73] The author who best succeeded in capturing this *Zeitgeist* in moral theology was Bernhard Häring, whose *Das Gesetz Christi* (1954) has often been taken as the charter of the new moral theology. It might better be described the systematic putting to work of the *re-sourcement* that had already been going on in moral theology – the return to its sources, notably the Bible. And this has inevitably had the result of concentrating interest on the more positive and personal, concrete and historical aspects of the Christian moral teaching. In this perspective the natural law – or rather the classical interpretation of the natural law – fares poorly in spite of Scriptural references to it, including the *locus classicus* in *Romans* 2: 14–15.

One of the theological objections to the natural law is that, even if the concept can be made philosophically respectable, it

[73] See the short bibliography in E. McDonagh, "Moral Theology, the Need for Renewal" in *Moral Theology Renewed*, p. 20.

must still fall short of Christian morality.[74] How can the natural law, by very definition a secular concept, do justice to the Christian scheme of things? When all is said and done, is the natural law not simply a watering down of the ethical teaching of the New Testament?[75] This is ground that has been fought over almost since the time when St. Paul excoriated the Romans for their sexual depravity; that they had not had the benefit of Revelation was no excuse, for they had the chidings of their conscience to guide them. The question was again posed by Gratian, in the twelfth century, in the definition that dominated the *Corpus Juris Canonici* – "natural law is what is found in the Law and the gospel."[76] It was posed, in yet another way, in the twentieth century controversy about the possibility of a Christian philosophy. Gilson has found the notion of "philosophizing within Christianity" a useful schema for explaining the thought of the great schoolmen; and Maritain, in contemporary terms, argued that to neglect the supernatural is to neglect the most important dimension in human existence. Adequate philosophizing means taking account of the highest and the most important truth, available to us in Revelation; and if this does not fit the technical definition of philosophy, then so much the worse for philosophy; let's talk instead of Christian wisdom. More particularly, as we have already observed, 'pure human nature' is an abstraction of the philosophers. It never really existed. The nature of man was either elevated in original justice, or fallen by original sin and in need of redemption. In either case supernatural grace is relevant – and does it not render nature almost irrelevant?[77]

[74] F.S. Carney, "Outlines of a Natural Law Procedure for Christian Ethics" in *Journal of Religion* 47 (1967), p. 27: "... the content of natural law is different from or falls short of the insights of Christian morality. It is said that, even if natural law were so conceived that its content were identical to the insights of Christian morality, action according to it would be considerably frustrated because of its failure to give adequate attention to the impairments of radical sin. It is said that action according to natural law arises from a different and less satisfactory motivation than that of appropriate Christian responsiveness to God's creating, saving and sustaining grace. It is said, finally, that natural law doctrine lacks the supporting context of the Christian church that characterizes Christian morality, especially the shared communal experience of judgement, confession, forgiveness and moral guidance."

[75] Cf. B. Schöpf, "Das Naturrecht in der katholischen Moraltheologie" in *Naturordnung* (1961), p. 99.

[76] *Decretum Gratiani* I, 1: "Jus naturale est quod in lege et evangelio continetur."

[77] This is the objection brought by N. Monzel against J. Messner; cf. J. Fuchs, *Natural Law, a Theological Investigation*, pp. 181–193, originally published as "Christliche Gesellschaftslehre" in *Stimmen der Zeit*, 164 (1959), pp. 161–170.

One answer to this objection is that given by Johannes Messner. He points out that "Christian moral law differs from natural moral law in that the latter is given to man through natural revelation, the former through supernatural revelation.[78] This is, of course, simply a special case of the distinction between theology and philosophy. Messner goes on to say that "In the Ten Commandments, confirmed and expounded in the teaching of Christ and the apostles, there is laid down no more than the natural law itself contains." What, then, one might ask, is the scope of Revelation?

> Supernatural revelation provides man with the full and clear understanding of his true nature, so that he may not mistake for natural in human existence what is really owing to the impairment of his nature by original sin, that is to say, mistake the lesser elements of his nature for his whole nature. For supernatural revelation informs man unmistakably of the spiritual character of his soul, of its immortality, of his eternal destiny, of God as man's Creator and Judge, last End and highest Good.[79]

The snare of making a radical distinction between a natural law independent of revelation and a supplementary natural law for Christians is not one into which Messner falls. That it is a snare had been pointed out long before by Jacques Leclercq[80] who spoke of distinguishing, in a particular precept, between what is natural and what comes from revelation (whether as an added force of obligation or as presenting a new situation to which a natural precept must apply). But it is not easy to say just how much is natural and how much goes beyond nature. Think of the difficulty, or impossibility, of disentangling notions like the natural equality of men and the spiritual fraternity of Christians, the natural unity and indissolubility of marriage and the obligations arising out of the Christian sacrament, the rights and duties of parents in education and the supernatural obligation of handing on the Faith and so forth.

The problem remains, although it is not discussed today in quite those terms. Leclercq and Messner see very well that there cannot be any question of two human natures, one a pure human

[78] J. Messner, *Social Ethics: Natural Law in the Modern World*, pp. 84–87, "Christian Moral Law."

[79] J. Messner, *op. cit.*, p. 84.

[80] *Leçons de droit naturel*, I, pp. 72–84, "Droit naturel et droit chrétien."

nature regulated by the natural law and the other human nature elevated by grace and illuminated by revelation. The implications of this are drawn out more fully in a writer like Josef Fuchs, who sees the natural law as naturally cognoscible while having regard to a human nature that is supernaturalized. But the elements of nature and supernature require careful delineation. An obligation may be known by reference to man's nature; but we cannot tell its precise contour until we consider man's situation in a supernatural order.[81] The historicity of human existence includes, above all, the supernatural order; and the problems posed for the natural law by man's situation in grace resemble those posed by his situation in culture and in history, in space and in time. These are the problems that prompted Karl Rahner, in his brief, sometimes cryptic and highly influential note on the natural law, to recommend a transcendental method of study to do justice to the nature of man.[82]

(ii) *The Question of 'Law'*

In the past the claim of the natural law to be genuinely a law has often proved a stumbling-block; and now, it appears, unnecessarily. Positivist legal philosophers tended to allow that moral or religious principles, or ideologies, may be relevant to law-making and law-interpretation but regarded it as provocative when such systems of ideas claimed to be 'law,' and superior law at that. It is nowadays abundantly clear that, no less than the word 'nature,' the word 'law' is Janus-headed. There is no need to point the finger (with John Stuart Mill) at Montesquieu who, in the beginning of his *Esprit des lois*, gives the impression that the similarities between the Law of Gravitation and the moral law are more important than their differences;[83] it is a misunderstanding that much modern scholastic writing on the natural law found it difficult to avoid, stressing as it did the universality and uniformity of natural law. On the other hand, it is equally a misunderstanding to assert that an unjust civil law is not a law, on the ground

[81] *Natural Law – a Theological Investigation*, pp. 52–58, "The Philosophical Concept of Nature"; see the same author's *Theologia moralis generalis*, Pars Prima, pp. 66–68.

[82] *Lexikon für Theologie und Kirche*, Band 7, col. 827–828.

[83] Montesquieu, *De l'esprit des lois*, Partie I, livre I, ch. 1; J.S. Mill, "Nature" in *Three Essays on Religion*, 3rd ed. London, 1923; H.L.A. Hart, *The Concept of Law*, pp. 182–183; F.S. Carney, "Outline of a Natural Law Procedure for Christian Ethics" in *Journal of Religion*, 47 (1967), p. 28.

that a law must, by definition, be just. This is to take too literally St. Thomas's famous phrase about the will of the prince, unregulated by right reason, being *magis iniquitas quam lex.*[84] The disadvantages of having to fight a rearguard action in defence of the 'legality' of natural law was long ago seen by writers like Jacques Leclercq and Odon Lottin, who can hardly be accused of undermining the natural law. Leclercq suggests that St. Thomas's enthusiasm for synthesis carried him away when he put eternal law and natural law, together with divine law and human law, in the *Summa;* and in support he calls on Lottin's observation that the Thomistic definition of law is analogical and, in order to apply to the natural law, in need of adaptation in all its elements.[85]

The fact of the matter is that 'law' is an analogical term, which leads to confusions unless the analogy is understood. One of these confusions is that between natural law in the scientific sense and natural law in the moral sense. The uniformities of behaviour that the physicist, or chemist, or astronomer, or biologist, discovers are commonly formulated as 'laws of nature.' Indeed standard works of reference like the *Encyclopaedia Britannica* or, more surprisingly, Hastings' *Encyclopaedia of Religion and Ethics* tend to concentrate upon these laws of nature.[86] Uniformity or pattern in behaviour must be an important ingredient in law. It is when we leave physical bodies, or chemical elements or living organisms, and consider the behaviour of human beings that uniformity or pattern takes a new shape. For man is unique in his capacity for self-conscious reflection and his power of free choice. These are the powers exercised by that 'rational animal' who is man and, in

[84] 1–2ae q. 90, a. 1 ad 3: see the commentary in S. Cotta, *Il concetto di legge nella Summa theologiae di S. Tommaso d'Aquino*, pp. 22–27.

[85] J. Leclercq, *La philosophie morale de saint Thomas d'Aquin devant la pensée contemporaine*, pp. 386–388; O. Lottin, *Principes de morale*, II, pp. 102–103: "Que conclure? Puisque nous n'avons de Dieu qu'une connaissance analogique, disons d'abord que la définition thomiste de la loi ne s'applique qu'analogiquement à la loi éternelle. Puisque, pour être appliquée à la loi naturelle, la définition thomiste a dû être adaptée en chacun de ses éléments, concluons ensuite et d'une manière plus générale que la définition thomiste n'est pas une notion univoque, s'appliquant absolument dans le même sens aux diverses espèces de lois."

[86] *Encyclopaedia Britannica*, 1956 edition, s.v. 'Natural Law.' There is a quarter of a page devoted to the natural law in the moral sense, à propos of Hugo Grotius in the article on the history of ethics. Hastings' *Encyclopaedia of Religion and Ethics*, 13 volumes, Edinburgh, 1908–26, s.v. 'Natural Law' (volume 10, 1917) does refer to the moral law, but the main emphasis of the article is on the laws of physical nature. Cf. volume 7, (1914) and volume I (1908) where there is a passing and favourable reference to Aquinas on 'law.'

consequence, one cannot think of the regularities of human behaviour in the same way as one thinks of those of animate or inanimate nature. Human behaviour is not as regular as that of atoms or molecules or the heavenly bodies. This makes us look for a way of expressing patterns or regularities we would wish to see in human behaviour, and to a considerable extent do see, without excluding the exercise of human freedom. So the law of human nature is said to be prescriptive (in contrast with the laws formulated by positive science which are descriptive); or it is said to be proposed to man (in contrast with the laws imposed upon irrational beings).

This battle about how natural law is a law is now being fought in a new way; or, rather, the natural law has found unexpected allies and the battleground has altered. It is no longer regarded as necessary to demonstrate that the natural law is law, just like civil law, and of a superior kind that must take precedence over civil law. It transpires, on the other hand, that certain concepts enshrined in civil law – 'legality,' or 'due process' or 'equality before the law' – turn out to be very like, if not actually assimilable to, a doctrine of natural law. I.T. Ramsey, for example, leans heavily, for his thesis that the natural law can be rehabilitated in Christian ethics, on H.L.A. Hart's well-known 'Minimum Content of Natural Law,' already considered.[87] And it is, indeed, striking that Hart should make such a case. It is not, however, the only natural law gesture (if the phrase may be used) in positivist legal literature. The chapter in which Hart expounds his minimum content of natural law is entitled: "Law and Morals" and the earlier part is concerned with natural law and legal positivism. This reminds one of the great debate about the enforcement of morals, in which the principal protagonists were Hart himself and Lord Devlin. Devlin's *The Enforcement of Morals* (1959), which engendered the debate, may be taken as a forceful exposition of the view that the law cannot abdicate a moral responsibility. This is, however, not the place to pursue this line or to argue that there is here another example of covert natural law thinking.

Reference may be made once again to Philip Selznick's essay, "Natural Law and Sociology,"[88] of which it might almost be said

[87] "Towards a Rehabilitation of Natural Law" in *Christian Ethics and Contemporary Philosophy*, pp. 382–396; H.L.A. Hart, *The Concept of Law*, pp. 189–195. Cf. A. P. d'Entrèves, "A Core of Good Sense: Reflection on Hart's Theory of Natural Law" in *Natural Law*, pp. 185–203.

[88] In J. Cogley et al., *Natural Law and Modern Society*, pp. 154–193.

that the theme is that

> The subtlety and scope of legal ideas and the variety of legal materials should give pause to any effort to define law within some simple formula. The attempt to find such a formula often leads to a disregard for more elusive parts of the law and excessive attention to specific rules.[89]

Selznick's handling of terms like 'the rule of law,' the 'legal order,' 'legality,' 'judicial creativity' and 'justice' itself (all of which, he points out, are value-terms and insufficiently investigated by sociology) is instructive. The point is that these concepts, doctrines or principles, however one may like to describe them, support the view that the legal order has "an implicit internal morality."[90] This, admittedly, begins discussion rather than ends it. For it must be possible to distinguish between good and bad law and to distinguish between the bad law that is merely bad policy and the bad law that violates, or only incompletely realises, the ideals of legality. In a word – and here Selznick quotes Morris Cohen – it must be possible to appeal from the law that is to the law that ought to be, from positive law to the principles of justice.[91]

This is the area in which the natural law can play its part; and it is here that we have seen the relevance of sociology. If the proper aim of the legal order and the special contribution of legal scholarship are "progressively to reduce the degree of arbitrariness in the positive law," then the method of natural law "because it offers a rule, a guide to enquiry" is welcome. It is worth remarking that the placing of limits upon the arbitrary exercise of political or legislative power may well be said to have been the historical function of the doctrine of a natural law and, in fact, the thread of continuity linking its various forms in successive historical epochs.[92] And it should scarcely be necessary to add that the

[89] P. Selznick, *op. cit.*, pp. 175–176.

[90] Selznick quotes the phrase with approval from Lon Fuller, "Positivism and Fidelity to Law – a Reply to Professor Hart" in *Harvard Law Review*, 71 (1958), p. 645.

[91] P. Selznick, *op. cit.*, p. 178: "This is sometimes put as an appeal from 'laws' to "the law" and there is merit in that approach. But it has the disadvantage of suggesting that "the law" is something disembodied and unspecifiable, when in fact all we mean is that general principles of legality are counter-posed to more specific legal materials." The suggestion is attributed to Roscoe Pound. See also Pound's "The Revival of Natural Law" in *Notre Dame Lawyer*, 17 (1942), pp. 287–372.

[92] This is the theme of A.P. d'Entrèves' *Natural Law*.

natural law Selznick has in mind is not a rigid pre-fabricated natural law but a flexible one. He affects the celebrated phrase of Rudolf Stammler – a natural law with "variable content"[93] – and indicates that, in the natural law, there is a "dialectic of continuity and change." The fact that the natural law varies is not tantamount to saying that it is arbitrary; natural law may presume changing legal norms, but this does not involve the abandonment of "the quest for universals or the assertion of them when they are warranted."[94] In a word, one must remember that, as the enquiry proceeds, it is always possible that the basic premisses will be revised; and that, as society changes, new rules and doctrines are needed in order to give effect to natural law principles by adapting them to new demands, new circumstances, new opportunities. The net result is a conclusion, which can come as no surprise after the exploration of the difficulties presented by the concept of 'nature':

> These perspectives demand that we detach natural law from illusions of eternal stability.[95]

C. AREAS OF DISCUSSION

The fact that the natural law, as expounded in the thirteenth century by St. Thomas Aquinas, is capable of being re-shaped to the needs of moral philosophy and moral practice of the twentieth century, is not of itself a proof of validity. But it is a good indication. And if our attention today is focussed upon certain areas of discussion, we ought not forget that these are the features of adaptation; side by side with them, and taken for granted, are the permanent features, like the hard-won relationship between natural law and the first principles of the practical intellect and the acceptance of moral variations. This, of course, does not mean that no difficulties remain; it means simply – and this is the greatness of the achievement – that the difficulties are discussed within an accepted framework.

Some of these difficulties and areas of discussion may be indicated briefly in this section. In the next section we may endeavour to see how the concept of the natural law meets the presentday situation. These topics of discussion are simply to

[93] P. Selznick, *op. cit.*, p. 184.
[94] P. Selznick, *op. cit.*, p. 184.
[95] P. Selznick, *op. cit.*, p. 185.

illustrate the kind of debate that goes on about the natural law today; two are taken from the practical sphere (the questions of evolution and ethics and of the natural inclinations) and two from the more theoretical (the naturalistic fallacy and the problem of moral absolutes).

(i) *Evolution and Ethics*

The evolutionary objection to a morality based upon human nature has already been noticed. It will be useful to consider whether human evolution, instead of being the ultimate refutation of the natural law, may not help to refine the concept. This is the argument of C. Fay, who in an article entitled "Human Evolution: a Challenge to Thomistic Ethics" chides the reluctance of Thomistic ethicians to come to terms with evolution and anthropology. The article makes certain assumptions: (a) that evolution provides a partial explanation not alone of the development of the human body, but of much of human culture; (b) that human evolution is "bio-cultural" i.e. both organic and superorganic; and (c) that it is meaningful to speak of progress in human as well as in organic evolution. Fay's finding is that, in general, the evolutionary approach confirms and complements the traditional conception of basic, unchanging principles in nature expressed, however, with different modalities.[96]

He begins by describing the mutual relations of bodily and cultural factors in human evolution and justly remarks that this interplay of the organic and the "more than organic" is precisely what a Thomist, given his theory of the soul, ought to expect. The fact that man has evolved in this fashion shows that he has a nature, and, so, an end, different from that of brutes. In the course of evolution life is lived at ever higher levels; but no essentially new mode of activity has arisen since Zijnjanthropos. The changes introduced as man evolved are accidental to his nature as a rational animal – a more upright posture, a less simian face, a central nervous system better organized for symbolic life. In contemporary humans there is abundant evidence for a common nature, despite racial and cultural diversities; language, technology, family, art, religion, are the universal traits of cultural life. These traits vary greatly, and some of the variations are more significant than others; but there is a limit to variation. Up to the present the changes introduced by culture in the direction and

[96] *International Philosophical Quarterly* 2 (1960), pp. 50–80.

pace of human evolution worked, for the most part, unconsciously: the genetic mechanisms involved were not understood. Work at present being done on genetics may yield the knowledge necessary to regulate the further course of evolution – a possibility that presents new problems in moral philosophy.[97] Before coming to it, Fay examines the effects of "bio-cultural evolution," which modifies human nature as it concretely exists, so that "its signification for ethics involves some sort of evolution in the sphere of morals.

The natural law is based upon man's nature; moral goodness is conformity to human nature *as it actually exists*, i.e. as affected by the conditions of time and place. In the course of bio-cultural evolution such conditions have modified, even radically modified, human nature. Primary urges, like those towards food and sexual activity, are differently experienced, even by contemporary men, as a result of differences in cultural conditioning. If the family, for example, represents a universal human situation, its determinate character is due to the particular circumstances obtaining when and where it is founded. In general, human morality has its universal and invariable aspect and its aspect relative to this or that particular culture. The conflict is more apparent than real; for it is simply a consequence of viewing human nature either abstractly and universally (and, so univocally common to the entire human species) or concretely and realistically existing in individual men (and, so, subject to bio-cultural evolution as well as to the individuation by matter). In the first case the natural law will be invariable; in the second, variable as is the nature on which it depends.

At this point Fay cites St. Thomas's phrase: *Natura autem hominis mutabilis est*[98] and suggests that here at least St. Thomas is taking the second of the above views of human nature. Further, this view would be more prominent if St. Thomas were writing today. For some of the changes introduced by bio-cultural evolution

so alter the meaning of human knowledge and power (for example, agricultural and industrial revolutions), so transform relations between

[97] He cites Teilhard de Chardin's saying that we are the players as well as the cards and the stakes in this great game and goes on (p. 78): "While this moral perspective ethos is as yet inchoate in the minds of most people, it does exist in the evolutionary humanists such as Julian Huxley, Herman J. Miller, as well as in Teilhard de Chardin's Christocentric approach." Cf. J.C. Flugel, *Man, Morals and Society*, pp. 316–317.

[98] 2–2ae. q. 57, a. 2 ad 1.

men and men (the urban revolution) and between man and nature (atomic energy, polymer chemistry) that certain acts which were formerly good become bad and vice versa. I do not deny that the species of morally significant acts are determined in the light of universal human needs which are stable; lying, stealing and murder are bad of their very nature, precisely because they frustrate universal human appetites. But I do deny that the species of moral acts is determined exclusively in the light of such needs; the species of good and bad acts are also determined by a constellation of biological and cultural conditions and emergent needs which are both variable and relative.[99]

The changes introduced by bio-cultural evolution may be accidental in the ontological sense; but morally they may be extremely important – as the ontological accident of relationship makes the same act with one person adultery and with another fornication. One example of a change introduced in evolution is provided by social organization, at one time based exclusively upon kinship. In a modern society it would be wrong to favour relatives in the distribution of offices; formerly it was not alone right but necessary. The difference is in the different ways in which men existed then and now, the changed historical situation. There are, nevertheless, some things that can be judged irrespective of the cultural situation, so that an individual in one culture can correctly judge an action performed in an alien culture as morally evil, despite his unfamiliarity with the cultural surroundings of the act. This is because, as well as the changing factors stressed by bio-cultural evolution, there are also universal and unchanging factors:

Every society forbids lying, murder and stealing because of needs experienced by all men. But some acts are regarded as unjust homicide or theft in one culture but not in another: nevertheless, a stranger to a certain culture can ordinarily recognize that an act of theft, say, is stealing and is unjust; and he disapproves in the light of appetites shared with the members of the alien culture. There are cross-cultural parallels in human appetition, and these parallels impose limits on variability and evolution in morals....[100]

[99] C. Fay, *op. cit.*, pp. 65–66. Compare P. Lumbreras, *De Lege*, p. 49: "... etsi evolutionis qui dicuntur philosophi naturalem legem ... mutabilem praedicent, nobis indubium est naturam humanam non subdi mutationi, neque propterea legem huius naturae comitem."

[100] C. Fay, *op. cit.*, pp. 64–65. Cf. C. Wellman, "The Ethical Implications of Cultural Relativity" in *Journal of Philosophy*, 1963 (60), pp. 169–184, where it is argued that a human nature relative to culture does not entail ethical relativity. "One may wonder whether the only alternatives are an entirely fixed and an entirely plastic human nature. It might be that enculturation could mould a

These views on the mutability of human nature are worth considering at some length because they represent an interpretation of evolution sympathetic to the demands of a natural law ethics; most evolutionary approaches to ethics are destructive of any system like the Thomistic one. Fay's conclusion should be taken to heart, that human needs and acts are proportionally similar rather than univocally the same, that, while there are profound similarities in human life and its moral requirements, "to come to grips with similarities in moral philosophy will require a more extensive use of the data and theories of the sciences of man than ethicians have been accustomed to."[101]

(ii) *The Natural Inclinations*

Some consideration has been given to this problem under the heading of 'biological nature.' There it was suggested that the matter is deceptively simple. What, after all, is a natural inclination? Man's urges to eat or to procreate are in a fundamental sense natural. And we have seen the longer lists of natural urges drawn up by writers like Messner or Grisez. The difficulty and the discussion centre upon when such inclinations ought to be followed and when not. Here reason enters. When St. Thomas, in the *Summa Theologiae*[102] discusses the three levels of human nature, substantial, animal and rational, is clear that the rational nature of man has the overriding authority; inclinations attaching

---

human being, but only within certain limits. These limits might exist because certain parts of human nature are not at all plastic or because all parts are only moderately plastic. For example it might turn out that the need for food and the tendency to grow in a certain way cannot be modified at all by enculturation, or it might turn out that every element in human nature can be modified in some ways but not in others. In either case what a man becomes would depend partly upon enculturation and partly upon the nature of the organism being encultured. ..." (pp. 173–4).

[101] C. Fay, *op. cit.*, p. 67. Cf. A. Verdross, *Abendländische Rechtsphilosophie*, Springer, Wien, 1958, p. 231: "Jeder Mensch besitzt aber nicht nur die allgemeine Menschennatur, er is immer auch ein konkretes Einzelwesen, das Glied eines bestimmten Volkes in einer bestimmten Zeit und einer bestimmten Kultur ist. Im Laufe der Geschichte ändern sich aber nicht nur die Verhältnisse, sondern auch die Menschen selbst da uns die Geschichte lehrt, dass primitive Völker allmählich zu Kulturvölkern heranreifen können. Daher muss das natürliche Rechtsgesetz, wenn es eine dem Menschen entsprechende Normenordnung ist, auch den Verschiedenheiten Rechnung tragen, die im Laufe der Geschichte eingetreten sind."

[102] 1–2ae, q. 94, a. 2.

to human nature at the other levels are to be followed only in the measure in which they are reasonable. But here is the rub. When are such inclinations reasonable? Are they reasonable because natural, or natural because reasonable? There are two points of discussion here. The first is concerned with the manner of avoiding the circular argument of using nature and reason to prove each other; this is the aspect already considered. The second point goes to the heart of the matter and asks why should an inclination, identified, let us say, as natural and reasonable in the circumstances, present a moral obligation? Or why should its frustration, or its partial indulgence, or its exercise with the exclusion of what has been identified as one of its purposes, be forbidden? The intuitive element in morality – St. Thomas's *prima principia per se nota* – is relevant here; but whence this moral obligation of which man has knowledge somehow related to his nature? Is it because we need a legislator that we call it the natural moral law? Evidently there is here abundant matter for discussion.[103]

(iii) *Deriving 'Ought' from 'Is'*

A more theoretical difficulty urged against the natural law, particularly in English language writing and in philosophy of the logical positivist or analytic school, is that the naturalistic fallacy is inevitably committed. The fallacy is usually traced to David Hume. Hume, however takes it rather less seriously than moderns; his reference is in a throwaway passage at the end of a section of his *Treatise of Human Nature.*[104] It was G.E. Moore, at the beginning of this century who drew attention to the fallacy and gave it its name. It has since occasioned extensive debate, without much sign of agreement. It may be admitted that if the natural law were to consist essentially in deriving a conclusion containing a moral term from premisses that are purely factual, then the reasoning would be fallacious. But this is far from being the only possible understanding of the natural law. It is more in the nature of a travesty of the natural law. One recalls the position given to the first principle of the moral order: 'Good should be done and evil avoided,' in the natural law theory of St. Thomas. He was certainly not one of those who believed that the moral term was introduced surreptitiously in the conclusion; he belongs to the large number of philosophers who hold that there

[103] Cf. supra Chapter VII, notes (43), (44).

[104] Book III, Part 1, Section 1.

must be an intuitional element in every ethical system. And as we have seen, he spoke in his earlier works of *synderesis* and, in his later works, of the habitual knowledge of the first principles of the practical reason, which are the first precepts of the natural law. Here, once again, is a large territory of debate.[105]

(iv) *Moral Absolutes*

Here, again, one may be brief in staking out an area of current natural law controversy. The problem is: Are there any moral norms which are absolute in the sense of admitting no exceptions of any kind? Broadly there are three parties to this debate. There are those who believe that it is precisely the function of the natural law to formulate such norms and to bring them to the notice of men. There are the situationists (whether they accept the label or not) who deny that there can be such norms, given that human conduct is always conditioned by circumstances and intentions. And there are those who take the view that the function of the natural law is not to produce universally valid norms, but rather objective norms (which may, for all practical purposes, be exceptionless).[106] One more specialized field of moral enquiry, in which the relevance of this debate is seen, is that of the moralists' 'Principle of the Double Effect.' The principle is foreshadowed in St. Thomas, in his discussion of the ethics of legitimate self-defence; the man who kills his unjust aggressor as the only means of saving his own life acts lawfully – for he intends the preservation of his life and not the death of his adversary.[107] The technical elaboration of the principle came later, with writers like John of St. Thomas (1589–1644); and down to modern times it has played a major part in the resolution of moral perplexities, particularly, in our day, in the field of medical ethics. There would clearly not be the need for the principle, which has frequently been challenged, were it not for

[105] G.E. Moore, *Principia Ethica*, chapters 1–2; cf. A.P. d'Entrèves, "Le droit naturel" in *Annales de philosophie politique*, III, pp. 153–157; A.N. Prior, *Logic and the Basis of Ethics*, cf. IX 'The Naturalistic Fallacy and the History of its Refutation," pp. 95–107; E.D'Arcy, *Conscience and its Right to Freedom*, pp. 49–71; A. Donagan, "The Scholastic Theory of the Natural law in the Modern World" in A. Kenny (ed.), *Aquinas: A Collection of Critical Essays*, pp. 325–339, etc.

[106] For a summary of the debate see J. Fuchs, "The Absoluteness of Moral Terms" in *Gregorianum*, 52 (1971), pp. 415–457; cf. also T.E. O'Connell, "The Question of Moral Norms" in *American Ecclesiastical Review*, 169 (1975), pp. 377–388.

[107] 2–2ae, q. 64, a. 7.

the presupposition that there are some actions, or ends of action, that may never, in any circumstances, be directly willed. The dissatisfaction of many moralists with the double-effect principle has led them to examine that presupposition very critically – and therefore to look critically also at the interpretation of the natural law upon which it is founded. Here, too, the literature is extensive – and all that is intended here is to point to the area of the debate.[108] The time has come, however, to return to the main issue of the natural law.

D. A REHABILITATED NATURAL LAW?

Some of the common ground shared by supporters and opponents of the natural law has been indicated. It will be useful now, by way of conclusion, to look at some of the more positive efforts of contemporary theology to rehabilitate the natural law. In effect, this means looking at the kind of answer that can be made to the most pervasive objection noted to the 'traditional' natural law, the objection, to put it in a phrase, that it lacks historicity.

There is no doubt that many of the traditional expositions of the natural law – the 'manualist' natural law – proceeded as if human nature had no history and were a non-temporal and imperceptible thing.[109] This, in a way, was its strength; its resistance to changes depending upon time and space seemed to guarantee a universality and an immutability that enabled it to sit in judgment on the temporal and the spatial in human conduct. But this no longer carries conviction: too many currents of contemporary thought, existentialism, personalist philosophies, phenomenology, agreeing in hardly anything else, proffer the insight that human existence is conditioned by temporality and culture. The best complexion that can be placed on the older accounts of the natural law is that the emphasis was wrong; too much upon the qualities of universality and immutability, believed to be necessary, and too little upon the subjectivity involved. The danger inherent in this one-sided emphasis was remarked upon, in somewhat sybilline fashion, by Karl Rahner, in a celebrated half-page article on the natural law in *Lexikon für Theologie und Kirche.*[110] F. Böckle makes the same point, stres-

[108] Cf. J.T. Mangan, "An Historical Analysis of the Principle of the Double Effect" in *Theological Studies*, 10 (1949), pp. 40–61; and, for a survey of the contemporary literature, R.A. McCormick, *Ambiguity in Moral Choice* (The 1973 Pere Marquette Theology Lecture).

[109] C.E. Curran, *New Perspectives in Moral Theology*, pp. 5–22.

[110] Band 7, Freiburg, 1962, col. 827–828.

sing that nothing is more damaging to the proper founding of the natural law than falsely 'absolutizing' what is, in fact, relative to history and to culture.[111]

Historicity, then, is inescapably part and parcel of any conception of a natural law that is to have any chance of acceptance today. In Catholic theology, for example, the traditional schematism of the natural law, with references to Scripture and tradition, was usually elaborated with the help of, and within the scope of, the tract on law in the *Summa Theologiae* of St. Thomas (1–2ae, qq. 90–108) – but how often with an unawareness of the subtlety and flexibility with which Thomas handles his concepts?[112] The static conception of human nature that emerged was all too vulnerable to the criticisms of our time. A closer reading of Aquinas would have helped; or indeed of the Scriptures, which give little encouragement to thinking in terms of an abstract nature of man.[113] Man is a social being; and as social is involved in historical development; his actions cannot be judged by reference to an abstract metaphysical nature. Man's nature is part of the development; it is changing and man himself is in some way author of the change. This increases, rather than diminishes, man's responsibility. There is here, according to Rahner, need for a new 'transcendental' method for the study of human nature and natural law.[114] And if it be asked how standards or criteria of behaviour may be established on the basis of a changing nature,

[111] *Das Naturrecht im Disput*, p. 14 – "falsche Verabsolutierungen"

[112] J. Gründel, "Naturrecht" in *Sacramentum Mundi*, III, 1969, col. 707–719.

[113] Cf. W. Pannenberg, "Toward a Theology of Law" in *Anglican Theological Review*, 55(1973), p. 397: "Contemporary theology has not yet accepted the comprehensive significance of the historical character of all human reality, despite the fact that it was disclosed by the biblical understanding of God."

[114] K. Rahner, "Heutige Aufgaben hinsichtlich des Naturrechts" in *Lexikon für Theologie und Kirche*, Bd. 7, 1962, col. 827: "Das wirkliche bleibende, sein sollende Wesen des Menschen kann darum nur in einer transzendentalen Erkenntnis als solches erfasst und von dem bloss universal Faktischen an ihm unterschieden werden. Es wäre weiter genauer zu unterscheiden zwischen einer bloss physisch-physiologischen Struktur des faktischen Menschen und einer als sein sollend transzendental nachweisbaren Struktur im menschlichen Seinsgefüge. Von da aus musste genauer durchdacht werden, wie weit eine solche transzendentale Wesenserkenntnis des Menschen reicht und ob von da aus jene Konkretheit der sittlichen Normen erreicht werden kann, die die Schultradition als noch unter das Naturrecht fallend betrachtet, oder ob solche mehr konkreten Normen in einer mehr sekundären und abgeleiteten Weise (wie?) an das 'transzendentale' Naturrecht gebunden werden können. Solche Überlegungen sind heute darum vor allem wichtig, weil der Mensch von heute den (nicht schlechthin falschen, aber unangemessenen) Eindruck hat, er sei gerade das Wesen, das 'sich selber macht', also seine 'Natur' verändern könne."

the answer must be that the recognition of the changing character of man's existence, and the developments of human nature, brings also the realization that there is a human subject of those changes.

This is not a quibble; here contemporary writers believe that they touch on the most profound truth in this matter. The moral theologian cannot neglect the historical changes in man and society, nor dismiss them as accidental, because it is precisely these changes and possibilities of change that exhibit man's shaping as a human person. The development is not completed; nor can it be predicted which data will be of importance tomorrow for their effect upon the future development of human existence. In a word, the knowledge of the natural law is itself an historical process.[115]

If this seems excessively radical, to be, in effect, the abandonment of any recognisable natural law, the impression will be corrected by a study of the contemporary approach to the vexed question of moral variations. This problem is not a discovery of our age – although historical, anthropological and cultural studies have given it a new urgency. St. Thomas, as we have seen, was aware of the difficulty presented by moral variations – the different codes and different moral convictions depending upon time and place and circumstance – to a law making claims to universality and immutability. We have seen his explanations under the three main headings; (1) the influence of the passions; (2) the unequal development of human reason; and (3) the diversity of background, situation and circumstance. Modern upholders of the natural law are saying the same thing, but with more insistence and in more sophisticated terminology. It is insisted, to begin with, that more precision is available – and demanded – in the expression of moral precepts. The auxiliary studies of anthropology and sociology help us to avoid the trap of an over-hasty identification of precepts as timeless and unchanging when, in fact, they are time-conditioned and culture-bound. One would be far more circumspect today than in the past in asserting, for instance, that private property is a matter of the natural law, or that to take interest on money is unnatural or that woman comes under the natural dominion of man.

Again, today's writer on the natural law is much more alive to the effects of changed situations on morals – the different function

[115] K. Rahner, *op. cit.*: "Die Erkenntnis dieser Natur ist selbst ein geshichtliches Prozess. . . ."

of money, for example, in a modern industrial and in a medieval rural economy; or the reality of warfare before and since the advent of nuclear weaponry, or before and since the (still rudimentary) organisation of international authority; or capital punishment or the indissolubility of marriage against backgrounds of social complexity formerly unknown. But, most importantly of all, there is the change in man himself. This consideration excites most suspicion because it has been used to undermine the doctrine of a natural law. But it should be recalled that St. Thomas taught that human nature is changeable – *natura humana mutabilis est* – without, however, having to spell out this mutability in the detail required today.[116]

What remains, then, of the unalterable natural law? One can say that the moral law is unalterably the law of man's (changing) nature. Or if this appears too paradoxical, one may say, with Bruno Schüller, that the only absolute is the connection between obligation and being, between *Sollen* and *Sein*. The correlation between man's duty and what man is does not decide the issue whether man's nature changes. This latter question is not one for ethics or moral theology at all, but for metaphysical anthropology.[117]

If it looks, then, as if many modern theologians and moralists are adopting a standpoint intermediate between absolutism and relativism, this does not spell the end of the natural law. It spells the end of a natural law based upon an eternal and unalterable human nature; but that natural law can no more resist the contemporary critique than the eighteenth century rationalist natural law could survive the onslaughts of the historical schools of the nineteenth century.[118]

[116] J. Gründel, *op. cit.*, col. 711–713, "Geschichtlichkeit."

[117] B. Schüller, "Wie weit kann die Moraltheologie das Naturrecht entbehren?" in *Lebendiges Zeugnis*, 1/2 (1965), cited in F. Böckle, *Das Naturrecht im Disput*, P. 128.

[118] L. Monden, *Sin, Liberty and Law*, p. 89: "Nor is the natural law in its classical meaning the collection of abstract principles or formulations to which textbook morality has often reduced it, under the influence of the seventeenth and eighteenth century theories of natural right. Historically the appeal to the natural law has arisen precisely from the resistance of personal conscience to the arbitrariness of written laws; it appealed to an *unwritten law*, an inborn knowledge of what man ought to do and ought not to do in order to be and to become authentically himself. Among the great classical authors that meaning of the natural law has been maintained in all its integrity," And the example taken by Monden is St. Thomas.

We may review the mistakes of the past, the recent past as well as the remote past, the misconceptions and the misleading definitions that disfigured the profile of the natural law. But it is not enough to shed a facile and self-flattering tear for this sins of our predecessors. We have enough of our own to weep for. And despite the insights of modern thought and the lessons of the past, who shall say that we have properly understood, and applied to the conditions of our time, the genuine natural law, the law of reason, whose features we have glimpsed in the work of the great scholastic writers?

BIBLIOGRAPHY

The literature on the natural law is enormous and the bibliographies are abundant. One may refer to the following:

A. KAUFMANN (ed.), *Die ontologische Begründung des Rechts*, Darmstadt, 1965, Bibliography, pp. 664–742.

W. MAIHOFER (ed.), *Naturrecht oder Rechtspositivismus?*, Darmstadt, 1972, Bibliography, pp. 580–622.

J.M. AUBERT, "Herméneutique du droit naturel" in *Recherches de science religieuse* 59 (1971), note bibliographique, pp. 490–492

A. MOLIEN, "Loi naturelle" in *Dictionnaire de théologie catholique*, t. 9, 1926, col. 878–890, bibliography, col. 909.

F.H. ETEROVICH, *Approaches to Natural Law from Plato to Kant*, New York, 1972, Bibliography, pp. 177–186.

G. FASSÒ, *Storia della filosofia del diritto*, Bologna, Notizie bibliografiche, I, 1966, pp. 311–353; II, 1968, pp. 411–453: III, 1970, pp. 425–460.

The *Natural Law Forum*, since 1969 re-named the *American Journal of Jurisprudence*, has for the past decade maintained a current bibliography of publications, in the field of natural law and related areas, from Germany, Austria, France, Italy and Switzerland.

What follows here is not a systematic bibliography but merely an alphabetical list to identify the authors cited, directly or indirectly, in text or notes. Authors from classical antiquity have been consulted in the Loeb Classical Library edition, where such exists, and have not been listed. Plato is quoted in the translation of Benjamin Jowett, 4th edition revised under the general editorship of D.J. Allan and H.E. Dale, I–IV, Oxford, 1953; and Aristotle in the Oxford Translation, edited by W.D. Ross, I–XII, Oxford,

1908–1952. Church Fathers and ecclesiastical writers are quoted from J.P. Migne, *Patrologia Series Graeca* (=P.G.) or *Patrologia Series Latina* (=P.L.). St. Thomas Aquinas is quoted, where possible, in the Leonine edition of his *Opera Omnia* and Francisco Suarez *De legibus ac Deo legislatore* in the new critical edition, *Corpus Hispanorum de Pace.* Otherwise standard editions are used. Useful collections of texts are found in O. Lottin, *Le droit naturel chez saint Thomas d'Aquin et ses prédécesseurs;* Id., *Psychologie et morale aux XIIe et XIIIe siècles;* R. Weigand, *Die Naturrechtslehre der Legisten und Dekretisten von Irnerius bis Accursius und von Gratian bis Johannes Teutonicus;* G. Fassò, *La legge della ragione.* Encyclopaedias and works of reference are not included, except in the case of signed articles of exceptional importance e.g. K. Rahner, "Heutige Aufgaben hinsichtlich des Naturrechts" in *Lexikon für Theologie und Kirche.*

ADLER, M.J., "A Question about Law," in R.E. Brennan (ed.) *Essays in Thomism*, New York, 1942.

ALBERT, St., *B. Alberti Magni ... Opera Omnia*, cura et labore A. Borgnet, Paris, 1890–1899.

——, *B. Alberti Magni Opera Omnia ad fidem codicum manuscriptorum*, Münster, 1951– .

ALEXANDER OF HALES, *Summa theologica ... Alexandri de Hales*, Quaracchi, 1924–1948.

ALLAN, D.J., "The Practical Syllogism" in *Autour d'Aristote; Recueil d'études ... offert à A. Mansion*, Louvain, 1955, pp. 325–340.

AMBROSETTI, G., *Diritto naturale cristiano*, Roma, 1964.

——, *Il diritto naturale della riforma cattolica: una giustificazione storica del sistema di Suarez*, Milano, 1951.

ANSELM OF LAON, F. Bliemitzrieder (ed.), *Anselms von Laon systematische Sentenzen*, Münster, 1919.

ARISTOTLE. *The Works of Aristotle* translated into English under the editorship of W.D. Ross, Oxford, 1908–1952.

ARMSTRONG , A.H., *Introduction to Ancient Philosophy*, London, 1947.

ARMSTRONG, R., *Primary and Secondary Precepts in Thomistic Natural Law Teaching*, The Hague, 1966.

ARNIM. Johannes ab, *Stoicorum veterum fragmenta*, I–IV, Stuttgart, 1903–1924; Photomechanic-reprint, Stuttgart, 1964.

ARNOLD, F. X., *Zur Frage des Naturrechts bei Martin Luther: Ein Beitrag zum Problem der natürlichen Theologie auf reformatorischer Grundlage*, München, 1937.

ARNOLD, F., "Die Rechtslehre des Magister Gratianus" in *Studia Gratiana*, 1 (1953), *pp.* 451–482.

ARNTZ, J.T.C., 'Die Entwicklung des naturrechtlichen Denkens innerhalb des Thomismus' in F. Böckle (ed.), *Das Naturrecht im Disput*, Düsseldorf, 1966, pp. 87–120.

——, "Natural Law and its History", in *Concilium*, 5 (1965), n. 1, pp. 23–32.

AUBERT, J.M., *Le droit romain dans l'oeuvre de saint Thomas d'Aquin*, Paris, 1955.

AULARD, A. and MIRKENE-GUETZEVITCH, B., *Les déclarations des droits de l'homme*, Paris, 1929.

AUSTIN, J., *Lectures on Jurisprudence*, 5th ed., revised and edited by R. Campbell, London, 1885.

AYER, A.J., *Language, Truth and Logic*, London, 1936.

BAINTON, R.H., *Studies on the Reformation*, London, 1964.

BALL, W.E., *St. Paul and the Roman Law and other Studies on the Origin of the Form of Doctrine*, Edinburgh, 1901.

BANNER, W.A., *Origen and the Tradition of Natural Law Concepts*, Dumbarton Oaks Papers, VIII, Cambridge, Mass., 1954.

BARKER, E., *The Politics of Aristotle*, Oxford, 1946.

BAUR, L., "Die Lehre vom Naturrecht bei Bonaventura" in *Festgabe Baeumker*, Münster, 1913, pp. 217–239.

BIECHLER, J.E., "Gabriel Biel on *Liberum Arbitrium:* Prelude to Luther's *De servo arbitrio*," in *The Thomist*, 34 (1970), pp. 114–127.

BLÄSER, P., *Das Gesetz bei Paulus*, Neutestamentliche Abhandlungen, Band XIX, Münster, 1941.

BOBBIO, N., "Quelques arguments contre le droit naturel" in *Le droit naturel*, Annales de philosophie politique, III, Paris, 1959, pp. 175–190.

BÖCKLE, F., (ed.), *Das Naturrecht im Disput;* Drei Vorträge beim Kongress der deutschsprachigen Moraltheologen 1965 in Bensberg, Düsseldorf, 1966.

——, "Rückblick und Ausblick" in *Das Naturrecht im Disput*, Düsseldorf, 1966, pp. 121–150.

BOEHNER, Ph., *Collected Articles on Ockham*, St. Bonaventure, New York, 1958.

BONAVENTURE, St., *Doctoris Seraphici S. Bonaventurae Opera Omnia*, Quaracchi, 1882–1902.

BONKE, E., "Doctrina nominalistica de fundamento ordinis moralis apud Gulielmum de Ockham et Gabrielem Biel," in *Collectanea Franciscana*, 14 (1944), pp. 57–83.

BONUCCI, A., *La derogabilità del diritto naturale nella scolastica*, Perugia, 1906.

BOURKE, V.J., *St. Thomas and the Greek Moralists*, Marquette, Milwaukee, 1947.

BRACTON, W., *Bracton on the Laws and Customs of England*, ed. G.E. Woodbine, with Translation, revisions and notes by S.E. Thorne, I–II, Harvard, 1968.

BRADY, I., "Law in the *Summa fratris Alexandri*" in *Proceedings of the American Catholic Philosophical Association*, 24 (1950), pp. 133–136.

BREDVOLD. L. I., *The Brave New World of the Enlightenment*, Michigan, 1961.

——, "The Invention of the Ethical Calculus" in R.F. Jones and others, *The Seventeenth Century: Studies in the History of English Literature and Thought*, Stanford, 1951.

BUCKLAND, W.W., *Text-Book of Roman Law from Augustus to Justinian*, 3rd ed., Cambridge, 1963.

BUDZIK, G., *De conceptu legis ad mentem Joannis Duns Scoti: Pars theseos*, Romae, Antonianum; Burlington, Wisconsin, 1954.

BURNET, J., *Early Greek Phiosophy*, 4th ed., London, 1948. *Greek Philosophy: Thales to Plato*, London, 1943.

CAIRNS, H., *Legal Philosophy from Plato to Hegel*, Baltimore, 1948.

CALMERER, R.R., "The Natural Law: a Theologian's View" in *Colloquy on Law and Theology*, St. Louis, 1962.

CARLYLE, R.W. and A.J., *A History of Medieval Political Theory in the West*, I–V, Edinburgh, 1903–1936.

CARNEY, F.S., "Outline of a Natural Law Procedure for Christian Ethics" in *Journal of Religion*, 47 (1967), pp. 26–38.

CATHREIN, V., *Moralphilosophie*, I–II, 6. Aufl., Leipzig, 1924.

CHENU, M.D., *L'éveil de la conscience dans la civilisation médiévale*, Conférence Albert le Grand, 1968, Montréal-Paris, 1969.

Chroust, A.H., "Hugo Grotius and the Scholastic Natural Law Tradition" in *The New Scholasticism*, 17 (1943), pp. 101–133.

——, "The Philosophy of Law from St. Augustine to St. Thomas Aquinas" in *The New Scholasticism*, 20 (1946), pp. 26–71.

Clement, L., "Le ius gentium" in *Revue de l'Université d'Ottawa*, 10 (1940), section spéciale, pp. 100–124, 177*–195*.

Clementinus a Vlissingen, *De evolutione definitionis juris gentium: Studium historico-juridicum de doctrina juris gentium apud auctores classicos saec. XVI–XVIII*, Romae, 1940.

Clarke, D.W., "William of Ockham on Right Reason," in *Speculum*, 48 (1973), pp. 13–36.

Cogley, J. and others, *Natural Law and Modern Society*, Cleveland-New York, 1963.

Composta, D., "Il diritto naturale in Graziano" in *Studia Gratiana* 2 (1954), pp. 151–210.

——, "Il diritto naturale in S. Ireneo" in *Apollinaris*, 45 (1972), pp. 599–612.

——, "Il diritto naturale neo-testamentario" in *Monitor Ecclesiasticus*, 97 (1972), pp. 95–114.

——, *Natura e ragione: studio sulle inclinazioni naturali in rapporto al diritto naturale*, Zürich, 1971.

Copleston, F.C., *History of Philosophy*, I–VIII, London, 1946–1975.

Cotta, S., *Il concetto di legge nella Summa theologiae di S. Tommaso d'Aquino*, Torino, 1955.

Courtenay, W.J., "John of Mirecourt and Gregory of Rimini on Whether God can undo the Past" in *Recherches de théologie ancienne et médiévale*, 39 (1972), pp. 224–256, 40 (1973), pp. 147–174.

——, "Nominalism in Late Medieval Thought" in *Theological Studies*, 33 (1972), pp. 716–734.

Cranston, M., "St Thomas as a Political Philosopher," in *History Today*, 14 (1964), pp. 313–317.

Crowe, M.B., "Human Nature – Immutable or Mutable?" in *Irish Theological Quarterly*, 30 (1963), pp. 204–231.

——, "The Term *synderesis* and the Scholastics" in *Irish Theological Quarterly*, 23 (1956), pp. 151–164, 228–245.

——, "St Thomas and Ulpian's Natural Law" in *St Thomas Aquinas Commemorative Studies*, I, Toronto, 1974, pp. 261–282.

Curran, C.E., "Absolute Norms in Moral Theology" in G.H. Outka-P. Ramsey (edd.) *Norm and Context in Christian Ethics*, London, 1968, pp. 139–173.

——, "Moral Theology: the Present State of the Discipline" in *Theological Studies*, 34 (1973), pp. 446–467.

——, *New Perspectives in Moral Theology*, Notre-Dame, 1974.

D'Arcy, E., *Conscience and its Right to Freedom*, London–New York, 1961.

Darmor, J., "A travers les grandes déclarations" in *Revue de l'action populaire*, janvier, 1964.

Davitt, T. E.; *The Nature of Law*, St. Louis–London, 1951.

de Blic, J., "Conscience ou synderèse?" in *Revue d'ascétique et de mystique*, 25 (1949), pp. 146–157.

——, "L'oeuvre exégétque de Walafrid Strabon et la Glossa ordinaria" in *Recherches de théologie ancienne et médiévale*, 16 (1949), pp. 5–28.

Delhaye, Ph., *Permanence du droit naturel*, Lille. 1961.

Deman, Th., "Le *De officiis* de saint Ambroise dans l'histoire de la théologie morale" in *Revue des sciences philosophiques et théologiques*, 37 (1953), pp. 409–424.

——, *La prudence*, Somme théologique, ed. de la *Revue des jeunes*, II–IIae, q. 47–56, Paris–Tournai–Rome, 1949.

Demmer, K., *Jus Caritatis: Zur christologischen Grundlegung der augustinischen Naturrechtslehre*, Roma, 1961.

d' Entreves, A.P., "A Core of Good Sense: Reflections on Hart's Theory of Natural Law" in *Natural Law*, 2nd edition, pp. 185–203.

——, "Le droit naturel" in *Le droit naturel*, Annales de philosophie politique, III, Paris, 1959, pp. 147–157.

——, *Natural Law: An Introduction to Legal Philosophy*, 2nd edition revised, London, 1970.

Diels, H., *Die Fragmente der Vorsokratiker*, I–III, 8. Aufl. Berlin, 1956.

Deploige, S., *Le conflit de la morale et de la sociologie*, 4me ed., Paris, 1927.

De Siano, F., "Of God and Man: Consequences of Abelard's Ethic" in *The Thomist*, 35 (1971), pp. 631–660.

Dihle, A., *Die Goldene Regel: Eine Einführung in die Geschichte der antiken und frühchristlichen Vulgärethik*, Göttingen, 1962.

DONAGAN, A., "The Scholastic Theory of the Natural Law in the Modern World" in A. Kenny (ed.) *Aquinas: A Collection of Critical Essays*, London, 1969, pp. 325–339.

DOUCET, V., "Prolegomena in librum III necnon in libros I et II" in *Summa fratris Alexandri*, t. 4, Quaracchi 1948.

DUPONT, J., "*Syneidesis* aux origines de la notion chrétienne de conscience morale" in *Studia Hellenistica*, 5 (1948), pp. 119–153.

DURANTEL, J., *Saint Thomas et le pseudo-Denis*, Paris, 1919.

EDELSTEIN, L., *The Meaning of Stoicism*, Cambridge, Mass., 1966.

EHRENBERG, S.V., *Die Rechtsidee im frühen Griechentum*, Leipzig, 1921.

EMOND, H., *La notion de lao naturelle chez Origène*, Dissertation, Université catholique de Louvain, Faculté de Philosophie et Lettres, 1970.

ENSSLIN, W., "The Senate and the Army," in *Cambridge Ancient History*, XII, ch. 11, Cambridge 1939, pp. 57–68.

FASSÒ, G., "Dio e la natura presso i decretisti ed i glossatori" in *Diritto ecclesiastico*, 67 (1956), pp. 3–10.

——, *La legge della ragione*, Bologna, 1964.

——, *Storia della filosofia del diritto*, I–III, Bologna, 1966, 1968, 1970.

FAY, C., "Human Evolution: A Challenge to Thomistic Ethics" in *International Philosophical Quarterly*, 2 (1960), pp. 50–80.

FECHNER, E., "Die Bedeutung der Gesellschaftswissenschaft für die Grundfrage des Rechts" in W. Maihofer (ed.), *Naturrecht oder Rechtspositivismus?*, Darmstadt, 1972, pp. 257–280.

FENNESSY, R.R., *Burke, Paine and the Rights of Man*, The Hague, 1963.

FIELD, G.C., *Plato and his Contemporaries: A Study in Fourth Century Life and Thought*, 2nd edition, London, 1953.

FLÜCKIGER, F., *Geschichte des Naturrechtes*, I, Altertum und Frühmittelalter, Zollikon-Zürich, 1954.

FLUGEL, J.C., *Man, Morals and Society*, Harmondsworth, 1962.

FORCELLINI, A.E., *Lexikon totius latinitatis*, I–VI, Patavii, 1940.

FOULQUIÉ, P. and SAINT-JEAN, R., *Dictionnaire de la langue philosophique*, Paris, 1962.

FRANSEN, G., "La date du Décret de Gratien" in *Revue d'histoire ecclésiastique*, 51 (1956), pp. 521–531.

Freeman, K., *The Pre-Socratic Philosophers – A Companion to Diels' Fragmente der Vorsokratiker*, Oxford, 2nd edition, 1949.

Friederich, C.J., *The Philosophy of Law in Historical Perspective*, Chicago-Cambridge, 1958.

Friedmann, W., *Legal Theory*, 4th edition, London, 1960.

Fuchs, J., "The Absoluteness of Moral Terms" in *Gregorianum*, 52 (1971), pp. 415–457.

——, "Christliche Gesellschaftslehre" in *Stimmen der Zeit*, 164 (1959), pp. 161–170; translation in Id., *Natural Law*, Dublin, 1965, pp. 181–193, "The Problem of a Christian Sociology."

——, *Natural Law: A Theological Investigation*, Dublin, 1965 (translation of *Lex Naturae: Zur Theologie des Naturrechts*, Düsseldorf, 1955 and *Le droit naturel, essai théologique*, Paris–Tournai, 1960).

——, *Theologia moralis generalis*, Pars prior, Gregoriana, Roma, 1960.

Fuller, L., "Positivism and Fidelity to Law – a Reply to Professor Hart" in *Harvard Law Review*, 71 (1958), pp. 630–672.

Gagner, S., *Studien zur Ideengeschichte der Gesetzgebung*, Stockholm, 1960.

Galan y Gutierrez, E., *Jus Naturae*, Valladolid, 1954.

Gaudemet, J., "La doctrine des sources du droit dans le Décret de Gratien" in *Revue de droit canonique*, 1 (1951) pp. 5–31.

Gauthier, R.A., "La date du commentaire de saint Thomas sur l'Ethique à Nicomaque" in *Recherches de théologie ancienne et médiévale*, 18 (1951), pp. 66–105.

Gauthier, R.A., and Jolif, J.Y., *L'Ethique à Nicomaque: Introduction, traduction et commentaire*, I–II, Louvain, 1970.

Gibbon, E., *The History of the Decline and Fall of the Roman Empire*, ed. J.B. Bury, I–VII, London, 1896–1900.

Gierke, O. von, *Johannes Althusius und die Entwicklung der naturrechtlichen Staatstheorien*, Breslau, 1929.

——, *Natural Law and the Theory of Society 1500–1800*, translated and introduced by E. Barker, I–II, Cambridge, 1934.

——, *Political Theories of the Middle Age*, translated with an introduction by F.W. Maitland, Cambridge, 1938.

Gilby, T., (ed.), *Law and Political Theory*, (*Summa theologiae*, volume 28, 1–2ae, q. 90–97), London–Cambridge–New York, 1966.

——, *Principality and Polity: The Rise of State Theory in the West*, London, 1957.

GILSON, E., *Introduction à l'étude de saint Augustin*, 3me édition, Paris, 1949.

——, *Jean Duns Scot: Introduction à ses positions fondamentales*, Paris, 1951.

GINSBERG, M., *On the Diversity of Morals*, London, 1962.

GLOVER, T.R., *The Ancient World*, Cambridge, 1935.

GRABMANN, M., "Die Lehre des hl. Thomas von der scintilla animae in ihrer Bedeutung für die deutsche Mystik im Predigerorden" in *Jahrbuch für Philosophie und spekulative Theologie*, 14 (1900), pp. 413–427.

——, "Das Naturrecht der Scholastik von Gratian bis Thomas von Aquin" in *Mittelalterliches Geistesleben*, I, München, 1926, pp. 65–103.

——, *Mittelalterliches Geistesleben: Abhandlungen zur Geschichte der Scholastik und Mystik*, I–III, München, 1936–1956.

GRANERIS, G., *La filosofia del diritto nella sua storia e nei suoi problemi*, Roma, 1961.

GREENWOOD, D., "Saint Paul and Natural Law" in *Biblical Theology Bulletin*, 1 (1971), pp. 262–279.

GREGORY OF RIMINI, *Gregorius de Arimino in librum Sententiarum*, Paulus de Genezano (ed.) Venetiis, 1503.

GRISEZ, G., *Contraception and the Natural Law*, Milwaukee, 1964.

——, "The First Principle of Practical Reason: a Commentary on the *Summa theologiae*, 1–2, question 94, article 2" in *Natural Law Forum*, 10 (1965), pp. 168–196 (reprinted in abridged form in A. Kenny (ed.), *Aquinas: A Collection of Critical Essays*, London, 1969, pp. 340–382).

GROTIUS, H., *De jure belli et pacis libri tres*, i– photographic reproduction of 1646 text, Washington, 1913; ii– translation of text by F.W. Kelsey and others, with introduction by J.B. Scott, Classics of International Law, 3, Oxford, 1925.

——, *Prolegomena to the Law of War and Peace*, reprinted from Classics of International Law, 3, Indianapolis, 1957.

GRUBE, G.M.A., *Plato's Thought*, London, 1935.

GRÜNDEL, J., "Naturrecht" in *Sacramentum Mundi*, II, Freiburg-Basel-Wien, 1969, col. 707–719.

GUALAZZINI, U., "Natura idest Deus" in *Studia Gratiana*, 3 (1954), pp. 411–424.

GUÉRIN, P., *L'idée de justice dans la conception de l'univers chez les Grecs de Thalès à Héracleite*, Paris, 1955.

GUTHRIE, W.K.C., *The Greek Philosophers from Thales to Aristotle*, New York, 1960.

HAMBURGER, M., *Morals and Law – The Growth of Aristotle's Legal Theory*, Yale–London–Oxford, 1951.

HAMEL, E., *Loi naturelle et loi du Christ*, Bruges-Paris, 1964.

HAMILTON, B., "A Developing Concept of Natural Law" in *The Month*, 235 (1975), pp. 196–200.

——, *Political Thought in Sixteenth Century Spain: A Study of the Political Ideas of Vitoria, Soto, Suarez and Molina*, Oxford, 1963.

HAMMER, F., "Bemerkungen zur Sexualanthropologie des Thomas von Aquin" in *Zeitschrift für katholische Theologie*, 98 (1976), pp. 1–8.

HARDIE, W.F.R., *Aristotle's Ethical Theory*, Oxford, 1968.

HARDING, A.L., (ed.), *Natural Law and Natural Rights*, Dallas, 1955.

——, *Origins of the Natural Law Tradition*, Dallas, 1954.

HARRIS, C.R.S., *Duns Scotus*, I–II, Oxford, 1927.

HART, H.L.A., *The Concept of Law*, Oxford, 1961.

HEBING, J., "Ueber 'conscientia' und 'conservatio' im philosophischen Sinne bei den Römern von Cicero bis Hieronymus" in *Philosophisches Jahrbuch*, 35 (1922), pp. 121–135, 215–231, 298–326.

HEELAN, P.A., "Nature and its Transformations," in *Theological Studies*, 33 (1972), pp. 486–502

HENQUINET, F., "Ist der Traktat de legibus et praeceptis in der Summa Alexanders von Hales von Johannes von Rupella?" in *Franciskanische Studien*, 26 (1939), pp. 1–22, 234–258.

——, "Vingt-deux questions inédites d'Albert le Grand dans un manuscrit à l'usage de S. Thomas d'Aquin" in *The New Scholasticism*, 9 (1935), pp. 312–322.

HIRZEL, R., *Agraphos Nomos*, Leipzig, 1900.

——, *Themis, Dikè und Verwandtes: Ein Beitrag zur Geschichte der Rechtsidee bei den Griechen*, Leipzig, 1907.

HÖLSCHER, E.E., *Vom römischen zum christlichen Naturrecht*, Augsburg, 1931.

Hörmann, K., *Leben in Christus–Zusammenhänge zwischen Dogma und Sitte bei den apostolischen Vätern*, Wien, 1954.

Horvath, B., "Die Gerechtigkeit der Vorsokratiker" in *Studi dedicati a Giorgio Del Vecchio*, I. Modena, pp. 336–372.

Hume, D., *A Treatise of Human Nature* (ed. L.A. Selby-Bigge) Oxford, 1967 (reprint).

Hurley, N., "The Natural Law and Man's Open-ended Nature" in *New Catholic World*, 216 (1973), Nov.–Dec., pp. 259–263.

Huxley, J., *Evolution in Action*, London, 1953.

Jaeger, W., "Die Anfänge der Rechtsphilosophie und die Griechen" in *Zeitschrift für philosophische Forschung*, 3 (1948), pp. 321–338, 512–529.

——, *Paideia: The Ideals of Greek Culture*, translated from the 2nd German edition by G. Highet, Oxford, 1939–1944.

Jeanson, F., *Le problème moral et la pensée de Sartre*, 2me édition, Paris, 1965.

Jolowicz, H.F., *Historical Introduction to the Study of Roman Law*, Cambridge, 1965.

Jones, R.F. and others, *The Seventeenth Century: Studies in the History of English Literature and Thought*, Stanford, 1951.

Justinian, *Corpus Juris Civilis*, I–III, apud Weidmannos, Berolini, 1928.

Kantorowicz, H., *Studies in the Glossators of the Roman Law*, Cambridge, 1938.

Kaufmann, A. (ed.), *Die ontologische Begründung des Rechts*, Wege der Forschung, Band XXII, Darmstadt, 1965.

Knoll, A.M. *Katholische Kirche und scholastisches Naturrecht*, Wien, 1962.

Kölmel, W., "Das Naturrecht bei Wilhelm Ockham" in *Franziskanische Studien*, 35 (1953), pp. 39–85.

Krakowski, E., *Les sources médiévales de la philosophie de Locke*, Paris, 1915.

Krieger, L., *The Politics of Discretion: Pufendorf and the Acceptance of Natural Law*, Chicago–London, 1965.

Küng, H., *Infallible? An Enquiry*, New York, 1971; London, 1972.

Küppers, W., *John Locke und die Scholastik*, Berne, 1894.

Kuhlmann, B.C., *Der Gesetzbegriff beim hl. Thomas von Aquin in Lichte des Rechtsstudiums seiner Zeit*, Bonn, 1912.

KUTTNER, S., *Repertorium der Kanonistik (1140–1234): Prodromus corporis Glossatorum*, I, Città del Vaticano, 1937.

LALANDE, A., *Vocabulaire technique et critique de la philosophie*, 8me édition, Paris, 1960.

LANGEMEIJER, G.E., "Philosophie du droit" in R. Klibansky (ed.), *Philosophy in the Mid-Century* III, Firenze, 1958, pp. 102–116.

LAUN, A., *Die naturrechtliche Begründung der Ethik in der neueren katholischen Moraltheologie*, Wien, 1973.

LAZZARINI, A., "Gratianus de Urbe veteri" in *Studia Gratiana*, 4 (1956), pp. 1–15.

LE BRAS, G., "Le triomphe de Gratien" in *Studia Gratiana*, 1 (1953), pp. 1–14.

LECLERCQ, J., *Les grandes lignes de la philosophie morale*, édition nouvelle, Louvain-Paris, 1954.

——, *Leçons de droit naturel*, I–IV, 2me édition, Namur-Louvain, 1953.

——, *La philosophie morale de saint Thomas d'Aquin devant la pensée contemporaine*, Louvain–Paris, 1955.

LEES, H.D.P., "The Legal Background of Two Passages in the Nicomachean Ethics" in *Classical Quarterly*, 31 (1937), pp. 129–140.

LEGRAND, J., *L'Univers et l'homme dans la philosophie de saint Thomas*, Bruxelles, 1946.

LEIBER, R., "Name und Begriff der synteresis in der mittelalterlichen Scholastik" in *Philosophisches Jahrbuch*, 25 (1912), pp. 372–392.

LEITMAIER, C., "Das Privateigentum im gratianischen Dekret" in *Studia Gratiana*, 2 (1954), pp. 361–373.

LEVY, E., "Natural Law in Roman Thought" in *Studia et monumenta historiae et juris*, 15 (1949), pp. 1–24.

LEVY, E. and RABEL E., *Index interpolationum quae in Iustiniani digestis inesse dicuntur*, Weimar, 1929.

LIEBAERT, J., *Les enseignements moraux des pères apostoliques*, Gembloux, 1970.

LLOYD, D., *The Idea of Law*, Harmondsworth, 1964.

LOCKE, J., *Essay concerning the Human Understanding*, I–II, London–New York, 1961.

——, *Essays on the Law of Nature*, Latin text with translation, introduction and notes by W. von Leyden, Oxford, 1954.

——, *Two Treatises*, ed. P. Laslett, 2nd edition Oxford, 1967.

LONGPRÉ, E., *La philosophie du B. Duns Scot*, Paris, 1924.

LOTTIN, O., *Le droit naturel chez saint Thomas d'Aquin et ses prédécesseurs*, 2me édition, Bruges, 1931.

——, "La loi en général: la définition thomiste et ses antécédents" in *Psychologie et morale aux XIIe et XIIIe siècles*, II, Gembloux-Louvain, 1948, pp. 11–47.

——, *Principes de morale*, I–II, Louvain, 1947.

——, *Psychologie et morale aux XIIe et XIIIe siècles*, I–III, Gembloux-Louvain, 1942–1949.

——, "La valeur des formules de saint Thomas d'Aquin concernant la loi naturelle" in *Mélanges Maréchal*, II, Bruxelles, 1950, pp. 345–357.

LUIJPEN, W., *Phenomenology of Natural Law*, Pittsburgh, 1967.

LUMB, R.D., "Law, Reason, Will" in *Philosophical Studies*, 10 (1960), pp. 179–189.

LUMBRERAS, P., *De lege (1–2ae, 90–98)*, Praelectiones scholasticae in Secundam Partem D. Thomae, V., Madrid-Buenos Aires-Romae, 1953.

LUSCOMBE, D.E. *Peter Abelard's Ethics*, Edition, with introduction and English translation, Oxford, 1971.

MCCABE, B., "Francis Bacon and the Natural Law Tradition" in *Natural Law Forum* 9.(1964), pp. 111–121.

MCCORMICK, R.A., *Ambiguity in Moral Choice*, The 1973 Père Marquette Theology Lecture, Marquette, Milwaukee, 1973.

——, "Human Significance and Christian Significance" in G.H. Outka-P. Ramsey (edd.), *Norm and Context in Christian Ethics*, London, 1969, pp. 233–261.

MCDONAGH, E., *Invitation and Response: Essays in Christian Moral Theology*, Dublin, 1972.

——, "Moral Theology: the Need for Renewal" in *Moral Theology Renewed*, Dublin, 1965, pp. 13–30.

——, (ed.), *Moral Theology Renewed*, Dublin, 1965.

MCDONNELL, K., "Does William of Ockham have a Theory of Natural Law?" in *Franciscan Studies*, 34 (1974), pp. 383–392.

MCGRATH, P.J., "Natural Law and Moral Argument" in J.P. Mackey (ed.), *Morals, Law and Authority*, Dublin, 1969, pp. 58–78.

MACKEY, J.P., (ed.), *Morals, Law and Authority*, Dublin, 1969.

MACQUARRIE, J., *Three Issues in Ethics*, New York, 1970.

MAES, B., *La loi naturelle selon Ambroise de Milan*, Roma, 1967.

MAIHOFER, W., (ed.), *Naturrecht oder Rechtspositivismus?*, Wege der Forschung, Band XVI, Darmstadt, 1972.

MANGAN, J.T., "An Historical Analysis of the Principle of the Double Effect" in *Theological Studies*, 10 (1949), pp. 40–61.

MANSER, G.M., *Das Naturrecht in thomistischer Beleuchtung*, Freiburg/Schweiz, 1944.

MANSION, A., "Autour de la date du commentaire de S. Thomas sur l'Ethique à Nicomaque" in *Revue philosophique de Louvain*, 50 (1952), pp. 460–471.

——, *Introduction à la Physique Aristotélicienne*, 2me édition, Louvain, 1945.

MARITAIN, J., *On the Philosophy of History*, London, 1959.

MATTHEW OF AQUASPARTA, *Fr. Matthaei ab Aquasparta... Quaestiones disputatae... de legibus*, Quaracchi, 1959.

MAURER, A., "The Unity of a Science: St Thomas and the Nominalists" in *St. Thomas Aquinas Commemorative Studies*, II, Toronto, 1974, pp. 269–291.

MAUSBACH, J., *Die Ethik des hl. Augustinus*, I-II, Freiburg/Breisgau, 1909.

MEERSSEMAN, G., "Le droit naturel chez S. Thomas d'Aquin et ses prédécesseurs" in *Angelicum*, 9 (1932), pp. 63–76.

MERLEAU-PONTY, M., *Sens et non-sens*, Paris, 1948.

MESSNER, J., *Social Ethics: Natural Law in the Modern World*, translated by J.J. Doherty, St Louis–London, 1949.

MEYER, Th., *Institutiones Juris Naturalis*, I–II, Freiburg, 1885.

MIDGLEY, L.C., *Beyond Human Nature: the Contemporary Debate over Natural Moral Law*, Brigham Young University Press, Utah, 1968.

MILL, J.S., *Three Essays on Religion*, 3rd edition, London, 1923.

MONDEN, L., *Sin, Liberty and Law*, translated by J. Donceel, London–Dublin, 1966.

MONTESQUIEU, C.J. de S., *Oeuvres complètes*, I–II, R. Caillois (ed.), Paris, 1949–1951.

MOORE, G.E., *Principia Ethica*, Cambridge, 1903.

MULDOON, J., "The Contribution of the Medieval Canon Lawyers to the Formation of International Law" in *Traditio*, 28 (1972), pp. 483–497.

MULLIGAN, R.W., "Ratio superior and Ratio inferior: the Historical Background" in *The New Scholasticism*, 29 (1955), pp. 1–32.

MUÑOZ, H., *Vitoria and the Conquest of America*, Manila, 1938.

MUNTZ, W.S., *Rome, St. Paul and the Early Church: the influence of Roman Law on St. Paul's Teaching and Phraseology and on the Development of the Church*, London, 1913.

MUNZ, P., *The Place of Hooker in the History of Thought*, London, 1952.

MURRAY, J.C., *We Hold These Truths: Catholic Reflections on the American Proposition*, New York–London, 1960–1961.

NICHOLAS, J.K.B.M., *An Introduction to Roman Law*, Oxford, 1962.

NITZSCH, F., "Über die Entstehung der scholastischen Lehre von der Synderesis" in *Jahrbuch für protestantische Theologie*, 5 (1879), pp. 492–507.

NOONE, J.B., "Rousseau's Theory of Natural Law as Conditional," in *Journal of the History of Ideas*, 33 (1972), pp. 23–42.

NUSSBAUM, A., *A Concise History of the Law of Nations*, revised edition, New York, 1954.

OAKLEY, F., Medieval Theories of Natural Law: William of Ockham and the Significance of the Voluntarist Tradition" in *Natural Law Forum*, 6 (1961), pp. 65–

OBERMAN, H.A., *The Harvest of Medieval Theology: Gabriel Biel and Late Medieval Nominalism*, Harvard, 1963.

——, "Some Notes on the Theology of Nominalism: with Attention to its Relation to the Renaissance" in *Harvard Theological Review*, 53 (1960), pp. 47–76.

O'CONNELL, T.E., "The Question of Moral Norms" in *American Ecclesiastical Review*, 169 (1975), pp. 377–388.

O'DONOGHUE, D., "The Thomist Concept of Natural Law" in *Irish Theological Quarterly*, 22 (1955), pp. 89–109.

O'MALLEY, J.W., "A Note on Gregory of Rimini: Church, Scripture, Tradition" in *Augustinianum*, 5 (1965), pp. 365–378.

ONCLIN, W., "Le droit naturel selon les romanistes des XIIe et XIIIe siècles," in *Miscellanea moralia A. Janssen*, II, Louvain-Gembloux, 1948, pp. 329–337.

Osborn, E., *Ethical Patterns in Early Christian Thought*, Cambridge, 1976.

Ott, G., "Recht und Gesetz bei Gabriel Biel: Ein Beitrag zur spätmittelalterlichen Rechtslehre" in *Zeitschrift der Savigny-Stiftung für Rechtsgeschichte*, 69 (1952), pp. 251–296.

Ottenwälder, P., *Zur Naturrechtslehre des Hugo Grotius*, Tübingen, 1950.

Outka, G.H. and Ramsey, P., (eds.), *Norm and Context in Christian Ethics*, New York, 1968; London, 1969.

Ozment, S.E., *Homo Spiritualis: A Comparative Study of the Anthropology of Johannes Tauler, Jean Gerson and Martin Luther (1509–16) in the Context of their Theological Thought*, Leiden, 1969.

Paniker, R., *El concepto de naturaleza: análisis histórico y metafísico de un concepto*, Madrid, 1931.

Pannenberg, W., "Toward a Theology of Law" in *Anglican Theological Review*, 55 (1973), pp. 395–420.

Pascal, B., *Pensées*, ed. V. Giraud, Paris, 1943.

Pelster, F., "Wann hat Petrus Lombardus die Libri IV Sententiarum vollendet?" in *Gregorianum*, 2 (1921), pp. 387–392.

Pelzer, A., "Le cours inédit d'Albert le Grand sur la Morale à Nicomaque recueilli et rédigé par S. Thomas d'Aquin" in *Revue néo-scolastique de philosophie*, 23 (1922), pp. 333–361, 479–520; reprinted in A. Pelzer, *Etudes d'histoire littéraire sur la scolastique médiévale*, Louvain, 1964, pp. 272–335.

Philippidis, L.J., *Die 'goldene Regel' religionsgeschichtlich untersucht*, Leipzig, 1929.

Piernikarczyk, E., "Das Naturgesetz bei Johannes Duns Scotus" in *Philosophisches Jahrbuch*, 43 (1930), pp. 67–91.

Piguet, J.C., *Le vocabulaire intellectuel*, Centre de documentation universitaire, Paris, 1957.

Pohlenz, M., *Die Stoa*, I–II, 2. Aufl., Göttingen, 1959 (Band I), 1955 (Band II).

Pollock, F., "History of the Law of Nature," in *Jurisprudence and Legal Essays*, selected and introduced by A.L. Goodhart, London, 1961, pp. 124–157.

Pound, R., *Justice According to Law*, Yale, New Haven, 1951.

——, "The Revival of Natural law," in *Notre-Dame Lawyer*, 17 (1942), pp. 287–372.

PRENTICE, R., "The Contingent Element Governing the Natural Law on the Last Seven Precepts of the Decaloque according to Duns Scotus" in *Antonianum* 42 (1967), pp. 259–292.

PRIOR, A.N., *Logic and the Basis of Ethics*, Oxford, 1949.

PUFENDORF, S., *Elementorum jurisprudentiae universalis libri duo*, Classics of International Law, Oxford, 1931.

——, *De jure naturae et gentium libri octo*, Classics of International Law, I–II, Oxford, 1934.

QUINN, J.F., "St. Bonaventure's Fundamental Conception of Natural Law" in *S. Bonaventura 1274–1974*, III, Grottaferrata-Roma, pp. 571–598.

QUIRMBACH, J., *Die Lehre des hl. Paulus von der natürlichen Gotteserkenntnis und dem natürlichen Sittengesetz*, Freiburg/Breisgau, 1906.

RADBRUCH, G., "Die Erneuerung des Rechts" in *Die Wandlung*, 2 (1947), pp. 8–16, reprinted in W. Maihofer (ed.), *Naturrecht oder Rechtspositivismus?*, Darmstadt, 1972, pp. 1–10.

——, *Rechtsphilosophie*, 4. Aufl., Stuttgart, 1950; 5. Aufl., (ed. E. Wolf), Stuttgart, 1956.

——, *Legal Philosophy*, translation of *Rechtsphilosophie* by K. Wilk, in *20th Century Legal Philosophies*, IV, Harvard, 1950, pp. 47–224.

RAHNER, K. "Heutige Aufgaben hinsichtlich des Naturrechts" in *Lexikon für Theologie und Kirche*, Band 7, Freiburg/Breisgau, 1962, col. 827–828.

RAMIREZ, S., *El derecho de gentes: examen crítico de la filosofía del derecho de gentes desde Aristóteles hasta Francisco Suarez*, Madrid, 1955.

RAMSEY, I.T., "Towards a Rehabilitation of Natural Law" in *Christian Ethics and Contemporary Philosophy*, London, 1966, pp. 382–396.

——, (ed.), *Christian Ethics and Contemporary Philosophy*, London, 1966.

RAMSEY, P., *Nine Modern Moralists*, Englewood Cliffs, New Jersey, 1962.

REIBSTEIN, E., *Die Anfänge des neueren Natur- und Völkerrechts: Studien zu den "Controversiae illustres" (1959), des Fernandus Vasquius*," Bern, 1949.

——, *Johannes Althusius als Fortsetzer der Schule von Salamanca:* Untersuchungen zur Ideengeschichte des Rechtsstaates und zur altprotestantischen Naturrechtslehre, Karlsruhe, 1955.

REHRL, S., "Grundlegung der Moral bei Johannes Duns Scotus" in *Salzburger Jahrbuch für Philosophie und Psychologie*, 3 (1959), pp. 137–228.

REINER, H., "Die 'goldene Regel': die Bedeutung einer sittlichen Grundformel der Menschheit" in *Zeitschrift für philosophische Forschung*, 3 (1948), pp. 74–109.

REYNOLDS, L.D. and WILSON, N.G., *Scribes and Scholars: a Guide to the Transmission of Greek and Latin Literature*, 2nd edition, Oxford, 1974.

RICKABY, J., *Of God and his Creatures*, translation of the *Summa contra Gentiles*, with some abridgments, Westminster, 1950.

RITCHIE, D.G., *Natural Rights*, London, 1903.

ROBINSON, N.H.G., *The Groundwork of Christian Ethics*, London, 1971.

ROBY, H.J., "Roman Law" in *Cambridge Medieval History*, II, ch. 3, Cambridge, 1913.

ROLAND OF CREMONA, *Summa theologica: Summae Magistri Rolandi Cremonensis, Liber Tertius*, Editio princeps curante A. Cortesi, Monumenta Bergomensia, VII, Bergamo, 1962.

ROMMEN, H., *The Natural Law; A Study in Legal and Social History and Philosophy*, St. Louis–London, 1947.

ROSS, A., *On Law and Justice*, London, 1958.

ROSS, W.D., *Aristotle*, 5th edition, London, 1949.

——, *Plato's Theory of Ideas*, Oxford, 1951.

——, "The Greek Philosophers" in M. Platnauer (ed.), *Fifty Years of Classical Scholarship*, Oxford, 1954, pp. 130–149.

RUFINUS, *Summa Magistri Rufini zum Decretum Gratiani*, ed. J.F. von Schulte, Giessen, 1892.

SABINE, G.H., *History of Political Theory*, 3rd edition, New York, 1961.

ST. LEGER, J., *The 'Etiamsi Daremus' of Hugo Grotius: A Study of the Origins of International Law*, Roma, 1962.

SALOMON, M., "Le droit naturel chez Aristote" in *Archives de philosophie du droit et de sociologie juridique*, 7 (1937), pp. 120–127.

SÁNCHEZ DE LA TORRE, A., *Los Griegos y el derecho natural*, Madrid, 1962.

SAUTER, J., *Die philosophischen Grundlagen des Naturrechts; Untersuchungen zur Geschichte der Rechts- und Staatslehre*, Wien, 1932.

SCHMIEDER, K., "Die Synderesis und die ethischen Werte" in *Philosophisches Jahrbuch*, 47 (1934), pp. 145–159, 297–307.

SCHNEIDER, C., *Geistesgeschichte des antiken Christentums*, I–II, München, 1954.

SCHÖPF, B., "Das Naturrecht in der katholischen Moraltheologie" in *Naturordnung in Gesellschaft, Staat, Wirtschaft*, Festschrift Messner, J. Höffner-A. Verdross-Drossberg-F. Vito (edd.), Innsbruck-Wien-München, 1961, pp. 99–110.

SCHUBERT, A., *Augustinus Lex-aeterna-Lehre nach Inhalt und Quellen*, Münster, 1924.

SCHÜLLER, B., "Wie weit kann die Moraltheologie das Naturrecht entbehren?" in *Lebendiges Zeugnis*, 1/2 (1965).

SEJOURNÉ, P., *Le dernier père de l'église: Saint Isidore de Séville, son rôle dans l'histoire du droit canonique*, Paris, 1929.

SELZNICK, P., "Natural Law and Sociology" in *Natural Law Forum*, 6 (1961), pp. 84–108; reprinted in J. Cogley and others, *Natural Law and Modern Society*, Cleveland–New York, 1962–1963, pp. 154–193.

SENN, F., *De la justice et du droit*, Paris, 1927.

SHELLENS, M.S., "Der Gerechtigkeitsbegriff des Thrasymachus" in *Zeitschrift für philosophische Forschung*, 7 (1953), pp. 481–492.

SIEGFRIED, W., *Der Rechtsgedanke bei Aristoteles*, Zürich, 1947.

SIMON, Y.R., *The Tradition of Natural Law: A Philosopher's Reflections* (ed. V. Kuic), New York, 1965.

SIMONITI, P., "Ueber die *Responsio contra Apologiam Melanchthonis:* Ein wiedergefundenes Werk des Augustiner Eremiten Bartholomaeus Arnoldi von Usingen" in *Augustiniana*, 25 (1975), *pp.* 48–57.

SOHNGEN, G., *Grundfragen einer Rechtstheologie*, München, 1962.

SOTO, DOMINGO DE, *De legibus*, (Puy, F., and Nuñez, L., edd.), Granada, 1965.

SPANNEUT, M., "Stoicism: Influence on Christian Thought" in *New Catholic Encyclopaedia*, vol. XIII, 1967, pp. 719–721.

STELZENBERGER, J., *Die Beziehungen der frühchristlichen Sittenlehre zur Ethik der Stoa*, München, 1933.

——, *Conscientia bei Tertullianus*, Düsseldorf, 1956.

STEPHANUS, H., *Thesaurus Graecae Linguae, I–VIII*, Paris, 1848–1854.

STEUBING, H., *Naturrecht und natürliche Theologie im Protestantismus*, Göttingen, 1932.

STOCKUMS, W., *Die Unveränderlichkeit des natürlichen Sittengesetzes in der scholastischen Ethik: eine ethisch-geschichtliche Untersuchung*, Freiburg/Breisgau, 1911.

STONE, R., "Dr. Johnson: Philologist or Philosopher?" in *Cambridge Review*, Nov. 14, 1964, pp. 114–121.

STRATENWERTH, G., *Die Naturrechtslehre des Johannes Duns Scotus*, Göttingen, 1951.

SUAREZ, Francisco, *De legibus ac Deo legislatore*, (Pereña, L., Abril, V, Suñer, P. and others: edd.) Corpus Hispanorum de Pace, XI– , Madrid, 1971– In progress.

SUÑER, P., "Teocentrismo de la ley natural" in *Francisco Suarez De legibus ac Deo Legislatore*, Corpus Hispanorum de Pace, XIII, Madrid, 1974, pp. xxxviii–lv.

SURLIS, P., "Natural Law in Richard Hooker" in *Irish Theological Quarterly*, 35 (1968), pp. 173–185.

TAPARELLI D'AZEGLIO, L., *Saggio teoretico di diritto naturale*, 8a edizione, Roma, 1949.

TAYLOR, A.E., *Plato: the Man and his Work*, 5th edition, London, 1948.

TELLKAMP, A., *Das Verhältnis John Locke's zur Scholastik*, Münster, 1927.

THAMIN, R., *Saint Ambroise et la morale chrétienne au IVe siècle*, Paris, 1895.

TIERNEY, B., "Natura idest Deus: A Case of Juristic Pantheism?" in *Journal of the History of Ideas*, 24 (1963), pp. 307–322.

TIERNEY, M., "The Antigone of Sophocles: A Problem Reviewed" in *Studies*, 32 (1943), pp. 327–337.

TJONG, Z.U., "Uber die Wendung zum Naturrecht bei Gustav Radbruch" in *Archiv für Rechts- und Sozialphilosophie*, 56 (1970), pp. 245–262.

TRAPP, D., "Augustinian Theology of the 14th Century: Notes on Editions, Marginalia, Opinions and Book-lore" in *Augustiniana*, 6 (1956), pp. 146–274.

——, "Gregory of Rimini, Manuscripts, Editions and Additions" in *Augustiniana*, 8 (1958), pp. 425–443.

——, Gregorio de Rimini y el nominalismo" in *Augustinianum*, 4 (1964), pp. 5–20.

——, "Peter Ceffons of Clairvaux" in *Recherches de théologie ancienne et médiévale,* 24 (1957), pp. 101–154.

TRUDE, P., *Der Begriff der Gerechtigkeit in der aristotelischen Rechts- und Staatsphilosophie,* Berlin, 1955.

TRUYOL Y SERRA, A., *El derecho y el estado en San Agustín,* Madrid, 1944.

——, *Historia de la filosofia del derecho y del estado: De los orígenes a la baja edad media,* 3e edicion, Madrid, 1961.

UTZ, A.F., *Recht und Gerechtigkeit,* Kommentar zur Band 18 der deutsch-lateinischen Ausgabe der *Summa Theologiae,* 2-2ae, 57–79, München-Graz, 1953.

VAN DEN EYNDE, D., "Nouvelles précisions chronologiques sur quelques oeuvres théologiques au XIIe siècle" in *Franciscan Studies,* 13 (1953), pp. 71–118.

VAN HOVE, A., *Prolegomena in Commentarium Lovaniense in Codicem Iuris Canonici,* Malines-Rome, 1945.

VAN MELSEN, A.G.M., "Natur und Moral" in F. Böckle (ed.), *Das Naturrecht im Disput,* Düsseldorf, 1966, pp. 61–85.

VAN STEENBERGHEN, F., *La bibliothèque du philosophe médiéviste,* Louvain-Paris, 1974.

——, *La philosophie au XIIIe siècle,* Louvain-Paris, 1966.

VERBEKE, G., "Authenticité et chronologie des écrits de S. Thomas d'Aquin" in *Revue philosophique de Louvain,* 48 (1950), pp. 260–268.

——, "La date du commentaire de S. Thomas d'Aquin sur l'Ethique à Nicomaque" in *Revue philosophique de Louvain,* 47 (1949), pp. 203–220.

——, *L'évolution de la docrine du pneuma du stoicisme à saint Augustin,* Louvain-Paris, 1945.

VERDROSS, A., *Abendländische Rechtsphilosophie, ihre Grundlagen und Hauptprobleme in geschichtlicher Schau,* Wien, 1958.

VEROSTA, S., *Johannes Chrysostomus, Staatsphilosoph und Geschichtsstheologe,* Wien-Graz-Köln, 1960.

VIGNAUX, P., "Nominalisme" in *Dictionnaire de théologie catholique,* t. 11, Paris, 1930, col. 717–784.

——, *La philosophie au moyen-âge,* Paris, 1958.

VILLEY, M., "Abregé du droit naturel classique" in *Archives de philosophie du droit,* 61 (1961), pp. 25–72.

——, "Le droit naturel chez Gratien" in *Studia Gratiana*, 3 (1954), pp. 83–99.

——, "Les fondateurs de l'école de droit naturel moderne" in *Archives de philosophie du droit*, 61 (1961), pp. 73–105.

——, *Leçons d'histoire et de la philosophie du droit*, nouvelle édition, Paris, 1962.

VIOLARDO, G., *Il pensiero giuridico di san Girolamo*, Milano, 1937.

VITORIA, FRANCISCO DE, *De Indis et de Jure Belli Relectiones*, being parts of *Relectiones Theologicae XII*, edited by E. Nys, I–IV, Classics of International Law, Washington, D.C., 1917.

——, *Commentario al Tratado de la ley*, edited by V. Beltrán de Heredia, Madrid, 1952.

VOGGENSPERGER, R., *Der Begriff des 'jus naturale' im römischen Recht*, Basel, 1952.

WALDMANN, M., "Synteresis oder syneidesis?: Ein Beitrag zur Lehre vom Gewissen", in *Theologische Quartalschrift*, 119 (1938), pp. 332–371.

WARD, L.R., "Natural Law in Contemporary Legal Philosophy" in *Proceedings of the American Catholic Philosophical Association*, 33 (1959), pp. 137–143.

WATSON, G., "The Early History of Natural Law" in *Irish Theological Quarterly*, 33 (1966), pp. 65–74.

——, "The Natural Law and Stoicism" in A.A. Long (ed.), *Problems in Stoicism*, London, 1971, pp. 216–238.

WEIGAND, R., *Die Naturrechtslehre der Legisten und Dekretisten von Irnerius bis Accursius und von Gratian bis Johannes Teutonicus*, München, 1967.

WELLMANN, C., "The Ethical Implications of Cultural Relativity" in *Journal of Philosophy*, 60 (1963), pp. 169–184.

WELZEL, H., *Naturrecht und materiale Gerechtigkeit*, 4. Auflage, Göttingen, 1962.

——, *Die Naturrechtslehre Samuel Pufendorfs, Ein Beitrag zur Ideengeschichte des 17. und 18. Jahrhunderts*, Berlin, 1958.

——, *Die 'socialitas' als oberstes Prinzip der Naturrechtslehre Samuel Pufendorfs*, Heidelberg, 1930.

WHITEHEAD, A.N., *Process and Reality; An Essay in Cosmology*, New York, 1969.

WILD, J., *Plato's Modern Enemies and the Theory of Natural Law*, Chicago, 1953.

WILMS, H., "De scintilla animae" in *Angelicum*, 14 (1937), pp. 194–211.

WINCH, P., *Ethics and Action*, London, 1972.

WOLF, E., *Das Problem der Naturrechtslehre*, Karlsruhe, 1955.

——, *Griechisches Rechtsdenken*, I-III, Frankfurt, 1954–1956.

WU, J.C.H., *Fountain of Justice: A Study in the Natural Law*, New York, 1955; London, 1959.

NAME INDEX

SUBJECT INDEX